D1301574

THE MATADOR'S CAPE

The Matador's Cape delves into the tangled causes and devastating consequences of American policy at home and abroad since 9/11. In a collection
of searing essays, the author explores Washington's seemingly chronic inability to bring "the enemy" into focus, detailing the ideological, bureaucratic,
electoral, and (not least) emotional forces that have warped America's understanding of, and response to, the terrorist threat. He also shows how the
gratuitous and murderous shift of attention from al Qaeda to Iraq was shaped
by a series of misleading theoretical perspectives on the end of deterrence, the
clash of civilizations, humanitarian intervention, unilateralism, democratization, torture, intelligence gathering, and wartime expansions of presidential
power. The author's breadth of knowledge on the War on Terror leads to conclusions about present-day America that are at once sobering in their depth
of reference and inspiring in their global perspective.

After receiving his Ph.D. from Yale in 1976, Stephen Holmes taught briefly
at Yale University before becoming a member of the Institute for Advanced
Study in Princeton in 1978. He then moved to Harvard University's Department of Government, where he stayed until 1985, the year he joined the
faculty at the University of Chicago.

At Chicago, Holmes served as Director of the Center for the Study of Constitutionalism in Eastern Europe and as editor-in-chief of the *East European
Constitutional Review*. In 1994–96, he was the Director of the Soros Foundation program for promoting legal reform in Russia and Eastern Europe.
From 1997 to 2000, he was Professor of Politics at Princeton University.

Holmes' research centers on the history of European liberalism, the disappointments of democracy and economic liberalization after communism, and
the challenge of combating transnational terrorism within the bounds of the
rule of law. In 1984, he published *Benjamin Constant and the Making of Modern Liberalism*. Since then, he has published numerous articles on democratic
and constitutional theory. In 1988, he was awarded a Guggenheim Fellow-
ship to complete a study of the theoretical foundations of liberal democracy.
He was a member of the Wissenschaftskolleg in Berlin during the 1991–92
academic year. His *Anatomy of Antiliberalism* appeared in 1993. And in 1995,
he published *Passions and Constraint: On the Theory of Liberal Democracy*. In
1999, his *The Cost of Rights*, coauthored with Cass Sunstein, appeared. For
his research on the deraling of Russian legal reform, he was named a Carnegie
Scholar in 2003–05.

THE MATADOR'S CAPE

America's Reckless Response to Terror

STEPHEN HOLMES

Walter E. Meyer Professor of Law
New York University School of Law

CAMBRIDGE
UNIVERSITY PRESS

CAMBRIDGE UNIVERSITY PRESS
Cambridge, New York, Melbourne, Madrid, Cape Town, Singapore, São Paulo

Cambridge University Press
32 Avenue of the Americas, New York, NY 10013–2473, USA

www.cambridge.org
Information on this title: www.cambridge.org/9780521875165

First published 2007

Printed in the United States of America

A catalog record for this publication is available from the British Library.

Library of Congress Cataloging in Publication Data

Holmes, Stephen, 1941–
The matador's cape : America's reckless response to terror / Stephen Holmes.
 p. cm.
Includes bibliographical references and index.
ISBN-13: 978-0-521-87516-5 (hardback)
ISBN-10: 0-521-87516-1 (hardback)
1. War on Terrorism, 2001– 2. Terrorism – Government policy – United States.
3. United States – Politics and government – 2001– 4. United States – Foreign relations –
2001– 5. Terrorism – Religious aspects – Islam. 6. Anti-Americanism. 7. September 11
Terrorist Attacks, 2001 – Influence. I. Title.
HV6432.H653 2007
973.931 – dc22   2006039195

ISBN 978-0-521-87516-5 hardback

For Francesco

ACKNOWLEDGMENTS

Most of the ideas in this book were first elaborated in the Law and Security Colloquium at the New York University School of Law. To Richard Pildes, David Golove, and Noah Feldman – my brilliant friends and co-directors in the Colloquium – I therefore owe an enormous debt. For their incisive and often humbling comments on various chapters I need to thank not only Golove and Feldman, but also many other friends and colleagues, including Bruce Ackerman, Samuel Beer, Tom Carothers, Kiren Chaudhry, Arista Cirtautas, Amos Elon, Jon Elster, John Ferejohn, Diego Gambetta, Venelin Ganev, David Garland, Tom Geoghegan, Moshe Halbertal, Helen Hershkoff, Helge Høibraaten, Jamie Holmes, Ivan Krastev, David Luban, Bernard Manin, John McCormick, Claus Offe, Pasquale Pasquino, Patrizia Pinotti, Richard Posner, Adam Przeworski, Adam Shatz, Paul Starr, Tzvetan Todorov, Leon Wieseltier, and David Woodruff. I am grateful to them all. Only Katie Sticklor knows what mortifications I have been spared by her unerring proofreader's eye. Heartfelt thanks also go to John Berger, my editor at Cambridge University Press, who gently coaxed me into producing this book in record time. To Karen Greenberg, the founding Director and guiding spirit of the Law School's Center on Law and Security, my debt, as much personal as professional, is simply too costly to repay.

Most of the chapters in this book are reconceived and rewritten versions of earlier publications. For the right to use this material, I thank the original publishers. The earlier versions first appeared as follows: Chapter One in Diego Gambetta (ed.), *Making Sense of Suicide Missions* (2005); Chapter Two in *The American Prospect* (April 2003); Chapter Three in *The American Prospect* (June 2006); Chapter Four in *The Nation* (May 10, 2004); Chapter Five in *The London Review of Books* (May 6, 2004); Chapter Six in *The London Review of Books* (April 24, 1997); Chapter Seven in *The London Review of Books* (November 14, 2002); Chapter Eight in *The Nation* (November 14, 2005); Chapter Nine in *The London Review of Books* (October 5, 2006); Chapter Ten in *The New Republic* (February 28, 2005); Chapter Eleven in *The New Republic* (November 19, 2001); Chapter Twelve in Karen Greenberg (ed.), *The Torture Debate in America* (Cambridge University Press, 2005); and Chapter Thirteen in *The Nation* (May 1, 2006).

INTRODUCTION

> "Terrorism wins only if you respond to it in the way that the terrorists
> want you to, which means that its fate is in your hands."
> – David Fromkin

This book is an attempt to understand and explain America's reckless response to the terrorist attacks of 9/11. It builds on many previous efforts to get the story straight about the al Qaeda attack, the invasion and occupation of Iraq, and American counterterrorism policy more generally. Learning how to think clearly about the 9/11 provocation and America's response to it is an obvious first step toward correcting the tragically misguided course on which the nation has embarked. What follows is my modest contribution to that collective and ongoing endeavor.

A few prescient sentences, written in 1990 by Bernard Lewis to downplay the threat posed at that time by radical Islamists to the West, succinctly convey the extent to which America's response to 9/11 has grievously backfired:

> We should not exaggerate the dimensions of the problem. The Muslim world is far from unanimous in its rejection of the West, nor have the Muslim regions of the Third World been the most passionate and the most extreme in their hostility.... Certainly nowhere in the Muslim world, in the Middle East or elsewhere, has American policy suffered disasters or encountered problems comparable to those in Southeast Asia or Central America. There is no Cuba, no Vietnam, in the Muslim world, and no place where American forces are involved as combatants or even as "advisers."[1]

Today, American policy has suffered a disaster comparable to those it suffered earlier in Southeast Asia and elsewhere. The principal cause of that disaster is the involvement of American forces as combatants in the Middle East. As a consequence of the U.S. occupation, the Muslim world is increasingly passionate in its hostility to the West. Another consequence is that Professor Lewis is no longer counseling his audiences to dial down their expressions of alarm.

How did we get to this point?

To understand the cascading misconceptions, deceptions, and mistakes of the Bush Administration, we need to start with the al Qaeda attack itself. Part I, Chapter One examines in some detail the possible motivations of the 9/11 organizers and perpetrators. It aims to cast doubt on the common assumption that religious extremism "caused" the attack. There are several reasons for approaching the issue from a different angle. Identifying the single dominant purpose of any complex action, whether the 9/11 plot or the invasion of Iraq, will always be difficult. Although they obviously played an important role in motivating the al Qaeda plotters, religious sentiments and commitments were not the only forces at work. Case studies of the operation's instigators, organizers, and perpetrators reveal a complex web of unstable and contradictory impulses and convictions. One theme that constantly resurfaces, nevertheless, is a craving to avenge real and imagined injuries inflicted by the United States on the Muslims of the world. Emphasizing religious extremism as the motivator for the plot, whatever it reveals, also terminates inquiry prematurely, encouraging us to view the attack ahistorically, as an expression of "radical Salafism," a fundamentalist movement within Islam that allegedly drives its adherents to homicidal violence against infidels. Emphasizing the craving for revenge, by contrast, whatever it conceals, opens up a wider and more historical perspective on past conditions and future consequences. It directs our attention to concrete events, such as Israel's crushing defeat of numerically superior Arab armies in 1967, which gave rise to a need for payback and retribution. It has another advantage as well, reminding us of the emotionally powerful lure of murderous retaliation, of the trite but cruelly accurate observation that violence breeds violence in an unending cycle, a primitive pattern that all civilization, including liberal civilization, is ceaselessly struggling to overcome. By implication, a focus on reprisal draws attention not only to the alleged injuries that the 9/11 plotters believed themselves to be avenging, but also to the possibility that America's response was derailed by pre-rational impulses and muddled causal thinking. The 9/11 attack was an act of mass murder that can be analogized to a matador's cape in the hands of a malevolent and crazed provocateur. Bin Laden himself has boasted that it is "easy for us to provoke and bait this administration."[2] That the United

States would be tempted to react viscerally rather than with a cool head, that it would be "goaded into a self-defeating reaction"[3] such as an indiscriminate use of force, was not inevitable. The psychological quirks of a few power wielders made it perfectly possible, however. Far from assessing threats accurately, human beings typically overestimate or underestimate the dangers around them. Keeping such potentially fatal cognitive biases in mind is, therefore, the first step toward rethinking America's overall response to 9/11.

Despite a slew of carefully researched and insightful books on the subject, the reason why the United States responded to the al Qaeda attack by invading Iraq remains to some extent an enigma. The Conclusion to this book represents my own attempt to unravel that mystery. Many of the crucial factors influencing the fateful choice for war are previewed in Part II. The Pentagon's irresponsible failure to prepare for the postwar reflects Cheney and Rumsfeld's facile optimism first of all. It also reflects their inveterate September 10th mindset, namely a lifelong and unrevised conviction that hostile dictatorships are the only serious threats to American security in the international environment (Chapter Two). Their indifference to the very real threat posed to U.S. interests by state collapse, sectarian warfare, and violent criminalization in Iraq was so blithe that the Cheney-Rumsfeld group did almost nothing, when destroying Saddam's iron-grip on his military arsenal, to prevent an unprecedented proliferation disaster (Chapter Three). That disaster did not occur only because, unbeknownst to the administration, Iraq did not possess the stockpiles of WMD that served as the original *casus belli* for the invasion. In compensation, the war party's obliviousness to the serious threat that state collapse can pose to U.S. security interests produced a social and political disaster.

It is dismaying to contemplate the role of historical accident in the making of such a momentous and consequential decision as the invasion of Iraq (Chapter Four). By sheer misfortune, a personal alliance between Vice President Dick Cheney and then Secretary of Defense Donald Rumsfeld created a policymaking process insulated from and impervious to the strong doubts being expressed by knowledgeable executive-branch officials cut out of the loop (Chapter Five). Insiders were never compelled to provide a coherent and plausible rationale for the invasion. As a consequence, the military and other government agencies assigned to carry out the policy were never provided a comprehensible explanation of what they were supposed to achieve and how they were supposed to achieve it. The Cheney-Rumsfeld group's fatally selective perception of the threat environment resulted from personal prejudice, bureaucratic politics,

ideological rigidity, and electoral calculations. The catastrophic consequences will be felt for generations, and not only in what will be left of Iraq.

The Administration's response to 9/11 was also shaped to some extent
by a number of sophisticated theoretical attempts to define America's role
in the world after the Cold War. Several important examples are examined
and criticized in Part III. Samuel Huntington did not intend his theory of
the clash of civilizations, which seemed to predict a conflict between Islam
and the West, to be descriptive merely (Chapter Six). He also meant it to
provide new bearings for a U.S. foreign policy that, he feared, was falling
into incoherence. America's internal discipline and global authority would
be lost, he suggested, unless a new enemy could be found to reoccupy the
place vacated by the Soviet Union. Rereading Huntington's extraordinary
book in the aftermath of 9/11 and while the Iraq conflict still rages helps
us understand how a deep psychological need for confrontation with a
malign global enemy, typical of the Cold War holdovers who are only now
reluctantly releasing their grip on U.S. foreign policy, continues to distort
American perceptions of both the terrorist threat and Islamic civilization
today.

The American invasion and occupation of Iraq has led to the deaths
of tens and perhaps hundreds of thousands of Iraqi civilians who never
harmed America or Americans. This hellish toll of death and destruction is nevertheless a nonissue in U.S. domestic politics, perhaps on the
principle – if it is a principle – that out of sight is out of mind. According to the Baker-Hamilton Commission, the American military makes it a
policy not to count Iraqi killed and injured: "A roadside bomb or a rocket
or mortar attack that doesn't hurt U.S. personnel doesn't count."[4] And
the American public, having applauded its own willingness to liberate a
brutally abused nation, now seems oddly indifferent to the cruel suffering it has inflicted on people for whose sake this "war of liberation" is
purportedly being waged. Cheney and Rumsfeld are not the only ones
inured to the mayhem and carnage that the United States has inflicted on
perfectly innocent foreigners, in other words. Their appalling numbness
has deep roots in U.S. public consciousness. Whatever this tells us about
American political culture more generally, it also leads us to ask about
the role of liberal intellectuals in the run-up to the Iraq war (Chapter
Seven). Humanitarian intervention has probably never had so many passionate advocates as it had in the 1990s. Their commitment to stopping
genocide at all costs made them willing to bypass the UN system in order
to "end evil" by sending American soldiers to topple tyrants inside nominally sovereign states that had not attacked the United States. This posture

seemed less morally ambiguous in the 1990s than it has come to seem after March 2003. The same can be said about the suggestion, floated by at least some liberal hawks, that opposition to the invasion of Iraq verged on tacit complicity in the savagery of Saddam (Chapter Eight). Antitotalitarian activists and humanitarian interventionists bear no responsibility for the Administration's reckless response to 9/11, but they did help muffle liberal outrage at the decision to invade Iraq. Their moral lapse was not to peer more deeply into the twisted motivations and limited capacities of the public officials who were going to be carrying out the policies that they, the liberal hawks, were embellishing with their good intentions.

The idea that the United States should devote blood and treasure to spreading democracy around the world has not always been fashionable among strong-on-defense American conservatives. Its extraordinary prominence in justifying the Iraq war, although in large measure hypocritical, is therefore worth exploring. What it illuminates, in the end, is the deep incoherence of the U.S. response to 9/11 (Chapter Nine). The idea that jihadist terrorism is caused by lack of democracy in the Arab Middle East deserves to be evaluated and criticized on its own merits. It is a theory officially endorsed by the U.S. President, however. What is remarkable, therefore, is that this theory implicitly acknowledges a strain of justice in the jihadist cause. It assumes that terrorism is an understandable by-product of American-backed autocracy, that is, of the absence of serious opportunities for political participation in much of the Muslim world. The proposal to democratize the Arab Middle East also implies that any durable solution to the terrorist threat must be political, not military. The violent clash of these "neoconservative" assumptions with the working convictions, reflexes, and strategies of Bush's war cabinet has not been sufficiently appreciated.

Part IV addresses the Administration's implicit claim that the rule of law and due process are sources of weakness, hamstringing the executive branch and removing the flexibility it needs to conduct the war on terror. This approach to law is theoretically simplistic and empirically shaky. For one thing, law is best understood not as a set of rigid rules but rather as a set of institutional mechanisms and procedures designed to correct the mistakes that even exceptionally talented executive officials are bound to make and to facilitate midstream readjustments and course corrections. If we understand law, constitutionalism, and due process in this way, then it becomes obvious why the war on terror is bound to fail when conducted, as it has been so far, against the rule of law and outside the constitutional system of checks and balances.

The intuitive claim that grave emergencies require discretionary authority to act outside and against inherited rules and standard operating procedures is much less plausible than its defenders seem to believe. Visit the emergency room in a hospital and you will find nurses at the bedside of a comatose patient following strict procedures to avoid making a fatal mistake, say, about the correct blood type to administer. Such rules evolve over time because the errors that professionals make in situations of stress and panic are predictable. That politicians and bureaucrats are just as susceptible to avoidable error as doctors and nurses (or airplane pilots or fire-fighters) goes without saying. Grave emergencies do not suspend the laws of human fallibility or eliminate the need for checklists, devil's advocates, second opinions, after-action reviews, and orderly adversarial procedures.

What is wrong with allowing the executive branch to make important decisions on the basis of undisclosed information? The answer is a general one, not restricted to court proceedings but applicable to all governmental decision making. Secret government invariably increases the rate of potentially fatal error. The rule of law enforces an uncomfortable degree of transparency on the executive. It requires that the factual premises for the government's resort to coercion and force must be tested in some sort of adversarial process, giving interested and knowledgeable parties a fair opportunity to question the accuracy and reliability of evidence. That is how due process serves the public interest and helps reduce the risk of error. To reject the rule of law is reckless because it frees the government from the need to give reasons for its actions before a tribunal that does not depend on spoon-fed disinformation and is capable of pushing back. A government that is not compelled to give reasons for its actions may soon have no plausible reasons for its actions. The distressingly obtuse decisions produced by such an undisciplined and hunch-driven process are on public view today.

The central threat posed by the Cheney-Rumsfeld response to 9/11 is not the violation of civil liberties. The real danger is the bunker mentality that inevitably develops when the executive branch pulls back into a partisan echo chamber, withdrawing from scrutiny and eschewing consultation with anyone outside a small circle, purportedly for fear of delays and leaks. Even in ordinary times, executive-branch officials often express contempt for congressional oversight, viewing committee members as grandstanding ignoramuses with whom as little information as possible should be shared. During a national-security crisis, even this weakened form of checks and balances risks going by the wayside, but an executive branch that undergoes no independent scrutiny and hears no objections is not necessarily well-positioned to make intelligent decisions about the conduct of national affairs.

Echoing Bush, Cheney, and many others, Karl Rove, too, has frequently suggested that anyone who wants to fight terrorism within the bounds of constitutionalism and the rule of law is proposing to coddle America's most vicious enemies: "Conservatives saw the savagery of the 9/11 attacks and prepared for war; liberals saw the savagery of the 9/11 attacks and wanted to prepare indictments and offer therapy and understanding for our attackers."[5] The crass demonization of political rivals is less interesting here than the attempt to steer public craving for revenge into a repudiation of due process. This topic is treated at greater length in Part IV, but a stylized example can be introduced here to suggest what is at stake.

Experts of all political stripes agree that the war on terror depends essentially on information. We should therefore ask about the effect of various proposed policy innovations on the quality and quantity of information concerning possible terrorist activity flowing from private individuals to responsible government agencies. What is the effect on the willingness of private citizens to inform on their neighbors, for example, of loosening ordinary evidentiary standards for arresting and detaining suspects? Two probable consequences stand out. First, malicious individuals, bearing private grudges, will lodge false accusations, expecting that the police will pounce without carefully vetting the evidence. Second, honest individuals will hesitate to report their suspicions, fearing that these suspicions will turn out to be baseless and expecting that the police might do something drastic, such as sending an innocent neighbor to Guantánamo, without carefully vetting the evidence. Loosening evidentiary standards, in other words, discourages honest informants and encourages dishonest ones. The point of this example is not that evidentiary standards should never be loosened. The point is that the Administration's public contempt for the rule of law reveals a dismaying ignorance of the way due process is designed to increase governmental effectiveness in the struggle to protect public safety.

An historical overview of the curtailments of liberty for the sake of security in American history not only reminds us how often international disputes and foreign wars have been turned, domestically, into tools of savagely partisan politics (Chapter Ten). It also raises forcefully the very question that concerns us most: Is it really possible to increase American security in the war on terror by curbing the right of American citizens to examine and criticize their government? Recent experience suggests the contrary, confirming the underlying premise of the Founder's Constitution, namely that an unwatched power, sheltered from outside input and criticism, will almost never perform well.

Frustration with international law and multilateral institutions is justified in part. It is nevertheless folly to hope that the United States can, without international cooperation, successfully break up terrorist conspiracies or interdict the clandestine transfer of fissile materials. A doctrinaire preference for unilateral responses to security threats, in fact, can lead to a fatal underestimation of the gravity of those threats that can be parried only cooperatively (Chapter Eleven). Conversely, it can lead to a fateful exaggeration of the urgency of problems, such as a hostile dictatorship in Baghdad, which at first glance appear very easy to handle unilaterally.

An additional perspective on unilateralism is this: An individual who lives alone and never communicates with others can easily become autistic and disconnected from reality. Self-insulation, for nations too, is unlikely to breed clear-eyed realism. It should not be forgotten that allies have ideas and insights as well as interests, and sometimes these ideas and insights are better than the ones we have on our own. Moreover, ongoing cooperative and consultative relations, especially with America's partners in Europe, can provide a reality check, helping American policymakers overcome debilitating blind spots and tunnel vision. American television, it should also be mentioned, has shown a completely different picture of the conflict in Iraq than has been seen on European television (not to mention Arab satellite TV). How can American democracy function properly in a globalized world if American citizens have a picture of the effects of U.S. policy abroad that bears almost no resemblance to what others, in allied nations especially, see? It is not a question of submitting to the opinions of others. It is simply a matter of having some modest understanding of what others, enemies as well as allies, think and why.

The law must obviously adapt, on an ongoing basis, to technological change. There is no reason why this should not also be true of the traditional distinction between American citizens, whose rights should be protected, and aliens abroad, who have no rights at all not to be harmed by American officials. Such a hard-and-fast distinction made some sense in a world where the vast moats of the Atlantic and Pacific insulated the United States from most of mankind. Does it still make sense today, in an age of globalized transportation, migrant labor, and massive flows of anonymous tourists? A nimble and flexible leadership, examining the present-day threat of transnational terror, might well conclude that extending some minimal legal protections to foreigners overseas (that is, to people who live one cheap plane ticket away from U.S. shores) may well serve the security interests of Americans in America.

Abusive treatment of detainees, many of them innocent of any offense, has become a trademark of Bush's war on terror. By toppling a weak dictatorship in Iraq, the Cheney-Rumsfeld group apparently hoped to display America's ferocity to the world, frightening others and consoling U.S. citizens for the 9/11 wound. This background raises the concern that American custodial personnel have been replicating macro-politics at the micro level, inscribing America's superior strength on the bodies of the weak and defenseless, not to extract actionable intelligence, but to vent outrage and display power. That hypothesis may seem farfetched, but it becomes more plausible when we look at the Administration's problematic rationale for what it calls unconventional methods of interrogation (Chapter Twelve). This rationale dissolves upon inspection. Its fatal flaw lies in a shoddily constructed "necessity defense." There are many reasons to doubt the word of an individual who, claiming to have committed homicide in self-defense, insists that he could not have saved himself in any other way. For a state, with vast resources at its disposal, to prove that it was compelled to torture captives because it could not have unearthed vital information in any other way is very difficult, if not impossible. This consideration does not settle the issue of how custodial authorities must act in every conceivable situation, but it does reveal something about the slipshod analysis of Bush's hired-gun lawyers for torture.

From his experiences in the Nixon and Ford administrations, Vice President Cheney apparently concluded that America would be able to behave as a dominant world power only if the executive branch were freed from legislative oversight and interference. An eccentric attempt to read Cheney's longed-for imperial executive into the dreams of the American Framers is interesting chiefly for what it inadvertently reveals (Chapter Thirteen). What it helps us understand, in fact, is that the authors of the Constitution had excellent and still valid reasons for refusing to concentrate all power, even in wartime, in a single individual and his immediate entourage. They refused to assign unchecked power to the executive branch because they believed that public officials, even when elected, were just as fallible and susceptible to cognitive bias and emotionalism as ordinary citizens. All human beings, especially politically powerful ones, are reluctant to admit the grave mistakes that they inevitably make. To improve the chance that human fallibility will not inflict irreparable harm on the country, the Framers placed in Congress and the courts the right and the power to compel the executive to give reasons for its actions and, when necessary, to correct the executive's egregious errors. That any attempt to dismantle or weaken the constitutional system of checks and balances would produce a cascade of policy disasters is exactly what the Framers would have predicted.

Neoconservative defenders of the administration's gloves-off response to 9/11, when backed into a corner, regularly reach for Chapter Seventeen of *The Prince* where Machiavelli famously remarks that it is better to be feared than loved.[6] Ridiculing a writer who argues for "greater respect for international law," for example, Max Boot states that this simple-minded author, "like other critics of the Bush administration, ignores Machiavelli's dictum that 'it is much safer to be feared than loved.' George W. Bush may not have increased the love for the United States, but if he has increased respect for American power, that's an underappreciated achievement."[7] Apart from the shrewdly placed "if" in the last phrase, this passage nicely summarizes a viscerally antiliberal and historically dubious view, typical of the Cheney-Rumsfeld group and its defenders, that violence begets compliance, simply because frightened people will kneel before their intimidator and do whatever he wishes. It also, incidentally, reveals the author's curious ignorance of Chapter Seventeen of *The Prince* which argues, yes, that it is better to be feared than loved, but which adds pungently: It is worst of all to be hated. The same violent and repressive actions – that was Machiavelli's point – may simultaneously provoke fear and hatred. Because hatred is more volatile and quick to spark action than fear, provoking hatred alongside fear can be immensely dangerous. Power-hungry groups that try to work their will by inducing fear may even end up hastening their own ruin through the revolutionary violence and murderous rage that their swaggering brutality unintentionally arouses. America's bellicose response to the 9/11 provocation was not only dishonorable and unethical, given the cruel suffering it has inflicted on thousands of innocents, but also imprudent in the extreme because it was bound to produce as much hatred as fear, as much burning desire for reprisal as quaking paralysis and docility. Some of the sickening effects are unfolding before our eyes. That even more malevolent consequences remain in store is a grim possibility not to be wished away.

PART I

THE TERRORIST ENIGMA

1 DID RELIGIOUS EXTREMISM CAUSE 9/11?

"We're not facing a set of grievances that can be soothed and addressed. We're facing a radical ideology with inalterable objectives."

– George W. Bush (October 6, 2005)

The way a nation's leaders choose to interpret a violent provocation will determine how that nation responds. So how did America's government choose to interpret the murderous attacks of 9/11? How should it have interpreted them? Diagnosis matters because it dictates remedy. If a diagnosis is inaccurate, it can motivate and justify a toxic course of treatment. That something of the sort occurred after 9/11 is by now widely understood. America's excruciatingly self-defeating response to 9/11 provides a very practical reason to revisit the al Qaeda attack and probe the causes behind it. Human motivation is intrinsically opaque and inscrutable. Explaining the motives behind a conspiracy as complex as 9/11 necessarily involves speculation and guesswork; it should always be attempted with a tentative spirit and a constant readiness to revisit and revise working hypotheses. There will never be a definitive account of the motives of the 9/11 organizers and perpetrators. We can aspire to acknowledge the complications, however, and correct oversimplified views. This chapter takes aim at one of these simplified views, namely the claim that religious extremism caused 9/11. This claim is not totally baseless, but it is one-sided and less accurate than its proponents believe. The purported causal relation between extreme religious views and the political violence committed in their name is easier to assert than to demonstrate. Many individuals with radical religious beliefs never commit acts of political violence, and many perpetrators of political violence (including suicide terrorism) are not motivated by religion. These facts place the burden of proof on those who wish to locate in religious extremism, rather than in personal psychology or political context, the most basic explanation of 9/11. Their causal claim cannot be disproved; but it cannot be proved, either. Certainly the 9/11 hijackers were obsessed with Islamic texts and observances, but others who are equally obsessed never fly airplanes into buildings. This creates doubt about the causal influence of religious obsession in driving the plotters and hijackers to commit mass murder. On the other hand, in justifying their attack on the United States, both the perpetrators and the instigators of 9/11 make ample references to the "crimes" and "injustices" allegedly committed by America. They also consistently describe the attacks as reprisal killings. Some of the crimes they claim to have been punishing or avenging are real (the destruction of Hiroshima), whereas others are imaginary (the ongoing destruction of Islam). They do not dwell, in any case, on the charge that Americans live outside the faith. Pious Muslims may see injustice and impiety as closely interconnected, to be sure. They may be convinced that a Muslim jailer who tortures his religious prisoners is behaving with such rank injustice precisely because he is impious – that he is willing to torture, in other words, because he is not a good Muslim. The invocation of America's crimes and injustices as free-standing justifications for 9/11, in any case, should be taken seriously. If we do not take such allegations seriously, we will never be able to understand why the vicious killing of 3,000 innocents was applauded by many Muslims who would never have committed such an atrocity themselves. Real or imagined injustices attributed to America have almost certainly enlarged the recruitment pool of anti-American jihadists. At the very least, any pragmatic response to 9/11 should take this possible dynamic into account. A counterterrorism policy that corroborates the inculpatory narratives about America that circulate widely in the Muslim world today will almost certainly prove counterproductive. Even if those involved in 9/11 were personally motivated by religious extremism, the wider Islamic community has a choice between disciplining or tolerating its own radicals. Ordinary Muslims will no doubt feel greater sympathy for extremists if the latter can plausibly present themselves as righteous defenders of Islam against indiscriminately violent and aggressive Western powers. A selective emphasis on religious extremism as the cause of 9/11 obscures this crucial principle by implicitly diminishing the importance of humiliation, rage, and the craving for vengeance in generating sympathy for anti-Western violence.

It is impossible to establish with any precision the role played by such volatile emotions in driving young Muslims into jihadist conspiracies. Still, no response to 9/11 that further enflames the revenge impulse in young Arabs and Muslims worldwide, as the Administration's response clearly has, is likely to make Americans substantially safer. Those who trace the 9/11 attacks to religious extremism do not intend such a consequence, but their tunnel vision has contributed significantly to the failure of U.S. counterterrorism policy by reinforcing the belief that America's only feasible option – because it is dealing with apocalyptic fanatics – is to slash and burn its way to security. Exposing the limits of the "religious" interpretation of the al Qaeda provocation can be a useful exercise if it encourages, even modestly, a rethinking and recalibration of America's excessively violent, too broadly targeted, and patently counterproductive response to 9/11.

On September 11, 2001, nineteen young men – fifteen from Saudi Arabia, two from the United Arab Emirates, and one each from Egypt and Lebanon – seized control of four large commercial airliners departing from Boston, Newark, and Washington, D.C. At 8:47 a.m., mission leader Mohammed al-Amir Atta piloted American Airlines flight No. 11 into the North Tower of Manhattan's World Trade Center (WTC), and at 9:05 a.m., with the world's television cameras now trained on the site, a second group barreled United Airlines flight No. 175 into the South Tower. Finally, after a third suicide squad had crashed American Airlines flight No. 77 into the Pentagon at 9:39 a.m., the fourth team, under assault by a group of passengers, ditched United Airlines flight No. 93 into the Pennsylvania countryside at 10:03 a.m. These transcontinental flights apparently were selected because of the negligible number of passengers likely to be on board and the 10,000 gallons of aviation fuel that, upon impact, transformed the planes into immense incendiary bombs. At the World Trade Center, the hydrocarbon fires caused by the burning fuel overcame flimsy fireproofing and, after a very short time, brought the massive skyscrapers crashing down, killing close to 2,750 people. One hundred and ninety-eight more were killed in the Pentagon attack. Although suicide terrorists had been loading vehicles with explosives and ramming them into buildings for decades, this was the first time that hijacked airplanes had been successfully deployed for such an assault. The political after-effects have been so massive that we can, without much exaggeration, describe 9/11 as the suicide mission that shook the world.

We know that passengers on some of the flights were lulled into passivity by being informed that the aircraft were returning to the airports. We also know that the hijackers murdered some pilots and members of the crew before impact, probably by slitting their throats. But except for information gathered from a few cell-phone conversations, mostly from United Airlines flight No. 93, we have little direct evidence about what actually happened on board. Common sense, however, supplemented by the massive inquiries made after the fact, supports one elementary proposition, namely, that this was a carefully planned operation conducted efficiently by trained and disciplined operatives. Not only did the hijackers or their dispatchers choose these specific flights to minimize passenger resistance and maximize the fuel load; they also carried on board lethal weapons that were inconspicuous enough to pass undetected through lax baggage screening. In the weeks leading up to the attacks, some of the hijackers made dummy runs on these same transcontinental flights to case flight procedures and crew behavior. This detail, too, suggests that the hijackers were cool professionals. They were not simply zealots, but disciplined zealots, capable of patience and able to execute a dangerous plan without attracting attention.

To succeed in such an audacious operation, the perpetrators also needed, besides instruction in terrorist tradecraft, logistical support from a variety of co-conspirators positioned around the world, especially in Europe and the Middle East. Money funneled through Dubai, among other places, allowed the future suicide pilots to take flying lessons on one-engine aircraft and practice on a flight simulator for commercial jets. The final go-ahead for the 9/11 attack was probably given when a handful of men around Osama bin Laden met Atta and other members of the Hamburg cell in Afghanistan in November or December 1999. As the plot unfolded and members of the Hamburg cell moved to the United States, supervisors abroad kept track of their doings, and eventually coordinated the just-in-time arrival of the rest of the squad. But not even a highly detailed chart of the 9/11 chain of command would answer the most important questions, namely: Why did the operational chief behind 9/11, Khalid Sheikh Mohammed,[1] decide to deploy a suicide team to attack these specific American targets? Why did he not instead send hit-and-run commando teams, as his nephew, Ramzi Yousef, did in 1993?[2] And why did the hijackers, particularly the fully informed pilots, agree to follow his instructions in this case, even though it involved participation in a predictably terminal mission?[3]

The importance and exact role of religious beliefs, sentiments, and codes of conduct in the 9/11 plot remain a matter of dispute. Many commentators insist that "what bin Laden has said and done has every-thing to do with religion."[4] Admittedly, religious convictions can lead young men to grow beards, avoid supposedly unclean foods, and embark on pilgrimages. But can we plausibly assert that the religious beliefs of the 9/11 terrorists *caused* them to plan and carry out the attack? This crudely formulated question arises because many of those involved in the plot have let the world know that they did it to express devotion to God or to curry favor with God.

Professions of piety deserve a respectful hearing, no doubt, but they alone clearly do not settle the issue. Sometimes people do what they do for the reasons they profess, but private motivations cannot always be gleaned from public justifications. The problem is not that individuals with secretly secular (personal or political) purposes may feign religious goals to bur-nish their reputations for purity. The problem, instead, is that one and the same decision could have been taken for either religious or secular reasons. In that case, it is often impossible to tell which motive played a preponderant role. For instance, emotions with a religious tinge, such as dread of contamination, might conceivably induce some individuals to face death without blinking; but so can non-religious emotions, such as the craving for blood revenge. Duty to God can desensitize a believer to ordinary costs and benefits; but so can boiling rage. An Islamic husband, living in Germany, may lock his wife inside the house because he wants to be pious and thinks that female sequestration is what piety demands; but he may also do it to exercise arbitrary power and thereby compen-sate psychologically for feelings of impotence and passivity that afflict the rest of his miserable life. According to one account, Islamic beliefs and sensibilities govern his behavior but, according to the other and no less plausible account, Islamic beliefs merely provide a pretext. So how can we decide which account is more persuasive in any particular case?

Did Osama bin Laden plot to eject the United States from the Arabian peninsula because American troops were desecrating sacred soil? Or was he aggrieved, much as any anticolonialist or nationalist insurrectionist might be, that the United States was "plundering" Arabia's natural resources? Or did he begin to hate the United States in 1991, not because the Americans had just stationed troops in Arabia, but because the Soviet Union had left Afghanistan, and bin Laden, for psychological or political reasons, needed another superpower on which to vent his enmity?

Does Ayman al-Zawahiri aspire to overthrow Mubarak because the latter is an apostate, or because he is a tyrant? Do extreme religious views cause political violence, or does terrorism occur when young men feel compelled to erase perceived personal or group shame by an act of homicidal rage? Violent youths who viscerally enjoy fighting and killing have a powerful motive to re-describe as "a religious duty" acts of cruelty that they perform for wholly nonreligious reasons? When secular and religious rationales are equally credible and would each independently trigger the action to be explained, we cannot know with any certainty that the decisive factor was religion.

Underestimating these methodological difficulties, some commentators have argued, without qualifications or disclaimers, that 9/11 was a religious act. When confronted by doubters, they may even complain, as do Daniel Benjamin and Steven Simon, that "so much of what was heard from al Qaeda after the attacks sounded to Americans like gibberish that many chords of the apocalypse were missed."[5] Americans are simply too secular to appreciate the grip of religion on the minds of militants and fanatics, they contend. But is this correct? Not necessarily. In fact, the opposite may be true. Some Americans, at least, think more easily in Biblical than in secular terms. They probably know more about "the end of days" than about political intrigue in Jeddah or Peshawar. Shared by the terrorists and their targets, Biblical phraseology may therefore have attracted too much, not too little, attention, obscuring nonreligious factors and motivations.

Why, for example, did the attackers target the World Trade Center? According to Nancy Kobrin, the targeting decision can be explained only by the planners' religious beliefs. Her analysis assumes, correctly, that knocking down great towers in lascivious cities is a Biblical theme. Radical Islamists, she goes on to say, viewed the Twin Towers as idols worshipped by the pagans. Assuming (falsely, it appears) that an earlier al Qaeda operation had targeted the Seattle Space Needle, she speculates that the organizers of the 9/11 attack saw the Twin Towers as deliberately mocking Islamic minarets. From the minaret, five times a day, all Muslims are called to prayer, that is, to total submission to God. Operating inside the Islamic belief system, Kobrin claims, the terrorists interpreted America's great skyscrapers as an affront to God, as a refusal to submit to God, or even as a supremely blasphemous attempt to become God.[6]

This fanciful analysis cannot be refuted, but it cannot be confirmed, either. Moreover, the targeting of the World Trade Center can quite comprehensively be explained without any reference to Islam. Haughty pride may be a sin before God, but it also can independently arouse resentment in human beings whose piety is erratic or nonexistent. Moreover, the 2001 attack on America's "pillars of pride" was a return visit. Khalid Sheikh Mohammed (KSM) may have wished to redeem his arrested nephew's botched toppling of the WTC in 1993 for much the same reason that

George W. Bush wished to redeem his ousted father's botched toppling of Saddam in 1991. The need to mop up unfinished business, and therefore to communicate in blood the dogged persistence of one's own side, is an independent reason for action. The same can be said of the desire to do for a kinsman what he is no longer able to do for himself.

True, the attack took place in a symbolic space against meaningful targets where the high density of human life may even have been secondary to the perceived symbolism of the buildings themselves. "Edificide," especially the destruction of sacred temples (such as the Askariya Mosque in Samarra, Iraq), apparently appeals to premodern minds. By bringing New York City's twin capitalist campanili crashing down, bin Laden and KSM may have hoped to prove to adversaries and supporters alike that their principal enemy's divinities were powerless or imaginary.

The symbolism was not necessarily Biblical, however. The Twin Towers could have been targeted simply as emblems of the United States, embodiments of American pride. To attack the WTC was to attack America in effigy. Bin Laden suggested as much, referring to the towers as "icons" less of America's infidelity or blasphemy than of America's supercilious power.[7] Depicting himself and his co-conspirators as rods of the Lord, devoted to shattering American arrogance, he claimed that "God Almighty hit the United States at its most vulnerable spot. He destroyed its greatest buildings. Praise be to God."[8]

Located in the country's greatest urban centre, these architectural advertisements of America's self-importance were militarily impossible to defend. Yet in his attempt to explicate the symbolic meaning of the towers, bin Laden lavishes less attention on America's presumptive "war against God" than on America's hypocrisy: "Those awesome symbolic towers that speak of liberty, human rights, and humanity have been destroyed. They have gone up in smoke."[9] So far as Arabs are concerned, the United States' steady support for Arab autocrats shows that its talk of "liberty" and "democracy" is hollow propaganda. This suggests, once again, that the WTC was chosen as a symbol not of unbelief but of the supposedly false liberty that the United States shows to the world even while colluding with nondemocratic regimes to oppress and despoil Muslims and indeed the majority of mankind.

Many of the key actors in the 9/11 drama, admittedly, articulate their grievances using archaic religious language. But the very fact that the code involved is ancient whereas the behavior we want to explain is recent gives reason to doubt causal theories that overemphasize the religious element. If suicide missions are a consequence of Islamic fundamentalism, why did not previous waves of Islamic fundamentalism give rise to suicide missions? If Russian anarchists, Japanese Kamikaze, and the Black Tigers of Sri Lanka have all undertaken suicide missions for secular reasons, how can we be confident that the 9/11 terrorists would have undertaken their suicide mission only if the religious reasons they allege were their deepest reasons? This skeptical line of thought suggests that nonreligious motives may have just possibly been predominant in the 9/11 mission as well. To pursue this suggestion, it will be helpful to divide our inquiry into two parts, looking first at the perpetrators and then at the instigators and supervisors of the plot.

The Hijackers

According to David Hume, "such is our natural horror of death, that small motives will never be able to reconcile ourselves to it."[10] So what were the large motives that reconciled the hijackers to their impending deaths? Many commentators offhandedly assert that the hijackers were simply programmed for death, having been socialized inside a cultural system that normalizes suicide terrorism. About al Qaeda, some even assert that "the culture of martyrdom is firmly embedded in its collective psyche."[11] Such appeals to social norms or a culture of martyrdom are not very helpful, however. They are tantamount to saying that suicide terrorism is caused by a proclivity to suicide terrorism. A less tautological approach starts elsewhere, with the observation that, at some level, Atta and the others did what they did because they were recruited, trained, and instructed to do so by their commanders in a quasi-military hierarchical organization that had "declared war" on America. That is to say, their murderous act must be explained organizationally and not merely ideologically or psychologically, or even sociologically. They were told what to do and behaved like soldiers, obeying superiors and dying for their (imaginary) country.

They were no doubt recruited, in part, because of their observed zeal for the cause and their evident willingness to follow orders, especially after sworn and recorded pledges made obedience into a matter of personal honor. But a willingness to follow orders, even when sealed by vows, needs a special explanation when it entails a willingness to face certain death. The most commonly fielded explanation for this staggering readiness is also the most straightforwardly religious. The nineteen hijackers "loved death," it is repeatedly alleged, not because they were nihilists but because they wholeheartedly believed that, in their case, death did not exist. Each pilot allegedly interpreted the crash site as a doorway through which he would slip into another and happier life. They thought that the impact would vaporize them instantly into the presence of the Prophet, that death in jihad was a pathway to redemption, a ticket to everlasting life. To keep their heads cool, they did not even need to be exceptionally courageous, since they were oblivious to the danger ahead. They did not have to overcome their fear of death, because they had no idea that they were about to die.

Under some circumstances, presumably, young men with an exclusively technical education could genuinely believe something of this sort. Recruiters for the plot were no doubt looking for candidates who could at least entertain on occasion the hope of a rewarding afterlife. A naive belief in paradise, as Voltaire waggishly remarks, can induce young "imbeciles" to risk their lives:

> Ce sont d'ordinaire les fripons qui conduisent les fanatiques, et qui mettent le poignard entre leurs mains; ils ressemblent à ce Vieux de la Montagne qui faisait, dit-on, gouter les joies du paradis à des imbèciles, et qui leur promettait une éternité de ces plaisirs d'ont il leur avait donné un avant-gout, à condition qu'ils iraient assassiner tous ceux qu'il leur nommerait.[12]

Let us call this "the Voltaire thesis." In religious conflicts, cunning priests exploit the blind folly of foot soldiers, particularly their fantasy of a never-ending afterlife. This irreverent charge assumes, in typical Enlightenment style, that charlatans and swindlers can easily "run" young men who are gullible and easy to string along.

A sharp distinction between brazen dupers and their credulous pawns can sometimes be extremely illuminating. Such a contrast may even help us understand something essential about the relation between leaders and followers in the 9/11 plot. Perhaps the hijackers died with their eyes shut, without realizing that death was on the horizon. But we cannot be satisfied, at the outset, with the conclusion that the 9/11 hijackers were "imbeciles" in this sense. Their belief that they were taking a plane ride to paradise cannot end all inquiry into the multiple causes of their extraordinary behavior. So, what other factors could contribute to their willingness to die? Another simple answer comes immediately to mind. Perhaps some of them were willing to die because, for highly personal reasons, they wanted to die.

Professional terrorist organizations presumably aim to recruit effective and reliable killers, not maladjusted misfits. On the other hand, the need to find volunteers for self-destruction may occasionally force them to compromise the highest standards of mental health. Here is one account

(of uncertain reliability) of Wail Alshehri and Waleed Alshehri, two brothers in Atta's crew, described as unmotivated and not very smart, devout to
some degree but also willing to indulge in smoking and listening to pop
music.

> A turning point came late in 1999 when Wael, 25, fell into a deep
> depression, Abdel Rahman said. His friends say it was not just depres-
> sion, but perhaps even a suicidal tendency, and he was forced to take a
> leave of absence from his work as a gym teacher. He went to see a faith
> healer in Mecca accompanied by Walid, 21, who was "just drifting in
> life," his brother said. It was at this point that the two apparently fell
> under the sway of a militant Islamic cleric who counseled both to read
> the Koran, to fast, and to take up jihad.[13]

Although they prove nothing, such anecdotes are suggestive. Personalities
prone to self-destruction may be impeded from acting as they wish by
a powerful social norm that declares suicide disgraceful. In the Islamic
tradition, as in Christian and Jewish traditions, suicide is also understood
as "a sin because only God has a right to take the life he has granted."[14]
Man is God's property, and therefore self-murder is a form of theft. So
how might individuals inclined to kill themselves find a circuitous path
around such powerful prohibitions?

One way would be to enlist in a cause that redescribes suicide as honorable, pious, and heroic, as self-sacrifice for a "higher" cause. The social
stigma of suicide, if not the divine prohibition itself, may deter some clin-
ically depressed youths in Muslim societies from taking their lives. The
ideal of militant jihad provides an opportunity to circumvent this taboo.
By enlisting in a suicide mission, a suicidally depressed individual could
kill himself or herself with social approval. All he or she has to do is agree
to kill an enemy of Islam in the process. Needless to say, if Wail Alshehri
or another one of the 9/11 hijackers were suicidally depressed, he would
also have had overpowering reasons to conceal his depression. Suicide
terrorism patently undertaken to escape from personal despair would not
only violate Islamic norms; it would also destroy the "social meaning" of
the act, which must appear to involve sacrifice (and that means giving up
something of value) for a higher cause. Seeking death to avoid the tribulations of life is a sign of cowardice, not courage.[15] The incentives in such a
case for deceptive signaling are so great, in fact, that no public pronouncements by a suicide terrorist can provide decisive evidence about his private
motivations. Religion may explain the hijackers' willingness to die, or it
may have simply made their nonreligious desires more socially acceptable.

It is hard to imagine discovering proof that demonstrates conclusively which explanation holds true.

Mohammed Atta

The most exhaustively studied member of the hijacking squad is the 33-year-old Egyptian team leader Mohammed Atta. He has been the focus of much attention not only because he played a central role in the plot, but also because his home bases of Cairo and Hamburg are accessible cities where foreign policemen and journalists have considerably less difficulty in conducting probes than they would, say, in Saudi Arabia's Asir province. Nothing we have learned suggests that he was suicidally depressed, so what might his motive have been for joining a plot that would end his life? He may have been motivated by religious belief, as many commentators contend, or by nonreligious desires wrapped in religious rhetoric, or by some combination of religious and nonreligious commitments and convictions. How can we decide?

Atta's family was not exceptionally pious, and the women in the family did not wear the veil. His father was a relatively prosperous lawyer, without any apparent affiliation to the Muslim Brotherhood. His childhood was punctured in 1981 (Atta was 13), when Anwar Sadat, President of Egypt, was assassinated by Islamic militants. Whatever he felt about them at the time, as the years ticked by he may have gradually come to see Sadat's assassins as role models who laid down their lives to "slay the Pharaoh." In the manual consulted by the pilots before the attack, the terrorists are told to imagine that they are reenacting the heroic exploits of famous Islamic heroes and martyrs. But, for an Egyptian such as Atta, Sadat's assassins may have provided more easily understandable models than the early caliphs and imams.

Atta graduated in 1991 from Cairo University with a degree in architecture, but seems to have had no sustained contacts with militant Islamic organizations while there. He began his studies in city planning in Germany in 1992, at the Hamburg-Harburg Technical University, working part-time at a German company for the next five years. His path to radicalization is uncertain, and, although some observers have tried to pinpoint the precise moment when Atta started marching to a different drummer, to do so is probably impossible.[16] We do know a little more about his outward turn toward religious observance. Soon after arriving in Hamburg, for instance, a presumably homesick Atta quickly began acting more devoutly than he had done back home in Egypt. He displayed his devoutness, in a perfectly conventional manner, by establishing cultural distance, isolating himself from his surroundings, "refusing to touch food prepared in pots used to cook anything that was not halal, and avoiding contact with dogs and women."[17]

In August 1995, Atta arrived back in Cairo for a three-month study visit just as the Egyptian government was unleashing a violent crackdown on the Muslim Brotherhood in response to an attempted assassination of President Mubarak in Addis Abbaba. Having recently undertaken a pilgrimage to Mecca, Atta now sported a full beard, and when he returned to Hamburg in November 1995, he was even more outwardly devout. Apparently, his mastery of Islamic texts was rudimentary but, already in April 1996, he swore before acquaintances to die as a martyr. The "last will and testament" that he signed at the time at a radical mosque near Hamburg railroad railway station is telling, particularly because of the anxiety it expresses about posthumous pollution by females ("I don't want any women to go to my grave at all during my funeral") and because it asks the men who would be washing his dead body to avoid unshielded contact with his genitals.[18]

By late 1998, Atta and his fellow conspirators had rented an apartment at 54 Marienstrasse in the Harburg district of Hamburg. This flat served as a headquarters, where three of the 9/11 pilots ironed out details of the attack.[19] Sometime around November 1999, Atta visited Afghanistan in the company of Ramzi bin al-Shibh, Marwan al-Shehhi, and Ziad Jarrah. Plans for 9/11 were apparently finalized during this trip, which included a meeting with Osama bin Laden. Upon returning to Germany, Atta reported his passport stolen to expunge all traces of his travels to Afghanistan and elsewhere. Continuing to follow instructions, he moved to the United States in early June 2000, joining Marwan al-Shehhi, who was one of his companions and roommates in Germany. With the money wired to them from Germany and the United Arab Emirates, the pair began to take flying lessons in Florida in November 2000, and received their pilots' licenses in December. Immediately afterwards, they spent some hours on a Boeing flight simulator.

It would be possible, but not necessarily helpful, to flesh out this thumbnail sketch of Atta's career. The important question for us is: Why did such a man choose to enlist in such a deadly mission? The sexual torments suggested by the "will" he signed in 1996 have convinced many commentators that his motivations must have been deeply religious, rooted in a dread of sin, impurity, and contamination, and we should not dismiss this hypothesis out of hand. Before we accept it, however, we should consider some alternatives.

The many investigators who, after the attack, attempted to piece together a psychological portrait of Mohammed Atta during the 1990s agree on one striking point – namely, that the grievances he loudly and frequently articulated against America and the Muslim autocracies that America supports were almost entirely secular. Most of those who knew him before 1996 stress not Atta's religious piety, but his implacable fury at the plight of the poor and the indifference of the rich: "Atta could get exercised by the world's shortcomings, big and small. He spoke out impulsively against injustice."[20] He was bitterly angry at the visible juxtaposition in Cairo of extravagant and frivolous luxury with mass squalor and hopelessness. Egypt's elite, in particular, was hypocritical, he believed. They talked one way and acted another, they showed a "democratic face" to the West, but displayed complete indifference to the misery of ordinary people at home. They had sold their country to the West for trinkets.

Interviews with German fellow students of Atta at Harburg reveal that, around 1995 (that is, only a short time before he signed his "last will"), Atta was still expressing fury at the way the homes of poor people in Cairo were being torn down to make way for tourist parking. Egypt's city planners were refashioning a few choice neighborhoods in overcrowded Cairo into a kind of Disneyland for Americans and Europeans. The inequalities that caught Atta's attention were also global, of course. A German friend reports Atta's assertion that Egypt "had opened up to Western influence and market capitalism regardless of the real needs of the people." This friend also recalls a telling detail: "He told me it was grotesque that strawberries were being grown in the Nile delta for the European market, luxury goods, while the poor could not afford to buy wheat imported from America."[21]

There is obviously nothing distinctively Islamic about such laments. The same German acquaintance, trying to explain Atta's "embitterment," explicitly concluded: "I don't think it was religious. Religion provided the vocabulary, not the cause. The cause was political."[22] A generation earlier, the same burning indignation could have been expressed in Marxist or nationalist idioms. In the mid-1990s, it is also worth noting, Atta repeatedly promised to return to "Arabia" to help build better communities. Much like his anger, his ambition seems to have been quite secular at the time. He frequently expressed his desire to help fellow Arabs improve their worldly condition, which makes him sound like a perfectly ordinary nationalist or egalitarian and is difficult to reconcile with his later rhetorical turn to an intensely religious ideology that doubts the ultimate worth of anything that occurs in this world.

Joseph Conrad famously described terrorist motivations as "personal impulses disguised into creeds." Infuriated by the world's refusal to recognize his merit, the suicide terrorist in *The Secret Agent* inflates his personal disappointments into a general theory of the corruption of modern society. Having been personally undervalued had "opened his eyes to the true nature of the world, whose morality was artificial, corrupt, and blasphemous."[23]

A similar psychological dynamic may have been at work in Atta's case. During his brief stay in Cairo in 1995, Atta experienced personally the sting of religious discrimination. His technical credentials had been unfairly devalued, he thought. Doors were slammed in his face simply because of his religious appearance and behavior: "Adding to Atta's distress was his realization that Cairo's planning administration was a nest of nepotism. Jobs were handed down from generation to generation, and none was about to be handed to an upstart who sympathized with the fundamentalists."[24] He was being treated unjustly, he concluded, by an "apostate" Muslim regime. But such rejections seem only to have made him more defiant: "Atta informed two German traveling companions that he would not be cowed by the country's 'fat cats,' who he believed were criminalizing religious traditionalists while bowing shamefully to the West in foreign and economic policies."[25] It is impossible to know if he was bothered more by the injustice or the apostasy of Egypt's public power. The two issues seem to have been inextricably intertwined in his thinking. The problem here is a general one. Personal motivations are often experienced subjectively as murky, jumbled, and unstable. The human psyche is a tangled skein, and what is true for the rest of us was presumably true in Atta's case as well. Resentment at unfair personal treatment and indignation at elite selfishness were no doubt promiscuously mixed together in his mind with religious distress over personal and social disobedience to God's will. Such a blurring of personal frustration, political protest, and religious convictions makes it very difficult, if not impossible, to demonstrate the specifically religious roots of Atta's commitment to jihadist violence. When the rich and powerful are accused simultaneously of impiety and injustice (or of apostasy and tyranny), we cannot be certain how much relative weight to ascribe to each charge. It is at least possible that Atta hated Cairo's "fat cats" more for their selfish greed and indifference to the poor than for their disbelief. It may even be true that the repression of Islamic radicals *represented*, in Atta's mind, the suffering of all Egyptians, religious or not, at the hands of Egypt's cruel and corrupt elite.

Another minor story bears retelling in this context. It involves Atta's apparent belief that traditional Muslim cities had been desecrated by modern high-rise buildings: "In his view skyscrapers were symbols of a Western civilization that had relegated his own culture to the sidelines."[26] He repeatedly "bemoaned Western influence – specifically, the rise of skyscrapers – in Arab cities."[27] Did Atta really feel this way about skyscrapers? If so, did this idiosyncratic aversion motivate him to enlist in an attack on the World Trade Center? Did he want to desecrate New York City's landscape to avenge the way "Americanization" had desecrated Cairo's? Such speculations are farfetched, or at least unverifiable, but his palpable anger at the destruction of ancient cities may nevertheless provide an important clue to Atta's thinking.

His 1999 German dissertation focused adoringly on the 5,000-year-old *souk*, or marketplace, of Aleppo (now Halab, Syria), with its miles of labyrinthine covered streets that had developed organically, without the deadening influence of modern rationalism.[28] Much has been made of his last-minute inscription to the dissertation, reading: "my prayer and my sacrifice and my life and my death are all for God, the Lord of the World."[29] Less attention has been given to the fact that ancient Aleppo was a pre-Islamic or, as Sayyid Qutb would describe it, a *jahili* city. Nostalgia for a bronze-age pagan society is not piously Islamic. Today's radical Islamists, in particular, do not feel especially squeamish about attacking pre-Islamic traditions, however venerable. Militant Islam does not honor local customs and traditions, but smashes them zealously to bring them into conformity with God's will. Thus, Atta's intense concern to preserve *non-Islamic traditions* that were being destroyed by modernization is, at best, only tenuously connected to his Islamic radicalism. Perhaps the "authentic" values that Atta perceived to have been traduced in the modernization of Aleppo had more to do with the lachrymose German romanticism of some of his Harburg professors than with a root-and-branch fundamentalism like Qutb's.

What originally attracted Atta toward Islamic militancy was not necessarily its doctrinal stringency. What drew him to Hamburg's al-Quds mosque, in all likelihood, was the rage that he encountered there toward the odious oligarchies of the Arab world and their American supporters. In such an incubator of animosity and insurrection, his bitter class-based resentments must have resonated powerfully with the similar fury of a group of likeminded, angry young men. If Atta became a jihadist because Islamic militancy was the only feasible way to express his hatred of Egypt's elite and their foreign backers, however, then we cannot say that his religious beliefs in any way caused him to join the 9/11 attack. It would be more accurate to say that the same secular fury against the privileged that led him to join the plot had propelled him at an earlier stage to affiliate with radical Islamist groups.

This pattern is not limited to Atta. Throughout the nominally Islamic world and beyond, individuals who are spoiling to fight against the established powers are turning to extreme versions of Islam because radical Islamic sects appear to be the only organizations that are sending out a call to arms. Such individuals are naturally attracted to the aggressive passages in the Qur'an, but the source of their aggressive feelings cannot be found in scripture. Rather than Islamic traditions producing militancy, currents of militancy are finding their way toward previously marginal streams of Islam, boosting their membership and driving them into increasing bellicosity and violence. This is not to deny, of course, that religious teachings can intensify and coordinate preexistent anger. Least of all is it meant to question the "sincerity" of Atta's religious beliefs. But such considerations should make us doubt the causal efficacy of religious beliefs, however sincere, in a context where secular anger and frustration could explain, on their own, why young men would embrace violent militancy. To pursue this line of inquiry, it will help to look briefly at some of the others who voluntarily died in the attack.

Social Background

The two other suicide pilots in the Hamburg cell, Marwan al-Shehhi (from the United Arab Emirates) and the Ziad Jarrah (from Lebanon), both arrived in Germany in 1996. Their backgrounds and characters cannot be described here in any detail, but we should at least mention that their personalities seemed quite unlike Atta's. They were, at least reportedly, as convivial as he was priggish. Jarrah, in particular, lacked Atta's punitive rectitude and burning sense of social injustice.[30] Such differences even within the Hamburg cell suggest the futility of trying to draw a composite portrait of "the 9/11 suicide pilot." These young men had different psychological make-ups, and it is quite unlikely that any single common motive explains why all three proved willing to die. Perfectly ordinary people, as is well known, become capable of committing unspeakable atrocities when caught up in group dynamics. This observation suggests the limited utility of psychological profiling as a predictor of who will become a terrorist.

Despite their clashing personalities, the Hamburg three shared several traits in common.[31] First and foremost, they all seem to have been radicalized while living as expatriates in Germany. According to many experts, "the radicalization that led them to carry out the attacks appears to have occurred while they were living in Europe."[32] That they were drawn to the al-Quds mosque as a welcoming oasis in an unwelcoming society is easy enough to imagine, and Europe's latent – and sometimes quite explicit – Islamophobia certainly increases the appeal of political Islam among Muslims living there. But discrimination and cultural exclusivity were not the only potential sources of personal hurt. Atta, for instance, seems to have experienced acute culture shock when he first moved from puritanical Egypt to anything-goes Germany.

Whether or not they were disoriented by Western license, young Muslims who came to Europe in the 1990s probably proved easy pickings for radical imams and jihadist recruiters simply because they were cut loose from family monitoring and control. Unlike other modern suicide terrorists (such as members of the Black Tigers or the al-Aqsa brigade), these three young men operated in the lengthy run-up to the attacks as a criminal conspiracy, isolated from older relatives and with almost no psychological or logistical support from a wider national community. When the smoke cleared, moreover, their families did not boast about their deeds. Many of the parents vehemently denied their sons' participation. Their mothers certainly did not celebrate their deaths, as have some mothers of Palestinian suicide bombers.

All the members of the Hamburg cell also came from middle-class backgrounds. This is why they are so often said to defy "the stereotypical profile" of the young terrorist as poor, uneducated, and desperate. Their fairly prosperous families presumably had no need for a "martyrdom allowance" such as that which has allegedly played a role in encouraging Palestinian suicide bombing. Still, their relatively privileged upbringing makes their willingness to commit suicide somewhat mysterious. These young men did not have their backs to the wall, as did the "jumpers" from the WTC on 9/11. They were not suffering from survivor's guilt. Nor did they face an imminent choice between dying passively and dying actively, exiting from the world pointlessly or taking some enemies with them. They were in a very different situation, in short, than the suicide bombers of Palestine. Their life prospects were not hopeless, and therefore the opportunity costs of suicide, especially in a mission with such an uncertain outcome, seem quite high. So what led them to overcome their instinctive fear of death?

In recent decades, the middle classes in many Middle Eastern countries have been living under a constant threat of downward mobility. According to his acquaintances at the time, "by the early '90s, Atta felt the intense pressures on middle-class Egyptians not to slip social rank. His friend Khalifa says Atta grew frustrated because he was unable to fulfill his academic ambitions in his homeland. He believed that political favoritism at Egyptian universities would keep him from the top spots."[33] That similar anxieties may have afflicted the Saudi members of the team is made at least superficially plausible by the dramatic drop in per capita Saudi GDP during the 1980s and 1990s.[34] The expatriate children of middle-class Lebanese, Egyptian, and Emirate families, although they could not have been as desperate as some Palestinian suicide bombers, may have carried inside them their families' class anxieties or their generation's fear of tumbling down the social ladder. They may also have been psychologically traumatized by their move to Europe, where they may have experienced, overnight, a bruising loss of status and prestige.

That middle-class apprehensions, reflecting precarious economic conditions in the Middle East, played some role in the inner lives of the 9/11 pilots is quite probable. But again, we obviously have no way of gauging the relative influence of such anxieties on their eventual decision to join an unforgiving jihad against America. We simply cannot know if the endangered privileges of their class made them especially concerned to redeem what they considered to be the lost dignity of the world Islamic community, as they imagined it.

What we can say, however, is that their middle-class backgrounds recall, to some extent, the social profile of members of the Red Brigades, the Baader-Meinhof gang, and other European terrorist groups who, while perfectly secular, were apparently indifferent to parochially nationalist goals. The members of the Hamburg cell certainly lacked the kind of community support received by the national-liberation terrorists of IRA, ETA, and Hamas. They were a vanguard without a mass following. There was no global intifada to buoy them up. In that sense, they eerily resemble the European radicals of the 1970s and even the anarchists active in Russia at the end of the nineteenth century and the beginning of the twentieth.[35] Such analogies, although playful, make us ask, once again, if radical Islamic ideology was really a necessary condition for their decision to embrace self-sacrificial violence in a cause that transcends the nation.

Psychological Background

None of these alternate motives is meant to deny the influence of religiously tinged indoctrination upon the hijackers' behavior and thought.

As mentioned, all nineteen hijackers seem to have spent some time in Afghanistan. In the training camps, among other skills, they learned to kill ritualistically, apparently by slitting the throats of goats and camels. They were also given instruction in another military "technique" with unquestionably religious connotations, namely, martyrdom. But the promise of paradise was not the sole inducement offered to those who signed up. Their indoctrinators no doubt pitched martyrdom to them by stressing the brevity and vanity of life, the certainty of death, and the need, in the face of life's all-consuming flux, to attach oneself to something imperishable.

That "something" could have been God, of course, but it could just as well have been the Islamic nation. After all, in modern times, the "nation" has significantly outperformed organized religion as an altar upon which young men have sacrificed themselves for a higher cause. This is why, as Michael Mann has written, "most suicide bombers have been nationalists, not fundamentalists." The reason he gives is that "the immortality offered by sacrifice for the nation is much more real than any religious notion of heaven."[36] This may not be universally true, but it applies to 9/11 if we admit that the worldwide Islamic community or umma (to whose "army" the hijackers thought they belonged) appeared to its members to be just as much of a "nation" as the dreamlands of Kurdistan or Palestine.

As an empirical matter, incidentally, and quite apart from the teachings of Islam, life *is* brief, and therefore the human impulse toward self-preservation invariably, in the end, proves futile. This may be the single most effective way in which training-camp revelations may have contributed to the willingness of these young men, already inclined in that direction, to scrap their dim lives for a radiant cause. While in Afghanistan, they were no doubt reminded incessantly of dismaying truths about mortality that most members of our self-delusional species prefer to ignore. Lengthening their lifetimes, they were told, would in no way shorten the amount of time that they would be dead. The future hijackers may have been reminded of other secular truths as well, for instance, that they could just as well be killed any day in a fluke accident; and they were surely encouraged to draw the logical conclusion that it would be better to make their deaths meaningful rather than meaningless, to exit life on a combat mission, for their community's honor, rather than as insignificant observers doing nothing, bored, sitting in cafés. Because death is inevitable in any case, there is nothing of "infinite value" to lose in dying for a cause. This is true whether the cause is secular (bloodying the enemy) or religious (serving God). What all this boils down to is that mankind's natural horror of death may be overcome or diminished by a perfectly realistic focus on death's inevitability, without any religious certainty that a sacred explosion will rocket a would-be martyr instantly to paradise.

The hijackers may also have blunted their natural fear of death with a strong dose of visceral hatred for the people whom they were about to obliterate. One of the most effective painkillers known to tribesmen is the imagined pain and death of those who, in the past, have harmed and killed members of their tribe. Revenge is famously "sweeter than honey." To satisfy their blood lust, the vengeful will throw themselves heedlessly into life-threatening conflicts. Single-minded focus on redressing past grievances may crowd out strategic consideration of unintended (even if predictable) future consequences. This is why we cannot conclude, when observing how suicide terrorists deviate from the ordinary canons of instrumental rationality, that they are acting from religious motives. It is equally plausible to conclude that they are driven by revenge, which may look "irrational" simply because it rivets the gaze to a past injury needing to be redressed, diminishing consciousness of both present and future.

A strong personal need to slake the craving for vengeance is universally thought to motivate some Palestinian suicide bombers, but most commentators downplay this possibility when discussing 9/11 because of the seemingly attenuated nature of the revenge motive in this case. Unlike the Palestinian suicide bombers, none of the 9/11 pilots seems to have been trying to avenge the blood of a friend or a relative killed by the target society. Because of the "long fuse" of the plot, it is also said, the 9/11 terrorists acted in cold blood, and could not have felt much visceral craving for revenge.

This analysis is reasonable, in a way, but it may also underestimate the power of artfully contrived "narratives of blame" to capture the imagination of uprooted young men in search of meaning and purpose and to give focus to their otherwise diffuse impulse to punish someone, anyone, for their feelings of frustration and humiliation. An ideology can refashion subjective perceptions of self-interest and it can also, presumably, rechannel the hard-wired revenge impulse, retargeting it toward a hitherto unappreciated enemy, even one who is distant or merely imagined rather than personally known. That something of the sort may have happened is suggested by one of the hijackers, who left the following message behind: "It is time to kill the Americans in their own backyards, among their sons, and near their forces and intelligence."[37] It is time to kill Americans in their own backyards not because of their impiety but because Americans have been killing Muslims in the Muslims' own backyards. The archaic principle of an eye for an eye, far from gaining legitimacy from Allah's approval, is prior to and deeper than any religious doctrine, and indeed attracts revenge-minded supporters to any religious tradition that sacralizes vengeance as a holy duty. Islam enters the picture here not as a religious creed, therefore, but as a political marker, identifying the imaginary community that has been wronged and that therefore has a natural right – that is, a nonreligious or prereligious right – to retaliate in kind.

How could so much rage build up in these men's hearts against a country that was so far away? TV images of Palestinian children killed by American-backed Israelis provide a vicarious experience of "pan-Arab victimhood" to a worldwide viewing audience. The gripping narrative built around these images demonizes America as a heartless oppressor and rinses clean "the Arab nation," making it seem innocent, humiliated, and despoiled. Intensified by envy of America's prosperity and power, such a widely repeated storyline is probably enough to inflame the desire for wreaking revenge on America, even in individuals who never personally experienced U.S. violence. The five-year lag between Atta's vow to die a martyr and the attacks of 9/11 does not demonstrate conclusively that he felt no desire for revenge. It only suggests that whatever hatreds he brought with him from the Middle East had to be kept simmering for years as they were gradually retargeted. For complex reasons, the focus of his rage shifted from the Cairo elite to those he came to see as the vicious, disdainful, indifferent, and essentially inhuman Americans.

Martyrs Are Soldiers

Yet, "narratives of blame" that demonize America, even when supplemented by a heightened awareness of the brevity of life, do not seem to be sufficient explanations for the decision by young men with no outward reasons for desperation to undertake a suicide mission. What other nonreligious factors might have been involved? Another likely reason why they were willing to die, even though they were not psychologically desperate, is that the hijackers thought of themselves as soldiers. There is nothing unusual about young men stationed far from home and cut off from palpable community support who are willing to sacrifice their lives in a violent conflict with personally unknown enemies. What is unusual is only that the unified army to which the 9/11 hijackers apparently thought they belonged was largely imaginary. The Muslim idea of martyrdom itself is closely associated with a soldier's death. Throughout the Middle East, "whether in Arabic, Turkish, Persian or Pashto Muslim society, *shahid* [martyr] is today used for any man who falls in battle."[38] The soldier's self-sacrifice for his country also associates Muslim suicide terrorists with secular terrorists such as the Japanese Kamikaze during the Second World War and the Black Tigers of Sri Lanka.

Is not martyrdom (*istishad*) also, or even primarily, a religious ideal? Is it not an important part of the cultural repertoire of the Islamic tradition? Were not the 9/11 hijackers simply enacting a venerable religious practice? Not exactly. In the Islamic tradition, in fact, "*shahid* is the warrior who was killed by the enemy in battle, not the one who killed himself."[39] Deliberately killing oneself in battle is not the same as being killed by an enemy in battle. When defenders of 9/11 assert that "it is wrong to call such operations a 'suicide',"[40] therefore, their defensive tone betrays lingering doubts. They are protesting too much. In reality, "self-martyrdom" lies somewhere between martyrdom and suicide, and does not reflect any well-established Islamic practice. Self-martyrs are not reenacting any traditional social role, certainly not that of the too frequently cited medieval "assassins." Mass casualty attacks in which the attackers kill their victims by killing themselves are, more or less, a twentieth-century innovation: "This form of jihad, in which the body is used as a weapon, is a recent development in the annals of Islamic warfare, even if the concept of holy war and martyrdom is as old as the religion itself."[41] It was basically unknown to Muslims until developed in Lebanon during the early 1980s. The influence of old religious traditions on the choice of suicide missions as a technique for conducting terrorism, therefore, remains unproven and implausible.

Not only suicide, but the killing of thousands of innocent civilians, too, is difficult to reconcile with traditional Islamic morality. To gauge the importance of this consideration, consider the rumor, apparently common throughout the Islamic world, that the CIA or Mossad orchestrated the attacks. Completely incompatible with the Muslim pride in the attacks that is also registered in some public opinion surveys, this fantasy suggests qualms about mass-casualty suicide terrorism. So how did the hijackers, assuming that they shared these conventional Islamic qualms to some extent, manage to quell them?

One paradoxical, but interesting, line of thought on this matter is that suicide itself provides a way to overcome the norms, including religious norms, which prohibit the killing of innocents. In *Les justes*, Albert Camus describes such a strategy for assuaging the guilty conscience of killers. His idea, put succinctly, is that *dying justifies killing*. At one point, the Russian anarchist hero of the play, Ivan Kaliayev, says: "if I did not die, I would be a murderer."[42] In other words, doubts about the morality of murder can be stilled by the willingness of the killer to die. Readiness for self-sacrifice establishes the Christ-like purity of the assassin. It shows that he is not a common criminal and that he is, above all, not a murderer. Willingness to die demonstrates publicly that a noble cause larger than any personal interest or caprice is at stake: "The truth of the cause is established by the individual's willingness to sacrifice everything in its behalf."[43] On this account, suicide attacks are, psychologically speaking, self-justifying. That is to say, in a hit-and-run terrorist attack, the "moral cause" that overrides the ordinary prohibition against the killing of innocent civilians must be extraordinarily compelling, even to the point of admitting no doubts. In suicide attacks, at least according to Camus, the cause need not be so obviously compelling, for the willingness of the killers to die demonstrates their subjective belief in the righteousness of their cause. Third-party observers may disapprove of the cause, but no one can plausibly deny that the terrorists themselves were convinced that the ends justified the means. For those with a moral conscience, if Camus is right, suicide terrorism is psychologically easier than hit-and-run terrorism.

Did such thoughts play any role in the 9/11 attacks? Did the foreknowledge of certain self-sacrifice help assuage the hijackers' guilt, arising at least in part from a religious sensibility, at the prospect of killing innocent civilians? Did suicide allow the perpetrators to dramatize their perverse belief that, even while committing mass murder, *they* were the ultimate victims?[44] Something of the sort might be possible, I suppose, but the conspirators had available to them a much less roundabout way to justify mass murder. If the hijackers felt a twinge of guilt at the thought of murdering innocent civilians, this guilt could be most easily assuaged by the thought that they were "at war." A soldier can kill a wholly guiltless conscript in the enemy's ranks without being labeled a murderer. Soldiering is a high-risk profession; and there is nothing at all rare about young soldiers believing that they are dying for their country.[45] It seems likely, in fact, that the martial distinction between the courageous and the cowardly was just as important to the 9/11 terrorists as the religious distinction between the saved and the damned. Willingness to face death unflinchingly, and scorn for materialists who cling pathetically to life, has more to do with martial ethics than with religious ethics, even though the two moral codes often overlap. There is nothing uniquely Islamic about bravado and fealty, in any case, nor is there anything uniquely Islamic about the desire to uphold manly honor or to display courage in battle.

In al Qaeda statements, the suicide hijackers are referred to not only by the term "martyr" (*shahid*) but also by the term "holy warrior" (*mujahid*).

The "holiness" in question no doubt has something to do with scriptural religion, but the proximate reference is to the pan-Arab fighters in the Afghan war. All soldiers, in any case, whether holy or not, have a right to kill. They are authorized to kill aggressors and other enemies of the community, just as executioners have a right to put to death criminals convicted of capital crimes. Rather than dying justifying killing, therefore, we have the more traditional pattern (well-known to all revenge cultures) of killing justifying dying. The foreseeable but unintended death of fellow Muslims in the course of an attack on infidels, too, can be explained away, in banally secular terms, as friendly fire, without reference to any expected or hoped-for welcome into paradise.

The warrior ideal, in sum, goes a long way towards explaining how the hijackers managed to armor themselves psychologically against the fear of death. They surely felt the warrior's pride at having been selected to participate in an important mission. They expected to win glory and be celebrated for their valor. They hoped to become role models whom only the bravest young Muslims would have the courage to emulate. There is nothing especially religious about desiring to make a splash, to be involved in large affairs, or to be celebrated all over the world.[46] Even if they were not certain that they had starring roles in the Last Judgment, they were embarked on a remarkable rite of passage, putting themselves to the test and demonstrating their worthiness of adult respect.

For psychologically complex reasons, their own personal honor and dishonor became wrapped up with the honor and dishonor of the umma as they imagined it. They may have been willing to die simply because they identified strongly with an enduring community that they expected to benefit from their deaths, a community that might eventually sing their praises. This would have been a perfectly secular way to overcome the fear of death. Far from exalting death above life, they may have found dying bearable because they thought it would help their community to live and flourish. Perhaps they managed to imagine death away, not by focusing on paradise, but by focusing on the honor to be enjoyed by their dishonored community after the enemies who had dishonored them were humiliated, choked in flames, and drenched in blood.

Sustaining Determination

It is one thing to explain why the 9/11 hijackers agreed to enlist in a suicide mission. A somewhat different question is how they managed to stay on course, without flinching, even as their fiery end drew near. According to one expert on suicide terrorism, "it is reasonable to assume that volunteers for such missions have to be used rapidly lest they change their mind, an eventuality that becomes more likely the greater the distance in time and place from their launching point."[47] Human desires are chronically unstable and ephemeral, shifting from situation to situation. A fleeting desire can wash over an individual's mind and disappear, without giving rise to action, never to return. Alternatively, the same fleeting desire, if the circumstances are right, can trigger an action that can alter a person's life, and perhaps even the course of history, forever. This analysis presumably applies to the desire to die for Islam.

On the spur of the moment, many people may feel committed enough to a cause to volunteer to die for it, but fewer will wake up the next morning with the same fierce determination. This observation raises a vital question for students of 9/11. Behind-the-scenes handlers could not keep watch on the hit team, punish would-be defectors, give periodic pep talks, stiffen the future hijackers' resolve, or escort them to the site. So how did al Qaeda, at a distance, make its volunteer commandos stick to their extravagant promises, unruffled, even as the moment of death drew near? What we need to explain, in other words, is how the attackers were kept on track, far behind enemy lines, without the usual forms of external monitoring and opportunistic intervention practiced to prevent a predictable and perfectly natural last-minute recoiling in the face of death.

One answer to this question is team spirit, or small-group loyalty. The sheer excitement of a cloak-and-dagger life behind enemy lines presumably helped keep the Hamburg cell together in the run-up to the attacks. The pleasure of partaking in a secret combat mission is an independent motivation for action, as is the chance to be, for once, a member of a highly select group, a killer elite.

Team spirit can thrive in isolated circumstances. The life of the Hamburg cell was built around concealing and masking. The conspirators looked like hapless students, but that was only because no one around them knew that they had been inducted into the black arts in Afghanistan. The contrast between their insignificant appearance (in their neighbors' eyes) and the shocking reality of their "true lives" presumably allowed the cell's members to experience a sense of elation and deep purposefulness. As Georg Simmel remarks, "the secret produces an immense enlargement of life." And he continues: "The secret offers, so to speak, the possibility of a second world alongside the manifest world."[48] Loyalty to their small countersociety was reinforced by the pleasures of cloaked intrigue. Although members of the enemy society around them viewed them as

marginal men, they knew better – they knew that they were chosen by
bin Laden himself for starring roles in what would soon be considered the
greatest spectacle on earth.

The group loyalty developed before the attack presumably influenced
the hijackers' behavior on 9/11 itself. There is no reason why the same
reasoning that applies to high-risk military attacks should not apply to
suicide missions too: "It probably takes more courage to stay behind
when one's platoon rises for assault than to charge with the others."[49]
Peer pressure and norms of solidarity would not affect a lone terrorist, of
course, but the 9/11 hijackers could certainly draw upon the "intragroup
commitment" found in "chain or concurrent multiple suicidal attacks."[50]
Fraternal bonds, even without supervision from above, help explain the
lunatic bravery of warriors, in this case just as in the case of conventional
war. Mutual pledges and vows, sworn ahead of time, before instinctive fear
at approaching death had a chance to set in, may also have contributed an
independent reason for steadfastness. The al Qaeda trademark of synchronized attacks may, among its other rationales, have allowed group solidarity to function as a precommitment device to help thwart last-minute
bail-outs. All these factors, perhaps combined with the pilots' alleged
incompetence at landing hijacked Boeings, could presumably have kept
the team on mission without close-up supervision by behind-the-scenes
handlers. Their desire to please God, however authentically felt, would
have been almost redundant in such a case.

The Religious Dimension of the 9/11 Plot

Secrecy and surprise are the principal assets of the weaker party in an asymmetrical conflict. To ask how religion contributed to the plot, therefore,
is also to ask how it contributed to secrecy and surprise. Formulated that
way, it suddenly seems much easier to answer, for religious practices obviously helped maintain a veil of secrecy around the plot. Membership in
a non-Christian sect in a majority Christian country enhanced the isolation and relative impenetrability of the cell behind enemy lines. Both
the al-Quds mosque in Hamburg and the Islamic "study room" at the
university in Harburg provided difficult-to-penetrate walls behind which
the future suicide pilots could map out their plan. At the al-Quds mosque
in Hamburg and in the Marienstrasse apartment, the conspirators sometimes appeared to be wrapped in a mantle of devoutness, which may well
have been perfectly sincere. Even in Atta's case, however, daily prayers
performed the auxiliary function of detaching the militant extremist from

his unsuspecting civilian surroundings. As one of his co-workers reported, Atta "would get his prayer mat out five times a day. During that time he was utterly absorbed – he wouldn't hear you if you spoke to him."[51] Although initially devotional in its purpose, such a walling-out of the surrounding society likely came to serve conspiratorial objectives as well.

Whether they took spiritual exercises and other religious practices seriously as a matter of piety, in other words, members of the Hamburg cell certainly came to take them seriously as a matter of security. The conspirators were able to protect themselves very effectively against infiltration, because they had a ready-made religious excuse for barricading themselves from non-Islamic neighbors and observers.

That religious practices – as opposed to religious beliefs – played yet another role in the success of 9/11 is suggested by the "manual" outlining preparations for the attack, apparently written by Abdul Aziz al-Omari and discovered in Atta's luggage that, by sheer chance, did not make it onto AA flight No. 11. (How many of the hijackers read this document is disputed.) In this manual, several items stand out. The most important instruction is to keep reciting prayers and incantations and passages from the Qur'an – understood as an "absolute text" that cannot be interpreted – during the entire operation: "Keep busy with repeated invocation of God." The kind of prayer recommended here seems more like behavior than thought. Indeed, ritualistic praying can obstruct thought and prevent the spontaneous upsurge of disobedient impulses and inclinations. Soldiers who pray before battle are often said to use prayer less as a motivator than as an anesthetic.[52] It helps keep fear under control. Chanting supplications and religious poems and reciting scripture acts as a sedative. Repetition can even induce a sort of trance or "dissociative" state of mind. Also, unlike daydreaming, prayer is a regulated behavior. Reading the Qur'an into one's palms and then rubbing one's hands all over one's body, in a ritual self-blessing, takes time and crowds out other thoughts. Mantras, much like the practice of counting sheep, are standard techniques recommended by psychotherapists for managing anxiety and keeping psychological demons at bay. Unflappability, composure, and total focus on the job at hand can be enhanced by robotic repetition. Shutting down most cognitive functions can minimize the danger of last minute faltering. Self-induced cognitive shut-down, in turn, can be facilitated by mechanically recited prayers.

An additional interesting detail in the manual is the instruction to stay awake all night. Even young and healthy men, presumably, would feel somewhat loopy after more than thirty hours without sleep. They might even have begun to hallucinate to some extent. The sleep-deprived may be especially susceptible to the numbing or sedating effects of religious rituals, perhaps even to the point of self-hypnosis. At the very least, the mental spontaneity of sleepwalkers is dimmed. Their grasp of context is attenuated and they may easily lapse into default mode, performing frequently practiced operations by rote. Like the desire to injure one's imagined enemies, in other words, religious rituals may blunt the sting of death even when the promise of paradise seems uncertain. The capacity of religious ritual to deaden the senses or narrowly restrict mental focus was probably important in the 9/11 case, because the hijackers' fear of death had to be subdued not forever, but only for a few hours.

Expiation by Suicide

The promise of paradise may not be the most effective instrument of control wielded by religious authorities. According to Thomas Hobbes, the power of priests has a much deeper source than the gullibility of "imbeciles." Preachers control their flocks, he argued, by first making people feel guilty about their own natural impulses, such as sexual desire, and then offering to protect them from sin and damnation in exchange for obedience to spiritual authority.[53] Searing guilt about sexual desire may become psychologically intolerable. At war with himself, a young man taught to regard sex as essentially Satanic will want and not want the same thing at the same time. Trapped in such a self-divided state, he will be unable to make important life decisions autonomously and will therefore naturally reach for an external crutch or authority figure, such as a religious guru, to lead him through life. The shakier people feel, the more readily will they submit to dogmatic religious instruction and control. Their intolerable inner conflict is what makes young imbeciles so susceptible to the wiles of older scoundrels, according to Hobbes. To escape their inner civil war, they will do whatever their "priests" tell them to do. To escape self-blame they will also, presumably, embrace the suggestion that the source of their torments is a malicious external aggressor who can and must be killed.

Although speculative, this Hobbesian analysis seems rather promising. In his study of Mohammed Bouyeri, the young Moroccan-Dutchman who assassinated Theo van Gogh in 2004, Ian Buruma reports his conversation with a psychiatrist who attributes

> the high incidence of schizophrenia among Muslim males in Europe to the "cognitive wiring" that goes wrong when faced with bewildering temptations. While many women embrace the liberties of Western life,

men, faced with rejection and frustration, turn away to a fantasy of tribal honor and religious rectitude. A teenage desire for 'easy' women makes way for disgust and rage.[54]

Could not the very same diagnosis apply to the 9/11 suicide pilots? Due to their relatively privileged backgrounds and, especially, their higher education, they were able to travel quite far on the road from the Middle East to Western Europe. They mastered foreign languages, for instance, and they were able to blend imperceptibly into a Western environment. This was undoubtedly a decisive consideration for those who recruited them into the plot. Having lived for some years in the West, however, they had also become, to some extent, limbo men. They were unable to arrive, we might say, yet also unable to return home. They were too Westernized to feel completely comfortable in the Middle East but not Westernized enough to feel accepted by a socially bigoted Europe.

Not without reason, some commentators speak of a "love-hate relationship" to explain the ambiguous attitude of such young men toward the Western societies that both attract and reject them. A further psychological key to our puzzle could lie here. The jihadist narrative of blame that channels anger toward America has a perverse codicil – the same radical worldview that reviles America simultaneously rebukes those Muslim youths who find America alluring. The ripest recruits for suicide missions, this analysis implies, would be half-way men, stuck in transit between the Middle East and the West, whose frustration is mingled with a feeling of being tainted by a society that continues to tempt them. The hijackers' felt need to erase, eradicate, purge such a stain from their souls could conceivably have become so obsessive that it finally eclipsed all thought of future consequences.

One way to think about the political effects of such a stressful psychological condition is to recall the classical Islamic distinction between the Greater Jihad and the Lesser Jihad. Embarked on the Lesser Jihad, holy warriors confront infidels on the field of battle. In the Greater Jihad, by contrast, struggling Muslims fight a private battle against their own carnality. Perhaps the 9/11 mission allowed the hijackers to fuse the two jihads into one. They could kill the despicable enemy and, simultaneously, end their own torment, eliminating the vile traces that the enemy had deposited in their souls. If this fanciful analysis has any validity, the 9/11 hijackers may have actually preferred suicide terrorism to hit-and-run terrorism, because a suicide mission, to speak crudely, allowed them to kill two birds with one stone. The potency of the connection between killing the enemy and purifying one's own soul by self-slaughter depends, according to Qutb's writings, on tracing personal temptations, experienced as shameful, to massive "cultural aggression" by the West.

One advocate of this admittedly convoluted approach is Malise Ruthven: "The jihad (struggle) against kufr (disbelief) which the hijackers and other Islamists espouse is not so much a 'war between civilizations' as a struggle waged over contested identities within the individual self."[55] Psychological conflicts within the minds of suicide terrorists are also stressed by Benjamin and Simon:

> Atta was a man flagellating himself. At some point, how and when are not clear, he had a brush with temptation; perhaps he felt he had succumbed. Whatever touched him, he identified with the West. It might have been something as simple as a personal desire to be part of the West that caused him to feel contaminated. His repulsion was powerful, and he felt somehow humiliated. . . . All these jihadists react to the taint or seduction they felt by espousing a violent Islamism, as though that overcorrection would erase the sin of their earlier lives.[56]

We are obviously treading on empirically unverifiable ground at this point. But the hypothesis entertained by these and other writers does have the ring of plausibility. The 9/11 pilots may have stayed on mission, despite the long incubation time of their plot and the remoteness of their masters, not only because they were devoted to redeeming collective honor (for which their deaths would have been a necessary evil) but also because they were devoted to self-mortification (for which their deaths would have been an intrinsic good).

It is at least conceivable that the hijackers were recruited into al Qaeda because these young men, in particular, combined bitter anger at the West with psychologically stressful self-contempt and self-blame. There is no reason to doubt that the idea of sin can have a powerful effect on human behavior. Whatever psychological processes lead a person to feel inwardly besmirched or contaminated, such self-disgust can be taken up, cultivated, and crystallized by religious indoctrination and training. Candidates for a suicide mission might or might not believe that the first drop of their blood shed in martyrdom will wash away their blackest sins, but they will quite realistically expect that suicide terrorism will put an end to their wanting and not wanting the same thing at the same time. Their burning sense of guilt, they knew, would not survive their deaths. What is attractive about this line of thought is that it allows us to imagine a connection between the uprootedness of the hijackers, their envy of America, their blind obedience to their superiors, and their extraordinary eagerness to die.

Such a connection feels plausible but remains unproven. Nevertheless, knowledgeable commentators insist that 9/11 "was a sacrifice made for the most common reason: expiation, the removal of a sin through an act of giving."[57] If so, then religious belief had a direct effect on the behavior of the suicide terrorists. Mark Juergensmeyer makes a similar point in another context:

> It is one thing when the moral sanction of religion is brought to bear on such worldly and non-spiritual matters as political struggles. It is quite another when the struggles themselves are seen primarily as religious events. The crusades, for instance, are examples from Christian history when a military expedition was carried out with religious zeal. To engage in such a struggle was a salvific act.[58]

If someone could conclusively show that the 9/11 hijackers performed the attacks as religious rituals to cleanse themselves of what they believed to be their sins, they would have demonstrated that the hijackers' religious faith was a principal cause of the attacks.

Although such speculations are probably indemonstrable, they are fully consistent with Olivier Roy's influential interpretation of Islamic fundamentalism: "the literature of jihad places less emphasis on the objective (to create an Islamic state) than on the mystical dimension (to sacrifice one's life); it is the act of supreme devotion."[59] Kanan Makiya and Hassan Mneimneh, too, emphasize the mysterious appeal of "sacrifice" in their analysis of the instruction manual presumably consulted by the terrorists before the attack. Their principal and debatable point is that the hijackers no longer saw martyrdom as a weapon in a wider war or an instrument serving an ulterior purpose but instead as an end in itself. They did not see themselves as defending their community against aggression by infidels, but were instead caught up in a personal act of worship meant to please God: "There is no mention of any communal purpose behind [their] behavior."[60] We might even speculate, taking this hypothesis a step further, that the hijackers were offering themselves, along with their victims, as burnt offerings to God. If so, archaic myths impinged upon their belief systems to the point of delirium. Of course, there is no way to verify this speculation either, even though it is made plausible to some extent by a striking supplication, uttered by one of the hijackers in his preattack video-recorded message: "Oh Allah, take from our blood today until you are satisfied."[61] The idea that on-looking divinities enjoy gorging on human blood is archaic indeed.[62]

Such extraordinary archaisms suggest another way in which sentiments with a religious tinge might have helped neutralize the pilots' fear of death.

In the manual, the hijackers are reminded that fear is a form of worship and that fearing anyone or anything besides God (including a militarily superior enemy) is a mortal sin that will damn them to everlasting hell. This instruction suggests that an effective way to manage fear is to focus one's mind, obsessively, on fear of God. Makiya and Mneimneh extend their diagnosis in this very direction:

> for the author of this manual an overpowering fear of God must rule in the mind of the True Believer, a fear that so focuses the mind as to rid it of all mundane considerations arising from experience and observation, thus enabling the Believer to remain utterly concentrated on his mission. In support of this the manual cites the Koranic verse, "Fear them not, but fear Me, if you are Believers."[63]

That their fear of God may have enhanced the hijackers' operational discipline is an interesting hypothesis. A hint that something more was going on, in any case, comes from multiple stories about the Hamburg team in the months leading up to the attacks. Many commentators have been titillated by the scandal of fundamentalists occasionally lapsing into mundane forms of fun, but another paradox is even more revealing. These young men, who ostensibly believed that fear should be reserved for God, were, at the same time, intoxicated by the thought of making other people fear them. They behaved as if they were somehow channeling God's infinite anger at the infidel. To cite a perfectly banal example, when Atta first arrived in the United States he reportedly visited a federal Farm Services agency in Florida to request a loan to buy an airplane. Hanging on the wall was an aerial photo of Washington, D.C., where the agent remarked that she had many friends. After his request for a loan was politely refused, Atta looked at the photo and asked the agent: "How would you like it if somebody flew an airplane into your friends' building?"[64] If Makiya and Mneimneh are correct, anyone operating within a radical Islamist worldview must identify the desire to instill fear with the presumably blasphemous desire to be godlike or perhaps to be God. The hijackers may have sought refuge from the all-corrosive flux of time by identifying themselves mentally with a God who was "the vanquisher of the arrogant."[65] They hoped for victory against a powerful enemy by imagining that they had a still more powerful, even all-powerful, ally at their side. Aiming to punish America, they probably pictured themselves as dispensers of divine justice, hitching a ride on His Terrible Swift Sword.

Such fantasies allow sadists to feel noble. They are also deeply incoherent, reflecting a simultaneous embrace of two clashing self-images. The hijackers, in all probability, saw themselves both as memorable heroes and as expendable assets. They were omnipotent and impotent, thunder gods and despicable sinners. They were liberating their people in the name of total personal enslavement, conquering and surrendering at the same time. Perhaps the psychological strain of maintaining mutually exclusive self-images was still another anesthetic, adding to the other emotions, beliefs, and rituals that numbed them to their impending deaths. This conjecture has the ring of truth, but it, too, can neither be proven nor ruled out.

The Masterminds

While Osama bin Laden, Ayman al-Zawahiri, and others instigated, encouraged, and blessed the 9/11 attacks, the plot's organizational commander was Khalid Sheikh Mohammed (KSM).[66] His Arabic code name was *Mukhtar*, or "the Brain." We now turn to the question of why KSM and his confederates chose to send suicide commandos on this particular mission. What considerations influenced their decision to mount a "martyrdom operation?" Did the mission's planners see the death of the hijackers merely as a necessary evil? Or did they ascribe a deeper, perhaps religious, meaning and purpose to the suicide of their operatives?

The Voltaire thesis, discussed earlier, implies that the motives of the 9/11 masterminds were not the same as the motivations of the 9/11 hijackers. A contemporary exponent of this thesis reformulates it as follows: "Even if many suicide attackers are irrational or fanatical, the leadership groups that recruit and direct them are not."[67] The latter, according to this approach, are shrewd calculators of costs and benefits, even if the former are robotic fanatics in the grip of myth. Yet such a contrast seems too sharp to capture the ambiguous undercurrents of the 9/11 plot. For one thing, the hallucinatory statements of al Qaeda's leaders suggest that, whatever their skills as organizers of terror, they too have been living somewhat disconnected from reality. After all, they have been hiding like hunted animals for years, surrounded only by people who think like themselves, insulated from the kind of heterogeneous community that can provide mentally stabilizing sanity checks. It would not be surprising, therefore, if their worldview contained some unrealistic beliefs.

Nonetheless, the Voltaire thesis probably applies to 9/11 to some extent. It is only reasonable to assume that al Qaeda masterminds, who apparently had little inclination to throw themselves into the flames, carried into the conspiracy a set of convictions, emotions, and dispositions rather unlike those of the suicide hijackers themselves. The masterminds, arguably, were neither so personally wrought up nor so eager to escape into an afterlife purified of temptation. Their basic rationality can be inferred from their decision to mobilize fast-moving light forces acting in secrecy. This is a highly efficient way for the weaker side in an asymmetrical struggle to deploy the modest resources at its disposal. Their targeting decisions, too, seem highly rational. By organizing the 1998 U.S. embassy bombings in East Africa, for instance, Khalid Sheikh Mohammed managed to degrade the United States' intelligence-gathering capacities, to al Qaeda's advantage, by compelling the Americans to shutter their embassies around the world. Such shrewd plots and ploys make the conspirators seem to be more the children of Lenin than the children of Mohammed. One commentator describes al Qaeda in exactly such terms: "Using techniques drawn from Leninism and operating on the Marxist militant model, it uses noms de guerre, adheres strictly to a cell structure, follows the idea of a cadre party, maintains tight discipline, promotes self-sacrifice and reverence for the leadership and is guided by a program of action."[68]

Their basic strategy may even have been the one most commonly alleged. Ample evidence exists that 9/11 was meant to provoke Washington into an unthinking emotional response. A spectacular attack would predictably draw America into imperial overstretch and would entice U.S. soldiers to become sitting ducks in remote shooting galleries. Terrorism might even goad the President into engaging the country's security establishment in a global guerrilla war on so many distant battlefronts in foreign lands that America's cognitive capacities – not its military and fiscal capacities alone – would be overtaxed. Whatever consequences it would unleash, a murderous attack on American civilians inside America would predictably shake up the world order and open opportunities for the fleet of foot. The 9/11 masterminds were certainly anticipating their own next moves. Their subsequent plans may or may not have come to fruition, but the fact that they bothered to make them provides a good measure of the distance between the scheming minds of the behind-the-scenes planners and the mission-fixated minds of those who personally carried out the attack.

Why Did the Planners Send a Suicide Squad?

In 1993, Khalid Sheikh Mohammed's nephew, Ramzi Yousef, led a hit-and-run team in a failed attempt to topple the World Trade Center.[69] In that "prequel" to 9/11, the commandos did not seek to die in the attacks. By contrast, the teams sent to carry out both the East Africa embassy bombings and the 2000 sea-borne attack on the USS Cole were suicide terrorists.[70] From the standpoint of the designers and organizers of such attacks, however, the distinction between hit-and-run terrorists and suicide terrorists may not have been especially salient. Like any high command in wartime, they may view men and materiel indifferently, as resources to be consumed in pursuit of urgent military aims. If high-level commanders consider their foot soldiers to be expendable surplus youth, then, for them, a suicide mission is just another form of remote-control terrorism.

Today, conspirators loosely affiliated with or inspired by al Qaeda continue to recruit suicide operatives to carry out lethal missions.[71] They do so, in part, because they have come to believe that suicide terrorism is a very effective way to achieve their strategic goals. But does expediency alone provide an adequate and exhaustive explanation for Khalid Sheikh Mohammed's decision to send suicide squads to conduct the 9/11 attacks?

Diego Gambetta draws a distinction between suicide terrorism as a military strategy and suicide terrorism as a way to communicate a message.[72] A good example of the former is the suicide assassination on Sept. 9, 2001, of Ahmad Shah Massoud, the Northern Alliance commander who posed a serious threat to the Taliban regime then hosting Osama bin Laden in Afghanistan. A suicide squad had a better chance than a hit-and-run squad to overcome Massoud's security precautions and was therefore presumably chosen for tactical reasons alone. Bin Laden's pre-9/11 gift to the Taliban, the assassination presumably demoralized the Northern Alliance and gave a last-minute boost to the spirits of the jihadists on mission inside the U.S. But employing suicide as an assassination technique probably provided no added value in this case.

Suicide missions, in fact, are often chosen on purely military grounds since "suicide attacks on average kill four times as many people as other terrorist acts."[73] It is a cost-effective way for a militarily outclassed group to attack hardened targets. Al-Zawahiri's writings provide evidence that this sort of rationale influenced the decision making of the 9/11 plotters: "Suicide operations are the most successful in inflicting damage on the opponent" and they are "the least costly to the mujahideen in terms of casualties."[74] Religious beliefs may ease recruitment into suicide missions, therefore. But religious beliefs can be said to *cause* suicide terrorism only in tandem with other powerful causes, especially an overwhelming asymmetry of military power.

Suicide missions, it is worth adding, greatly simplify planning because the suicide commandos who penetrate heavily defended security perimeters do not have to find an escape route. Suicide attacks are relatively inexpensive as well, and their costs well within the financial resources of modestly financed terrorist groups. Another consideration that may heavily influence the dispatchers of such missions is that, when suicide terrorists are used, no operatives remain to be captured and so there is no danger that they may reveal operational secrets under torture and thereby put the organization and its higher-ups in personal danger. This is why it makes sense to say that interrogatory torture, as discussed in Chapter Twelve, was one of the principal causes of the emergence and survival of suicide bombing as a trademark weapon of violent jihad.

For tactical and instrumental reasons of this sort, terrorist planners may opt for suicide terrorism over hit-and-run terrorism. But when is suicide terrorism *intrinsically* superior to hit-and-run terrorism? One plausible answer is when self-sacrifice adds value as propaganda, directly affecting the emotions and beliefs of allies and enemies, as well as conveying important information about the cause that could not be delivered, or delivered so memorably, by a nonsuicidal attack.

The distinction between suicide terrorism as a military strategy and suicide terrorism as a way to communicate a message should not, of course, lead us to neglect the strategic and military value of communication itself. Sending a message is itself an action that can have serious and, to some extent, predictable psychological consequences. The "war" between al Qaeda and the United States, in which 9/11 was only an episode, is one of those asymmetrical confrontations in which the superpower's challenger has few weapons besides publicity. Murdering almost 3,000 people did not have any direct effect on the military power of the United States, strictly considered. But communicating a message can itself be, latu sensu, a military maneuver if it changes the equation, weakening the strong and strengthening the weak. It can frighten and panic the enemy, steel the resolve of partisans, and weaken the resolve of opponents. An examination of al Qaeda's own statements makes it clear that the group's leadership mounted the 9/11 mission hoping that it would have precisely such effects.

Whether suicidal or not, terrorism is usually aimed at an audience rather than at its direct victims.[75] Whatever else it accomplishes, it seeks to publicize a cause. Explaining "the centrality of the urban setting in the history of early martyrdom," one historian remarks that "martyrdom in a city provided the greatest possible visibility for the cause of the nascent

Church."[76] The events of 9/11 did the same, providing unprecedented visibility for the cause of anti-American Islamic militancy because the main attack occurred in what is not only a great city, but the capital of the world's media. Islamic insurgencies throughout the world have struggled for decades to break through the walls of indifference and censorship that, they alleged, prevented them from attracting public attention to their causes. These walls of indifference came down with the WTC on 9/11.

Not only can suicidal terrorism electrify the public, it also reaps the benefits of "martyrdom." Etymologically, a "martyr" is a witness giving testimony before listeners on a jury or tribunal. Their desire to bear witness before a world audience seems to be an essential reason why 9/11's planners decided to mount an exploit of such staggering magnitude. Referring to the attacks as "speeches," bin Laden himself boasted that "the speeches are understood by both Arabs and non-Arabs – even by Chinese."[77] Addressing himself to the jihadists, al-Zawahiri wrote that anti-Western terrorism is a way to communicate with an enemy who understands only the language of force: "Cause the greatest damage and inflict the maximum casualties on the opponent, no matter how much time and effort these operations take, because this is the language understood by the West."[78] Finally, in a preattack videotape, one of the nineteen hijackers, Ahmad al Haznawi al-Ghamidi, declared: "We left our families to send a message, which has the color of blood, to reach the whole world."[79]

Suicide Terrorism as a Communicative Act

What was this bloody message, and what was its intended effect? The communicative strategy adopted by the 9/11 plotters can be inferred from various features of the attack itself, as well as from prior and subsequent pronouncements by bin Laden and others. Particularly telling is the plotters' decision to mount four simultaneous hijackings. Al Qaeda did not invent this method of synchronized attacks but borrowed it from the precursors of Lebanese Hezbollah. (One of the very first acts of suicide terrorism in modern times, the October 1983 operation by Lebanese Shiites, involved synchronized strikes, one against U.S. marines and the other against the French.) But it has since become an al Qaeda trademark. One of its functions, presumably, is to demonstrate the skill and resolve of the attackers. A sneak attack that obviously required careful planning by multiple actors over many months broadcasts to the world the chronic blindness of the targeted regime and the helplessness of its intelligence services. The basic communicative strategy behind 9/11, however, was probably more subtle still.

Their published pronouncements suggest that the attack's instigators and organizers assumed, fascinatingly, that military power can be destroyed non-militarily because all such power is ultimately based on myth. Various al Qaeda spokesmen have repeatedly claimed that the dominance of a military superpower, such as the U.S.S.R., depends on its reputation for invincibility, which lulls oppressed and abused groups into passivity, fatalism, and acquiescence. For the ambitious organizers of insurgencies, therefore, the strategic question is how to disenthrall the mesmerized masses, to dispel their acquired fatalism, and thereby to rouse a sleeping army against a dominant and oppressive power. Belief systems are military assets, to be invested in and targeted, because beliefs can sedate or inflame the emotional wellsprings of violent resistance. To dispel the paralyzing false consciousness that lulls the oppressed into a state of passive resignation, a vanguard must crack the superpower's protective shield and, by so doing, excite the desire of freelance warriors around the world to set the dominant power's besieged fortress on fire. The effectiveness of this strategy remains doubtful, but the organizers of the 9/11 attack seemed to have sincerely believed that they could politicize and radicalize a scattered "army" of Islamist youth by exploiting instruments of mass communication to shatter another myth of superpower invincibility.[80]

On the same preattack video just cited, Ahmad al Haznawi al-Ghamidi says that "the United States is nothing but propaganda and a huge mass of false statements and exaggeration. The purpose of this propaganda was to make the United States big in the eyes of the world."[81] By implication, 9/11 was counter-propaganda. Its purpose was to cut the United States down to size, to tip over the hollow idol. A successful mission would demoralize the Americans and encourage the Islamists by revealing how a poorly armed David can cut to the quick of a heavily armored Goliath. Admittedly, a small fighting force cannot hope to defeat a mighty adversary by delivering a knockout blow. The smaller force can do so indirectly, however, by eliciting an overreaction, inspiring copy-cat attacks, and sparking a popular insurrection. The organizers of 9/11 seem to have had all of these possibilities in mind. We have already discussed the frighteningly effective provocation strategy – the triggering of an overreaction. Even a relatively weak group can throw a superpower off balance by a shocking and murderous gesture – flashed before the eyes like a matador's cape. But what about the messages delivered to fellow Muslims?

By tossing a stone, the 9/11 plotters apparently hoped to loose a worldwide Islamic insurgency against insufficiently pious Muslim rulers as well as against non-Muslim forces occupying Muslim lands. They hoped that 9/11, or the string of attacks of which 9/11 was only the most spectacular, would break "the shackles of fear"[82] that kept the oppressed Islamic nation docile and quiescent, thereby sparking a revival of the warrior spirit in Muslim youth.

The strategy was double: to provoke America and awaken the sleeping umma. The attack itself would send a first jolt through Muslim communities worldwide, and then America's predictable overreaction would awaken the Muslim masses even more. By provoking the United States into lashing out indiscriminately against Muslims everywhere, the attack would politicize and radicalize groups that had hitherto remained passive and inert. Based on documents discovered on al-Zawahiri's desktop computer, it seems highly probable that al Qaeda's principal aim was to tempt the United States "to strike back in a way that would create sympathy for the terrorists."[83] Al-Zawahiri looks forward to the brutal repression that invariably follows a terrorist attack as the spark that, he hopes, will ignite a popular uprising.[84]

There was nothing especially Islamic about this playbook. The same trite and predictable plotline surfaces in almost all literature about terrorism, including non-Islamic terrorism. Conrad has his suicide terrorist say that nothing would please him more than to goad the police into "shooting us down in broad daylight with the approval of the public. Half our battle would be won then."[85] The principal purpose of much spectacular terrorism, it seems, is to elicit exactly such a lawless overreaction. Making this very point, David Fromkin describes the strategy of Irish and Jewish as well as Algerian terrorists as follows: "Their theory has been that their terrorist attacks would force hitherto liberal regimes to become repressive, a change which in turn would alienate the masses, thus setting the stage for revolution."[86] A terrorist will commit a murderous atrocity not because he wants these random civilians dead but "in order to provoke a brutal police repression that he believes will lead to political conditions propitious to revolutionary agitation and organization aimed at overthrowing the government."[87] This anticipated scenario is so common that it even turns up in Timothy McVeigh's favorite novel: "One of the major purposes of political terror, always and everywhere, is to force the authorities to take reprisals and to become more repressive, thus alienating a portion of the population and generating sympathy for the terrorists."[88]

If the organizers and instigators of 9/11 thought in this way, it was not because they were Islamic fundamentalists, but because they were mass murderers playing chess. They may have thought that U.S. military retaliation, with massive collateral damage to civilian bystanders, was inevitable. If provoked by a terrorist attack, the United States would surely bomb a Muslim country, such as Afghanistan. If this bombing was sufficiently indiscriminate, in turn, it would appear to Muslims worldwide as America's callous attempt to punish all Muslims collectively, whether guilty or not of the initial attack. This impression of America's animus against Islam would then, presumably, cause the Arab and Pakistani "street" to boil over, delegitimating the American-supported regimes of the region and rallying even more popular support to the jihadist cause.

The 9/11 plotters may have been brandishing a matador's cape, therefore. On the other hand, they may have been hedging their bets, calculating that the Americans could react to their audacious provocation either by weak retreat or by unfocused (and therefore self-defeating) retaliation. The planners might even have admitted that the exact response to their "message" was unpredictable and have welcomed either possible outcome: ignominious capitulation or panicky escalation.

The strength of the U.S. government, including its ability to project force abroad, not only depends on its reputation for invincibility abroad, it also relies on its domestic legitimacy, which provides a further context in which to situate the communicative strategy behind 9/11. The plotters killed American civilians, according to bin Laden, because America is a democracy, a system in which ordinary citizens wield political influence. Democratic citizens are legitimate targets not because they refuse to acknowledge the truth of Islam, but because they pay taxes and vote for a regime that conducts an unjust foreign policy.[89] One way to undermine America's capacity to project force abroad, therefore, is to attack the civilians who must finance and vote for deployment of U.S. troops abroad. After being bloodied by the jihadists, private citizens will begin to pressure their leaders to stop supporting the Egyptian and Saudi regimes. That nothing of the sort happened (or could have happened) does not contradict the proposition that this is probably what the 9/11 plotters hoped.

No government is legitimate unless it can effectively protect its citizens from violence. Some al Qaeda pronouncements suggest that the 9/11 conspirators also aimed to unravel the American social contract, the elemental exchange of protection for obedience. They wanted to show Americans that their government could not protect them. But the question remains: How did the *suicide* of the attackers contribute to this aim? Would not a hit-and-run attack that successfully toppled the WTC have provided all the publicity that Osama bin Laden and Khalid Sheikh Mohammed craved? Was the suicide of the attackers really indispensable for disheartening the Americans and rallying Islamic youth to al Qaeda's cause?

Once they took up the audacious idea of using civilian airliners in the attack, of course, the suicide of the operatives was dictated as a means to an end. Only the willingness of the hijackers to die allowed a certain kind of psychological victory. How else could they have forced Americans to watch endless reruns of their fellow citizens being express-delivered like so many sheep to the slaughter? The willingness of airborne terrorists to sacrifice their lives in the attack allowed the organizers of the 9/11 attacks to maximize the audience for their provocative call to arms by mounting a spectacular urban operation destined for worldwide television coverage.

The death of the perpetrators may have been meaningful, however, as well as instrumental. It may have conveyed a message that would have been lost on the watching world if delivered in any other way. To escape personal shame, someone who has been treated as a slave and who inwardly worries that he may still be one at heart, can prove to others and himself that he is not a slave only by risking and perhaps sacrificing his life. To make the move from a feeling of enslavement to a feeling of freedom, people must show that they will no longer be paralyzed by fear. How can they do this? Unlike hit-and-run terrorism, suicide terrorism publicly communicates the perpetrator's decision to face down the quaking fear that, throughout history, has kept subordinates on their knees before their masters.

The suicide of the perpetrators also displays the futility of using normal tactics to fend off enemy attackers. If disheartening the enemy was one strategic objective, then the suicide of the hijackers on 9/11 also may have been chosen for its value as an intensifier of enemy despair. Suicide terrorism, among other things, makes visible the contrast between the attackers who braved death coolly and their victims, weeping helplessly and fleeing in panic. Arguing that cultural stereotypes may play a role in the decision to mount suicide missions, one commentator defines the message of such attacks as follows: "The enemy is also a coward. Why is he perceived as a coward? Because Western society [is] primarily made up of pleasure seekers who fear death and suicide. These fears, combined with the quest for 'the good life,' are viewed as the basic tenets of Western culture."[90] If this analysis is sound, then the suicide of the perpetrators may have been part of a media campaign to propagate the myth – to which bin Laden subscribes – of an irreconcilable clash of civilizations.[91]

Osama bin Laden's ability to induce young men to die for him is striking testimony to his "Pied Piper" mystique and, by inference, to the persuasiveness of his cause. In a December 2001 videotape, bin Laden noted: "When people see a strong horse and a weak horse, by nature they will like the strong horse."[92] In the case of 9/11, the killing of Americans made Americans look weak, and the suicide of the hijackers made the hijackers look virtuous. The purity of motives implied by self-sacrifice helped recruit future terrorists and inspire imitators. It was a classic case of proselytizing by deed. The organizers may have hoped that the astonishing willingness of nineteen young men to give up absolutely everything would set a bandwagon in motion. The unidentified Sheikh from Saudi Arabia who appears with bin Laden in the December videotape boasts: "Hundreds of people used to doubt you and few would follow you until this huge event happened. Now hundreds of people are coming out to join you."[93] Such a recruitment bonanza was evidently what at least some of the plotters aspired to achieve.

To the extent that it enhanced the recruitment effect of the attacks, the suicide of the terrorists can be understood not only as a cost of the operation but also as part of the "message" it communicated. The simultaneous death of the attackers also added to the mission's demoralizing effect. The plotters may have chosen a suicide mission rather than a hit-and-run mission because it was a more corrosive form of psychological warfare. They used suicide to push America's panic button. The voluntary death of the hijackers, for one thing, communicated the futility of deterrence. This was a frightening message, especially for a national security community that, for half a century, had assumed that the only barrier between itself and nuclear annihilation was deterrence. The implication was especially rattling when coupled with bin Laden's saber-rattling about weapons of mass destruction. "It would be a sin for Muslims not to try to possess the weapons that would prevent the infidels from inflicting harm on Muslims."[94] If loose talk about loose nukes was part of a campaign to strike the fear of God into America's foreign policymakers, it succeeded only too well.

The suicide of the hijackers may also have conveyed another psychologically disturbing message. A terrorist who lobs a grenade into a café and darts away is just as frightening as a terrorist who explodes himself among his victims. Carnage produces nightmares however delivered. What makes suicide terrorism more disheartening than hit-and-run terrorism is that the former denies the victims' kin their ordinary after-the-fact consolation of inflicting pain upon those who have inflicted pain on them.

There is no concrete evidence that this consideration influenced the 9/11 plotters, but the logic behind it is suggestive. The chance for psychologically satisfying revenge is thwarted by suicide missions because the perpetrators have deliberately placed themselves out of the reach of human justice. Punishment of a murderer is cathartic, providing the victim's kin with some measure of psychological relief. The elimination at the outset of all possibility for exacting vengeance upon the immediate perpetrators arguably makes suicide terrorism more dismaying – harder to recover from psychologically – than hit-and-run terrorism.

Suicide terrorism also compels the targeted group, faute de mieux, to redirect its craving for revenge onto the living kin of the now-dead killers. This is why mass murder that simultaneously lifts the mass murderers beyond the reach of retribution also reorders the moral universe of the victims. It encourages a terrible moral regression, reawakening primitive desires for collective punishment because targeted punishment based on individualized findings of culpability has become impossible.

Roughly speaking, modern law replaces group revenge by the punishment only of those individuals found personally guilty of committing culpable acts. By targeting generic Americans, wantonly and indiscriminately, 9/11 resuscitated dark preliberal impulses, including a regressive craving to retaliate indiscriminately against the attackers' entire community, be it Arab or Muslim. The suicide of the terrorists excited this primitive longing for collective punishment not only by making it impossible to punish the hijackers individually, but also by communicating the message that the killers considered their own deaths not as a dreaded punishment but as a coveted reward. This is how suicide terrorism leads the attacked community to "mirror image" the crude racism and tribalism of the attacking community. The dismaying results may be exactly what the terrorists intended. Poorly targeted retaliation against the wider community of Arabs and Muslims comes close to corroborating the terrorists' implicit claim that they committed their atrocity not for personal or criminal reasons but from political devotion to an unjustly injured and victimized community.

The 9/11 attacks did not have exactly the results for which its designers had hoped, however. No Muslim government has fallen to fundamentalists, and no general uprising of Muslim peoples has occurred. One reason why 9/11 did not have such effects may be that the "message" it conveyed was much more garbled than those who sent it imagined. The self-erasing incoherence of the message as delivered was not an accident, moreover, but followed from a profound contradiction in the jihadist project itself.

Bin Laden, al-Zawahiri, and KSM wanted to stage an act of "martyrdom" that would display Muslims simultaneously as suffering victims and warlike aggressors. This was harder to do than they thought.

Jesus Christ managed to win a mass following and posthumously convert a mighty empire by assuming the dual roles of sacrificing priest and sacrificial lamb. But no one, least of all Mohammed Atta, can be both a sacrificial lamb and a mass murderer. The cognitive dissonance is too great. Savage victimizers cannot retain an aura of innocent victimization. A clear message does not get through. Accordingly, the wanton murder of 3,000 people from over 100 countries did not unleash a great wave of sympathy for bin Laden and al Qaeda or trigger a revolutionary uprising of Muslim masses. Rather than drawing attention to Muslim grievances, it stimulated immediate emotional identification with the innocent victims of the attackers' audacious cruelty. Even some radical Islamists, as mentioned, expressed their deep ambivalence about 9/11 by stating, incoherently, that they were proud of the attacks and that Mossad or CIA had orchestrated them. This last conceit is interesting less as a sign of demented conspiracy thinking than as a reflection of an almost universal disapproval of homicidal lunacy.

Retaliation and Self-Defense

To deepen our understanding of why Khalid Sheikh Mohammed chose to mount a suicide mission on 9/11, we need to inspect the "war aims" publicly announced by al Qaeda. Bin Laden, al-Zawahiri, and others have been fairly articulate about the purposes of their decade-long struggle against America, a campaign that has included hit-and-run attacks as well as suicide missions and has aimed at military as well as civilian targets. The war aims they have announced are ambiguous, contradictory, and constantly evolving, but not much more so than, say, the war aims announced by the United States in Iraq.

In the public statement of 1998, heralding the creation of the World Islamic Front for Jihad against Jews and Crusaders, bin Laden joined others in declaring: "The ruling to kill the Americans and their allies – civilians and military – is an individual duty for every Muslim who can do it in any country in which it is possible to do it, in order to liberate the al-Aqsa mosque and the holy mosque [in Mecca] from their grip, and in order for their armies to move out of all the lands of Islam, defeated and unable to threaten any Muslim."[95] Summarizing this and other pronouncements, we can say that al Qaeda's principal aims in its "war" with America, announced before 9/11, were to drive U.S. forces out of the Arabian peninsula as a prelude to seizing power in Saudi Arabia, to end U.S. support for Mubarak as a prelude to seizing power in Egypt, and to end U.S. support for Israel. The first half of the first mission has been accomplished, the rest not. But, accomplished or not, each of these aims is perfectly secular and, indeed, could easily be supported by Arab nationalists engaged in a struggle to end Western "colonization" of the Middle East.

Admittedly, bin Laden has also described the conflict in overtly religious terms. He has said, for example: "Under no circumstance should we forget this enmity between us and the infidels. For the enmity is based on creed."[96] To assert that the enmity between Islam and the West is based on creed is to deny that it is based on deeds. To fight non-Muslims "until they say there is no God but Allah"[97] is different from fighting Americans until they decamp from Arabia or stop supporting Israel. So how can we explain this back and forth between national-liberation terrorism and all-consuming religious war? Does the very mention of religious war prove that the 9/11 masterminds were irrational "fanatics"?

Most of bin Laden's public statements, as mentioned at the beginning of this chapter, emphasize secular not religious rationales for 9/11. The principal purpose of the attack, he repeatedly says, was to punish "unjust and tyrannical America."[98] He repeatedly justifies anti-American terrorism not by invoking American impiety but by reciting a litany of wrongs that America has inflicted on Muslims. True, he occasionally remarks that America has declared war on God, but such statements would carry little conviction if not fused with claims that America is tyrannizing and exploiting Muslim peoples. Under the Western boot, Islam is being persecuted and oppressed: "Its sons are being killed, its blood is being shed." To these fairly secular accusations, bin Laden adds, "its holy places are being attacked." He also mentions that Islamic nations are "not being ruled according to what God has decreed." The charge of apostasy is rhetorically prominent here, but its real importance is somewhat undermined by what comes next: "Despite this, nobody cares."[99] This revealing aside suggests that bin Laden's audience, if not bin Laden himself, experiences Western indifference to Islamic suffering as a very hurtful form of aggression against the Islamic world. Passages of this sort even seem to signal an unacknowledged need for recognition by the West, a need that would be superfluous, or even blasphemous, for anyone who genuinely believed that the West was an enemy of all things sacred.

Be this as it may, bin Laden seldom describes anti-Western terrorism as a way to convert Western unbelievers to the true faith. Instead, he almost always justifies terrorism against the West as a form of legitimate self-defense. The events of 9/11 were part of a "defensive jihad."[100] They embodied the perfectly secular need to punish America for its arrogance toward Muslims and to retaliate for American enmity and aggression and for what the jihadists consistently refer to as American and Israeli terrorism. In the Islamic tradition, wars of self-defense are easier to justify than wars of aggression,[101] but there is nothing specifically Islamic about this norm. Indeed, the superior legitimacy of wars of self-defense is virtually universal. If a community suffers a vicious attack, it can justly respond in whatever way its leaders judge proportionate.

In his videotape of Oct. 7, 2001, bin Laden savored the impact 9/11 had on Americans: "What the United States tastes today is a very small thing compared to what we have tasted for tens of years. Our nation has been tasting this humiliation and contempt for almost eighty years."[102] Following this rationale, the 9/11 attack on America should be understood as an act of retaliation – disgrace for disgrace, hurt for hurt. Three years later, he implied that the idea of toppling the World Trade Center first occurred to him in Beirut in 1982, "when America allowed Israel to invade Lebanon." Present in Beirut at the time, he helplessly observed as "houses were being destroyed and tower blocks were collapsing, crushing their residents." His craving for revenge was therefore natural and irresistible, he explains: "As I looked at those destroyed towers in Lebanon, it occurred to me to punish the oppressor in kind by destroying towers in America, so that it would have a taste of its own medicine."[103]

According to this account, Americans were forced, on 9/11, to ingest some of their own foul medicine, compelled to witness the mass murder of fellow citizens on home soil. Indeed, the backward-looking principle of retaliatory justice – do unto others as they have done unto you – looms much more prominently in al Qaeda statements than the expectation of a revived Caliphate. The 9/11 plotters adapted this basic tenet to the age of mass communications: Show the world that you can inflict bodily harm on others the way they have shown that they can inflict bodily harm on you. For years, CNN had beamed vivid footage throughout the Muslim world, picturing Arabs humiliated, as they saw it, and killed by the United States and its allies. In reply, the plotters decided to hand-deliver a colossal snuff flick to America's doorstep.

Of all the emotions and impulses driving the 9/11 conspirators, the intense craving for retaliation and the (real or imagined) imperatives of self-defense may turn out to have had the most decisive impact. A month after the attack, an al Qaeda spokesman complained that "when the victim tries to seek justice, he is described as a terrorist."[104] The 9/11 suicide operatives were not terrorists, from his perspective, but seekers of justice, righters of wrongs, punishers of crime. America deserved the attack because it has committed a "huge criminality."[105] What crimes do bin Laden and his companions have in mind? "The United States is the leader of the criminals in the crime of the establishment of Israel," Ayman al-Zawahiri explained, adding: "It is a crime that continues to take place and that has been repeating itself for the past fifty years. The Muslim nation cannot accept the continuation of this crime."[106] Like other criminals, the United States must be punished by the legitimate authorities. From this perspective, the hijackers were simply executing a death sentence passed by an al Qaeda high court. The crimes that the jihadists sometimes hype as crimes against God are invariably crimes against the Arab people or a Muslim nation. The executioners who carried out the death sentence on 9/11 needed no divine authorization for their action because they believed the execution of "the Americans" was justified by the primordial right of every community to punish criminal injuries to itself.

Like Jesus Christ and George Orwell, bin Laden speaks in animal fables to make his ideas accessible and memorable. The following characteristic passage about the American crime of supporting Israel is worth citing in its entirety. The impulse to punish criminal acts, here again, suggests a secular rationale for retaliation against previous American acts of injustice.

> What is taking place cannot be tolerated by any nation. I do not say from the nations of the human race, but from other creatures, from the animals. They would not tolerate what is taking place. A confidant of mine told me that he saw a butcher slaughtering a camel in front of another camel. The other camel got agitated while seeing the blood coming out of the other camel. Thus, it burst out with rage and bit the hand of the man and broke it. How can the weak mothers in Palestine endure the killing of their children in front of their eyes by the unjust Jewish executioners with US support and with US aircraft and tanks?[107]

Islamic law certainly justifies punishing the unjust, but the avenging camel of bin Laden's fable has no need to consult a religious principle to justify his instinctive – and therefore natural – retaliation. For the same reason, Islamic militants do not need the Shari'a to give them permission to shed American blood if America is, in their minds, committing criminal atrocities against Muslims.

Identifying the Enemy

Those who locate the source of anti-American violence in religious extremism often stress the jihadists' Manichaean worldview. One way to reply is to cite George W. Bush's idea, to which we will return, that America today is at war with "evil." Without doubting the influence of religion on Bush's rhetoric, we can confidently state that American enmity has been aroused by al Qaeda's actions, not by its beliefs. Why cannot the same be true of bin Laden?

An essential point to keep in mind is that a Manichaean religious framework, although dividing the world into good and evil, does not specify a religious community's military enemy of the moment. Bin Laden's decision to declare war on the United States was provoked by concrete historical circumstances, therefore, not foreordained by religious doctrine. To understand the motivations in question, the best place to begin is probably the Afghan war. Although it failed miserably in the Middle East, pan-Arabism was spectacularly successful, at least in popular perception, in the multinational effort to drive the Soviet Union out of Afghanistan. An international brigade drawn from diverse Arab countries helped to defeat a superpower. After the Soviet retreat in 1989, however, this "homeless phalanx"[108] of demobilized Arab warriors was left in the lurch. Its members became mujahideen drifters in search of a jihad. Many of the Arabs who gathered around bin Laden in Afghanistan during the 1990s had nowhere else to go because they faced death sentences or imprisonment back home. (Some of them chose to join guerrilla campaigns in Bosnia, Chechnya, and Kashmir.) Although it provided a short-term remedy locally, in other words, the exile of radical Islamic insurgents from the Middle East produced a long-term problem globally, creating a pool of angry déracinés willing to enlist in violent causes around the world.

Self-selected "warriors" are not the only dangerous political exiles from the Arab world. They have been joined abroad by self-selected "priests" as well. As part of their governments' counterinsurgency strategies, the security apparatuses of Egypt, Jordan, Syria, Algeria, and other Arab countries have exiled many homegrown radical imams not to Afghanistan but to Western Europe. The resulting Europe-based diaspora of angry preachers was able to prey especially upon deracinated Arab youths who were cut off from their families, feeling the sting of discrimination, and looking for some colorful purpose to orient their drifting lives. Searching for pungent myths that could appeal simultaneously to the Algerians, Moroccans, Egyptians, Yemenis, Jordanians, Libyans, and Syrians living in

Europe, these preachers naturally idealized the jihad in Afghanistan, where a pan-Arab force had, as they recounted the story, brought a superpower to ruin.

If political Islam almost died in the Arab Middle East, as some have argued, it was revived in the Arab diasporas of Western Europe thanks precisely to this lethal syndicate of self-anointed preachers and would-be warriors inspired by the myth of the Afghan jihad. Islamic beliefs may or may not motivate terrorists, but they certainly increase the "interoperability" of multinational terrorist cells. It is not surprising that Algerians, Syrians, and Yemenis concur more readily on what they oppose than on what they favor. Even if they disagree completely about the ultimate positive aim of violent jihad (what sort of Caliphate? run by whom?), they can collaborate today on short-term goals such as bloodying the perceived enemies of Islam. Al-Zawahiri, for instance, states that the one "slogan" above all others that has been "firing up the feelings of the Muslim nation from Morocco to Indonesia for the past 50 years" is "the call for the jihad against Israel."[109] The same logic helps explain the pan-Islamic demonization of the United States. Radical imams in Europe, preaching to young Muslims with different backgrounds and from a variety of Muslim countries and cultures, need a common enemy. Next to Israel, the only obvious candidate for the role of a unifying enemy is America. In the imagination of Islamic militants, the United States apparently reoccupied the space vacated by the Soviet Union.[110] The United States was not merely "the remote enemy." It was also the *shared* enemy. A jihad against America sounded appealing, among other reasons, because it would allow radicalized Muslim youth to reenact the celebrated victory of the Afghan war, but this time on a global scale.

These concrete historical events, not some underlying religious Manichaeism, explain why the 9/11 plotters directed their fury against the United States. Bin Laden was originally interested in overthrowing the Saudi regime, just as al-Zawahiri was focused initially on overthrowing the Egyptian regime. Unable to make any headway at home, they jointly evolved an indirect strategy of attacking their local autocrats' foreign backers: "we must move the battle to the enemy's grounds to burn the hands of those who ignite fire in our country."[111] By attacking U.S. interests, they hoped to force the United States to withdraw its troops from the Persian Gulf region and its support for Mubarak, just as attacks in Lebanon in 1983 and Somalia in 1993 had driven the Americans to pull out their troops. To successfully overthrow both Mubarak and the House of Saud, al Qaeda had to induce the Americans to abandon their clients

in the Middle East. The most effective way to undermine the near enemy
was to attack the distant enemy.

Plausible so far as it goes, this instrumental logic does not wholly
explain why the 9/11 plotters turned their fury against America, however. An additional consideration is the following. To attack "apostate"
regimes back home, bin Laden and al-Zawahiri first had to bulk up their
mujahideen army. To rally more troops, they had to adjust their "war
aims." Their thinking was not straightforwardly instrumental, therefore.
They were not simply seeking the most efficient means to achieve preset ends. On the contrary, they deliberately modified their ends to attain
more plentiful and lethal means. To some extent, recruitment seemed
to become an end in itself. They redefined their objectives to provide
them with the widest possible appeal, especially to Arab youths living in
Europe, who were insulated (to some extent) from abuses by the powerful and wealthy back in the Middle East. Only a battle against Israel,
the West in general, and, especially, America would permit al Qaeda to
draw recruits from across the varied spectrum of alienated Muslim youth.
America was cast as the principal enemy of Islam not only because of what
America is or what America does. America was also chosen as the enemy
because it was the best candidate to rally and hold together an incoherent
international grab bag of aspiring jihadists and their hangers-on.

What struck the United States on 9/11, therefore, was a "consortium,"[112] the pooled residue of the suppressed Islamist insurgencies of the
Arab Middle East. The fusing of what remained of these previously local
insurgencies took place largely among diaspora Arabs outside the Middle
East itself, in Afghanistan and Europe. The multinational or pan-Arab
Hamburg cell exemplifies how uprooting can effect an ad hoc blending of
the offshoots of underground local resistance movements. It also reveals
how the internal logic of this merger can compel a redefining of the enemy-
in-view.

Neither of al Qaeda's maximalist goals (destroying America and achieving Islamic domination of the world) is particularly reasonable or realistic.
But the 9/11 masterminds had to speak this way to their multinational
army of mujahideen. They could not plausibly say that their ultimate goal
in attacking the United States was to topple now Mubarak, now the House
of Saud. The backstage plotters could communicate with the hijackers only
by repackaging micropolitics as macropolitics. For radicalized Arabs living in Europe, the purpose of attacking the United States could not have
been simply to push America out of their various homelands, because they
had loosened their ties to their homelands – or, rather, they had, in some

sense, replaced their birth countries, where nationalism had failed, with an imaginary community of faith. The redefinition of al Qaeda's war aims from decolonization to religious war can best be understood, therefore, as a by-product of the organization's all-points recruitment drive aimed at young expatriates with no national homeland to defend against foreign occupation.

Transnational jihadism feeds off local insurrections. Those who "graduate" from national to transnational violence, or who lift their eyes from nearby to remote oppressors, seem to undergo a personal transformation. When national-liberation guerrillas or domestic rebels redirect their hostility from a local enemy to a global enemy, they may be doing more than merely switching tactics. They may be consolidating a new identity. This would help explain why the conflict between al Qaeda and the United States, far from being another rehashing of "ancient hatreds," seems historically unprecedented.

When articulating a positive goal, al Qaeda spokesmen often mention a world Caliphate. But such a Caliphate, with the West, India, China, and Russia reduced to tribute status before radical Sunni powers, is the religious equivalent of Marx's communist utopia. It is basically a pipedream, difficult to imagine in any detail as well as utterly impossible to bring about. To make a revived Caliphate into a distant aim of jihad, therefore, poses no threat at all to the unity of a shaky coalition of radical Sunnis from across the Middle East and the world.

From Decolonization to "Religious" War

The mobilizing ideology behind 9/11 was not Islam, or even Islamic fundamentalism, but rather a specific narrative of blame. Even despair must be interpreted to become politically effective. To dispel fatalistic illusions and stimulate feelings of aggression, it is necessary to focus the mind on an ostensibly guilty party. Those who downplay America's crimes, according to bin Laden, "anesthetize the nation."[113] Those who call attention to these crimes, by contrast, arouse the nation, readying it for battle.

Between the harm that people experience and their defensive reaction to it comes a narrative or interpretation. This intermediate factor can be decisive because the causes of suffering, viewed objectively, are almost always complicated and ambiguous enough to admit conflicting perspectives. If an injury is seen as a visitation of nature, it will be considered a misfortune, to which the only reasonable response is resignation. If people come to believe that an injury has been inflicted purposely by a malicious enemy, by contrast, they will call it injustice, not misfortune. The difference of interpretation is important here because perceived injustice excites a violent response, and perceived misfortune does not.

To sooth the rage of victims, political authority often tries to persuade the injured that their losses were caused by impersonal forces, such as fate or accident, and that struggling is futile. To enflame the rage of victims, radical leaders do the opposite. They focus attention on those who both caused and benefited from the victims' pain. An interpretation of suffering is especially apt to stir the will to violence if it focuses attention on a culprit who can suffer pain in turn. According to the classic study of resentment, "every sufferer instinctively seeks a cause for his suffering; more specifically, an agent, a 'guilty' agent who is susceptible of pain – in short, some living being or other on whom he can vent his feelings directly or in effigy, under some pretext or other."[114] If suffering is seen as natural or uncaused it will be coded as misfortune instead of injustice, and it will produce resignation rather than rebellion. The most efficient way to incite, therefore, is to indict.

Naming a particular enemy and reciting his crimes in gory detail transforms diffuse feelings of personal misery into focused rage. To rally Muslim youth to their cause, therefore, bin Laden and al-Zawahiri have indulged in a veritable orgy of blame. They have interpreted American actions as crimes by inserting them into an overarching narrative detailing the West's monstrous plot to dominate Muslims and plunder their wealth. They have embroidered and mythically heightened observed facts to make them appear to support a vast conspiracy theory. For instance, they implausibly but persistently interpreted "Operation Restore Hope" in Somalia in 1992–93 as another case of a Western power trying to occupy Muslim lands, and they wholly ignored the role of the United States in opposing Milosevic's malign ambitions against Muslims in Kosovo. But the ultimate charge that bin Laden levels against America is the charge of genocide. Before 2003, it seems, America's "occupation" of Saudi Arabia provided definitive proof that the United States was engaged in "a war of annihilation"[115] against Islam. Astonishingly, bin Laden repeatedly argued, prior to 2003, that the presence of U.S. troops in the land of the two holy mosques was a much graver offense than the Soviet invasion of Afghanistan, a conflict, remember, that killed one million Afghans and exiled five million more.[116] Demonizing America and all its inhabitants not only helps neutralize qualms about killing civilians. It also, presumably, helps intensify the otherwise lukewarm craving for blood revenge felt by jihadists who have had little personal contact with the United States. This is probably why entrepreneurs of Islamist violence spend so much energy mythically magnifying and embroidering on the real injustices committed by the United States, interpreting them as parts of a vast sinister plot to "destroy Islam," and concealing any information that might contradict the simplistic storyline. There is nothing specifically Islamic, of course, about the charge of genocide. Unlike impiety or blasphemy, genocide is a crime against humanity. To accuse America of plotting a *Vernichtungskrieg* against the Islamic nation, therefore, is to accuse it of violating a Western norm accepted by atheists and non-Muslim believers alike. That bin Laden resorts so regularly to this outrageous charge is a strong sign that his audience is more interested in American injustice than American infidelity.

This logic is impeccable so far as it goes. But the idea that the 9/11 masterminds really declared war on the United States for its odious foreign policy, which America could presumably abandon or modify, rather than for more existential reasons, does not mesh well with bin Laden's call to murder all Americans everywhere. Pressuring American citizens is quite different from wiping them out. Extreme talk about visiting hellfire on American urban centers and annihilating the American way of life makes nonsense of at least one interpretation of the strategy behind 9/11, whereby a pinprick attack on America would persuade the United States to withdraw its support for Muslim autocracies. Genocidal threats make more sense if the attack they accompanied was meant to provoke a reckless response.

Before al Qaeda, it is sometimes said, terrorist groups wanted a lot of people watching, not a lot of people dead, on the reasonable grounds that mass casualties will viscerally alienate potential supporters. When promising to deliver America "its Hiroshima," as a result, bin Laden is commonly taken to have turned a corner, closing the door to negotiation and unleashing a kind of zero-compunction terrorism that had never been seen before. Only a thoroughly religious mind that sincerely believed in "cosmic war" could have done this, it is inferred.

Although superficially plausible, this inference is too hasty. Bin Laden and his associates may have perfectly nonapocalyptic reasons for sounding apocalyptic. For one thing, such talk is frightening. They could certainly anticipate that allusions to an American Hiroshima would drive U.S. policymakers into a frenzy. The more crazed al Qaeda sounds, the more likely it becomes that the United States government will lose its equilibrium. During the Cold War, America's one source of psychological comfort was that its enemy, too, feared the apocalypse. A shared fear of nuclear disaster provided the basis for accommodation and compromise between

Washington and Moscow, even when relations grew tense. To take this solace away, as bin Laden has done, was an immensely shrewd form of psychological warfare.

It was shrewd, but not necessarily wise. The plotters' own folly was revealed by their total lack of preparation for the ferocity with which the United States destroyed al Qaeda's Afghan sanctuary. If they were playing matador, then the 9/11 masterminds got badly gored. But we should still not adduce the unrealistic goals that they announced as evidence that the masterminds of 9/11 were "irrational fanatics."

Here is an alternative way of looking at the matter. The organizers of 9/11 spent years in an underground revolutionary organization. Honed in conflict, their skills are no doubt wholly inappropriate to the mundane tasks of a postconflict situation. If apostate regimes fell down in Saudi Arabia and Egypt, what roles in ordinary governance would bin Laden and al-Zawahiri assume? For men such as these, terrorism is a profession that can be exercised only under conditions of ongoing hostility. Not only do they have a strong incentive to keep these conditions in place, they also have the means to do so. For instance, they can raise unreasonable demands that their declared enemies cannot possibly accept. The 9/11 masterminds surely want to keep up the value of their personal investment in terrorism. This desire alone, in the absence of irrational fanaticism, could explain why their demands seem hallucinatory and unrealistic. Impossible to satisfy may be exactly the way they want their demands to seem. By refusing to compromise on unrealistic goals, they may be angling to keep their jihad alive. After all, it is the only activity they really know.

This hypothesis does not imply that the plotters' thought processes were wholly rational. An additional reason why not has to do with "the fallacy of the instrument." This fallacy, to which I will return, causes people with a hammer to see every problem as a nail. An example of this fallacy is the American decision to combat nonstate terrorist groups using military force, not because military force is appropriate (it is not) but because military force is the "best" instrument at America's disposal. When a group of weak and angry men, with poor technology at their disposal, face a military superpower, suicide terrorism may be the only method available for inflicting noticeable harm. Suicide terrorism may have been al Qaeda's most effective "hammer," in other words. What drove them to use it, as mentioned, was less perennial religious extremism than a contextual asymmetry of power. The 9/11 masterminds may have vastly overestimated its utility, however. They may have imagined that it was more useful than it was because it was the only serious weapon in their arsenal and, like other political leaders, they "had to do something." The 9/11 plotters may have chosen mass murder by suicide terrorists not because such an attack would reliably produce important benefits but rather because it was the only action they could think of that would valorize the meager assets they had at hand. To the extent that their capacities dictated their intentions, they were deviating from ideal strategic rationality. Such deviations are historically ubiquitous, however, and have nothing at all to do with the plotters' religious beliefs.

What Is at Stake?

When designing an effective response to 9/11, policymakers have to clear their minds of rage and revulsion and hear the "message" delivered by the attacks. Leaping to see religious extremism behind 9/11 prematurely terminates a strategically vital search for other equally important reasons and motives. Overemphasizing apocalyptic religiosity also blocks the way forward. To see scriptural absolutism in the attacks, in fact, is implicitly to choose ruthless violence as the only feasible response to the terrorist threat. If America is facing implacable religious zealots who believe that Allah has told them to destroy America, then the only way to respond is with crushing military force, but if religion was only one factor among many others that shaped the jihadists' war aims and strategies, then the United States can decide to respond in a variety of ways.

Religious extremism obviously played a role in the 9/11 plot. If we do not overstate that role, however, we are likely to consider the influence of other forces in motivating the attacks. Psychologists sometimes trace violence to "an intolerable condition of human shame and rage."[117] That much jihadist violence, too, is fueled by feelings of indignity seems almost certain. Yet if the makers of America's counterterrorism policy had been compelled to take this hypothesis seriously, they would have made greater efforts to design a response to 9/11 that would have minimized the infliction of further indignities on ordinary Muslims, some of them picked up by accident in random dragnets. Self-restraint along these lines was not in evidence after 9/11, however.

An alternative and more promising framework is the following. Radicalization is driven not by underlying religious belief but by specific grievances, both real and imagined. Rage at perceived injury can be exacerbated by extraneous emotions such as envy, sexual guilt, and self-hate, but it is crystallized and disciplined by narratives of blame, promulgated by savvy entrepreneurs of political violence. Traditions of religious radicalism play some role in fomenting such rage, just as the institutions of organized Islam, such as *zakat* or obligatory almsgiving, provide resources that terrorists can exploit. Religious devotion detached from a vivid narrative of blame will not funnel diffuse rage toward a specific target. Any sensible response to 9/11 must therefore aim at unraveling, or weakening the plausibility of, the narratives of blame that implicate the West in general and the United States in particular in injuring and humiliating Muslims.

The Bush Administration's response to 9/11 assumes, on the contrary, that American immoderation will produce Muslim moderation. That the shortsightedness of this approach was not blindingly obvious reflects badly on the wisdom of those who designed the policy, for it is one of the most elemental truths about human nature that violence breeds violence, in a potentially endless cycle. Violent injury triggers rage and a need to erase the attendant shame. America's invasion of Iraq in response to 9/11 fits this pattern perfectly. The same will be said about the next attack on the United States, perhaps carried out in response to America's gratuitous invasion and horrifyingly bloody occupation of Iraq.

The hearts-and-minds dimension of the war on terror is so discouragingly difficult because no one knows how to dismantle and discredit the narratives of blame that crystallize and target the diffuse rage of Muslim youth. But it should at least be possible not to make things worse. Making things worse is exactly what the Administration has done by its reckless decision to militarize counterterrorism and plunge blindly into Iraq. Making things worse is also what the United States has done by suspending the presumption of innocence and sweeping up large numbers of young Muslims in indiscriminate police dragnets. Policies that fuel ever more homicidal rage against America and Americans appear less intelligent in retrospect than when they were first proposed and implemented. Even the Administration's "forward strategy of freedom" is humiliating to the extent that it implies, as it inevitably does to some extent, Western superiority and Muslim inferiority. Yet no action was more thoroughly self-defeating in this regard than the American invasion of Iraq. This is the topic to which we now turn. By tolerating spectacularly high levels of collateral damage in Iraq and allowing the slaughter to spread, the United States has inadvertently corroborated a central proposition in the jihadist narrative of blame, namely, that Americans feel contempt for Muslims and ascribe little or no value to Muslim lives. Sending such a message was not only despicably immoral. It was also a fatal mistake.

PART II

SHOW OF FORCE

2 | WHY MILITARY SUPERIORITY BREEDS ILLUSIONS

Much of what has gone wrong after 9/11 can be traced to the distorted picture of the threat environment entertained and promulgated by the Iraq war's plotters and planners. Their mental fog, especially the rationally unjustifiable priority they assigned to threats that could be countered only militarily, seems to have been, at least in part, a product of their emotional, not to mention professional and financial, investment in America's unchallenged military superiority. In the run-up to the war, Robert Kagan and others argued that Europeans and Americans did not understand threats to the West in similar ways because America was a military giant and Europe a military pygmy. This was an important insight, but its implications are not the ones that Kagan alleged. He bragged, basically, that America's enormous military power allowed it to see the world without illusions, whereas the militarily feeble Europeans were lost in wishful thinking. A massive difference in military capacity explained why the United States, in 2003, was able to see vividly the serious and urgent threat to the West posed by Saddam Hussein, and why the Europeans were blithely unaware of the same looming danger. Revisited today, after America's wholly baseless illusions about Iraq have been so violently dashed, this way of contrasting the United States and Europe seems implausible. It makes much greater sense now to flip Kagan on his head. Because the Europeans, protected after World War II by a U.S. military umbrella, invested heavily in the linguistic and cultural knowledge of their law-enforcement and intelligence services, they can now see more clearly than the Americans the true contours of the terrorist threat, especially the radicalization of second-generation Muslim youth in France, Britain, Germany, Spain, Holland, and Belgium. Because Americans, by contrast, have sunk so much of their national treasure into a military establishment fit to deter and perhaps fight an enemy that has now disappeared, they have an almost irresistible inclination to exaggerate the centrality of rogue states, excellent targets for military destruction, to the overall terrorist threat. They overestimate war (which never unfolds as expected) and underestimate diplomacy and persuasion as instruments of American power. Far from guaranteeing an unbiased and clear-eyed view of the terrorist threat, as Kagan contends, American military superiority has irredeemably skewed the country's view of the enemy on the horizon, drawing the United States, with appalling consequences, into a gratuitous, cruel, and unwinnable conflict in the Middle East.

France and Germany's refusal, in the run-up to the 2003 invasion, to accept the Bush Administration's definition of the Iraqi threat made publicly visible a gradual, decade-long weakening of the Atlantic alliance. Robert Kagan peers behind that diplomatic contretemps to discover why, after the end of the Cold War, Europeans and Americans "understand each other less and less."[1] Unbelievable as it may sound, his thesis is that Europeans and Americans have trouble coordinating their foreign policies because Europeans are utopian and deluded and Americans are tough-minded and unafraid to look reality in the face. He first advanced this anomalous claim in an essay, "Power and Weakness," published in the summer of 2002, which he then updated and expanded into a book. That essay quickly became a sensation among European diplomats and policy-makers.[2] But how did a conservative American polemicist such as Kagan manage to provoke such storms of soul searching among Europeans? He did so partly by suggesting that European nations, despite their endless squabbles, share more values with one another than they share with the United States, an idea that some Europeans, at least, devoutly wish to be true. He also attracted attention by implying, plausibly enough, that Europe's own foreign policy disarray contributes decisively to America's controversial unilateralism.

Although mentioning that "the crisis over Iraq has cast the transatlantic problem in the harshest possible light,"[3] Kagan seeks the roots of U.S.-European tensions in the different military postures of the world's two great economic powers. In his view, "The key difference is less a matter of culture and philosophy than of capability."[4] The premise of his argument here is quite intriguing. Rather than searching for tools to address new problems, both individuals and states, Kagan tells us, unconsciously redefine the problems they face to fit the solutions with which they feel most comfortable. He is essentially elaborating on the well-known principle: Capabilities create intentions. In this case, on-hand capacities to respond to threats distort an individual's (or a government's) perception of the threat environment. Because the United States is a military colossus and Europe is a military pygmy, he adds, they will never agree about the nature and gravity of the dangers they face. Kagan drives his point home with the following folktale:

> The psychology of weakness is easy enough to understand. A man armed only with a knife may decide that a bear prowling the forest is a tolerable danger, inasmuch as the alternative – hunting the bear armed only with a knife – is actually riskier than lying low and hoping the bear never attacks. The same man armed with a rifle, however, will likely make a different calculation of what constitutes a tolerable risk. Why should he risk being mauled to death if he doesn't need to? This perfectly normal human psychology has driven a wedge between the United States and Europe.[5]

This little passage contains the gist of Kagan's argument. It is not simply that Americans, being armed to the teeth, are willing to venture forth in search of monsters to slay while Europeans, being military weaklings, pusillanimously shun confrontations. It is rather that weak powers routinely fail to take the full measure of actual threats, indulging in the fantasy that looming dangers can be allayed by diplomatic finesse and international law, whereas strong powers are able to see the floodlit world as a frighteningly dangerous place where freedom will perish if not defended by force.

Some Europeans, at least, want us to interpret an exclusive devotion to multilateralism, diplomacy and international law as a sign of superior morality. Kagan, by contrast, disparages European fondness for multilateral solutions as a symptom of helplessness, or perhaps as an expression of resentment. Tacitly drawing on Nietzsche's genealogy of morals, he argues that Europeans are slyly trying to unman their American allies by employing "strategies of weakness."[6] They hope to hobble the United States by slow-walking it into diplomatic negotiations and international legal regimes. "In what may be the ultimate feat of subtlety and indirection," Kagan writes, "they want to control the behemoth by appealing to its conscience."[7] And, he warns, these devilishly crafty Europeans may even succeed in derailing the United States from sober realism into the pursuit of pacifist illusions, presumably with some help from homegrown Wilsonian idealists and Vietnam-era liberals.

This Euro-liberal attempt to charm the United States into abandoning war as an instrument of foreign policy, Kagan maintains, is a self-defeating folly. Even today, more than a half-century after the destruction of Nazi Germany, Europe's pampered civilians remain "dependent on the United States' willingness to use its military might to deter or defeat those around the world who still believe in power politics."[8] European leaders, therefore, should simply admit "the vital necessity of having a strong, even predominant America."[9] If Europeans would learn to defer politely to the United States, Kagan expects or hopes that American officials would return the courtesy by avoiding gratuitous put-downs that serve no purpose other than deflating the Europeans' preposterous self-importance.

America as Mars, Europe as Venus

Kagan's intellectual framework may seem rather unsophisticated, but it does boast a philosophical foundation. Its premise is that a domestic realm built along liberal lines, where force and fraud are repressed and the rule of law prevails, can be stabilized and defended only by a vigorous, even ferocious, foreign policy. Force and fraud must be deployed ruthlessly against unscrupulous adversaries abroad, and international laws and treaties should be respected only when convenient. That is the only way to protect civilization against barbarism, to defend the world's "good neighborhoods" against the world's "ghettos," he implies. Kantian dreamers of peace and reason may not know it, but their hyperliberal utopia always depends on a Hobbesian willingness to apply organized violence, without regard to rules, to fend off barbarians at the gate. It is naïve to believe that a dangerously turbulent world can be managed by United Nations resolutions, foreign aid, diplomatic negotiations, and a thickening of commercial ties.

That Kagan's argument has at least some force will be recognized even by those who most fiercely disagree with it. The same cannot be said for the emotionally charged mythology with which he decorates his basic claim. Just as prewar German nationalists loved to oppose *Helden* to *Händler* (Teutonic "heroes" to English "merchants"), so Kagan enjoys contrasting masculine Americans with effeminate Europeans: *Americans are from Mars and Europeans are from Venus.* Gun-shy Europeans are able to putter around their Kantian garden in sock feet only because lethally armed Americans are out there in combat boots patrolling the Hobbesian jungle to prevent the "post-historical paradise" from being destroyed by various ayatollahs, Saddam Husseins, and Kim Jong Ils.[10] Kagan brings his gendered interpretation of United States-European Union relations to a surprising culmination when, in his final paragraphs, he reinvents himself as a marriage counselor, urging the quarreling couple to kiss and make up, for their own sake and the world's.

This is amusing, in its way, all the more so because it is basically unserious. Unfortunately, Kagan's more sober attempt to trace transatlantic discord to differences in military capacity founders on the experience of the Cold War, when Americans and Europeans agreed on a definition of a common threat even though their military capacities were just as asymmetrical as they are today. Countries that are militarily weak will sometimes defer quietly to allies that are militarily strong. At other times they will vigorously dissent. Capabilities alone, therefore, do not bear the explanatory burden that Kagan places upon them. Moreover, a much simpler explanation suggests itself. Europeans no longer feel that the United States is protecting them from a dangerous threat because the likelihood of a military invasion from the East has disappeared. Without U.S. help, Kagan claims, Europe will be unable to prevent itself from "being overrun, spiritually as well as physically, by a world that has yet to accept the rule of 'moral consciousness.'"[11] But who, exactly, is about to overrun Europe "spiritually as well as physically"? There may be a good answer to this question, but if Kagan knows, he is not telling. Lack of a clear and convincing answer to the "What military threat?" question explains tensions in the alliance more economically than do differences in military capacity.

The European Enigma

Even if Kagan were right that different levels of military preparedness necessarily give rise in Europe and the United States to differing assessments of threats, how does he explain the vastly different levels of military preparedness? Europe is rich enough to be a military superpower, so why have European nations been so reluctant to increase their defense spending or even to assemble on schedule their much-discussed rapid-reaction force?

Kagan's answer to this critical question is a blur, partly because he cannot consistently invoke the objective disappearance of a shared military threat. Perhaps the United States after World War II successfully retired Europe from world history, reprogramming the once-militaristic Germans into harmless merchants, civilians, and welfare recipients. Perhaps bitter memories of *Machtpolitik* and chauvinistic militarism have dampened the European appetite for war. Perhaps other Europeans continue to fear that Germany's homicidal impulses could be reawakened in a remilitarized Europe. Perhaps the successful experience of building the European Union has given the Europeans an illusion that similarly legalistic methods could be used to fashion a new global order. Perhaps Europeans are simply free riders, smartly purchasing domestic tranquility by generous social spending in the expectation that American taxpayers will foot the bill for European security. Perhaps they are simply unable to switch quickly from the posture, to which the United States assigned them during the Cold War, of territorial defense to a policy of force projection, which is what it would take to compete militarily with the United States today. Or perhaps, as Samuel Huntington might say, the European population is simply aging, its animal spirits waning, a process of decay sometimes evidenced in negative population growth. Kagan rehearses these various factors but provides little guidance about how to interrelate or weigh them.

Yet the real weakness of his argument is something else. However we might explain European criticisms of American policy, it is unreasonable to suggest that the French, say, disagree with U.S. foreign policy because they are pacifists. The French are not watering tulips in their walled gardens; they are out there in the "jungles" of the Côte d'Ivoire. Kagan even admits that French and British (and even German) militaries have been, until recently, more willing to absorb casualties than their American counterparts, suggesting again that his eye-catching contrast between American "men" and European "women," although helpful for selling books, is bogus.

Kagan informs us repeatedly that "the new Europe really has emerged as a paradise...freed from the laws and even the mentality of power politics."[12] But what Europe is he talking about? Algerian youth in the *banlieues* of Paris have not been especially impressed by the humanitarian softness of the French police. Nor would most Poles and Hungarians agree that the new Europe is a realm rinsed free of power asymmetries where all peoples are treated equally under law. One source of Kagan's comprehensive confusions is his inexplicable tendency to treat law and force as antonyms. He knows that law is useless without enforcement, but he does not think through the implications of this simple truth. Contrary to the unrealistic formulas he thoughtlessly recites, moreover, law can never wholly erase asymmetries of power. The pervasive favoritism of every known rule-of-law system suggests that law expresses and stabilizes asymmetries of power. (Because no party is strong enough to rule without out a degree of voluntary cooperation, law often stabilizes asymmetries of power by moderating them to some extent.)

This tendency of law to look favorably on the interests of the powerful explains why, from Nuremberg to the International Criminal Tribunal for Yugoslavia, the United States, as the world's leading power, has been the champion of international law. That would be incomprehensible if law, as Bush-league Nietzscheans such as Kagan seem to believe, were simply a shackle placed by the weak on the strong. The United States created the current international legal regime and has used it for half a century to its own and its allies' advantage. The current crisis over Iraq came about not because the Europeans were trying to hobble U.S. sovereignty by imposing international law but rather for the opposite reason. Americans could not persuade Europeans in the 1990s to take international law (in the form of UN resolutions) seriously. In other words, the Iraqi crisis itself reveals how perversely misleading is Kagan's stylized contrast between Europeans living in a Kantian world of reason and rules and Americans living in a Hobbesian world of force and fraud.

The Military Lens

Kagan's basic argument keeps crumbling under inspection because it rests on an intellectual sleight of hand. Its elementary fallacy lies in the selective application of its theoretical premise, namely, the valid and important insight that a community's capabilities affect the way it prioritizes threats. What Kagan is pointing to can be described as a particularly subtle form of "confirmation bias," the general human proclivity to focus disproportionate attention on evidence that confirms preexistent prejudices and beliefs. In this case, the human mind attaches disproportionate importance to problems for which it has ready-made, off-the-shelf solutions. Intelligence that is not immediately "actionable," given available capacities for action, is frequently stuffed into the filing cabinet and forgotten, even if it is objectively quite disturbing. This particular cognitive failing is a "capabilities bias," commonly referred to as the Fallacy of the Instrument. It has the potential to skew irrationally the threat assessments of any organized group.

A country's foreign policy, in particular, can become unrealistic if specially favored instruments prevent policy-makers from facing up to threats that can be addressed effectively only by other, less-favored means. From this true premise, however, we cannot infer, as Kagan does, that Europe's meager military capacities make European assessment of threats unrealistic whereas the United States' formidable military capacities make American assessment of threats realistic. The illusions of the jungle are no less pernicious than the illusions of the garden. Kagan touches on this point when he allows, "The stronger may, in fact, rely on force more than they should."[13] But he does not integrate this important insight into his basic argument. Indeed, he devotes no attention at all to the role of irrationality in the making of American foreign policy, even though he knows full well that a missionary impulse pervades Washington's understanding of the United States' global role. Kagan himself seems intoxicated, not sobered, by his unvarnished view of today's dangerous world. That is the only way to explain his pose as a think-tank prophet standing on the ramparts to defend the fortress of human civilization from the teeming barbarian hoards. His own heroic posturing, in other words, definitively explodes his over-sharp contrast between the hard and the soft, between realistic Americans and utopian Europeans.

Kagan is right that a militarily weak society will typically underestimate problems that cannot be solved by civilian means alone. But his analysis is unbalanced because he slights the flipside, namely, that a militarily powerful society will typically underestimate problems that cannot be solved by military means alone. (The National Security Act of 1947 attempted to circumvent this capabilities bias by locating the CIA outside the military, so that it would not define the threat environment in a way that deliberately or inadvertently overvalued military solutions.) Both mistakes are possible, of course, and both can be fatal, but Kagan pays attention only to the former. Despite the occasional justice of his remarks about European self-delusion, therefore, he comes across as a Bush-Administration apologist making a pitch rather than as a foreign-policy analyst trying to make sense of a complicated problem. Are Paris and Berlin really more "in denial" than Washington? Do Europeans have a more distorted view of the contemporary security environment than Americans? Kagan says so, but he is wrong.

The United States' unrivaled military power is not just a "tool." It is also a warped lens distorting the way the Bush Administration has defined the direst threats facing the country. Acute problems that cannot be addressed by a unilateral deployment of American military power (such as North Korea's horrifying slide toward becoming a serial proliferator of nuclear weapons) get much less sustained attention than problems (such as Iraqi noncompliance with United Nation's resolutions) that can be addressed unilaterally and militarily. Oil dependency, underinvestment in foreign-language skills, contagious disease, state collapse, and global warming are disparate examples of neglected national-security threats that are not made any less acute simply because they cannot be managed by unilateral military force.

Kagan's talk of American heroes patrolling the Hobbesian world obscures these and other irrationalities afflicting George W. Bush's foreign policy. An ideological conviction that government is the problem and that laxly regulated private exchanges are the answer, for instance, has seduced the Administration into thinking that rogue states are invariably more dangerous than failed states. One consequence, explored further in Chapter Three, was the war party's failure to anticipate the possibility that Iraqi weapons of mass destruction might enter the clandestine arms market after Baghdad's centralized control was destroyed by an American attack and before our forces secured an Iraqi territory "the size of California," crisscrossed by well-developed smuggling routes. Deeply held Christian beliefs prevent the Administration from grasping the fatal threat posed to the United States by religious certainty. In addition, myopic domestic lobbies, interagency rivalries and Cold War habits of mind all distorted the Administration's understanding of the nation's new security environment, as we shall see.

Europe's Relevance

The most striking, and by far the most dangerous, misperception afflicting Bush's approach to foreign affairs concerns the war against transnational terrorism. Kagan asserts that Europe "has had little to offer the United States in strategic military terms since the end of the Cold War."[14] Widely shared inside the Administration, this view is based on the premise that the "end of the Cold War did not reduce the salience of military power."[15] Military power is just as central to American security today as it was during the Cold War – that is what Kagan would have us believe. And after the Cold War, "European military incapacity"[16] means that our former allies have become almost wholly irrelevant to U.S. security. That is the assumption behind *Paradise and Power* and, presumably, behind the unfathomably cavalier attitude of the Bush Administration toward our European allies.

That this assumption is fallacious is the very least that might be said. The 9/11 attacks were partly planned, organized, and financed in Europe. Europe's Muslim diaspora communities, into which terrorist cells can invisibly blend, remain the likeliest staging grounds for future al Qaeda attacks on the United States. The implications have been lucidly spelled out by Steve Simon and Daniel Benjamin:

> The rise of Islamic radicalism in the West is not something the United States can deal with militarily. At least as the world exists now, Washington will not be dispatching troops to fight in the Paris suburbs. But the growth of radicalism in Europe does require that the United States and its allies deepen their intelligence and law enforcement cooperation to the greatest extent possible to thwart terrorist operations.[17]

In other words, Europe remains a frontline region in the struggle against terrorism just as it was in the struggle against communism. As daily press reports also reveal, the European police have been acting in a perfectly Hobbesian manner, arresting scores of suspected terrorists. In other words, despite his pose as a no-nonsense realist, Kagan has apparently failed to realize the degree to which the contours of American national security have been redrawn since 9/11. The home front and the foreign front have now been disconcertingly blurred. National-security strategy must now operate in a domain where soldiering and policing have become of coequal importance. This profound change helps us diagnose the erroneous premise of Bush's foreign policy. In our new security environment, despite the prevailing cliché, the United States is *not* the world's only superpower.

The war on transnational terrorism depends essentially on information gathering and policing, and in these respects the Europeans are anything but security pygmies. Their capacities to respond effectively to today's greatest security threats easily rival those of the United States. America may not need any aircraft carriers from France, as has been pointed out, but it does need the French *services de renseignement.* Europeans' linguistic skills and cultural knowledge alone ensure that they can make indispensable contributions to U.S. security. Their law-enforcement and intelligence agencies can perform essential tasks of monitoring, infiltration, disruption, and apprehension for which our own unrivaled military machine is patently unfit. These realities can be denied only by ideologues convinced, contrary to logic and evidence, that harsher methods are inevitably more effective. The reason why it is usually a mistake to approach the threat of terrorism with a military mindset has been explained succinctly by Louise Richardson: "Speed and force are both critical elements in a successful military campaign; it is far from clear that they are necessary ingredients of a successful counterterrorism policy."[18] Dismantling terrorist networks and isolating violent radicals from their communities requires skill, persistence, intelligence, and caution, not explosive ferocity. As a consequence, the demilitarization of counterterrorism, characteristic of Europe, can be useful strategically as well as tactically. It is no surprise that, having had to deal with home-grown Islamic terrorism in the mid-1990s, the French police never shared the fatal American delusion that Islamic terrorism must always be state-sponsored.

Dismissing the "platitude" that the United States cannot protect itself without European help, Kagan concludes that "the United States *can* 'go it alone.'"[19] This is apparently the thinking (if you can call it that) behind the Administration's mindlessly denigrating remarks about Europe. True, European leaders can sometimes be hypocritical and foolishly condescending. But we certainly cannot afford, for the sake of a frisson, to undermine American security by further poisoning relations with capable allies in a time of unprecedented national peril.

A Monolingual Hegemon?

Apparently unnoticed by Kagan, the relative power of the United States has been paradoxically undermined by the spread of English as a world language. One result is that America has become highly transparent to outsiders (terrorist conspirators abroad can easily enroll in American flight training schools), while the rest of the world has become increasingly opaque to Americans. To cite a pertinent example: "Our embassy of 1,000 has 33 Arabic speakers, just six of whom are at the level of fluency."[20] How in the world can the United States save civilization from barbarism by "patrolling the jungles" of the world if American officials cannot speak any language except their own? The hopelessness of this assignment is brought home stunningly by an anthropologist, Army Reserve Maj. Christopher Varhola, commenting on the inability of American soldiers in Iraq to speak the language of the people they have been tasked to police: "It is not uncommon to hear American soldiers explain that the only thing the Iraqis understand is 'force.' For the most part, however, the people saying this do not speak Arabic."[21]

We are now in a position to examine directly the mindset of the Bush Administration officials who launched the Iraq war. They, too, personally exhibit what the Iraq Study Group laments as "Americans' lack of language and cultural understanding."[22] It is not surprising, therefore, that they too seem to believe that the world is populated by people who understand no language other than force. That their compulsive preference for war over diplomacy is rooted in such cognitive biases is one of the principal hypotheses to be explored.

"il ne suffit pas pour pouvoir gouverner une nation de l'avoir vain-
cue."
> – Tocqueville, *Lettre sur l'Algérie* (22 August 1837)

Tens and perhaps hundreds of thousands of innocent Iraqis have now
died violent deaths, and "the country that was once Iraq" now serves
as a haven for al Qaeda and a training ground for a new generation of
anti-Western jihadists. Israel's position has been weakened, and Iran's has
been strengthened. So why has the American occupation of Iraq ended
so disastrously for occupier and occupied alike? Dissenters in the uniformed military think they know why. In planning the Iraq campaign,
Donald Rumsfeld, U.S. Secretary of Defense 2001–06, clung to his theological certainty that, in modern warfare, speed is more important than
mass. One consequence was that the United States did not have enough
troops on the ground to secure the borders or prevent weapons storage sites (or even the al Tuwaitha nuclear storage facility) from being
looted. If Saddam Hussein had actually possessed the tons of chemical
and biological weapons that, in the president's talking points, constituted the *casus belli* for the invasion, Rumsfeld's slimmed-down force
would have abetted the greatest proliferation disaster in world history. In
lieu of the proliferation disaster that did not occur (because the WMD
did not exist), Rumsfeld's preference for speed over mass helped produce a social, economic, legal, political, and sectarian disaster. It never
seems to have occurred to him that, when stabilizing a traumatized
society after a tyrannical regime has been violently excised, mass might
prove more important than speed. For his part, L. Jerry Bremer, Jr.,
head of the Coalition Provisional Authority 2003–04, chose to throw
hundreds of thousands of armed men out of work, without discussing

his decision beforehand with the National Security Advisor or the Secretary of State. No one can be certain that the occupation could have been successful even if it had not been plagued by repeated failures to consider the potential downsides of irreversible decisions. Was it ever going to be possible for Sunni, Shiite, and Kurd to serve side-by-side inside the same army, police, and security units, all swearing their ultimate allegiance to a common Iraq state rather than to their separate ethnic, sectarian, or tribal groupings? As Colin Powell allegedly told President Bush, "if you don't have a government that you can connect these forces to, then Mr. President, you're not building up forces, you're building up militias."[1] Did the so-called "national" Iraqi institutions ever have a serious chance to attract allegiance from all groups, rather than being doomed from the start to become empty shells or to be seized and used by violent factions? Were the Sunni and Shiite communities likely to remain coherent enough internally, after Saddam's fall, to negotiate and maintain durable bargains with each other? If the answer to these questions is "yes," then the administration must be blamed for botching the occupation. If the answer is "no," the administration must be blamed for launching the war.

Cobra II **wraps a political bombshell inside a riveting tale.**[2] **Its central** chapters deliver a blow-by-blow account of the unstoppable American dash toward Baghdad, blinding sandstorms and all, in March and April 2003. The co-authors – Michael Gordon, the senior war correspondent for the *New York Times*; Bernard Trainor, a former Marine Corps lieutenant general – tell stories of skilled leadership, combat heroics, and the campaign's ultimate success at driving Saddam Hussein from power, without neglecting the inevitable battlefield snafus, poor coordination among combatant units, wildly misleading intelligence, and scenes of gruesome carnage.

False Starts

For the American invaders, the greatest surprise turned out to have been the unconventional tactics of the enemy. On the drive to Baghdad, U.S. forces did not initially confront, as they had been led to expect, either the demoralized regular army or Saddam's Republican Guard but rather the highly motivated Fedayeen Saddam: "The enemy faced by U.S. forces" was "largely amorphous, not in uniform, and rarely part of an organized military force." It leveled the battlefield, to some extent, "by ignoring the rules of conventional warfare." It fought "using guile, deception and ambush."[3] At one point, the Pentagon's original war plans looked to be in shambles thanks to "the work of an enemy who was not supposed to exist."[4] The decision to seize Baghdad at lightning speed and therefore to dart past pockets of unexpected guerrilla-style resistance in the south, rather than lingering to mop them up, remains one of the most controversial choices of the war.

Cobra II, however, would not be such an important book if it were merely a fascinating and unflinching work of military history. It is much more than that. Gordon and Trainor may have tossed the stone that loosed the avalanche of a generals' mutiny against the leadership of Donald Rumsfeld. Gordon and Trainor freely acknowledge that extensive interviews with military officers from all services shaped their perspective on the war. By publicly documenting the depth and breadth of military disenchantment with Rumsfeld, their book may have emboldened, in early 2006, a half-dozen dissenting generals to speak bluntly about what they considered the wretchedly incompetent performance of the defense secretary. This public dissent suggested intense conviction on their part, or at least white-hot anger, considering that it might well have jeopardized lucrative future employment in the defense industry.

Rumsfeld's military critics regularly take him to task not only for the many catastrophic decisions he made, but also for his overbearing decision-making style and even for a pathologically autistic personality. In one of the most hilarious passages of the book, Trainor and Gordon reproduce Rumsfeld's answer, in December 2005, to the question of what he had learned from the war in Iraq: "I think if I had to pull out one lesson that we've learned over the past four or five years, it would be that in the 21st century we're going to have to stop thinking about things, numbers of things, and mass, and think also and maybe even first about speed and agility and precision."[5] In other words, what Rumsfeld "learned" from the war in Iraq is nothing other than the military doctrine that he had been preaching for years.

Rumsfeld's commitment to a streamlined invasion force scandalously contradicted the *casus belli* that the Administration alleged for the war. Bush rallied political support for the invasion by presenting it as an act of pre-emptive self-defense on the grounds that Saddam Hussein possessed stockpiles of chemical and biological weapons and had cooperative relations with transnational terrorist groups. If Rumsfeld had taken such allegations seriously, however, he would have had to double the size of the invading force: "Securing the WMD required sealing the country's borders and quickly seizing control of the many suspected sites before they were raided by profiteers, terrorists and regime officials determined to carry on the fight." The force that Rumsfeld eventually assembled, by contrast, "was too small to do any of this."[6] In other words, Rumsfeld's fixation on slimming down the invasion force trumped Bush's wish to prevent WMD from falling into the hands of terrorists. A doctrinaire commitment to a peculiar method of war fighting contradicted and subverted the primary declared purpose of the war.

This inconsistency between methods and aims remains just as striking if we turn to the long-term war objective of creating a stable, pro-American regime in Iraq so as to transform the politics of the region and make the Middle East more hospitable to American national-security interests. When the aim of war is to stabilize a country politically, mass becomes more important than speed. Rumsfeld's failure to grasp this imperative or indeed to take any noticeable interest in the prerequisites of political stability explains, according to the authors, how he managed to snatch defeat from the jaws of victory. The "messy aftermath of a seemingly decisive war" was due mostly to "military and political blunders in Washington." The insurgency flared from a small spark into a raging conflagration – so the authors contend – because Rumsfeld did not commit enough soldiers to the Iraqi theater to damp it down.

Long before the invasion, Rumsfeld was granted full control of the postwar situation in Iraq, but it interested him so little that he did almost nothing to prepare for it. "After the Pentagon established its primacy in postwar Iraq, the Phase IV [i.e., postwar] planning effort slowed to a crawl." Rumsfeld is renowned as a chronically impatient micromanager. In this particular case, however, he "did not seem anxious about the lack of momentum." Why not? Absurd as it may sound, "Rumsfeld and his aides viewed the building of a new Iraq as a relatively undemanding pursuit." Alternatively, the defense secretary vaguely imagined that yet-unidentified subservient allies would miraculously appear in the wake of a spectacular American victory to perform the unglamorous chores of peacekeeping and nation building. These expectations seem to explain why, shockingly, "No military headquarters or staff was selected in advance to secure postwar Iraq."[7]

Neglect of postwar stability was a conscious choice, Trainor and Gordon insist, made in defiance of plentiful advice to the contrary. Army Chief of Staff General Eric Shinseki, who was publicly derided by Paul Wolfowitz after telling a congressional committee that hundreds of thousands of American troops would be needed in Iraq, is only the best-known example. Others inside and outside the Pentagon were arguing for a constabulary force at the ready to control the criminal anarchy likely to break out when the ghastly dictatorship collapsed, but Rumsfeld and his cadre of yes-men did not listen.

Speaking of yes-men, Rumsfeld's haughty impatience with dissent and disagreement apparently explains his choice of the self-effacing Richard Myers as chairman of the Joint Chiefs of Staff. "After hearing Rumsfeld testify on troop levels around the world," Trainor and Gordon recount, "Senator John McCain, the Arizona Republican, said cuttingly there was no need to hear from Myers as well since he knew the chairman was incapable of expressing an independent view."[8] The Gulf War in contrast, according to the authors, saw a robust and productive back-and-forth between Defense Secretary Dick Cheney and a strong chairman of the Joint Chiefs, Colin Powell. Rumsfeld preferred a deferential military leader, ensuring that his own ideas, however half-baked, invariably prevailed.

Like Myers, General Tommy Franks sallied forth from retirement to defend the defense secretary against his critics. However, the portrait of Franks sketched in *Cobra II* is no more flattering than the portrayal of Myers. For one thing, "Tommy Franks never acknowledged the enemy he faced nor did he comprehend the nature of the war he was directing."[9] He is also described as vainglorious, taking credit for a war plan developed by subordinates and "airbrushing" history when regaling journalists such as Bob Woodward with stories of the war. Even though he at first proposed dispatching more than 300,000 troops to Iraq, he allowed himself to be browbeaten by Rumsfeld into sending the streamlined force that proved unable to control the postwar anarchy.

Rumsfeld also seems to have had similar reasons for supporting the appointment of L. Paul Bremer III as administrator of the Coalition Provisional Authority in Iraq. Having no familiarity with the Middle East and no experience at all with nation building, Bremer could not talk back to his bosses in Washington with the confidence reserved for the knowledgeable. The original plan was to team Bremer with Zalmay Khalilzad, later to become ambassador to Iraq, 2005–07, who at the time was the only high-level member of the administration personally acquainted with all of the important players in the Iraqi diaspora. At this point Bremer (to the astonishment of Powell and others) pulled a Rumsfeld: "Determined to solidify his authority, Bremer squeezed out Khalilzad, the one official who knew the Iraqi politicians well."[10]

The defining moment of Bremer's Iraqi tour occurred in May 2003, when he issued his two notorious orders, first to "de-Baathify" the Iraqi bureaucracy and, second, to disband the Iraqi army. Bremer himself reports that the de-Baathification order came from policy undersecretary

Douglas Feith.[11] Whatever the ultimate source, by carrying out the order, Bremer not only made it very difficult for Sunnis to take part in the government being created, but he also ended up punishing people for being who they were rather than for what they did. What is more, he violated the sage advice, attributed to Machiavelli, that a new ruler should always try to retain those who were loyal to the old regime because such people are likely, because of their habitually servile character, to be loyal to the new occupants of authority. In disbanding the army, moreover, Bremer showed himself oblivious to the role of the military as an employment agency providing subsistence to hundreds of thousands of armed Iraqis and their families. The rationale for stripping so many armed men of their livelihood is still obscure. What we know is that the Joint Chiefs, Secretary of State Powell, and National Security Advisor Condoleezza Rice all learned about this momentous decision *after* it was made. Decision making by a small handful of men, behind closed doors and without consultation even inside the executive branch, may suit the authoritarian personality of the defense secretary. Yet can anyone argue that it promotes an intelligent approach to national security?

Elevating Loyalty above Capacity

During the invasion, Gordon was "embedded" with the Coalition Forces Land Component Command. It is not surprising, therefore, that Iraqi voices and perspectives are largely absent from *Cobra II*'s account of the fighting. The one marvelous exception is the authors' retelling of the invasion from the vantage point of the subsequently executed Saddam Hussein and his inner circle. Their account is based on postwar debriefings of high-ranking Iraqi officers, who were induced to talk not by harsh and humiliating treatment, it should be mentioned, but, on the contrary, by lavish banquets and buttering up.

The key revelation here is that Saddam was long convinced that the United States would never launch an all-out assault. He knew that he had no stockpiles of WMD and no working ties with Islamic terrorists targeting America. He was therefore perfectly confident that Bush had no serious *casus belli*. As a result, "He saw no reason why the Americans would want to invade Iraq."[12]

So fearful was Saddam of his own countrymen, by contrast, that he hesitated to arm Iraqi tribes to defend the country: "There was always a chance that he himself could end up as the target of the people's war."[13] By discouraging fraternization among his officers he made a coup less likely, but he also weakened the military's capacity for coordinated defense. One

Republican Guard commander explained exactly how autocracy breeds obtuseness, remarking that, in Saddam's Iraq, "the clever men learned not to involve themselves in any decision-making."[14] Saddam appointed one of his close cousins as commander of the Special Republican Guard forces responsible for the defense of Baghdad, even though the man was a militarily inexperienced drunkard, precisely because "he was not clever enough to put a coup together."[15] His subordinates dared not contradict Saddam for fear of death and worse. The regime operated with virtually no sanity checks. Saddam sometimes made even important decisions on the basis of his dreams.

The self-weakening nature of Saddam's autocracy was displayed most visibly in his elevation of loyalty over capacity: "Republican Guard and other senior officers were often chosen on the basis of family ties and loyalty, not competence."[16] Gordon and Trainor dwell on this theme, presumably to evoke an ironic comparison with the Bush administration. Of course, Rumsfeld merely fired the people who dared contradict him, while Saddam murdered them along with their families. So the comparison is loose, at best. To underscore both the sharp differences and remote similarities, the authors report an encounter that took place soon after Bush assumed the presidency between an Army colonel and Steve Cambone, Rumsfeld's chief aid at the time. "Cambone jested that Rumsfeld thought the Army's problems could be solved by lining up fifty of its generals in the Pentagon and gunning them down."[17] That joke was presumably funnier in George W. Bush's Washington than it would have been in Saddam Hussein's Baghdad.

Some commentators have alleged that Saddam planned an insurrection against the American conquerors, to be unleashed after he was toppled from power. Zero evidence supports such speculations, Trainor and Gordon tell us. "Saddam was no more farsighted than the Americans in preparing for the aftermath," they mordantly observe.[18] The real story is more complicated and more interesting. First, Saddam did not anticipate being ousted by force, but he did believe that the Americans might successfully ground the Iraqi Air Force, including its helicopter gunships, and then proceed to foment a Shiite rebellion in the south. To prepare in advance for such a dangerous development, Saddam distributed caches of small arms, guarded by Baathists, along with Fedayeen units, throughout southern Iraq. Although unit commanders were forbidden to communicate with each other lest they conspire against Saddam, the Fedayeen would presumably have been able to fight off local insurrections long enough to allow the Republican Guard to arrive by land. Once the American invaders had plowed through the south and on to Baghdad, driving Hussein from power, the potential dual use of both the prestashed arms and the Fedayeen's cell-like command structure came into view: "[T]he very force designed to counter an insurgency" ultimately became "the core of the insurgency against the Americans."[19]

Could Things Have Gone Differently?

Having absorbed the biases along with the insights of their principal informants, Trainor and Gordon tend to exonerate the uniformed military from serious responsibility for the Iraqi debacle. "The violent chaos that followed Saddam's defeat," they argue, "was not a matter of not having a plan but of adhering too rigidly to the wrong one."[20] If a better plan had been contrived, presumably incorporating higher troop levels and well-trained constabulary forces, violent chaos would not have erupted or, if it had erupted, it would have been contained.

That the uniformed military should not be granted blanket exoneration, however, is strongly suggested by the parade of officers who rallied in support of their besieged defense secretary. *Cobra II* itself acknowledges that Franks knew no more than the civilian Rumsfeld about "the actual structure of political power in Iraq."[21] Both are described as refusing to listen to experts and professionals who knew what needed to be known. Who exactly within the U.S. government knew better?

The CIA and U.S. Special Forces had many contacts in Afghanistan, dating back at least to the 1980s. Iraq, by contrast, had been a denied area, meaning the war was necessarily planned by amateurs with measly knowledge of the country that the United States was about to invade. Civilians in the administration were no more knowledgeable or thoughtful. After the American military had thoroughly destroyed the Tikriti clan that had ruled Iraq for decades, Rice explained, "the institutions" of the country (the ministries, the courts, the provincial governments, and the police) would go on working normally. Here are her own words: "The concept was that we would defeat the army, but the institutions would hold, everything from ministries to police forces." And she added, "You would be able to bring new leadership, but we were going to keep the body in place."[22] Such statements betray an appalling ignorance of the dependence of formal institutions on informal social networks.

Gordon and Trainor sometimes seem to suggest that the Iraq War could have ended successfully if only Rumsfeld had not been in charge. Does this make sense? Admittedly, a powerful argument can be made that a large peacekeeping force is more effective than a small one. Not only do small peacekeeping forces "encourage adversaries to think they could challenge the peacekeepers" but, even more important, they lead the peacekeepers "to rely more on firepower to make up for their limited numbers."[23] Although this is plausible, it is not a decisive argument. An equally persuasive case can be made that a "bigger footprint" will prove politically destabilizing. Larger numbers of rowdy and culturally ignorant American soldiers blasting heavy-metal music outside mosques on Friday afternoons will not necessarily calm down the population of an occupied country. In other words, a bigger footprint may be either stabilizing or destabilizing. It can cut either way. Because we cannot be certain ahead of time which of the two contrary effects will predominate, we cannot be sure that higher force levels would have prevented a disastrous outcome of the Iraq War.

The Baker–Hamilton commission, moreover, concluded intelligently that "Sustained increases in U.S. troop levels would not solve the fundamental cause of violence in Iraq, which is the absence of national reconciliation."[24] The same point was made earlier by John Gray: "if America is facing a strategic defeat in Iraq the reason is not that its forces there are insufficiently numerous. It is that their operations have never served any political goal that could be realized."[25]

This leaves open a related question concerning American war aims in Iraq and the armed wing of the Iraqi state bureaucracy: Was it ever realistic to expect Kurds, Sunnis, and Shiites to be melded together within fully integrated Iraqi police, military, and state security units – that is, within the core institutions of the state? If not, and there are good reasons to doubt it, the very project of turning power over to "the Iraqis" was unfeasible from the start. In any society deeply divided along tribal, sectarian, and ethnic lines, it is difficult to create a government that is both representative and coherent. (Saddam's government was to some extent coherent because it was in no degree representative.) When a society's basic subgroups not only fear and distrust each other but also are weakly organized and fragmented internally, they are unlikely to be able to negotiate stable bargains and share power.

The authors are on firm, not to mention well-trodden, ground when they claim that the occupation of Iraq has been disastrously mismanaged. They sometimes intimate, however, that it was realistic for Bush to try to reform the Middle East to America's advantage though a military attack. The problem here lies deeper than strategy or tactics. The Administration knew so little about the country it decided to invade that its expectations were basically indistinguishable from wild guesses. Its entire approach to the challenge also reflected an unwarranted confidence in the politically transformative power of superior force. That something even more dishonorable may have been going on is implied by a six-page article, "How and Where to Apply Shock and Awe," penned by Air Force General Charles Horner and forwarded to Franks by Rumsfeld in December 2001. Trainor and Gordon quote Horner's extraordinary concluding sentences: "In the end, if we are going to lead, then we must be considered the madmen of the world, capable of any action, willing to risk anything to achieve our national interests.... If we are to achieve noble purposes we must be prepared to act in the most ignoble manner."[26] This is how tyrants and terrorists think. That such ideas may have influenced the Administration's decisions in Iraq suggests that it has much more to answer for than its incompetence.

4 | RADICALS TRAPPED IN THE PAST

The mindset of those gung-ho officials in President Bush's first term who plunged the country into a Middle Eastern war remains to some extent enigmatic. Apparently preferring boldness to caution regardless of context, these self-styled security hawks were held hostage by their own Cold War obsessions and presuppositions, notably their conviction that American national security could be threatened, if at all, only by hostile states. This preconception was so deeply ingrained in their thinking that they seemingly could not relinquish it even after the United States was attacked by a nonstate terrorist group. The fatal leap from 9/11 to the Iraq war begins to make sense only in light of such a fundamental misperception of post-Cold War threats. Mystery also shrouds Bush's "forward strategy of freedom." That the desire to democratize Iraq had little or no influence on the thinking of Vice President Richard Cheney or then Secretary of Defense Donald Rumsfeld is by now widely acknowledged. Their scant interest in transparent and accountable government in the United States makes it extremely unlikely that they would have spent American blood and treasure to impose such a cumbersome arrangement on Iraqis. What remains worth exploring, on the other hand, is the enthusiasm of Paul Wolfowitz, U.S. Deputy Secretary of Defense 2001–05, and a handful of others, toward a project that conflicted so violently with the deep skepticism about democracy promotion that, after it was lucidly articulated in 1979 by Jeanne Kirkpatrick, seemed to have been hard-wired into the Republican worldview. The most plausible explanation for this flight of fancy is that Wolfowitz knew more about the deficiencies of international nuclear inspections than about the deficiencies of international democracy promotion, that he had read next to nothing about the troubled historical emergence of democracy, and did not bother to ask if any of the widely recognized historical preconditions of democracy existed in Iraq. Letting Wolfowitz rattle on about democratization may have suited Cheney's and Rumsfeld's purposes, in any case, because they were presumably happy to adorn their desire for violent "regime change" in Baghdad with a little idealistic rhetoric. Talk of a quick shift to Iraqi self-rule also permitted the single-minded war planners to deflect such irritating questions as how essential government services (electricity, water, sewage, trash pickup and so forth) were going to be delivered once the government in Baghdad had collapsed. As realists, however, Cheney and Rumsfeld must have foreseen that festering anarchy, as opposed to well-ordered democracy, was a possible consequence of the violent destruction of the Baathist government. If they did not dwell on the thought, it must have been partly because they believed that a power vacuum in Iraq would not end up posing any significant security threats to America. This last assumption, which seems in retrospect altogether unwarranted, remains the most plausible rationale, when combined with short-term electoral calculations, for what is now universally recognized as a reckless decision to destroy a tyrannical government without making serious plans to replace it.

Uncomfortable with the free flow of information, for reasons having as much to do with electoral politics as with national security, the Bush political machine labored mightily after 9/11 to impede public examination of U.S. foreign policy. Yet the dismaying reality could not be indefinitely hidden from view. A tiny group of individuals, with eccentric theories and reflexes, had recklessly compounded the country's security nightmare, launching a humanly disastrous and politically destabilizing military adventure on publicly untested assumptions. One of the first to pierce their veil of secrecy was James Mann. He did so by adopting a simple methodology, poring over the past words and deeds of Bush's first-term foreign policy team.[1] By interrogating the public record for clues about Cheney, Rumsfeld, Wolfowitz, Rice, Powell and Armitage, Mann provided a distressingly coherent account of the origins of the debacle still unfolding before our eyes.

We knew it already, of course, but it is nevertheless unnerving to read that fateful decisions, perhaps affecting the course of world history, are profoundly influenced by palace intrigue, turf wars, and petty personal rivalries, not to mention the outrageous practice of placing poorly qualified party loyalists in positions of grave public responsibility. If conservative

Congressmen had not blocked Tom Ridge's nomination as Defense Secretary, for the ludicrously immaterial reason that he was wobbly on abortion, then the Cheney-Rumsfeld group, including Wolfowitz and Feith, would have been in no position to hijack the administration's reaction to 9/11. By sheer chance, Rice and Powell – no doubt orderly managers – have pedestrian minds and perhaps deferential personalities. Neither provided a gripping and persuasive vision of the United States' role in the world that might have counteracted the megalomania of the neoconservatives, and neither was capable of outfoxing the hard-liners in an interagency power struggle. By sheer luck of the draw, therefore, and also because Rumsfeld's former assistant, Cheney, sat in the White House and commanded his own foreign policy staff, civilian leaders at the Office of the Secretary of Defense (OSD) managed to amass unprecedented influence over foreign policy, unbalanced by those in the State Department and elsewhere in the federal government who still believed that diplomacy was indispensable, even for a military superpower.

The fate of the country and the world, it is only a slight exaggeration to say, was abandoned to the personal eccentricities, obsessions, compulsions, and tunnel vision of a handful of political operatives who, by shrewd maneuvering, prevailed in a bureaucratic power grab. This self-important crew spent the Clinton years making money, of course, but with only occasional access to the corridors of power and often affiliated with one-sidedly partisan think tanks where researchers are paid to assemble evidence and arguments for preconceived policies. "Cherry picking" is not the vice president's personal idiosyncrasy, in other words, but business as usual for the American Enterprise Institute and the other simplification factories from which Bush continues to recruit many of his high-level appointees. Administration officials acquired their habit of politicizing intelligence (that is, trawling for evidence that substantiates what they politically, ideologically, and psychologically need to believe) from such politicized policy institutes. After 9/11, their bunker mentality – their doctrinaire exclusion of dissonant viewpoints and unsettling information – became so extreme that well-connected moderate Republicans such as Brent Scowcroft and James Baker were reduced to communicating with the White House through op-eds.

Francis Fukuyama's critical analysis of the Administration's "freedom agenda" will be discussed in Chapter Nine. But it is already worth mentioning here how thoroughly his semi-insider's diagnosis of Bush's war cabinet corroborates James Mann's more scholarly account. Partisan loyalists around Cheney and Rumsfeld, according to Fukuyama, not only exhibited "a fixed mind-set and unjustifiable self-confidence,"[2] but were also "excessively distrustful of anyone who did not share their views."[3] Rather than testing their ideas in a free-wheeling adversarial process, they barred the doors, lowered the shades and denigrated their critics, including distinguished Republicans who had served in the administration of Bush's father, sometimes smearing them as myopic appeasers of America's implacable foes. Making an implicit claim to infallibility, they also downplayed facts that challenged their preconceived ideas: "Their deeper fault was to not have any self-doubts or to engage in a more open-minded review of the evidence before launching a preventive war."[4] This retreat of the administration's principal decision makers into a windowless command center, with little creative input from critics and dissidents, entailed a self-stultifying loss of knowledge, causing the administration to dismiss out of hand "much of the accumulated knowledge that existed in the U.S. government."[5]

Permitting a clique of like-minded individuals to conduct the nation's foreign policy behind closed doors and to bypass the regular interagency process risks loss of contact with reality. Right-wing ideologues who identify with the Administration fret incessantly about "moral relativism," but pay little attention to the opposite and more treacherous inclination: False certainty. Unjustified certainty can be sustained only by reflexively blocking out doubt, dissent, and complexity.[6] The obstinate refusal of Administration officials to acknowledge even their most blatant mistakes, that is, their implicit claim to infallibility, has by now become a national and international embarrassment. It is also a slap at the Constitution, which established various mechanisms of self-correction (such as judicial and legislative oversight of executive action) on the premise that even the wisest men are sometimes wrong and desperately need, precisely when they find it discomfiting, the benefits of adversarial process.

The masterminds behind the Iraq war, as Mann shows, had been long devoted to America's military predominance. "The defeat in Vietnam," he writes, led them "to a preoccupation with first regaining and then maintaining American military power."[7] They are also well known for their scorn of arms control and impatience with what they considered to be Henry Kissinger's coddling of left-wing tyrants. Whatever the threat, they consistently preferred, and still do, confrontation to engagement. Speaking of Rumsfeld's earlier tour of duty in the Ford Administration, Mann remarks: "As secretary of defence he did more than anyone else to block détente and to stiffen American policy toward the Soviet Union."[8] Stiff-arming opponents has more consistently defined their shared approach than, say, seeking mutually beneficial compromises, profiting from disagreement, or questioning their own preconceptions.

The principal architects of the current calamity, in Mann's now generally accepted account, were Cheney and Rumsfeld, with Wolfowitz playing a strong supporting role. Having treated Powell as arm candy during the 2000 campaign, dangling him before the public to reassure moderate voters, they deftly sidelined him once Bush took office. Cheney, Rumsfeld and Wolfowitz had a reputation as radicals – ready to shake things up – with little reverence for the status quo. Yet, the reality was not so straightforward. For they were also prisoners of the past, hostages to outdated preoccupations and to habits formed decades earlier, when they first wielded power. Mann even calls them "backward-leaning."[9] What he means is that these no-longer young men could not stop fighting the Cold War. Their struggle with the Soviets, moreover, led them to mimic the enemy to some extent, making them shockingly at ease with lying publicly for a higher cause, indulging in public prevarications without scruples if it allowed them "to galvanize the nation into rapid action before it was too late."[10]

On Sept. 14, 2001, Wolfowitz declared defiantly that "*dictators* underestimate America's strength" (my emphasis).[11] This phrase, implicitly tracing the 9/11 attacks to some unnamed dictator, bespeaks a one-track mind chronically unable to absorb novel and dissonant information. Mann refers to Wolfowitz as "the leading conservative foreign policy thinker of his generation."[12] But with the country reeling, this purported thinker's immediate reflex was not to think but rather to strike a Churchillian pose, disclosing his psychological, or perhaps ideological, fixations. According to Richard Clarke's scathing memoir, Wolfowitz showed himself, in high-level White House meetings, wholly unable to bring the new threat into focus.[13] Faced with terrorists, he could see only "dictators." That is all he wanted to see. Such an undiscriminating view of the threat environment is connected to a more general degradation of public perception and discourse.

Soon after 9/11, the Administration's Orwellian corruption of thought and language surfaced not only in its deliberate blurring of al Qaeda and Iraq but also in its mantra that the U.S. was now engaged in "a conflict between terrorism and democracy." This is a highly confusing and unhelpful manner of speaking. For one thing, al Qaeda terrorists have violently attacked not only the United States but also, for example, Saudi Arabia. Since Saudi Arabia is not a democratic country, it is impossible to make sense of the current worldwide struggle by depicting it as a war between terrorism and democracy. Those who describe it this way confound not only the public but also themselves.

When the Soviet Union collapsed, the principal concern of Cheney and Wolfowitz, this time with the full support of Powell and Armitage, was to avert serious cutbacks in military spending. According to Mann, Powell signed off on the disastrous Somalia mission, from which he subsequently tried to distance himself, because he did not want to give the newly elected Democratic president and Congress an excuse for reducing the military budget after the end of the Cold War.[14] This rallying around defense appropriations could be explained by the biographies of all four men, who spent important stretches of their public lives at the Pentagon. But their support for military spending has roots deeper than agency loyalty. It is the fruit of a mindset and a worldview. By background and training, these security hawks could bring into focus only certain kinds of threats. Their disproportionate emphasis on building a missile shield reveals as much, since a spaced-based perimeter defense would obviously do nothing to protect against the threat of infiltrators and saboteurs in possession of a thermonuclear device. So what dangers did they emphasize? How did they set priorities? How did they rank the various threats facing the country?

The gravest threats, they decided, were those that could be countered effectively only by military force. They could see rogue states in bright colors, but nonstate conspirators remained indistinct, easy to dismiss, beneath their radar. This bias had some basis in fact. Never in history had a nonstate actor posed a serious security threat to the United States or any other great power. Bush's seasoned war cabinet could not shed this (outdated) truth. There is no other way to explain their inattention to terrorism in general and to Osama bin Laden in particular, not only before but even after 9/11.

How much relative weight should we assign to each of the various motivations ostensibly behind the original decision to invade Iraq? The most commonly mentioned motives are these: the desire to display America's intimidating military power by crushing a defiant and cruel but universally despised and basically defenseless enemy; the desire to eliminate a military threat to Israel; the desire to break up OPEC and/or prepare for the possibility of a political upheaval in Saudi Arabia that would put vast oil reserves into the hands of revolutionary jihadists; the desire to prevent Saddam from reinitiating his suspended weapons programs once the sanctions regime unraveled; and the desire "to get it right this time" – that is, to complete the unfinished business of the Gulf War. Which of these (or other) motives were decisive or dominant?

Mann does not answer this question, to which I will return at greater length in both Chapter Five and the Conclusion. But he does help us explore an important aspect of the same puzzle, namely: Did the desire to democratize Iraq have any influence on the decision to go to war? There are many reasons to doubt it, above all the fact that Bush spokespersons began to highlight the benefit to Iraqis of Saddam's ouster only after their original justifications for the war, stressing benefits to Americans, collapsed under scrutiny. It is also noteworthy that Bush campaigned in 2000 against the very idea of humanitarian intervention, associating the toppling of odious dictators with arrogant meddling and utterly futile attempts to impose the American system of government on faraway peoples who are perhaps unprepared for American-style democracy but whom, in any case, Americans understand barely, if at all. During his second debate with Gore, on Oct. 11, 2000, Bush stated, apparently without coaching: "I'm not so sure the role of the United States is to go around the world and say this is the way it's got to be. . . . I want to empower people. I want to help people help themselves, not have government tell people what to do. I just don't think it's the role of the United States to walk into a country and say, we do it this way, so should you." That 9/11, which so obviously excited the president's visceral craving for blood revenge, also converted Bush to a Mother Teresa foreign policy is hard to believe. There was certainly nothing even remotely eleemosynary about the threatening ultimatums that the Administration addressed, immediately after the attacks, to Islamic leaders such as Pervez Musharraf. Styling himself as a Warrior President, Bush was in no mood to echo the Clintonian idea that foreigners will love us if we are nice to them, even though that seems to be the only way to make sense of his Administration's subsequent claim that Arabs in particular will come to admire America (and accept Israel) if only we lend them a generous helping hand as they make themselves democratic and prosperous.

Did the expected benefits of democratizing the Middle East play any role in motivating the Iraq war? Or should we simply view talk of building democracy in Iraq as agitprop concocted after the fact by White House managers of public perception to stave off criticism of a ruinous policy? We should approach this topic methodically, if only because the Administration is still maintaining the pretense in 2007, even though the public and the mainstream press, after waiting four years for positive trends to emerge, have now abandoned the thought or hope that U.S. forces have a serious chance of helping to create a coherent, stable, and friendly democracy in Iraq.

No one imagines that either Rumsfeld or Cheney has ever lost any sleep over the misery of ordinary people in distant countries. That neither had any trouble, earlier in their careers, doing business with cruel tyrants is also well documented. The principal cheerleader for democracy promotion in the Middle East was Wolfowitz, a man who, as Rumsfeld's deputy during Bush's first term, was "the most influential underling in Washington."[15] His influence during this period was presumably augmented by the coincidence that both Cheney's deputy at the time, "Scooter" Libby (now on trial for perjury), and Rice's deputy at the time, Stephen Hadley (who succeeded Rice as National Security Advisor in Bush's second term), were Wolfowitz protégés.

What Mann shows, however, is that Wolfowitz himself was obsessed with Gulf oil and weapons of mass destruction (WMD) in the Middle East long before he revealed any humanitarian concern for the victims of tyranny in the region, much less any ambitions to implant American-style democracy in Mesopotamia. His dissertation, written in the late 1960s at the University of Chicago under the supervision of Albert Wohlstetter, argued that the Israelis should not be allowed to develop nuclear weapons (which they were clandestinely seeking to do at the time) because, if they did so, their neighbors would be compelled to pursue WMD for themselves. Commenting on the implicit irony here, Mann delivers a syntactically convoluted but politically pungent aside: "In public, at least, Wolfowitz in later years rarely, if ever, acknowledged his opposition to the Israeli nuclear program or the role that it had played in spurring on other countries in the Middle East to match it."[16] It is not surprising that the Administration officials who, in Bush's second term, have been most outspoken about the unacceptability of an Iranian bomb have been deadly silent on this historically fascinating detail.

Working in the Pentagon under Jimmy Carter as a holdover from the Nixon/Ford Administration, Wolfowitz soon turned his attention to the danger of the Soviet Union's move to militarily block U.S. access to Persian Gulf oil. If the energy-rich Soviets successfully did so, he and others argued, they could undermine and even destroy America's alliances with Japan and Europe, both perilously dependent on imported energy. His interest in the Gulf, at this point, was exclusively geopolitical and not at all humanitarian. When the U.S.S.R. began to buckle and eventually collapsed, it is true, Wolfowitz began to redirect his attention to the hostile dictatorship in Iraq. But here again, what alarmed him was less Saddam's cruel tyranny over helpless Iraqis than the potential threat he posed to the world's oil supply and also, incidentally, to Israel.

Why Wolfowitz became such an ardent advocate of democratizing a country that would be almost certain to have an anti-Israeli majority remains something of a mystery. The mystery is deepened if we reexamine, as Mann invites us to do, one of the founding documents of modern American conservatism, namely the late Jeane Kirkpatrick's 1979 *Commentary* essay, "Dictatorships and Double Standards." (After reading this article, Reagan began wooing Kirkpatrick and thereby started the migration of neoconservatives from Democratic to Republican ranks.) It is difficult to imagine a more powerful warning against the neoconservative fantasy of democratizing Iraq than this essay by a woman who was "first called a neoconservative sometime after 1972."[17] The few diehards who continue, in 2007, to fantasize about Iraqi democracy should all be compelled to ponder her bracing comments on "the dangers of trying to be the world's midwife to democracy when the birth is scheduled to take place under conditions of guerrilla war."[18]

Kirkpatrick went on to chastise President Jimmy Carter for his short-sighted attacks on both the Shah of Iran and Nicaragua's Somoza for human rights abuses. All that Carter managed to accomplish with his humanitarian posturing, she argued, was to help oust friendly dictators and install hostile ones. She attributed this self-defeating policy to Carter's unrealistic belief that, in countries such as Iran and Nicaragua, there existed "a democratic alternative to the incumbent government."[19]

It is worth lingering for a moment over Kirkpatrick's analysis for two reasons. First, it was immensely influential among conservative foreign-policy experts at the time. And, second, it speaks directly to the hopes for democratic regime change, once voiced so confidently by Wolfowitz and his circle and reiterated later by Secretary of State Condoleezza Rice. In a 2005 speech in Cairo, Rice said this: "For 60 years, my country, the United States, pursued stability at the expense of democracy in this region here in the Middle East – and we achieved neither. Now, we are taking a different course. We are supporting the democratic aspirations of all people."[20] America should promote Muslim democracy, we are encouraged to infer, even at the expense of stability.

For her part, a quarter of a century earlier, Kirkpatrick had attributed "the American effort to impose liberalization and democratization" on illiberal and nondemocratic countries to what she considered a hopelessly naïve but characteristic strand in American culture. "The preference for stability rather than change," she wrote, is "disturbing to

Americans, whose whole national experience rests on the principles of change, growth, and progress."[21] Moreover, for various historical reasons, Americans have no conception of the complex preconditions of democratic government:

> Although most governments in the world are, as they always have been, autocracies of one kind or another, no idea holds greater sway in the mind of educated Americans than the belief that it is possible to democratize governments anytime, anywhere, under any circumstances. This notion is belied by an enormous body of evidence based on the experience of dozens of countries which have attempted with more or less (usually less) success to move from autocratic to democratic government. Many of the wisest political scientists of this and previous centuries agree that democratic institutions are especially difficult to establish and maintain – because they make heavy demands on all portions of a population and because they depend on complex social, cultural, and economic conditions.[22]

Mann draws attention to this prescient passage for a purpose. He is urging us to look more deeply into the Administration's idealistic rationale for invading and occupying Iraq. Kirkpatrick composed her essay in the spirit of Edmund Burke and other paleoconservatives, who ridiculed the conceit of French revolutionaries who, in turn, believed they could impose their progressive ideas on other peoples by force of arms. History "clearly establishes that democratic governments are both rare and difficult to establish."[23] The problem with promoting democracy in a country such as Iraq is that "Decades, if not centuries, are normally required for people to acquire the necessary disciplines and habits."[24] We can overhear the same Kirkpatrickesque doubts about social engineering and the same respect for the cake of custom in Brent Scowcroft's remark, also cited by Mann: "I'm a skeptic about the ability to transform Iraq into a democracy in any realistic period of time."[25]

So what happened to such sober considerations? Has conservative aversion to root-and-branch revolution wholly vanished from the neoconservative worldview? Western models of liberal democracy can guide and inspire institutional reformers in nondemocratic societies. But this obviously does not imply that a military superpower can impose democratic reforms on any society anytime. So how could Wolfowitz, given his long association with conservative causes, have imagined that the United States could unilaterally remake Iraqi political culture by a six-week military campaign? How could a conservative of any stripe have lapsed into such facile optimism?

One common answer is that Wolfowitz is not really a conservative but rather a revolutionary. This pleasantry is seemingly confirmed by the fact that other bearers of the neoconservative label, such as Irving Kristol, were Trotskyists in their youth and, it is argued, favored an invasion of Iraq as the best way to bestow the blessings of liberty on the Middle East. But can we really believe that then Deputy Secretary of Defense Wolfowitz, whom Mann also calls "the least daring member of the neoconservative movement,"[26] was a revolutionary utopian, straining at the bit, unwilling to accept the imperfections of human life and expecting to solve the world's problems once and for all by democratizing the Middle East?

Mann provides an important clue for resolving this mystery: Wolfowitz never wholly renounced Kirkpatrick's argument. At times, he explicitly reaffirmed it. The inconsistency here is only superficial, in truth. It has long been a maxim among hard-liners to support friendly dictators and oppose unfriendly ones. Carter's mistake, from this perspective, was to oppose a friendly dictator, the Shah of Iran. If he had opposed an unfriendly dictator, such as Saddam, he would not have been chastised, but praised.

This point deserves elaboration. Skeptics about détente learned from the Helsinki process how effectively the United States could weaken the international stature of its principal military rival by invoking human rights. The political utility of demonstrative morality was not lost on the most bellicose among them. Already in 1975, as Mann reminds us, Cheney fought unsuccessfully against Kissinger to have Solzhenitsyn invited to the White House. This instrumentalization of human rights, once we penetrate beneath the surface, is perfectly compatible with Kirkpatrick's attack on Carter. For hard-liners, human rights serve as a stick with which to beat and weaken America's enemies. But the cudgeling should stop when it comes to America's friends. Human rights are a formidable tool in America's propaganda arsenal, but they are not really a blueprint for creating new regimes.

Circumstantial evidence suggests that the dominant figures in both Bush's first and second terms view human rights and democracy in the Middle East today less as guidelines for nation-building than as moral rebukes meant to humiliate and weaken our enemies. This radically instrumental approach to human rights and democratic ideals is perfectly compatible with a tacit acceptance of the Kirkpatrick doctrine. That the Administration's public embrace of democracy has always been opportunistic is also suggested by its forgiving attitude toward, say, Pervez Musharraf, an apparently friendly dictator whom Bush is understandably reluctant to criticize for Pakistan's obvious failure to live up to America's liberal ideals. Charles Krauthammer has theorized this reluctance more clearly than anyone else, arguing that America's attempts at promoting democracy must always be "targeted, focused and limited,"[27] that is to say, selective. There is nothing especially hypocritical, from the standpoint that neoconservatives share with Cheney and Rumsfeld, about democratizing (that is, overthrowing) our authoritarian enemies and propping up our authoritarian friends.

Such selective invoking of humanitarian ideals, however cynical, is not necessarily incoherent. It leaves the Administration's Iraq policy unexplained, however. What is the United States doing in Iraq, four blood-drenched years after Saddam's fall, if we are not trying to transform the country into a model democracy that could serve as an inspiration for the entire Middle East? Ambassador Paul Bremer, who may not be reading the papers, still justifies the American occupation in such dreamy terms: "Who can forget the moving image of thousands of Iraqi men and women waving their purple-stained fingers in pride."[28] No one contemplating these brave voters, he implies, could dream of regretting the invasion.

How anyone can still celebrate "baptismal elections" that have proved utterly incapable of producing a government capable of governing is difficult to understand. Be this as it may, the question remains: Should we believe the advocates of "the forward strategy of freedom" when they list Iraqi democracy as an ex ante reason for the war? After all, America's past indifference to the political oppression of ordinary Arabs has probably done more to stimulate anti-American rage in the region than U.S. support for Israel. So was not Wolfowitz right to call for a radical change of approach? Did not Iraq seem like the best place to display America's benign intentions?

The allegedly lofty aspirations of the war planners cannot justify the decision to invade Iraq. But can they at least help explain it? What makes such an explanation seem implausible is a simple detail. No one in the U.S. government had any idea how to create democracy in Iraq. Moreover, the Administration's behavior strongly suggests that the real decision makers, namely Cheney and Rumsfeld, were never committed to this farfetched undertaking. The ultimate evidence that the architects of the Iraq war were nonchalant about the goal of postwar democratization is provided by the paucity of troops they arranged to have in Baghdad after victory. There were very few soldiers, and none trained as a constabulary force, and as a result postwar looting and worse proved impossible to bring under control. After upending U.S. foreign and domestic policy for the sake of "security," Cheney and Rumsfeld proved shockingly oblivious to the need for basic security in Iraq. The predictable consequence of the power vacuum opened up by the invasion was the rise of private militias and armed gangs, usually based on clan, ethnicity, or sect, engaged in savagely predatory behavior and offering protection services in the absence of an effective controlling authority. In April 2003, Rumsfeld famously commented on this explosion of physical insecurity, from which the occupation has never recovered, by quipping cavalierly that "stuff happens."

This tasteless jest may have signaled that the civilian leadership in the Pentagon entertained no more interest in the fate of Iraq after Saddam's fall than in the fate of Afghanistan after the fall of the Taliban. That is the view of George Packer, for example, who claims that "no one at the top level of the administration was less interested in the future of Iraq than Donald Rumsfeld."[29] Alternatively, a cavalier attitude toward violent anarchy may reveal that ruthless bureaucratic infighters do not know the first thing about democracy, its preconditions, its history, or its inherent fragilities and disorders. Historical illiteracy and unsophisticated theory may go a long way toward explaining how experienced officials with no desire to fail could have confused the toppling of a dictator with the establishment of democracy, as if replacing Saddam with Chalabi was going to be as easy as replacing Clinton with Bush. Or then again, Cheney and Rumsfeld may simply have thought that the Iraqi democracy fantasized by Wolfowitz would be fine, in principle, but that a failed state in Iraq, if it came to that, would present no serious security threat to the United States or its principal regional ally. Richard Perle formulated just such a view shortly before Bush became president. The United States should get serious about replacing Saddam, he wrote, "even if the process required to bring about such a change carries some risk of Iraq breaking apart" or even of Iraq's "political disintegration."[30] A festering anarchy, unable to project power outside its borders, would surely be less dangerous than a threatening dictatorship, assuming that U.S. Special Forces could always enter at will and assassinate any troublemakers who subsequently emerged. The downstream political costs of botched democratization would be relatively low, while the upfront propaganda benefits of flying the democratic flag might be substantial. All told, that may be the most plausible reconstruction of Cheney's and Rumsfeld's ethically appalling prewar view.

A final observation completes the case against the claim that the United States invaded Iraq with democratization seriously in mind. The White House's allergy to criticism and zealous devotion to secrecy reveal its weak grasp of the fatal danger that false certainties pose to intelligent decision making and the timely readjustment of policy initiatives gone awry. This misapprehension, combined with a coarse identification of the national interest with a highly partisan agenda, bespeaks a profoundly antidemocratic turn of mind. While still in Congress in 1988, as Mann tells us, Cheney helped defeat a law to notify Congress forty-eight hours after the beginning of any covert operation. The notion that the executive branch performs best when uncriticized and unwatched will be discussed at length in Chapter Thirteen. It represents Cheney's novel and perverse contribution to American constitutional doctrine: The executive branch is most effective when it is never compelled to give reasons for its actions. The vice president's contempt for Congressional, judicial, and public oversight pervades the entire Administration even today. That Cheney's implicit claim to vice-presidential inerrancy is unwarranted is the least that might be said.

Moreover, how can an administration that regularly confuses criticism with betrayal be serious about creating democracy abroad? Indeed, the most glaring evidence of the Administration's antidemocratic instincts is the dependence of its foreign policy on high-tech weaponry and a volunteer army. Vietnam taught hawks of Rumsfeld and Cheney's generation that the U.S. government cannot sustain a bloody war in the teeth of public opposition. Frustrated by an antiwar movement that, in their view, had prevented the United States from "winning" in Vietnam, they thought deeply about how to blunt public hostility to unexplained military adventures. Eventually, they hit upon a simple strategy.

Public opposition would never flare up if precision weaponry could reduce casualties substantially and if the soldiers who were eventually killed or wounded were "volunteers," often driven to serve because they could not find equivalent economic opportunities in the civilian economy and who were drawn disproportionately from minorities or who were lower middle class whites with little political clout. To avoid the burden of explaining its irrationally targeted bellicosity, as a consequence, a crafty administration has assiduously avoided a draft, which could cause mainstream America to start asking embarrassing questions. For similar reasons, tax hikes to fund military expenditures were avoided, even if revenue shortfalls mean that future generations will be forced to repay massive loans from the Chinese Central Bank. The Bush Administration's firm opposition both to reinstating conscription and raising taxes, in other words, is rooted in a fierce Vietnam-era aversion to democratic accountability.

Could men who plotted to put the public to sleep in their own country have possibly hoped to bring democratic accountability to Iraq? That defies belief. The only reasonable conclusion is that they continued for so long to talk this talk because they could conjure up no other remotely plausible justification for their irresponsible gamble, and they hoped to prevent, by various distractions, a deniable fiasco from turning into the fiasco that everyone with eyes to see can observe today.

Mann seems to think that Cheney, Rumsfeld, and Wolfowitz introduced "broad, enduring changes in the underlying principles guiding American foreign policy."[31] But the bulk of his book confirms the opposite thesis, namely, that the Bush Administration has managed foreign affairs so ineptly because it has been reflexively implementing out-of-date formulas in a radically changed security environment. During the Cold War, even the most extreme hawks were chastened in their aggressive impulses by fear of provoking escalation into a full-blown conflict with the U.S.S.R. Once the Soviet Union collapsed, these healthy fears and inhibitions mostly disappeared, but the psychological and political need to confront "evil" enemies remained. In the areas of the world today where the possibility of deadly escalation cannot be excluded, such as North Korea and the Taiwan Strait, the Administration continues to tread fairly cautiously. But in Iraq, alas, the lack of a major military rival excited some aging hard-liners into toppling a regime that they did not have the slightest clue how to replace. They took the plunge with reckless disregard for the possibility that the invasion and occupation might not only remove a dictator but also unravel the very fabric of Iraqi society, not to mention diverting America's scarce national security resources away from much graver threats. We have only begun to witness the long-term consequences of their ghastly misuse of unaccountable power.

5 | A SELF-INFLICTED WOUND

The outcome of inter- and intra-agency battles in Washington, D.C., allotted disproportionate influence to the fatally blurred understanding of the terrorist threat shared by a few highly placed and shrewd bureaucratic infighters. Rumsfeld and Cheney controlled the military; and when they were given the opportunity to rank the country's priorities in the war on terror, they assigned paramount importance to those specific threats that could be countered effectively only by the government agency over which they happened to preside. One U.S. enemy whose power to do harm had been exaggerated and whom the American war machine could easily crush was Saddam Hussein. Drawing power to themselves, Cheney and his circle talked up the nightmare scenario of a nuclear handoff, whereby Saddam would transfer a thermonuclear bomb to al Qaeda, to explain why an invasion of Iraq was an absolutely appropriate and necessary response to 9/11. This remote but fearful possibility may have helped them justify, even to themselves, why they were so fixated on toppling the Iraqi dictator who had profoundly embarrassed the George H. W. Bush administration by surviving the 1991 war. Their simultaneous neglect of the wider problem of nuclear proliferation, in Russia and elsewhere, makes their handoff fantasy seem like a rationalization for, rather than a cause of, their decision to invade, however. Their one-sided emphasis on problems that can be solved by military means alone, it bears repeating, contributed fatally to their neglect of the daunting challenges of postwar Iraq. Dictatorships can be smashed militarily. But political order cannot be conjured out of sectarian, ethnic, and tribal chaos by sheer irresistible force. Another reason why Cheney and Rumsfeld may have devoted little sustained thought to the political stabilization of Iraq after the fall of Saddam was their undisguised disdain for "peacekeeping."

They surely agreed with Condoleezza Rice's assessment, offered in the run-up to the 2000 election: "The president must remember that the military is a special instrument. It is lethal, and it is meant to be. It is not a civilian police force. It is not a political referee. And it is most certainly not designed to build a civilian society."[1] Just as capacities create intentions, so do incapacities veil problems from view. Cheney and Rumsfeld neglected the question of postwar stabilization for another reason as well, because this onerous process would have required voluntary cooperation from the allies they derided. Finally, the decision for war was ultimately made by a handful of individuals who did not completely agree among themselves about the endgame. Some imagined a quick American exit after the fall of Saddam. Others dreamed of a long-term American commitment to remaking the entire region. This "overlapping agreement" about the wisdom of invasion among individuals who differed about the ends that an invasion promised to serve provides yet another reason for the war party's neglect of planning for the postwar. If the various actors who signed on to the invasion had openly discussed their mutually inconsistent plans for what to do next, the coalition for war might have rapidly come unraveled. If they had asked pointed questions about the postwar, they might have received disquieting answers about potential downsides and costs that could have weakened public enthusiasm for the invasion. Viewed in this light, the fateful refusal to discuss what to do after Saddam fell was not simply a mistake. Heedlessness about the postwar was also an improvised strategy for silencing doubters, suppressing hesitations, and keeping together an assorted alliance in favor of a war lacking a coherent rationale.

By the end of 2003, it had already become startlingly clear. The central reality that defined the international order was no longer 9/11. It had become instead America's increasingly bloody occupation of a disintegrating Iraq. So why did the Bush Administration shift its attention from tracking down Osama bin Laden and a limited number of al Qaeda fugitives to reordering the Iraqi political system in line with American interests and values? This diversion of resources from a clandestine war against a proven enemy to the uphill stabilization of a wretchedly abused and fractured society seemed, even at the time, extraordinarily illogical, if not self-defeating. Commentators seeking to make sense of it soon began filling the bookstores with volumes devoted to the American "empire." Although most of these works were critical, they essentially accepted Robert Kagan's image of the U.S. military, ensconced in forts and outposts, patrolling the imperial frontier. But do empires, in the countries they occupy, usually loose the centrifugal forces of factional violence, tearing the social fabric apart, breeding instability, criminalization, economic collapse, and civil war?

Fantasies of Omnipotence

A useful guide to the purportedly "imperial" nature of America's war on terror is Michael Mann's *Incoherent Empire*, a volume composed, we are told, "at breakneck speed."[2] Mann reports that he has been working for two decades as "a historical sociologist on the nature of power in human societies."[3] In his dense and lively book, he analyzes and evaluates the main strands of U.S. global influence, with separate chapters devoted to America's military, political, economic, and ideological power. To these he adds others on Afghanistan, international terrorism, North Korea, and Iraq. *Incoherent Empire* is a wide-ranging work, therefore, and one that repays close study, even by readers who will not find its perspective altogether congenial or convincing.

It was America's reckless foreign policy after 9/11, Mann explains, that compelled him to climb down from his ivory tower. He decided to make the leap from scholar to activist, he says, for "the sake of the world."[4] He pursued his project in his own bookish way, situating Bush's foreign policy in a broad historical context and exposing its pathologies without resorting to "high moral rhetoric."[5] Instead of denouncing American power as evil, he charges it with incoherence, exposing U.S. foreign policy as self-defeating rather than merely malevolent or deranged.

The irrationality of U.S. counterterrorism policy, Mann seems to believe, stems from a fatal self-misunderstanding. He has in mind the boast of Charles Krauthammer and others that America's power advantage over other countries is unparalleled in human history.[6] With bases in 132 countries, it is true, America has "the first military force deployable over the entire world."[7] Moreover, since 1991, the United States has faced no enemies of its own stature. This "lack of rivals," Mann concedes, "is truly unique in history."[8] But, he adds, it is a serious error to infer from the absence of peer competitors a complete absence of limits on American power.

Mann's political aim is to deflate the omnipotence fantasies that, in his opinion, have fueled the Bush Administration's rashly destabilizing behavior in the wake of 9/11. By drawing attention to the imprudently neglected confines of American power he hopes to moderate the scope of American ambition. To dial down the administration's megalomania, he first distinguishes among the various dimensions of U.S. power. Although its military power is genuinely daunting, America's political, economic, and ideological powers are much more modest.

Such discriminations are important because, as already noted, military power is not especially useful for achieving many of the United States' most important goals. This is true even in the realm of national security. The principal security threats identified by the White House itself are nuclear proliferation and elusive, nonstate terrorist cells dispersed in Western Europe, South-East Asia, and throughout the world. The Department of Defense is no better equipped to handle these problems than to take the lead in disrupting terrorist financing, curbing U.S. fossil fuel consumption, or reforming the madrassas of Pakistan. Such problems cannot be smashed by unilateral military deployments: They must be managed co-operatively, painstakingly, and inconclusively by diplomats and other civilians.

Over-Militarizing the Response to 9/11

The need to respond multidimensionally to a multidimensional threat has still not been fully appreciated by the hawks who made the toppling of Saddam into the number one priority of U.S. counterterrorism policy. Preferring military force to diplomacy and law, they inflated a (minor) threat that could be definitively solved by unilateral military action and played down other (more serious) threats that could only be managed over extended periods of time, with inevitable setbacks and little hope of finality, by patient multilateral diplomacy.

By now a commonplace, the folly of over-militarizing America's national security strategy should have been obvious even before the decision was made to invade Iraq. It already showed up clearly in the Bush Administration's early dealings with North Korea, "a threatened, failing regime driving towards nuclear weapons."[9] Soon after taking office, Bush informed the world that Kim Jong-Il was a "pygmy" whom he "loathed." The Administration went on to combine its call for disarmament with an aggressive demand for regime change. To ask for both simultaneously was breathtakingly provocative. It was as if the Americans were ordering Kim Jong-Il to put down his weapons so they could kill him more easily. How did they expect an isolated and presumably paranoid North Korean leadership to react?

This bullying approach, according to Mann, typifies the amateurishness of Bush's foreign policy. The United States should be extending "carrots," he suggests, rather than beating "would-be proliferators" with sticks, because this would give them "an alternative way out."[10] Yet instead of hammering out a serious strategy for dealing with North Korea, the Bush Administration spent its first two years operating with "no policy" at all. It indulged in juvenile name-calling not because it had concluded that insults were likely to trigger compliance but only to demonstrate that it cared little for appearances and wanted to be feared not loved, as allegedly befitted the greatest military superpower in history.

Unilateralism Explained

During the first months of Bush's first term, the debate between unilateralists and multilateralists took the form of an interagency power struggle between the Department of Defense and the Department of State for influence over United States foreign policy. The principal reason why the Office of the Secretary of Defense (OSD) prevailed, as mentioned, was the support it received from the Office of the Vice President (OVP). As a result, the Bush Administration became, in the words of James Risen, "the first presidency in modern history in which the Pentagon served as the overwhelming center of gravity for U.S. foreign policy."[11] This victory of Donald Rumsfeld and Dick Cheney over Colin Powell had far-reaching consequences. It guaranteed that America's response to 9/11 would be conceptualized and carried out not as a metaphorical "war," but as a real one. It led the Administration to put excessive emphasis on military force, even in circumstances where diplomacy and international policing would have been likelier to produce more favorable results with less backlash and fewer opportunity costs.

A closely related question concerns international law: Why do Administration hawks delight in blanket condemnation of international law? This is a mystery because the UN (an organization that bin Laden himself reviles as "a tool with which the plans of global unbelief against Muslims are implemented"[12]) has never presented a serious obstacle to U.S. ambitions. We might even say, with only slight exaggeration, that the United States retains a veto over international law. Multilateral institutions and international law as they currently exist were in effect created by the United States to serve U.S. national interests. The UN secretary-general, as Mann tartly remarks, is virtually a U.S. appointee.

If international law is either toothless or a pliant tool of U.S. power, why do Bush's hawks thunder at the restraints it allegedly places on U.S. power? Why, in the run-up to the Iraq war, did they show so little interest in a UN mandate which might have made it easier to secure allied soldiers, logistics, cash and help in postwar reconstruction? A morally dubious but politically useful benefit of multilateralism, according to Mann, is that it allows allied countries to "hide behind UN ideological authority," turning a deaf ear to their own publics in order to acquiesce in American wishes.[13] So the mystery deepens. Why did Bush's officials disparage such an asset in their hour of need?

One answer is that the international legal regime, as it existed when Bush came to power, interfered with two pet projects of his hawkish foreign policy team. The impregnable space-based weapons platform that the "new imperialists"[14] dreamed of creating under the cover of missile defense was inconsistent with the ABM treaty then in force. (Bush opportunistically abrogated this treaty in the aftermath of 9/11.) Customary international law had created a strong presumption against future nuclear weapons testing. This expectation exists only informally, it is true, but if it were ever codified – that is, if a comprehensive test-ban treaty were to be ratified by the U.S. Senate – the new imperialists would have to renounce their Stangelovian dream of developing a whole new generation of small first-strike nuclear weapons.

A less alarming explanation for the instinctive unilateralism widely shared in the Cheney-Rumsfeld circle is that multilateral instruments are not always as useful as their liberal proponents contend. On this subject Mann is commendably even-handed. Although the world's gravest problems, including treacherously unpredictable states, require international cooperation, these problems cannot be competently managed through an organization as "divided and ineffective" as the UN. The Security Council "often stalls amid wrangles between the permanent members,"[15] Mann remarks. As a result, "leaving everything to the UN might be a recipe for the deployment of high moral sentiments, endless political squabbles, and little action."[16] In fact, multilateral institutions and international law work best under "American leadership."[17] When America refuses to supply the power of enforcement, as is often observed, international law has no teeth. Mann therefore favors "combined U.S./UN activity" and laments that it is becoming rare.[18]

Why did OSD's understandable preference for unilateral military power over diplomacy become White House policy? The civilian leaders at the Pentagon presumably concluded soon after 9/11 that they could ride the public fear of terrorism to ever greater influence (and ever larger budgets) if they could persuade the unschooled president that the massive military machine created to deter and fight the Soviet Union could be transformed quickly to meet the challenge of transnational terrorism. Some evidence for this improbable contention was provided by the technically and tactically impressive destruction of the Taliban regime in Afghanistan. The Pentagon provided devastating air support and a small military ground force to help the CIA and the Northern Alliance destroy al Qaeda's training camps. However, why did the Department of Defense's crucial role in Afghanistan imply that OSD should become the lead agency in the overall American war on terror? Because the Pentagon was not as well-designed as other U.S. agencies to conduct police manhunts and obstruct nuclear smuggling, it made little sense, as a matter of substance, to give OSD such a central role in shaping America's fight against terrorism. Or so you might have thought.

After the fall of the Taliban, the OSD managed to seize the dominant role in the war on terror because the White House, under Cheney's influence, inflated the threat posed by rogue states, claiming that they are central rather than merely marginal players in the international terrorism aimed at the United States. This skewed threat assessment, to be examined in more detail below, rests on an imagined doomsday scenario, in which a rogue state might "hand off" a WMD to an elusive terrorist group which, in the grip of an apocalyptic ideology, could then devastate an American city. To pre-empt this eventuality, allegedly, the United States has the right to use military force to "change" any regime that might conceivably contemplate such a lethal transfer.

This argument should not be dismissed simply because it is advanced by OSD and its friends with an eye to increasing the power of OSD. It could be self-serving and nevertheless independently convincing. However, there are ample reasons to doubt its persuasiveness as well as its sincerity. For one thing, if Bush's officials were genuinely worried about WMD, they would also have been focused on other potential sources of proliferation, but they were not. As Mann helpfully reminds us, they initially opposed Nunn-Lugar, a program demonstrably making America safer by dismantling poorly guarded Soviet weapons and protecting highly enriched uranium (HEU) storage facilities inside Russia. Bush at first curtailed its funding. He proved willing to spend $300 billion and counting to protect America from the threat supposedly posed by a country that turns out to have had no WMD, but for much of his first term he could barely bring himself to spend $1 billion on a program aimed at reducing the threat from a country that everyone agrees is still over-flowing with unsecured HEU. The simplest explanation for why America gave greater attention to Iraq than to Russia was that OSD, charged with assigning priorities to various threats, saw a bigger role for itself in Iraq than in Russia. It was a clear case, to paraphrase Rumsfeld, of the whimsically assigned "lead agency" defining the mission rather than the mission, independently defined, determining the agency that should take the lead.

An even more alarming sign of the war cabinet's cavalier attitude towards proliferation was its proposal, still alive, to develop "new low-yield and variable-yield theatre nuclear warheads," including a small deep-penetrating device designed to destroy underground bunkers where the enemy leadership or its illegal nuclear arsenal might be stashed. The Departments of Defense and Energy have temporarily shelved their requests for funding to create such a new generation of small-yield first-strike warheads, although the program may be going forward covertly under another name. In any case, there has never been a new weapons system that has not eventually fallen into the hands of the enemy. The "new militarists" who strongly advocate a research initiative into the miniaturization of nuclear devices, even when the United States faces no serious military rivals, presumably know this. It is therefore difficult to believe that, in the run-up to the invasion, they were thinking carefully about ways to minimize the terrifying risks of nuclear proliferation.

What Military Power Cannot Achieve

So why did Bush embrace a lopsided militarizing of America's response to 9/11? Mann offers the following explanation. Dazzled by America's unquestioned military supremacy, Bush and his aides seem to have lost all realistic appreciation of what the military can and cannot do. This brings us to a curious fallacy, already touched upon above, namely the often cited cognitive bias that leads a man with a hammer to pay disproportionate attention to problems that resemble nails and even, at the extreme, to thwack all problems, regardless of their shape, as if they actually were nails.

The country with unrivaled military power sees its environment in a distorted way (Chapter Two). Highly attuned to threats posed by hostile states, the Cheney-Rumsfeld group seems to have perceived nonstate threats only obscurely. This predisposition was reinforced by ideological biases: Republicans have an easier time discerning and acknowledging threats posed by rogue states than threats posed, say, by unregulated arms markets or rogue religious charities with only minimal input from troublemaker states. They tend to deemphasize the way freedom of trade and religious education can jeopardize American security. Such blind spots, too, have contributed to an overemphasis on rogue states as supporters of terror, an overemphasis that played directly into OSD's reckless decision to transform Saddam's tyranny into the primary target of the war on terror.

Rumsfeld also seized on the invasion of Iraq as an opportunity to push forward his streamlining of America's military structure and doctrine. Indeed, he was so single-mindedly focused on his reform agenda, meant to improve the war-fighting capacity of U.S. troops, that he shrugged off the question of what to do after victory. Scandalously, U.S. soldiers were given no instructions about how to behave when the Iraqi military collapsed. Despite all the prewar talk about "huge" weapons stockpiles, only perfunctory preparations were made for a postwar proliferation disaster. Weapons depots were left unguarded. Borders were left unsecured. As they rolled through the country, invading forces did not even do anything to prevent the Al Tuwaitha Nuclear Research Center from being ransacked. Radioactive materials were carted off from this well-known site during a war ostensibly launched to prevent the proliferation of WMD.

More generally, no constabulary force was on hand to deal with predictable post-invasion looting and mayhem. And, in Mann's words, the United States "went into this invasion with no credible plan for political reconstruction."[19] Various reasons have been offered to explain why OSD did not plan seriously for the challenges of postwar Iraq. There were plenty of warnings. For example, George Kennan said in the fall of 2002: "I have seen no evidence that we have any realistic plans for dealing with the great state of confusion in Iraqian affairs which would presumably follow even after the successful elimination of the dictator."[20] So why were no serious preparations made?

Perhaps Rumsfeld believed that the country would stabilize itself after Saddam was removed with his entourage, but at the root of his cavalier approach must have been a tacit conviction that a failed, festering, chaotic state in Iraq, if it came to that, would not seriously threaten U.S. national security. The war planners must have been blocked, conceptually and psychologically, from appreciating the dangers involved if a power-vacuum were allowed to develop in post-invasion Iraq. Focused obsessively on the threat posed by rogue states, they were apparently oblivious to the threat posed by collapsed states. *Absence of power* was not a threat that appeared on their radar screen. Some possible reasons for this blindness were canvassed in the preceding chapter. Because OSD focused exclusively on problems that overwhelming U.S. military power can readily solve, it neglected, until it was too late, the problems of state collapse, political instability, and ineffective policing.

Reflecting on this debacle, Mann responds to those, like Robert Kagan, who scoff at Europe as an economic giant but a military midget: "In interventions inside nation-states, the U.S. is a political pygmy. After inflicting military devastation on a country, it cannot easily bring political order – as we see in both Afghanistan and Iraq."[21] In what he calls an "age of nationalism,"[22] he might have added, a foreign protectorate is more likely to be accepted when administered by a genuine coalition of states, operating perhaps under UN authorization, than when it appears to be imposed by a single conquering power. In other words, the Bush Administration's knee-jerk hostility to multilateralism may have contributed significantly to its failure to assert control over political processes in postwar Iraq. No one seems to have planned, in the run-up to war, for the UN to assume a political role after hostilities ceased, and no one seems to have anticipated that unilateralism, however much battlefield flexibility it allows, would also make it virtually impossible for the United States to blame others for unavoidable setbacks or to extricate its troops after routing Saddam's regime.

Terrorism versus Guerrilla War

Iraq has not been Bush's sole foreign policy calamity. Elsewhere, according to Mann, in the real struggle against 9/11-style terrorism, things have not gone any better. The general war on terror is just as "disastrous"[23] as the war in Iraq, he argues, because it is being conducted in a fundamentally indiscriminate way. Here again, Washington has failed to focus sharply on the real threat, extending its war to a miscellaneous collection of terrorist groups that obviously had nothing to do with 9/11. Indeed, Bush's war on generic terrorism reflects a fatal conflation of two very different types of threat: national-liberation terrorists, such as the Chechens, the Kashmiris, or Hezbollah, and international terrorists, such as al Qaeda, for whom ousting foreign troops or overturning local autocrats has apparently become secondary to global jihad against the West in general and America in particular. Territorially based guerrillas and rebels are numerous and very difficult to overcome. Members of al Qaeda, by contrast, are few and somewhat easier to incapacitate or kill. On 9/11, the United

States was attacked by international terrorists, but instead of focusing on those responsible, the government declared war indiscriminately on *all* terrorists, lumping together those who attacked the United States and those who did not, mixing up those that operate globally with those that operate only locally, and so forth. Because it fails to incorporate such elementary distinctions, the State Department's official list of terrorist organizations provides a poor basis for formulating an effective counter-terrorism policy. To understand the warping of America's foreign-policy priorities since 9/11, we need to start with this serious failure to clarify the conceptual prism through which the enemy is seen.

National terrorists are "guerrillas" who dwell "protected among their own people."[24] Such irregular fighters are difficult to wipe out precisely because they blend into the background and rely on local support. Most revolutionary turbulence in the world is caused by such rebels, who "are usually too deep-rooted to eradicate merely by repression." These "national struggles are almost endless."[25] Indeed, attempts to repress them often backfire. As a result, a counterinsurgency that hopes to succeed must be fine-tuned, applying enough force to repress the rebels but not so much that it alienates the local population.

Thwarted in their struggle against oppressive rule, a small subset of these nationalist insurgents escape or are ejected from their home countries and end up as "isolated extremist splinter groups, living in alien lands."[26] Unable to operate in their own countries, these uprooted freedom fighters decide, desperately but not irrationally, to redirect their rage against "states abroad whom they identify as allies of their local enemy."[27] Using Western cities as launch pads, however, "they cannot as easily operate as guerrillas." Instead, they are forced to "fight exposed amid alien communities."[28]

Mann's point seems to be that essentially rootless networks such as al Qaeda, because they are unable to draw on the unquenchable fires of nationalism, are inherently weak or unlikely to perpetuate themselves for long. Their power has been exaggerated only because a handful of them, by sheer luck, managed successfully to attack the United States. In reality, we "could easily win the war against existing international terrorists, who are very exposed to attack."[29] The search for the 9/11 conspirators is a worldwide police manhunt; it does not resemble those "guerrilla wars, deeply rooted among local populations."[30] In pinpoint law-enforcement operations, the United States will continue to capture or kill al Qaeda operatives, who are living on the lam. It can do this, mercifully, without slaughtering village-loads of innocent bystanders. This is a notable advantage, because the indiscriminate killing and crippling of bystanders is how poorly conducted counterinsurgencies inadvertently propel new recruits into terrorist conspiracies. Unfortunately, Bush has clamorously failed to exploit this advantage. Instead of de-linking fundamentalist and nationalist movements, he has driven them together. He has unwittingly channeled the powerful passions of frustrated nationalism into what would otherwise have remained a dangerous but uprooted and therefore manageable anti-American jihad. Instead of keeping aloof from the world's unwinnable guerrilla wars, he decided that America's war on terror is truly "global," meaning that the United States has to take sides against local Islamic insurgents everywhere, as when, in 2002, 3000 American soldiers went to help crush Abu Sayyaf, the Islamic secessionist movement in the southern Philippines. (Although these troops were eventually withdrawn, U.S. forces continue to work closely with the Filipino military in the fight against Abu Sayyaf.) And, of course, he has lit Iraq on fire, giving rise to, among other forms of violence, a wholly new guerrilla war.

American Autism

Although a handful of individuals in OSD and OVP made the decision to invade Iraq, they would not have been able to carry out such a disastrous policy without significant public support. The American public's well-documented ignorance of world affairs has contributed to its willingness to support Bush's rechanneling of the public desire for vengeance from al Qaeda to Iraq, on the one hand, and to national-liberation terrorists, such as Hamas, on the other. Since the U.S. public was poorly informed about political turmoil in, say, Saudi Arabia and Pakistan, it had the impression that, on 9/11, the United States was hit *from nowhere*. As a result, Americans were widely supportive of purportedly retaliatory attacks *anywhere* the government desired.

As Mann makes clear, however, uncritical public support for Bush's folly in Iraq has not exactly been spontaneous; it is to some extent a product of bowdlerized and biased media coverage. Most distressingly, the American public has never had a chance to see the invasion and occupation of Iraq that were broadcast to non-American publics around the world: "The disconnect between the American and foreign media during the Iraq invasion became quite extreme."[31] Political distortions in news coverage occur everywhere, of course, but whoever is at fault, the diluting and excising of shared experience, especially between the United States and its democratic allies, bodes ill for "international amity."[32] Because U.S.

citizens are "insulated within their self-censorship,"[33] they, as well as their leaders, show increasing signs of national autism.

As a dual citizen of the United States and the U.K., Mann is acutely conscious of the new American solipsism. He places some of the blame for it on Tony Blair, who is depicted as a "camp follower" with a "walk-on part" in Bush's war on Iraq.[34] Blair placed British soldiers in the service of a foreign power, "objectively" aligning the U.K. with Ariel Sharon and making it into an appealing target for radical Islamic terrorism. He did this in part because of his "Christian Soldier desire to bring good to the world by force."[35] Mann charitably adds that Blair, in the end, was so fixated on moderating Bush that he simply "got trapped inside the military tent."[36] This was "a world-historical mistake,"[37] allegedly, because only a common European front against the invasion of Iraq could have stopped Bush.

Will Blowback Be Fatal?

My account thus far does not do full justice to Mann's searching analysis and cascading insights. But it will nevertheless be useful, at this point, to examine some of his book's minor shortcomings. First, Mann does not distinguish clearly enough between the passing sins of the Bush Administration and deeply entrenched patterns of U.S. behavior that will change little even if a Democrat is elected to the White House in 2008. A President Gore probably would not have invaded Iraq. But plenty of Democrats voted for the war, and many liberal newspapers supported the military overthrow of Saddam.

Mann also oscillates confusingly between the claim that the United States lacks important powers and the allegation that the present government, for ideological reasons, refuses to use these powers. After explaining at great length that America is doomed to fail in its imperial ambitions because it has neither the resources nor the favorable conditions enjoyed by the British when they established and maintained their empire, he flips around and argues with equal confidence that the United States is not seeking a territorial empire on the British model.

If Mann's generally persuasive analysis has a serious flaw, it lies in the mechanical nature of his thinking about the "global blowback"[38] likely to follow from Bush's inept counterterrorism strategy. At various points he endorses the ancient notion that the hubris of the great inevitably precipitates their downfall. In a few passages, this prognosis sounds surprisingly like wishful thinking. The United States's "overconfident, hyperactive militarism," he predicts, "will soon destroy" America's global power.[39]

Elsewhere he refers to the Bush Administration's "ruthless arrogance leading to overconfidence, eventually leading to hubris and disaster."[40] That
he feels somewhat uneasy with this mythical-poetical style of thinking
comes out in his odd disclaimer, expressed as a dissent from Osama bin
Laden: "I doubt that God will strike down the Americans."[41] However,
he does not seem to doubt that the minor deity called "blowback" will
do something of the sort.

Or rather, he confidently asserts it in some passages, and in others flatly
denies it, but even where he insists that destruction is a real possibility,
he cannot quite decide about the mechanism by which America will be
punished for its sins. The general idea is that it will suffer for swimming
against "the tide of history,"[42] as if history had a single prevailing tide and
Mann knew what it was. Sometimes he says that a resurgent nationalism
will throw off America's imperial yoke the way it put an end to the British
Empire. The problem with this prediction is that America's pacification
efforts in Iraq, for example, have been derailed less by nationalism than by
violent centrifugal forces, by ethnic, sectarian, and tribal divisions – that
is, by the weakness of Iraqi nationalism.

Another of Mann's candidates for the role of empire-slayer is the international Islamic brigade which he predicts will be created, or recreated,
by the serial invasions of Afghanistan and Iraq. He confirms the danger
posed by this form of blowback, humorously enough, by introspection.
If he had been confined in Guantánamo, he reveals, "I would now be
tempted to become a terrorist mastermind!"[43] He even associates himself, if only weakly, with those who asserted that the United States had
it coming on 9/11. America has treated poor countries so badly that "it
should expect some of them to hit back, a few of them armed with the
weapons of the weak in the name of the poor and the oppressed of the
world. To a degree, the United States would have deserved it."[44]

Yet having thoroughly debunked the power of international terrorists,
he cannot turn around and make a strong case that they will bring the
United States to its knees. In another passage, he dismisses the idea that
either national insurgencies or international conspiracies could seriously
weaken America. Instead, he explains, the only true limit on American
power is the threat of capital flight. If Japan and OPEC abandon the dollar,
the American economy will collapse, spelling an end to the United States's
capacity to project its military power around the globe. This might happen,
he adds, if reckless militarism makes the world's investors see the United
States as a potentially insolvent debtor. There is obviously something
to this analysis, but its relation to the other mechanisms discussed and

dismissed is never made clear. Nor is it reconciled with the assurance else-where in the book that American power will obviously survive more or less intact, even though Americans will suffer grievously in the years to come.

Conceptual Politics

Looming in the background here is Mann's struggle to navigate the tricky transition from academic sociology to partisan polemic. His entire project makes sense only if he can trace what he sees as disastrous political choices back to conceptual blunders and factual inaccuracies about the world. By correcting these errors, he hopes to deliver a fatal blow to the immoral and violence-breeding policies built upon them.

This conceit may be noble, but it is not very reasonable. Mann argues, for instance, that the failure of the Bush Administration to distinguish between international terrorists who attack the United States and national-liberation terrorists is a conceptual mistake. But there are too many win-ners and losers involved for this to be an analytical mix-up that an alert professor can keenly identify and deftly correct. In actuality, the obfusca-tion is as much political as conceptual. By declaring war against generic terror, rather than against those terrorists who pose a direct threat to the United States, the Bush Administration is committing itself, for example, to the Israeli side in the Middle East conflict, but Mann persists in treating this fateful political choice as if it were the fruit of a conceptual slip rather than a political choice.

This is not to belittle his substantive commentary on United States–Israel relations. Mann calls the Israeli-Palestinian conflict "the running sore of U.S. foreign policy."[45] When he writes that "US failure to con-trol Israel is irrational,"[46] he means that he cannot explain it. Why should a global power takes sides in a blood feud and tribal dispute over land and water? American partiality in the Middle East conflict manifestly con-travenes Rumsfeld's precept, mentioned above, that the mission must determine the coalition rather than the other way round. In this case, quite obviously, the alliance determines the mission – but why? America's unbending loyalty to Israel buys it such virulent hostility around the globe that it cannot be explained on narrow national-security grounds alone, nor can it be explained by the ethnic loyalties of America's relatively insignifi-cant (and in any case divided) "Jewish lobby."

Mann's frank admission that he cannot explain Israeli-American rela-tions should encourage readers to ponder some of the less-than-rational forces that may underlie U.S. devotion to, even obsession with, Israel.

What we can say with some confidence is that this unusual alliance rests on deep feelings of affinity. No doubt the central role of "Israel" in the Protestant-evangelical interpretation of the Bible has not been lost on an administration that sees electoral advantage in satisfying the Christian Right. Having grown up with the myth of the American West, some hawks may also feel drawn to a frontier society of armed settlers, scratching the desert to make it bloom and gallantly thrusting forward against the hopeless resistance of an "inferior" people. Or perhaps they sympathize with a government that prefers hard military solutions to soft civilian alternatives and is constantly at odds with the UN. Those who are nostalgic for Cold War certainties might also identify psychologically with a democratic country caught in a struggle for survival against an implacable foe. Such unverifiable speculations do not resolve the mystery of the America-Israel bond, but they underscore Mann's assertion that it is both a pivotal factor in contemporary affairs and one that is painfully difficult to comprehend. They also contravene his assumption that the United States would quickly cut Israel loose if Americans only got a grip on the concept of "state terror," or if they were suddenly to learn that the Palestinian resistance had stopped targeting U.S. citizens back in the 1980s.

A related objection can be raised against Mann's claim that the international terrorists who attacked America are "easy" to separate from national-liberation terrorists. In reality, the al Qaeda network is Janus-faced, combining national-liberation struggles with transnational operations. As David Kilcullen has argued, "Al Qaeda and similar groups feed on local grievances, integrate them into broader ideologies, and link disparate conflicts through globalized communications, finances and technology."[47] Mann's discriminating approach will not completely de-link transnational terrorism from national-liberation struggles for the simple reason that the dangerous linkage in question, rather than being fomented solely by counterproductive American policies, is the unintended gift of globalization to jihad.

In any case, bin Laden's organization has roots inside Saudi Arabia and has been involved in sporadic terrorism there. Most of the 9/11 terrorists continued to live in Saudi Arabia until a few months before the attack, and came out, with clean records, for a one-time strike. They were not, therefore, fighting in exposed forward positions as Mann claims. Moreover, even those international terrorists who do operate in foreign countries, cut off from their home communities, are not as easily detectable as he implies, since they swim in the international waters of migrant labor, study-abroad programs, and international Islamic networks.

In the final paragraphs of the book, Mann gives the United States the following advice. To sustain its global influence and even guard itself from disaster, America must start withdrawing its troops from places "where they have no business."[48] It must also stop supporting Israel, stop "seeking extra-territorial control over oil supplies,"[49] and, of course, stop invading foreign countries. "No significant danger would occur if the United States stopped doing all these things," he says. "Quite the contrary."[50] How this advice comports with Mann's earlier pleas for America to remain engaged in the world as a "leader" and a "conciliator" is unclear.[51] But the real problem is that every one of his "proposals" is politically unrealistic. At some level, Mann writes as a utopian rather than as an activist – less to improve America politically than to rebuke it morally. This comes through in his description of the United States as "a disturbed, misshapen monster."[52] Such talk may deliver a welcome jolt in a seminar, but as propaganda meant to harm Bush politically, it is sure to have the opposite effect.

Warriors without a Strategy

More promising is Mann's attempt to identify the comprehensive plan that, in his opinion, underpins Bush's entire foreign and national security policy. "Do not think," he says, "that U.S. policy towards Kyoto, landmines, Star Wars, Iraq, Iran or the southern Philippines are ad hoc or unconnected. They are all part of the grand strategy for a global American empire, first envisioned as theory, then after 9/11 becoming reality."[53] The "theory" he has in mind was developed in the early 1990s by Paul Wolfowitz, Richard Perle, and others at the Project for the New American Century (PNAC), calling for the United States to increase military spending and to target rogue states (Iraq, Iran, and North Korea) preemptively, as well as to develop missile defense and a new generation of theater nuclear weapons.

Mann is onto something here, but he also risks giving the war planners too much credit. Indeed, we might say, turning his own phrase against him, that Bush's use of American power "to make the world a better place" is not coherent enough to be the embodiment of any strategy, grand or petty. No impartial examination of U.S. activities abroad, from foreign aid through bilateral trade agreements to military invasion, could conclude that the Administration has a clear and consistent set of priorities or that it knows how to rank, according to degrees of urgency or importance, the tangle of problems and threats facing the country today.

Thanks to the poorly prepared invasion, Iraq has become such a cauldron of sectarian, criminal, and factional violence that an American withdrawal would now risk destabilizing a strategically vital region of the world. That seems to be the Administration's last remaining rationale for "staying the course" in Iraq. But notice the dramatic change of purpose that this rationale implies. Staying in Iraq to prevent anarchy means giving up any hope of a showcase American victory. A tyranny can be defeated, but not an anarchy. Iraqi factions may lay down their weapons and chose peaceful coexistence. But such a settlement, even if it were possible, would be the product of political negotiation among the parties, not the product of an American military "victory."

So what was the long-term strategy behind the war? To answer this question, Mann looks to insiders associated with PNAC – especially Wolfowitz and Douglas Feith, but also Cheney and Rumsfeld. These longtime acquaintances had been discussing an invasion of Iraq for many years before 9/11. After the attack, they served up their preconceived policy of preventive war (alongside their preconceived policy of missile defense) as if it were a solution to the wholly new problem of international terrorism targeting U.S. territory. This fateful step is often described as cynical opportunism. But it could just as easily have represented a failure of imagination. The Bush team may have responded to the shock of the new by reverting to what was most familiar. They had paid no attention to al Qaeda before 9/11. Afterwards, they continued to slight it, perhaps because they simply could not bring themselves to focus seriously on a threat posed by nonstate actors.

What they *did* focus on was America's mission in the world after the collapse of the U.S.S.R. Some of them conceived U.S. hegemony as an expanded and improved version of British imperial domination. Here their motivations become obscure, inconsistent, and wholly unworthy of the name of "grand strategy." Bush may fantasize that the Almighty has assigned him the personal task of bringing "freedom" to mankind. Wolfowitz and Feith presumably had more secular dreams. Their proposal to use American power to compel the rest of the world to accept the U.S. understanding of human rights and democracy certainly sounds like megalomania, but it also provided a publicly acceptable motive for deploying U.S. military forces abroad. It is very difficult, as a consequence, to be certain who took it seriously as a motive and who merely invoked it, cynically, as a pretext.

Those who dream of democratizing the world may be righteous in their own minds, but the Iraq debacle has exposed the essential callowness of their messianic vision. Even in 2007, Administration officials continue to read from cue cards, reaffirming America's commitment to a genuinely democratic government in a sovereign Iraq. But no outside commentators are now saying that success in this venture will provide the ultimate vindication of "muscular Wilsonianism." No one is still expecting that, with sufficient American hand-holding, a model Iraqi democracy will emerge. No one now hopes that, in the decimated Iraq that emerges from the American occupation, due process and minority rights will be scrupulously respected and the oil economy managed without corruption. No one believes that happy Iraqis, grateful to the United States, will elect a government eager to comply with U.S. regional policies, including unbridled support for Israel. Finally, no one still thinks that a democratic Iraq will trigger a tidal wave of reform throughout the region, turning virulent anti-Americanism into heartfelt appreciation for American friendship.

It is hard to know how to assess the guileless optimism of the war's architects, especially when professed by men who vaunt their lack of illusions. Had they never heard of worst-case scenarios?[54] What sort of foreign policy assumes that democracy has no historical, cultural, economic, and psychological preconditions? Among the factors obstructing the emergence of democracy in Iraq is the fragmentation of the population. As Mann says, "this is not an easy country to hold together."[55] It is increasingly unlikely that the United States can gain Kurdish and Shiite acquiescence to the minimal condition for Iraqi nation-building: namely, reintegrating the alienated Sunnis into the country's police and military hierarchy. No one knows how an Iraqi "unity government" can be both representative enough to be legitimate and coherent enough to govern. That any foreign occupier could create "social and political cohesion"[56] in a country honeycombed with ethnic, sectarian, and tribal divisions is dubious. That the United States in particular has the skill, wisdom, and perseverance to create the "demos" presupposed by any functioning democracy, given the intrinsic difficulty of ethnic and confessional reconciliation in a country with Iraq's history, surpasses belief.

That promoting democracy in Muslim countries was ever going to be a consistent principle of U.S. foreign policy is farfetched. Bush's passion for electoral accountability, for example, never extended to Pakistan or Jordan, where majorities might beg to differ with U.S. regional interests. The global manhunt for sleeper agents affiliated with al Qaeda also reveals the limits of liberal messianism as a guide to Bush's policy, because tracking down terrorists requires the United States to sustain amiable relations with security apparatuses around the world, including those in undemocratic Muslim states. It is hard to believe that the Administration was ever so dedicated to spreading democracy that it would welcome elections even if they produce governments unwilling to comply with U.S. requests. Self-government is fine, but whatever a few messianic liberals say, Washington's preference has always been and remains for a world in which no state can comfortably say no to Washington.

Rather than searching for a grand strategy behind the invasion of Iraq, it is more fruitful to view the war as the consequence of a set of ad hoc compromises among various decision makers who were driven by unrelated and sometimes contradictory aims. The "mission" to bring democracy to mankind was only one aim among many, and not the dominant one by a long shot. Without trying to establish any particular hierarchy, let us pause for a moment to review what Mark Danner calls "the great, multicolored braid of reasons and justifications leading to the Iraq war."[57] These motives were not especially coherent or even mutually compatible but, at a particular historical moment, they all pointed to war.

An invasion of Iraq was embraced as a means serving the following disjointed ends: to frighten any group or state that might feel emboldened to replicate or outdo 9/11; to offer solace to American voters traumatized by 9/11 by letting them see U.S. military supremacy in action; to increase the power of the executive branch and shrink the power of Congress and the courts; to show that the United States was still responding aggressively to 9/11 even after "running out of targets" in Afghanistan, and thereby to improve the Republican Party's electoral prospects in 2004; to "get it right this time," that is, to finish a job that George H.W. Bush had left undone; to avenge Saddam's 1993 attempt to assassinate the first President Bush; to establish OSD primacy in the war on terror and, in the process, field-test Rumsfeld's proposals for military reform; to break OPEC by increasing output of Iraqi crude, perhaps via sweetheart deals with American oil companies; to evacuate U.S. troops from Saudi Arabia, thereby removing a focal point of anti-American rage, but nevertheless keeping U.S. forces within striking distance of the Saudi oil fields in case a fundamentalist revolution toppled the monarchy; to destroy an important regional threat to Israel; to make sure that Saddam would not acquire the capacity for nuclear blackmail after France, Germany, and other countries dismantled the UN embargo; to express America's self-love by offering to replicate American political institutions abroad; to counter "moral relativism" by revealing that the world really is divided between good and evil.

That different individuals and groups, embracing such a cacophony of aims, could come to agree on the invasion of Iraq seems plausible enough. That they would not easily concur about what to do after victory also makes perfect sense. Any attempt to achieve consensus about an endgame would have risked breaking up the ad hoc coalition for war. Hard-headed realists permitted democratic sloganeering to replace serious planning because they had no grand strategy and no ultimate aim.

Power Unchecked Is Power Deranged

This dismaying picture should be supplemented by one additional observation. During the Cold War, Soviet power not only threatened but also chastened the United States. Today, no such well-organized enemy is even on the horizon. A few challenges to U.S. power exist, but they are all what Mann calls "half-baked."[58] None compares even remotely with the former U.S.S.R. This means that U.S. policy-makers now face radically reduced incentives to think carefully about how they deploy their country's global power. Bellicose gamblers have always agitated U.S. foreign policy circles. But during the Cold War standoff they were held in check by more sober heads. The disappearance of a peer competitor, with global capacities for reaction and retaliation, eliminated compelling reasons for scrupulous forethought. If America were still disciplined by such a militarily powerful enemy, the Administration would not have become militarily entangled in Iraq without planning what to do next.

Incoherent Empire was one of the first works to argue explicitly that "the new militarism will also increase terrorism."[59] That Bush has accomplished this in Iraq is by now the consensus view. One consequence of his tragic miscalculation is that whole new cadres of snipers and bombers (including suicide bombers) have spent the past four years murdering Americans (as well as Europeans and other foreigners, not to mention Iraqis) on a regular basis. America's new-minted enemies have even seized a bit of moral high ground, to the extent that they have been targeting U.S. soldiers, and not American civilians as on 9/11. No Iraqis were doing anything like this before the collapse of Saddam's regime. Thus, by inflating the threat from rogue states and magically making them into the principal targets of America's counterterrorism efforts, Bush has managed to aggravate the very problem he ostensibly set out to solve. To call such a policy incoherent seems almost euphemistic. The bitterest twist of Bush's foreign policy is a different one however. After ridiculing Bill Clinton for confusing foreign policy with social work, Bush has ended up conducting foreign policy as social work of the most hazardous and hopeless kind. This may not be blowback, in Mann's sense, but it definitely has the feel of a serious self-inflicted wound.

PART III

FALSE TEMPLATES

SEARCHING FOR A NEW ENEMY AFTER THE COLD WAR

Al-Jazeera: What is your opinion about what is being said concerning the "Clash of Civilizations"?

Osama bin Laden: I say that there is no doubt about this. The [Clash of Civilizations] is a very clear matter, proven in the Qur'an and the traditions of the Prophet, and any true believer who claims to be faithful shouldn't doubt these truths.[1]

Made famous by Samuel Huntington, the intriguing but misleading theory of a "clash of civilizations" has been embraced, for analogous reasons, by extremists on both sides of the Western-Islamic divide. Huntington originally argued that the ideological conflict of the Cold War was destined to be (or at least should be) replaced by a conflict between civilizations. After 9/11, his book was reread as foretelling the emerging worldwide confrontation between Islam and the West – the very sort of confrontation that was allegedly illustrated by al Qaeda's attack on America. Islamic radicals, it should be noted, regularly describe "the West" as a single, coherent entity. For example, Sayyid Qutb, one of the most influential thinkers of radical Islam, "saw the West as a single cultural entity. The distinctions between capitalism and Marxism, Christianity and Judaism, fascism and democracy were insignificant by comparison with the single great divide in Qutb's mind: Islam and the East on the one side, and the Christian West on the other."[2] Huntington exaggerated the homogeneity of the Islamic world for much the same reason that Qutb exaggerated the coherence of the West. By painting their respective enemies as more unified and aggressive than they actually are, both Huntington and Islamic radicals hope to boost solidarity and awaken warlike passions on their own side. Huntington also echoes radical Islamists when he suggests that people who find political and private life today to be spiritually vacuous can find meaning in potentially fatal conflicts with deadly enemies, that is to say, in polarized confrontations where compromise is impossible and manhood is at stake. Huntington's famous remark that "Islam has bloody borders" should not be read critically, as a matter of fact, for he greatly admires civilizations capable of aggression and organized violence. He fears that the West has grown too old to fight furiously against youthful enemies such as Islam. Indeed, despite the combative spirit of his book (he rebukes Clinton for helping Muslims in the Balkans and suggests that the EU slam the door on Turkey), its ultimate drift is darkly pessimistic. For one thing, Huntington's attempt to make liberalism into the core of a neo-tribal Western identity obviously fails because liberalism is only one strand among many in Western history. Furthermore, the Enlightenment tradition does not permit the kind of unprovoked aggression against strangers that xenophobic tribalism encourages. Immigration into Europe and the United States has also advanced too far to permit a refounding of Western identity on a purely ethnic or mono-cultural basis. Anxiety about low Western birthrates compared to the rest of the world compounds Huntington's pessimism, as does his belief that the modern nation-state, which globalization continues to weaken, is the only known political form capable of disciplining violent chaos into some sort of stable social order. But one of Huntington's principal reasons for pessimism was his expectation, already in 1996, that a nuclear bomb might eventually fall into the hands of a transnational Islamic group that, lacking a fixed territorial basis, could not be deterred. This was perhaps the most prescient fear in his intellectually sparkling and emotionally fear-filled work.

Huntington's Clash of Civilizations

Renowned Harvard professor and self-styled defender of Western civilization, Samuel Huntington has been a dominant voice in American political science for forty years. Roughly contemporary, as a Harvard graduate student in security studies, with Henry Kissinger and Zbigniew Brzezinski, Huntington failed to achieve their spectacular level of political success in Washington, although he did rise to a second-tier position in the National Security Council under President Jimmy Carter. His intellectual achievements, by way of compensation, have outstripped those of his peers. His immensely influential *Political Order in Changing Societies* (1968), in particular, established his reputation as the country's most brilliant and accomplished theorist of political development. Although he passes as a conservative of sorts, he is anything but a libertarian, and has been an articulate critic of the tendency of Americans, in particular, to underestimate the contribution of political authority to individual liberty. His 1993 *Foreign Affairs* article, "The Clash of Civilizations?," was something of a departure.[3] It propelled him into even greater international prominence, not only because it provided a simple picture of the dangers of a post-Cold War world, but because he wrote of ethnic hatred and religious intolerance without the usual liberal discomfort, indeed without appearing to make value judgments of any sort.

Tribal Conflict on a Global Scale

The Clash of Civilizations and the Remaking of World Order is an elaboration of that article and a response to its critics.[4] Dazzling his readers with a masterly tour of world politics and a forecast of "tribal conflict on a global scale,"[5] Huntington all the while keeps one eye trained apprehensively on the "moral decline"[6] of the United States. He is distressed at an increasingly materialistic and multiculturalist America, at its "relativism, egotism and consumerism,"[7] among other blemishes and failings. Not unlike the writings of Oswald Spengler and other theorists of comparative civilizations, on whom he unapologetically relies, Huntington's scholarly endeavor is permeated by alarm at the current decay and possible extinction of his own culture and society. "The West's victory in the Cold War has produced not triumph but exhaustion."[8] We have lost not only our "self-confidence" but also our "will to dominate."[9] American society is marked by self-indulgence, a wasting work ethic, raging criminality, antisocial behavior, disrespect for authority, drug use, family breakdown, poor educational performance, and a general erosion of personal trust. He naturally asks if anything can be done to reverse these woeful trends.

"The Nineties," he claims, "have seen the eruption of a global identity crisis."[10] In characteristically different styles, Westerners and non-Westerners alike seek compelling answers to the crucial question: "Who are we?" For many other peoples, this quest for new bearings follows the dismantling of age-old village communities and local traditions. Driving such traumatic transformations are massive rural-urban migrations, the unprecedented demands of modern occupational roles, and the spread of transnational markets and telecommunications. But for the inhabitants of the United States (and of Western Europe), loss of a coherent self-understanding and sense of purpose has a different cause. We are in trouble because, after the flabbergasting disappearance of the Soviet Union, we lack a sustaining and ennobling enmity.

The unexpected implosion of the West's once-great rival was a mixed blessing because we often know who we are "only when we know whom we are against."[11] It is no surprise to hear Huntington, who thrives on controversy, argue that "people define their identity by what they are not," or that "it is human to hate. For self-definition and motivation, people need enemies."[12] If having an enemy gives us a reason for getting out of bed in the morning, then the Western, if not the global, identity crisis may be solvable. That is where the "clash of civilizations" comes in. By identifying our enemies, Huntington hopes to re-enchant the post-Cold War world, to restore our sense of purpose, and of course to raise the prestige of the military in Western societies. Dangerous battlefronts lend clarity, flavor, excitement, and meaning to human existence. Frayed solidarities and dissipated virtues can be recouped, but only with the help of a lethally hostile foe.

Superficially, Huntington's principal thesis, or hypothesis, is a descriptive one. A new age of disharmony is dawning, "an era dominated by ethnic conflict and fault-line wars between groups from different civilizations."[13] The secular optimism of those who believe that mankind is being drawn into peaceful coexistence and mutually beneficial cooperation by the growth of global markets is not just misplaced. It is downright suicidal. The leading actors in this new era, besides the West, will be China (understood to include the East Asian Chinese diaspora) and Islam, "the challenger civilizations,"[14] now resurgent, to our great peril, after centuries of impotence and passivity. (India, Japan and Russia are consigned to supporting roles, South America and Africa have negligible parts.)

China and Islam are not ideological communities, but cultural ones. China is unified by language and tradition as well as race; Islam by religion. They are arrayed against us by "blood and belief, faith and family."[15] Their emergence as major players confirms that "Cold War alignments are giving way to civilizational ones" and that, after the collapse of Communism, "culture replaced ideology as the magnet of attraction and repulsion."[16] With remorseless logic, cultural affinities are weaving new alliances between countries once at odds, while cultural remoteness is loosening alliances cemented only by ideology, and even tearing nations apart.

The most obvious example of this massive reorientation of peoples from doctrine to kinship is Yugoslavia, a society pasted together by Titoism that fractured into an array of mutually hostile tribes. To prepare to face our challengers, Americans and Western Europeans must reinforce our own "economic and political integration."[17] This renewed Atlanticism must be based not on universal principles, but on shared cultural roots and Western particularism.

Fatalism or Hope?

Eccentrically, Huntington interprets the approaching confrontation between the West and its new arch-enemies through the lens of what we might have thought was a superannuated philosophy of history. "All civilizations," he tells us, "go through similar processes of emergence, rise, and decline."[18] Being at the "peak" of power is unnerving, because it suggests that the United States and Western Europe will soon begin a preordained downward skid. Huntington may not actually believe that analogies with the biological life-cycle help to explain social change, but he writes as if he does. Westerners are now in a "golden age," marked by "low birthrates and aging populations."[19] Societies such as ours "do not have the youthful vigor to be expansionistic and offensively oriented."[20] By contrast, "when civilizations first emerge," and apparently when they re-emerge, "their people are usually vigorous, dynamic, brutal, mobile and expansionist."[21] A "maturing civilization" such as Western Europe is especially vulnerable to "surging civilizations," of the Islamic or Chinese types, full of piety and vinegar.[22]

This strange argument is made even stranger by Huntington's tendency to waver perplexingly between voluntarism and determinism. On the one hand, he toys with the philosophy of fate, admitting that, for the West, the bloom is off the rose, and suggesting that we discreetly withdraw into a gated community, like an old man who does not want to share, clamping down on immigration, and perhaps abandoning Asia to Chinese hegemony. This is a plausible strategy, he suggests, because the other great civilizations, too, may be attracted to global apartheid, to a system of mutually respectful spheres of influence in which "global power is obsolete."[23] The prospect is not very alluring. The decrepit West, he counsels sagely, must "learn to navigate the shallows, endure the miseries, moderate its ventures, and safeguard its culture."[24] In other, feistier passages, however, he insists that "nothing is inevitable."[25] Under more vigorous leadership, the United States could resume its role as "the leader

of Western civilization" and, most wondrously, given the moral deterio-
ration of our maturing societies and the purported obsolescence of global
power, the West as a whole could "reconfirm its position as the leader
whom other civilizations follow and imitate."[26]

This back-and-forth between hope of revival and fear of decline,
between appeals for renewed global leadership and for modest regional
retreat, seriously blurs the policy implications of the book. Do dismissive references to "the vacuousness of Western universalism"[27] mean that
we should give up on bodies such as the United Nations? The answer is
unclear. His waffling on the most desirable China policy is another case
in point. To the question whether the United States should attempt to
maintain military superiority in Asia, he answers both yes and no. In a
defeatist mood, he suggests that we should sidestep the hurtling train and
abandon any attempt to contain China: "a major war could occur if the
United States challenges China's rise as the hegemonic power in Asia."[28]
In other passages, when spoiling for a Western "revival," he urges us "to
restrain the development" of China's "conventional and unconventional
military power."[29] Finally, in a split-the-difference passage, he argues that
both allowing China to become the dominant power in Asia and trying to
prevent this would involve "major costs and risks" for the United States.[30]

Huntington's simultaneous embrace of hope and despair, voluntarism
and fatalism, prevents the main contours of his argument from coming
clearly into focus. Why, for instance, does he allow the blanket category "Islam" to obscure inner divisions between Arabs and non-Arabs,
or between Shiites and Sunnis? Why does he lump together within a single homogeneous civilization such disparate societies as, say, Indonesia,
Pakistan, Iran, and Algeria? The answer is that he finds homogeneity
because he is looking for homogeneity. He is less interested in describing
Islam with fidelity, in short, than in depicting it as a hair-raising, intransi-
gent foe of the West. If he wanted to generalize about the "basic attitude"
toward the West detectable in the non-Western world, might he not have
mentioned "ambivalence"? Is not the West hated and admired in much
the same measure and for much the same reasons? Is it not hated partly
because it is admired? This ambivalence is almost inaudible in *The Clash
of Civilizations*. To bring it up would muffle the clash.

Do Cultures Have "Souls"?

Huntington's catch-all categories also reflect his fanciful essentialism. Each
great civilization, he believes or pretends to believe, has an inner nature
(Spengler would have called it a "soul") that it is destined to unfold. "The

essence of Western civilization is the Magna Carta."[31] The essence of Islam, by contrast, is "Muslim bellicosity,"[32] apparently hard-wired into Islamic societies by the warrior example of Mohammed and the glorious traditions of conquest and expansion. "Wherever one looks along the perimeter of Islam, Muslims have problems living peaceably with their neighbors."[33] Similarly, "Muslims make up about one-fifth of the world's population but in the Nineties they have been far more involved in intergroup violence than the people of any other civilization."[34] And, "Confucians, Buddhists, Hindus, Western Christians and Orthodox Christians have less difficulty adapting to and living with each other than any one of them has in adapting to and living with Muslims."[35] Although he was lambasted for his earlier statement, in the *Foreign Affairs* article, that "Islam has bloody borders," Huntington remains unrepentant: "Islam's borders *are* bloody," he repeats, adding uncompromisingly, "and so are its innards."[36]

The Islamic militants who are often said to approve of Huntington's original article, recognize that this tough talk is not at all an expression of contempt. For he is not particularly squeamish about cut-throat aggression. Indeed, he often seems to admire Islam's driving-aspiring culture and "youthful"[37] barbarian energy. This is not surprising, since every good soldier desires a worthy foe. When Islamic leaders "see Western culture as materialistic, corrupt, decadent and immoral,"[38] Huntington can only nod in approval. Finally, he cannot consistently regret Islam's hostility towards us if it sharpens the battlefronts that will help us get a grip on ourselves.

The idiosyncrasy of this essentialist approach is most colorful in Huntington's discussion of "torn countries." The idea of a torn country – a category meant to be simultaneously descriptive and normative – apparently derives from Nikolai Danilevsky and other 19th-century slavophile writers who attacked Westernizing tsars for betraying Russia's soul. Spengler picked up the idea, objecting to the way Weimar's architects traduced Germany's soul by trying to anglicize an essentially un-English people. Now Huntington comes along, resuscitates this slavophile perspective, and applies it to Turkey.

Amazingly, he describes Kemal Atatürk as a betrayer of his country, as a defector and apostate, a Westernizer suffering from false consciousness, who plunged his countrymen into "cultural schizophrenia"[39] by trying to Europeanize an essentially Islamic people. Such attempts to repress one's own cultural heritage and replace it with Western imports are uniformly "destined to fail."[40] The rhetoric here is remarkably unguarded: "At some point, Turkey could be ready to give up its frustrating and humiliating role as a beggar pleading for membership in the West and to resume its much more impressive and elevated historical role as the principal Islamic interlocutor and antagonist of the West."[41] A truly great leader, he says, could "remake Turkey from a torn country into a core state" – which "might be desirable."[42]

This discussion of Atatürk's role in Turkish history, flawed by an implausible essentialism, acquires further unfortunate connotations in the context of Huntington's repeated insistence that those who do not cluster along civilizational lines will be cruelly punished for their trespasses. The failure of American foreign policy in the 1990s, for instance, was due to Clinton's inability to recognize "cultural and civilizational tides." "Those who do not recognize fundamental divides . . . are doomed to be frustrated by them."[43] The murders of Sadat and Rabin, two criss-crossers of civilizational dividing lines, are invoked in support of this proposition. If Australia gives priority to its trading relations with non-kin, it will suffer the fate of all those who defy the logic of things, becoming, in Lee Kwan Yew's charming phrase, "the new white trash of Asia."[44] And Huntington has this to say about cosmopolitan writers of non-Western origins who subscribe to the thesis that all the world's cultures are being gradually amalgamated into a single global super-civilization:

> As is often the case with marginals or converts, among the most enthusiastic proponents of the single civilization idea are intellectual migrants to the West, such as [V.S.] Naipaul and Fouad Ajami, for whom the concept provides a highly satisfying answer to the central question: Who am I? "White man's nigger," however, is the term one Arab intellectual applied to these migrants. If you are disloyal to your roots, you will pay the price.[45]

Approaching Turkey with this in mind, Huntington lays it down that the European Union is and should be a Christian club, and that NATO "should recognize the essential meaninglessness of having as members two states each of which is the other's worst enemy and both of which lack cultural affinity with the other members."[46] That Huntington's maps are somewhat eccentric is already clear from the fact that, following their guidelines, today's corrupt, criminalized, and anarchical Russia would be made "responsible for order"[47] in Romania and Bulgaria, and perhaps even in Serbia and Greece. More ominous is the suggestion that, to bolster the West's inward coherence, we need to slam the door in Turkey's face. Such a rebuff, a matter of choice not of destiny, would have serious consequences, as scores of commentators have protested; responsibility for delivering it should certainly not be hidden behind the search for an interesting new way of looking at international politics.

Noncultural Explanations

Thankfully, Huntington's detailed analyses do not follow the lines laid down by his broad generalizations. For instance, he does not explain Islamic violence, in the manner of Molière's doctor, by invoking the Islamic tendency to violence. Instead, in a perfectly conventional manner, he adduces a wide array of noncultural factors, especially "the demographic explosion in Muslim societies and the availability of large numbers of often unemployed males between the ages of fifteen and thirty."[48] He also stresses, in several engaging chapters, the ways in which modernization paradoxically reinforces neo-tribalist developments. Economic growth means that local traditions have been sapped at the same time as frustrated young job-seekers, "crowded into decaying and often primitive slums,"[49] are being bombarded by "cassettes, compact discs and videos glorifying Islamic history,"[50] delivered by an "Islamist international"[51] shamelessly exploiting Western technological advances in communications and transportation. A rise in literacy also increases the susceptibility of the young to social mobilization. Conscience money paid by oil sheikhs to Islamic radicals, training offered by Afghan veterans, and the destruction of secular opposition groups by myopic political rulers are also invoked but none of these factors has much to do with the essence, or inner destiny, of Muslim culture.

The only vaguely plausible thing Huntington has to say along essentialist lines concerns the relation between Islamic culture and state weakness. State incapacity, he argues, plays an important role in the spread of fundamentalism because, whenever political incumbents default on their most basic duties, Islamic organizations swoop down to play an active role in a whole range of areas, from education to sanitation, from care of the elderly to emergency relief. He might have added that incumbents who are themselves too disorganized or corrupt to provide these rudimentary public services may find it tempting to offer cheap dignity to frustrated citizens by indulging in anti-Western tirades and heaping blame on the Great Satan.

Even if we agree, however, that government incompetence provides fertile soil for fundamentalist militancy, we still need to explain that incompetence, and here Huntington points to the culture of Islam. Islamic nation-states are so consistently weak, he claims, because Islamic peoples are culturally indisposed to honor and obey state authorities. Even if honest and public-spirited leaders emerged, they could not secure mass support simply by providing vital social services, because the "loyalty intensity curve" in Muslim societies is culturally programmed to be U-shaped.[52] That is to say, Muslims tend to be intensely loyal to family-clan-tribe and to culture-religion-empire, but only weakly attached to their nation-states. One reason for this is the debilitating colonial rule which the West imposed on Islamic lands, but the deeper reason is that "the idea of sovereign nation-states is incompatible with belief in the sovereignty of Allah and the primacy of the *ummah*."[53] Such an analysis is erroneous, but it is at least more complicated and interesting than the suggestion that Islam is *essentially* violent and aggressive.

How Conflicts Shape Cultures

None of Huntington's arguments has arched more scholarly eyebrows than his equivocal suggestion that cultural similarities produce co-operation while cultural differences produce conflict. "People rally to those with similar ancestry, religion, language, values and institutions, and distance themselves from those with different ones."[54] Russia and Ukraine will never fight one another, he predicts, because they are religious and linguistic kin. China-Taiwan trade has been "greatly facilitated by 'shared Chineseness' and the mutual trust that resulted from it."[55] Just so, the European Union is economically successful because it is the legitimate heir of Christendom. Birds of a feather flock together, whereas relations between peoples of different civilizations are bedeviled by missed cues, jarring styles, feelings of superiority, and fear.

   This thesis is untenable on theoretical grounds alone. Similarity is not a relationship, and will not spawn a relationship without propinquity, interaction, mutual advantage, shared enemies, or widely accepted narratives chronicling common origins, sufferings, or opportunities. Likewise, difference alone will not generate hostilities without economic exploitation, territorial rivalry, or historical grievances. In addition, similarity and difference are a matter of interpretation and standpoint. Examined microscopically, no two snowflakes are identical while, observed from a distance, Protestants and Catholics in Northern Ireland appear indistinguishable. Thus, it is natural that "in the past Christians killed fellow Christians,"[56] for similarities mutate into differences, and vice versa, depending on shifting points of view.

   A common culture cannot be the main reason for the relative success of the European Union, moreover, since Europeans shared a common culture when they were cutting each other to ribbons. Faced with this obvious objection, Huntington rescues the principle that kinship fosters harmony by dusting off his quaint philosophy of history and explaining that, while all civilizations have a warrior phase, Europe has already passed through its period of internal strife and has now attained serenity. Lack of conflict turns out to be produced not by cultural brotherhood but by the "maturing" of Europe and the graying of its populations.

Fortunately, not to say typically, Huntington deals with the many objections to this point by ladling them obligingly into his book. Having first insisted that similarities do engender cooperation, he lurches into reverse, arguing that they do not, any more than differences stir conflicts. The dizzyingly mobile nature of his thought on this matter was already clear in the 1993 essay, where he wrote that "differences in culture and religion create differences over policy issues," only to add that "differences do not necessarily mean conflict."[57] In the book, the bulk of his analysis – as opposed to his memorable one-liners – follows the second, more plausible assumption, showing that the real sources of conflict lie in the struggle for control over territory, sea lanes, resources, markets, and power.

In another incautious generalization, he declares that today "cultural identity is what is most meaningful to most people."[58] This statement is worth pondering. Why would he want to specify, in such an undiscriminating way, the one loyalty that he knows in advance will be predominant everywhere, without inserting a qualifying reference to shifting contexts and situations? After all, human beings can easily manage a plurality of loyalties – to family, friends, school, locality, region, profession, class, political party, religion, linguistic community, nation-state, and so forth – without melting down psychologically or succumbing to multiple personality disorder. There is nothing particularly natural about sacrificing a plurality of allegiances on the altar of one ultimate identification. Indeed, a singular loyalty is likely to eclipse all others only in situations of crisis or emergency – a war, a natural disaster, a strike, a jihad, or an illness.

Huntington knows this perfectly well, which is why he focuses so intently on the clash of civilizations. In an intense confrontation pitting "them" against "us," "multiple identities fade and the identity most meaningful in relation to the conflict comes to dominate."[59] This is a useful admission. Identity does not give rise to conflict. On the contrary, intense and lethal conflict causes one salient identity to eclipse all others. Far from being the natural outgrowths of underlying cultural similarities and differences, friend/enemy relations can be used by political entrepreneurs (such as Osama bin Laden) to highlight or play down cultural affinities, depending on the mobilizational demands of the current situation. The unchanging "souls" of distinct civilizations are neither here nor there. Solidarity stems not from shared devotion to a common culture but from shared fear of a common enemy. To accept this thesis is to repudiate Huntington's entire framework. Cultural similarities do not guarantee peace any more than cultural differences necessitate war. The idea that friend/enemy relations are a matter of political choice, not historical destiny, although it contradicts the very idea of an inevitable clash of civilizations, is implicit in Huntington's own hope that civilizational conflict can be harnessed to solve the great identity crisis of our time.

What attitudes towards East Asia does Huntington's theory of civilizational blocs dictate? Whatever the importance of Japan, Taiwan, and South Korea as trading partners, he explains, the inexorable logic of homogeneous groupings requires us to reject "the elusive and illusory calls to identify the United States with Asia."[60] For "the fundamental cultural gap between Asian and American societies precludes their joining together in a common home."[61] In this context, he warms over a few stereotypes about the Chinese and other Asians being nonmoralistic, subtle, indirect, and devious. In any face-off with such cold and cunning poker players, Americans will be push-overs. Because of the American penchant to identify "good" relations with "friendly" relations, the United States is at a considerable disadvantage in competing with Asian societies who identify "good" relations with ones that produce victories for them. To the Asians, American concessions are not to be reciprocated, they are to be exploited. Without scruples or hypocrisy, moreover, "China has defined the United States as its principal enemy."[62] Huntington is not sure if the United States has what it takes to return the favor.

Yet there is ultimately something discordant about Huntington's insistence on "the fundamental cultural differences between Asian and American civilizations."[63] What makes it unconvincing, oddly enough, is the approval with which he greets East Asian theories of the decline of the West. He largely agrees with East Asian assertions that the West "is culturally and socially decadent."[64] Just as he seems to admire Islamic culture for mobilizing youthful aggression, Huntington seems to admire Lee Kwan Yew for denouncing Western secularism and egoism. At the very least, he cites Singapore as an exemplar of order, discipline, honor, diligence, sense of mission, abnegation, communitarianism, family responsibility, high savings rates, hard work, and group effort – of everything, in short, that America lacks and needs. Long ago, in *The Soldier and the State* (1957), Huntington extolled West Point as a glorious remnant of

Sparta surviving amid the Babylon of petty Yankee commercialism and bourgeois squalor. Forty years later, West Point has been replaced by Singapore, a city-state epitomizing the Asian virtues of authority, hierarchy, the supremacy of state over society, and the supremacy of society over the individual. Even those who think of Singapore less as an authentic expression of Asia's indigenous authoritarian capitalism than as a piece of real estate rented by foreign financial institutions, will be struck by the sincerity of Huntington's sympathy with Lee Kwan Yew's theory of Western decline – a sympathy which, by demonstrating the essential porosity of cultural divides, completely counter to Huntington's theory, vindicates the hope that individuals from one civilization can understand the underlying philosophies and ways of life of another.

On a less personal level, despite his talk about cultural incommensurabilities between Asian and American civilizations and his repeated suggestion that the distrust they spawn will naturally lead to hostility, Huntington eventually settles down to discussing future relations between the two great powers in utterly conventional terms: "The underlying cause of conflict between America and China is their basic difference over what should be the future balance of power in East Asia."[65] It may be true that "the Asia of economic sunshine will generate an Asia of political shadows, an Asia of instability and conflict," but civilizational differences are not decisive here since, whatever their cultural affiliations, "the emergence of new great powers is always highly destabilizing."[66]

We also learn, eventually, that even during the coming clash countries will not be slavishly positioned along civilizational lines. Conflicts within civilizations will remain just as common as alliances across civilizations. Drug cartels already routinely cooperate across civilizational lines. For similar reasons, weapons-selling nations and weapons-purchasing ones will continue to stretch out "arms across the sea." Political leaders and military strategists will seldom sacrifice national security to diffuse civilizational identifications felt by subject groups that are easy to manipulate and silence. Foreign policy will not cater to the psychological needs of confused citizens. The great powers have "their own more diversified interests"[67] to look after and, when forming alliances, will give kinship a backseat to perceived advantage. Islam and China, for instance, have less in common culturally than either has with the West, but they are busy forging a long-term alliance, in Huntington's view, because "in politics a common enemy creates a common interest."[68]

After posting eye-catching but implausible headlines, in short, Huntington introduces his reasonable and even uncontentious arguments in smaller typeface. But his repeated stand-downs make his book difficult to criticize by obscuring its principal claims. Seldom has so much old wine been poured into a new paradigm. We can nonetheless pursue his argument a step further if we examine how badly he stumbles when trying to identify the moral foundation of a renewed Atlantic alliance. Since the age of ideology is over, the West must recreate its coherence on the basis of its shared cultural heritage. Yet what is the civilizational core on which Huntington pins his hopes? One thing is sure, it cannot be an ideology. He mentions Christianity in passing, but quickly drops the subject, perhaps because secular Europeans and religious Americans are not likely to be united by faith. He also mentions some secular residues of Christianity, but when he inventories them in detail they turn out to be none other than liberty, democracy, individualism, equality before the law, constitutionalism, and private property. What this amounts to, of course, is liberalism, a thin creed not a thick culture – the same old ideology, plucked inexplicably from the waste-bin of history, that once united the West against Soviet Communism.

Is Liberalism the Tribal Culture of the West?

Huntington's identification of liberalism and democracy as the core of Western culture is implausible for many reasons. His claim that "the West was the West long before it was modern,"[69] for instance, also implies that the West was the West long before it was liberal. Thus, even if the West has an essence, it makes no sense to identify that essence with "Western concepts of human rights, liberalism and democracy"[70] or, for that matter, with Magna Carta. Historically, there is nothing remotely non-Western about religious intolerance or depriving racial minorities of basic rights, though these practices are blatantly illiberal. The pre-liberal West and the non-liberal West are still Western. The culture of the antebellum South was perfectly Western, although in good measure illiberal; the same can be said about important strands of German culture before 1945. Fascism is no less European than liberal democracy. Not only Savonarola and Torquemada, but Hitler and Mussolini were Western.

Now this is elementary stuff and it would be preposterous to suppose that Huntington is unaware of it, but his scholarly caution apparently yields to his political passion. He is looking for some basis on which the West can forge a unity as intense as that created by (what he sees as) the homogeneous monoculturalism of China or Islam. But the United States, at least, does not have the faintest chance of developing political unity on anything but an ideological basis. At this point, therefore, darkness descends:

> In an era in which peoples everywhere define themselves in cultural terms, what place is there for a society without a cultural core and defined only by a political creed? Political principles are a fickle base on which to build a lasting community. In a multicivilizational world where culture counts, the United States could be simply the last anomalous holdover from a fading Western world where ideology counted.[71]

The United States is not a nation-state. Its unity is creedal and only weakly cultural. Indeed, it is a cultural hybrid or perhaps a mishmash, unified only by abstract principles acceptable to people who have come from around the world.

As a struggle between "two superpowers, each of which defined its identity by its ideology and neither of which was a nation-state in the traditional European sense,"[72] the Cold War gave the United States an honorable role. As a struggle between two ideologically unified multi-cultural states, the Cold War played to America's strengths. The United States is not sufficiently tribal to deal in an appropriate style with the coming geotribalism, however, just as the West as a whole has become too multicultural to confront successfully such monocultural powerhouses as China and Islam. So how does Huntington deal with this situation? What alternative does he offer to pessimism and despair?

His initial proposal is first broached in a remarkable passage at the beginning of the book which cites Herodotus to the effect that Athenians and Spartans, bound by "blood, language, religion, way of life,"[73] will never turn against one another. Read ironically (and how else are we expected to read it?), this passage implies that kin groups, whatever their boasts on ceremonial occasions, will cooperate with each other only so long as terrifying enemies, such as the Persians, are bearing down on them. So Huntington, rather than throwing up his hands, toys with the idea that he can help solidify the Western alliance, however culturally heterogeneous Western societies have now become domestically, by painting Islamic and Chinese threats in lurid colors.

Although not accounting for every oddity in Huntington's analysis, his failed quest for a saving enmity helps to bring a bit of order into the confusion. The book would have been easier to follow, however, if not only this idea but two others had been more openly and critically assessed. First, the disproportional birthrate among Western and non-Western societies and, second, the weakening of nationalism and the nation-state.

Birthrate Wars

For Huntington, writing in the mid-1990s, the war in Bosnia symbolized the coming age, just as the Spanish Civil War, a battle of ideologies, was a symbol of the great age of ideological conflict between Liberalism, Fascism, and Communism. But what is Bosnia for Huntington? We can grasp what he has in mind only when we recall his explanation for the breakdown of Yugoslavia. Its principal cause was not the end of ideology, but something more down-to-earth. Although the intercivilizational wars in the former Yugoslavia had many causes, "probably the single most important factor leading to these conflicts . . . was the demographic shift that occurred in Kosovo,"[74] that is, the drop in the Serbian and the rise in the Albanian proportion of the population. This inversion was not limited to Kosovo, but took place in Bosnia as well. In 1961, according to Huntington's statistics, the Bosnian population was 43 per cent Serb and 26 per cent Muslim, while by 1991 it had become 31 per cent Serb and 44 per cent Muslim. What was going on, to put it crudely, was ethnic cleansing by procreation. When two ethnic groups share a single territory, a high birthrate in one group "induces countervailing responses"[75] in the other. To the slow-motion ethnicide committed against them, he adds less euphemistically, the Serbs responded in kind, not by having babies of their own, but by murdering the babies of their enemies: "Ethnic expansion by one group led to ethnic cleansing by the other. 'Why do we kill children?' one Serb fighter asked in 1992 and answered: 'Because some day they will grow up and we will have to kill them then.' "[76]

Huntington's model "does not sacrifice parsimony to reality,"[77] but the opposite. When human beings do not behave as his theory predicts, instead of modifying his ideas, he demands that people modify their behavior. Or rather, he warns them of dire consequences if they fail to do so. An egregious example of this keep-the-theory-and-change-the-facts approach is his claim that "Western sympathy" for the Bosnian Muslims was a mistake.[78] It was "a noncivilizational anomaly in the otherwise universal pattern of kin backing kin."[79] Like the American decision to help the Israeli Jews, whom Huntington audaciously and eccentrically labels as non-Westerners, the decision to help the Bosnian Muslims violated the most basic precept of the New World Order: blood and treasure should be expended only for civilizational kin. It also revealed that the Americans were dupes. By "wrapping themselves in the victim guise," the

Bosnian Muslims were "able to promote an image of themselves as helpless victims."[80] America's knee-jerk response to "the alleged genocide"[81] was not only a sign of gullibility, it was also a strategic folly, since the Iranians correctly see Bosnia as "the soft underbelly of Europe."[82] Huntington summarizes his complaints: "Pursuing the chimera of a multi-civilizational country, the Clinton Administration denied self-determination to the Serbian and Croatian minorities" – that is, curtailed their campaigns of ethnic cleansing – "and helped to bring into being a Balkan one-party Islamist partner of Iran."[83] What Clinton's foreign policy team failed to grasp was that "the fires of communal identity and hatred are rarely totally extinguished except through genocide" and that "fault-line wars are interminable" unless "one group exterminates the other."[84] No surprise, therefore, that in Bosnia, "the peace process was also helped by the ethnic cleansing which occurred."[85]

To understand Huntington's unusual approach to Bosnian-style ethnic cleansing, it helps to consider his discussion of Western colonialism. When the West was still young and vital, not to mention psychologically willing to exploit the Industrial Revolution for military gain, it conquered the globe by "applying organized violence."[86] Europe was so successful in this bloody business that "for four hundred years intercivilizational relations consisted of the subordination of other societies to Western civilization."[87] Indeed, "in 1920, the West directly ruled about 25.5 million square miles or close to half the Earth's earth."[88] Western expansion came in two basic forms. Non-Western peoples "were either subjected to rule from Europe or, except in South Africa, were virtually decimated by Western settlers."[89] The second form of colonialism recalls the Serb fighter's attitude towards Bosnian Muslim children. In colonized lands, such as the United States, where they "obliterated other peoples,"[90] Westerners are still today in proud command. Decolonization was not an option because the indigenous were almost all wiped out. By contrast, wherever they tried to dominate native peoples, while allowing them physically to survive, the descendants of Europeans have been humiliated, marginalized, or tossed out on their ears.

This contrast between two styles of European colonialism – between successful ethnic cleansing and failed ethnocracy – remains shadowy and unelaborated in the book. Indeed, it has to be pieced together from scattered asides. Bringing it into focus helps us penetrate one of the book's great mysteries – namely, what Huntington means by cultural competition. The struggle to control territory is understandable, but what is a struggle over values? What will winners win and losers lose in such a contest? Huntington refers repeatedly to half-hearted Western attempts to "impose" human rights on various corrupt, insolvent, incompetent, indifferent, and abusive regimes around the world. But while it generates an impressive flow of words, transnational human rights enforcement is not exactly a preponderant factor in global politics. Cultural competition might also conceivably involve Hollywood, McDonald's, rap music, Disneyland, and so forth. Huntington dismisses "Westoxification,"[91] the global metastasis of American popular culture, as of negligible importance, however. So what will the cultural competition he anticipates be about?

When applying the life-cycle metaphor to entire civilizations, remember, Huntington distinguishes between high-birthrate and low-birthrate societies. The former are "young"; the latter are "mature." Thus, even though "the West is overwhelmingly dominant now and will remain number one in terms of power and influence well into the 21st century," it has to fear the challenger civilizations. China and Islam pose such lethal threats because of the West's "stagnating populations."[92] Without saying that unchecked population growth is a sign of social vibrancy, Huntington certainly implies that, so far as cultural competition is concerned, an oversupply of the young is better than an abundance of the old.

The West now accounts for 13 percent of the world's population, 24 percent of its territory and 50 percent of world gross economic product. This might seem like a favorable ratio (especially in an age of high-tech weaponry, when mass armies no longer give an overwhelming military advantage), but Huntington appears not to think so. In a curiously worded passage, suggesting that overpopulation in the non-Western world is an arrow aimed at the heart of the West, he delivers the following bad news: in 2020, "the West will probably control about . . . 10 per cent of the total world population (down from 48 per cent)."[93] Even a casual perusal of demographic trends, in short, reveals the insidious way in which the West is being besieged.

Intensified interaction with non-Europeans, according to Huntington, has caused Frenchmen, Italians, and Germans increasingly to see themselves as cultural kin. To say that European identity has recently been heightened is to say that Arab and African immigration has loosed racism on Europe and fueled the rise of anti-immigrant parties. Faced with unsavory alternatives, the French have come to look with welcoming eyes on white and Catholic immigrants from Poland, who earlier seemed like aliens. Huntington also suggests that the more than 13 million Muslims who live in Western Europe today constitute unwelcome shadow members of the EU, impossible to integrate into the host cultures. It is totally unclear if, faced with such alien floods, Western societies will be able to maintain their "cultural, social and ethnic integrity."[94] And uneven population growth is a factor globally as well as domestically. Although Christians make up 30 per cent of the world's population today and Muslims make up 20 percent, the percentages will be reversed by the year 2025. In the contest between the world's two proselytizing religions, Mohammed wins out. This is because Christianity spreads primarily by conversion, while Islam spreads by conversion and reproduction. Spain's Maghrebi neighbors breed ten times faster than the Spanish and have one-tenth their per capita GNP. Fifty percent of births in Brussels are to Arabs. And don't even mention the Chinese.

Running like a red thread through *The Clash of Civilizations*, in other words, is demographic anxiety or birthrate envy. Every time we look in the mirror, we have shrunk. This is the Kosovo syndrome on a global scale. It is what Huntington's cultural competition is ultimately about and, in this race, the "maturing" civilizations are limping hopelessly behind. To prove that "the gap is narrowing"[95] between the West and the Rest, he notes that infant mortality continues to fall in non-Western societies. As an aspect of cultural competition, the comparative survival rate of newborns, too, is a zero-sum game. For the population of the West now comes in a global fourth – ranked below the Chinese, the Hindus and the Muslims. (The ranking here would have come out differently, incidentally, if he had included Latin America as part of the West.)

Just as Europe has an Islamic fifth column, so America has a Hispanic one.[96] As a result, America is now risking "cultural suicide."[97] Its door swung open to non-European ethnicities in 1965 when traditional barriers to Asian and Latin American immigration were removed. In the Fifties, two-thirds of immigrants into the United States were white Europeans, whereas now only 15 per cent are white Europeans. This is why the United States risks becoming "a cleft country."[98] A cleft country is any nation containing sizeable populations from different civilizational families. The concept itself, which is again both descriptive and normative, implies that countries of this unfortunate sort are schizophrenic and their situation unnatural as well as inherently unstable. Cultural heterogeneity may even put a nation's territorial integrity at risk, especially if the country sits astride a fault-line separating one major civilization from another. Infiltrated by non-Westerners, the now multicultural United States may be about to lose its identity. The "continuous Mexican society stretching from Yucatan to Colorado" poses the ultimate threat.[99] If its Hispanic inhabitants "continue to adhere to and propagate the values, customs, and cultures of their home societies,"[100] revanchist sentiments may eventually arise, and Mexico may reclaim the lands the United States seized by organized violence in the 19th century. Huntington takes the cultural category, "Hispanic," and colors it racially. During the next half-century, he informs us, the U.S. population will become "almost 50 percent white and 25 percent Hispanic," as if "white," too, were a civilizational term.[101] This slip of the pen recalls a phrase that Huntington cites from Lee Kwan Yew: "people feel a natural empathy for those who share their physical attributes."[102] In that spirit, he introduces a stunning map, labeled "The United States: A Cleft Country?,"[103] which vividly illustrates alien encroachment and the shrinking hegemony of Western culture across the country. Without a word of commentary, this map classifies black Americans among non-Western peoples.

The American sin is the sin of hybridity. Go to California or to New York City, and what you find is astounding ethnic co-existence and intermingling. The Americans supported the Bosnian Muslims, defying Huntington's consanguinity principle, because America is palpably a multicultural country and its policy-makers believe implicitly that a country can be both culturally heterogeneous and politically well-organized. This is a naive assumption, says Huntington, for "history shows that no country so constituted can long endure as a coherent society."[104] Countries with large numbers of peoples of different civilizations are candidates for dismemberment. So what is in store for the United States?

On the one hand, Huntington urges us to reaffirm the basic values of Western civilization. On the other, he urges us to abandon our universalism and settle comfortably into amoral familialism, elevating kinship above principle. Common allegiance to Enlightenment principles provides an unstable basis for neo-tribalism in the West. These two bits of advice are not consistent. How can the United States, in particular, reaffirm its identity as a liberal country if it jettisons the principle of tolerance for diversity and openness to strangers? In any case, there is no realistic alternative. It is far too late. America cannot now be reconstituted on the basis of common ancestry and a shared cultural heritage, no matter how cleverly it manages immigration and assimilation. An existential threat from a lethal enemy may force another nation to rediscover shared ethnicity as a source of solidarity under siege. This cannot happen in the United States. Multiculturalism is by now America's inescapable fate.

The alternative to a universal world civilization, which Huntington mocks, is not a neat division of the planet into homogeneous cultural groupings – spoons and forks in separate drawers – but interminglings and syncretisms and restless diasporas which, thanks to technology, keep in constant touch with their countries of origin. Western societies are magnets for members of all the world's civilizations not because their guard is down or because they are too debilitated by the ideology of "the open society" to protect themselves from infiltration. Immigrants flow westwards because the West is rich and offers jobs.

New Dark Ages

Here we encounter another latent theme, and a second source of Huntington's pessimism: the increasing weakness of nationalism and the nation-state. The best way to approach this subject is through the wholly unexpected concluding section, where *The Clash of Civilizations* begins to sound like a UNICEF brochure. In the last few pages, Huntington pleads for "understanding and co-operation among the political, spiritual and intellectual leaders of the world's major civilizations."[105] This could be read simply as an elaboration of the idea that "the world will be ordered on the basis of civilizations or not at all."[106] Although no common or universal civilization seems likely to emerge, a modus vivendi can be worked out among the great civilizations; the planet can be partitioned into territorially demarcated spheres of influence. An "international order based on civilizations"[107] would, on this understanding, require various forms of co-operation, especially border management and the disciplining of border states, because the great civilizational precincts would no doubt flare dangerously at the edges.

Huntington's final pages are much more dramatic than this, however, for they are motivated by the view that Civilization itself is in jeopardy: "On a worldwide basis Civilization seems in many respects to be yielding to barbarism, generating the image of an unprecedented phenomenon, a global Dark Ages, possibly descending on humanity."[108] At such a juncture, we must surely do something more radical than establishing a modus vivendi and superintending hot frontiers between rival civilizations. Instead, "peoples in all civilizations should search for and attempt to expand the values, institutions and practices they have in common with peoples of other civilizations."[109] After three hundred pages of confrontationalism, this call for reconciliation and harmony comes from out of the blue.

True, Huntington does not abandon his psychological premise that solidarity presupposes enmity. Humanity as a whole has an enemy of sorts – namely, "transnational criminal mafias, drug cartels and terrorist gangs violently assaulting civilization."[110] Even so, his plea for discovering commonalities across cultures throws the reader off balance. Why such a dramatic volte face? Has Huntington concluded that an international order based on civilizations, which the bulk of the book presents as a solution to the world's woes, will not only fail to protect us from a new barbarism but will actually deepen the darkness descending on mankind? It is the only plausible explanation.

A global identity crisis might conceivably be solved by homogeneous groupings, but such an arrangement will not solve a further problem, the "global crisis of governance."[111] Huntington's earlier statement that we are "moving into an era in which multiple and diverse civilizations will interact, compete and accommodate each other"[112] implies that civilizations are capable of action. Needless to say, this is a dubious proposition. A decent life for individual human beings and their families depends, first of all, on legitimate political authority. Only states, not civilizations, can govern human societies effectively. Only states, not civilizations, can govern societies decently. Yet for Huntington, the same economic forces that have gradually eroded loyalty to locality are now eroding loyalty to the nation-state. The identification of individuals with their nation-state, the allegiance of citizens to their political rulers, is everywhere weakening. While not always made explicit, this is one of the basic premises of *The Clash of Civilizations*. Like demographic anxiety, it provokes Huntington's unrelieved gloom.

In the West, "the nation-state has been the apex of political loyalty,"[113] eclipsing narrower and broader loyalties. Not surprisingly, the end of the age of Western domination is accompanied by the rise of regionalism and the enfeebling of the nation-state. Reflecting on this theme, Huntington remarks that "state governments have in considerable measure lost the ability to control the flow of money in and out of their country and are having increasing difficulty controlling the flow of ideas, technology, goods and people."[114] One cause or consequence of this weakening is the growing rootlessness of political élites, symbolized by devernacularization, or the tendency of indigenous governing classes to speak English, even when it is unintelligible to their constituents or subjects. Rulers around the world apparently identify and socialize increasingly with a tiny international peer group while losing contact with the people they are supposed to govern: "élites of non-Western societies are often better able to communicate with Westerners and each other than with the people of their own society."[115]

Growing popular distrust in government is not unrelated to the identification of peoples with transnational religions, on which Huntington lays such stress. Today's "global revival of religion"[116] is the flipside of a global retreat of citizenship. The fading of national identification is reflected in the fact that, today, the dominant identity of most people in the world "almost always is defined by religion"[117] – that is, by a diffuse cultural membership that does not coincide with any politically organized community. When Huntington says that "in the modern world, religion is a central, perhaps the central, force that motivates and mobilizes people,"[118] he implies that national loyalty is on the wane. Again: "As the world moves out of its Western phase, the ideologies which typified late Western civilization decline, and their place is taken by religions and other culturally based forms of identity and commitment."[119] Among the now obsolete ideologies once typical of the West is nationalism. Islam is so virulently anti-Western, and so inhospitable to Western values, because it inclines believers to a powerful "rejection of the powers that be and the nation-state."[120]

But the decline of nationalism and the nation-state will spell the end of Civilization *tout cour*. That, it seems to me, is Huntington's real, but only vaguely adumbrated, claim. How else explain his incongruous concluding paragraphs urging, hope against hope, the very sort of intercivilizational solidarity that he has repeatedly ruled out? Today's world can be stably governed on the basis of religions or not at all. Today's world cannot be stably organized, or well-governed, on the basis of religions, because religion is an inherently fissile and self-replicating force, that splits internally, leaps anarchically across boundaries, does not submit willingly to discipline, and eschews strategic caution. Hence, global ungovernability lies ahead. In such a hopeless situation, there is nothing left to do but pray.

One feature of the coming Dark Ages is worth singling out. "Islam is a source of instability in the world because it lacks a dominant centre."[121] The basic reason "the absence of one or more core states in Islam"[122] is such a problem is that "the Confucian-Islamic connection"[123] may eventually put a nuclear device at the disposal of fanatics devoted to inflicting harm on the West. "At some point, a few terrorists will be able to produce massive violence and massive destruction."[124] Weapons of mass destruction can be safely placed in the hands of national leaders, presumably, because they can be deterred from using them by a threat of retaliation against their home territory. In the clutches of self-appointed representatives of diffuse cultural entities (Osama bin Laden again comes to mind), nuclear weapons are much more dangerous, because an appropriate formula for deterrence does not exist. His fear of a Confucian–Islamic bomb, in any case, is one factor driving Huntington to see an "international order based on civilizations"[125] not as the last best hope of, but as a lethal threat to, Civilization itself. The concluding somersault, otherwise inexplicable, registers his belated understanding of this fatal dynamic.

However vacillating his arguments, let it be said in conclusion, Huntington is unwaveringly consistent about his ideals. He admires, without

regard to culture, well-disciplined and orderly societies, full of combative energy and proud of their uniqueness. Yet in seeking to deepen and
reinvigorate the Atlantic alliance, he comes up empty-handed. Neither
race nor religion nor the essence of the West can provide a reliable basis
for the social cohesion of Western societies. What then remains is his
proposal to reestablish clear battlefronts against dangerous rivals. If this
program were convincing, civilians, whether culturally similar or different, would be reminded of how they depend on each other in matters
of life and death, not to mention how beholden they are to the discipline, pride, and devotion of military men. But this argument, too, peters
out in self-refutation and hopelessness because, among other reasons, the
new battlefronts he envisages run between diffuse civilizational groupings, incapable of enlisting masses of individuals, in a disciplined fashion,
in sharply focused common projects.

If cultures have no essences to which, in a crisis, they can naturally
revert, and if cultural disentangling is beyond our powers, are we simply
destined to collapse into barbarism and incivility? Huntington thinks so
because he implicitly rules out the possibility of effective state-building in
conditions of cultural pluralism. The rest is a counsel of despair. Neither
civilizational homogeneity nor civilizational confrontation are as attractive as he sometimes makes them seem, however. That they are also stag-
geringly unrealistic is the basic flaw, if not the secret confession, of his
distressed and disturbing book.

Postscript

The principal policy makers who were compelled to improvise a forceful
response to 9/11 woke up earlier that morning with their own stubbornly
entrenched mental frameworks, theoretical commitments, and habits of
thought. Worldviews can be shaken by violent events, but they are unlikely
to be shed at a moment's notice. For all its academic subtleties and ambiguities, Huntington's bold 1996 book helps us understand the preexisting
prisms and ideological schemes through which Bush's top officials came to
view the still-smoldering disaster. This is important, once again, because
the way the war cabinet interpreted 9/11 decisively shaped its tragically
misguided response.

Writing of Vice President Cheney, for example, George Packer reports
that "his speeches after the terror attacks conveyed almost a sense of relief
that here finally was a global enemy on the scale of communism."[126]
That mental habits developed during the Cold War survived the demise
of the Soviet Union is not particularly surprising. In the United States,

the most important residue of that long and bitter conflict was probably the mythical assumption that the world was a battleground between the forces of good and the forces of evil. Although deeply etched in American self-understanding, the "morally clear" idea of an irredeemably wicked global enemy became suddenly useless in 1991. This discarded template was dusted off and put back to work on the afternoon of 9/11, however. Although the Administration's retrieval of a "paradigm lost" may have provided some sort of short-term psychological comfort to officials working under unbearable pressure, it also obscured and distorted, with fatal effects, the Cheney-Rumsfeld group's view of a wholly unprecedented threat.

Eight years before 9/11, as we have seen, Huntington boldly envisaged the possibility that a transnational Islamic enemy could reoccupy the position vacated by the Soviet Union. Searching for a new framework to help orient American policy makers after the Cold War, he even suggested that Americans should transfer their existential enmity from the now-defunct U.S.S.R. to the "upsurging" Muslim world.

Despite his verbal gestures toward Islam as a great and peaceful religion, Bush's policy after 9/11 closely tracked Huntington's "musical chairs" approach to shifting geopolitical threats. According to Gilles Kepel, moreover, this conscious or unconscious fidelity to the Huntingtonian fantasy helps explain why the American response to 9/11 has ended in bloody catastrophe. The impulse to see Islam as America's new global enemy is fatally misleading, Kepel argues, for the simple reason that Islam in no way resembles the Soviet Union. Mecca is not Moscow, al Qaeda is not the KGB, and the Islamic world is much too vast, disorganized, and heterogeneous – and its connectedness to the West much too intimate – to be thrust into the role of a unified enemy, the "evil" adversary of American "goodness." This misalignment of inherited categories and contemporary realities had disastrous consequences, according to Kepel:

> Huntington's clash of civilizations theory facilitated the transfer to the Muslim world of a strategic hostility the West had inherited from decades of Cold War. The parallel drawn between the dangers of communism and those of Islam gave Washington's strategic planners the illusion that they could dispense with analyzing the nature of the Islamist "menace" and could simply transpose the conceptual tools designed to apprehend one threat to the very different realities of the other.[127]

One implication of Kepel's diagnosis is that the Administration did not respond to 9/11 by tearing up the rulebook and radically rethinking

U.S. national-security policy. Rather, it clung obtusely to old patterns of thought and action, blinded by a false analogy between the old enemy and the new.

A second and equally brilliant French student of Islamic radicalism, Olivier Roy, agrees, explaining "the appeal in Muslim societies of Huntington's concept of 'the clash of civilizations' "[128] in roughly the following way. Feeling besieged by Western power and influence, Islamists seek to identify the one true essence of Islam that they need to preserve. Huntingtonians and radical Islamists make the same mistake, according to Roy. They both act as if there were a definitive answer to the question: "What is Islam?" As a result, they read too much unity and coherence into "Islam," treating this vast, sprawling and kaleidoscopically evolving tradition as if it were much simpler and coherent than it is: "Islam is seen as a discrete entity, a coherent and closed set of beliefs, values, and anthropological patterns embodied in a common society, history, and territory, which allows us to use the term as an explanatory concept for almost everything involving Muslims."[129] Centuries of disputation and diversity inside Islam (not to mention the variety of reactions within the Muslim world to 9/11, ranging from celebration to disgust and shame) should suffice to discredit this simplifying approach. Nonetheless, Anatol Lieven and John Hulsman are not wrong when they claim to discern, behind any number of Administration policies, "the lumping together of radically different elements in the Muslim world into one homogeneous enemy camp."[130] The same authors add that "Weak, isolated, and despised regional states with a tiny fraction of America's power are elevated into new equivalents of the Soviet superpower, and mortal threats to American dominance."[131] That such distortions, illusions, and false clarities can stubbornly survive the most withering criticism is just another distressing lesson of the post-9/11 world.

7 | HUMANITARIANISM WITH TEETH

Did liberal defenses of humanitarian intervention and pleas for the United States to assume an aggressively moral role in world affairs abet President Bush's decision to invade Iraq? Yes and no. In her award-winning historical account of Western responses to genocide, Samantha Power shows the limited influence of moral conscience on international politics. The reason why the United States reacted so slowly to the carnage in Bosnia is the same reason why the United States reacted not at all to earlier homicidal rampages, from the massacre of the Armenians in 1915 to the slaughter of the Tutsis in 1994. When its national interest, as the incumbents of the moment conceive it, is at stake, America intervenes abroad. It has seldom if ever intervened merely to relieve the suffering of others. Bosnia and Kosovo are exceptions that prove this rule. As a general principle, the humanitarian desire to relieve suffering and prevent gruesome atrocities will have but faint influence on the decision by great powers, including the United States, to send troops overseas. Nevertheless, a savvy prowar party may successfully employ humanitarian talk both to gull the wider public and to silence potential critics on the liberal side. That is what seems to have happened in the run-up to the Iraq war. Many humanitarian interventionists, with the best of intentions, helped the Bush Administration launch a disastrous and bloody military adventure with almost no public discussion. By making a rhetorically powerful case for casting aside existing decision-making rules and protocols to battle more effectively the "evil" of genocide, they may have emboldened the Bush Administration to fight the "evil" of terrorism outside the Constitution and the law. In a terrifyingly ironic twist, the burning guilt felt by liberals about Rwanda may have played at least a small role in turning Iraq into a second Rwanda, a Mesopotamian killing field that some well-meaning Americans helped prepare with the best intentions in the world.

Idealism is easy to abuse. Terrorist financiers, for example, can hijack *zakat* or religiously obligatory almsgiving. Similarly, bellicose nationalists can invoke humanitarian interventionism as a pretext for military campaigns aimed not at the relief of suffering but rather at displaying America's capacity for awesome destruction. In the 1990s, humanitarian interventionists argued that the battle with "evil" (namely, genocide) permitted and even commanded the United States to act outside the United Nations system and in contravention of international law. They made a strong case that moral ends justified otherwise dubious means. Even if an offending state had not crossed international borders in an act of aggression against its neighbors, invasion could be morally permissible and even obligatory to stop the butchery of innocent citizens inside a tyrannical state. Such a justification would be valid even in the absence of totally reliable evidence, of the sort that would stand up in court, that such butchery was going on. For some American liberals, this argument for the moral obligation to intervene seemed persuasive enough to erase the bitter memory of Vietnam. It reintroduced the idea that America could use its military power to save the weak, repressing what had been a healthy and realistic worry that such interventions unfold unpredictably and could end badly. The humanitarian interventionists, it should also be mentioned, were more concerned to end atrocities than to create democracies. They cultivated a habit of mind more focused on halting sickening crimes than on creating workable institutions once an abusive regime had been removed. Faced with genocide, in any case, they grew used to treating opportunity costs and side effects as matters of limited importance.

The humanitarian interventionists rose to a superficial prominence in the 1990s largely because of a vacuum in U.S. foreign-policy thinking after the end of the Cold War. They may have influenced President Clinton's decisions to intervene in Bosnia and Kosovo. Their influence was small, however, and after 9/11, that influence vanished altogether. For the most part, human beings are capable of sympathizing strongly with the pain of genuine "others" (that is, nonmembers of their own ethnic or sectarian or tribal group) only when they are not in acute distress themselves. Thus, the peaceful interlude of the 1990s provided a congenial environment in which humanitarian interventionism could flourish. Once they were injured by 9/11, as could have been predicted, Americans were no longer in an eleemosynary mood. The humanitarian impulse died out, but the humanitarian interventionist paradigm nevertheless left its mark on the foreign-policy thinking of American liberals.

Above all, it made liberals much more willing than they otherwise would have been to acquiesce, with a clear conscience, in a battle against "evil," including the military invasion of a country that had not attacked its neighbors, conducted outside the UN system, contrary to international law and in the absence of evidence that could stand up in court.

Humanitarian interventionists can certainly not be accused of giving "material support" to the Bush Administration's misbegotten war in Iraq. But they did, willingly or not, lend ideological and psychological support. How did neoconservative writers, such as William Kristol and Lawrence F. Kaplan, make the case for the Iraq war before it began? They copiously cited Amnesty International and Human Rights Watch to demonstrate Saddam's moral monstrosity and "genocidal" behavior.[1] Saddam's tactics in the Iran-Iraq war, they explain, "make up an encyclopedia of Geneva Convention violations."[2] So-called realists who believe that such a government "should be able to do as it pleases within its borders"[3] are morally bankrupt, they imply. Equally despicable, in their view, is the way "the international community turned a blind eye"[4] to chemical weapons attacks on Halabja, Goktaba, and other Iraqi villages.

Neoconservative appeals to the Geneva Conventions and Human Rights Watch may or may not have been cynical and strategic. Kristol and his circle may or may not have been involved in a calculated plot to weaken voices of dissent by pitting the anticruelty sentiments of liberals against their antiwar sentiments. We may never know. The question nevertheless remains: Do the palpably good intentions of the genuine humanitarian interventionists exculpate them totally from the way their approach was subsequently abused?

This question is probably unanswerable. But one factor ought to be considered in trying to make sense of the issue. Any student of history knows that universalistic norms and sentiments are politically weak. This emphatically includes Samantha Power, whose impassioned book on humanitarian intervention I will be examining in this chapter. Sympathy with human suffering has "political legs" only when it is selective. Pertinent examples of one-sided sympathy include sympathy with the Palestinians or sympathy with the Israelis, sympathy with Northern Irish Protestants or sympathy with Northern Irish Catholics, sympathy with the Tamils of Sri Lanka or sympathy with the Sinhalese. These moral and emotional identifications are tribalistic, not universalistic, exclusive, not inclusive. That is why they are politically consequential.

Military interventions occur, sometimes under a false flag of humanitarianism, when the national interests of the intervener are at stake. A common example is the fear of uncontrollable refugee flows from a turbulent zone. Bush's claim to have intervened in Iraq to help the Iraqi people is not only refuted by his evident desire to display American wrath. It is also contradicted by what sometimes seems to be the entire country's inexplicable and morally sickening indifference to the violent deaths, caused by the invasion, of tens and perhaps hundreds of thousands of Iraqis who had never done Americans any harm. The Administration's steadfast refusal to count the number of innocent Iraqi civilians killed under the occupation[5] is made additionally perverse by the claim that everything America does in post-Saddam Iraq is done to benefit the Iraqi people.

Muslim radicals devoted to anti-Western violence advertise their exclusive concern for the well being of fellow Muslims. The real firebrands among them even preach that non-Muslims deserve nothing but death and destruction. For such crazed extremists, the idea of sharing the earth with other human beings whose beliefs and aspirations are different than their own obviously holds no appeal. Even if most Americans do not think in such bloody-minded ways, their moral sentiments are far from being universalistic or humanitarian. True, Americans are not as tribalistic as Huntington would like. When they are attacked, however, they respond like other peoples. Their latent tribalism bursts forth. (This is presumably why Huntington himself finds lethal enmity so appealing.) That Americans, too, can see some humans as more human than others is suggested by the continued reference, to this day, of "the 3,000 Americans" killed on 9/11. Around 350 of those killed on 9/11 were non-Americans. Do they not count? Are Americans reluctant to mix their blood with the blood of non-Americans? Why did no politician stand up and say that Americans take special pride in their country's capacity to shelter refugees, immigrants, and travelers and that we all mourn the tragic deaths of our ill-fated foreign guests? One of the gravest injuries to the country that day was an injury to a national tradition, namely the shattering of the legend that the United States could offer safety to foreigners escaping from political turbulence and violence in the rest of the world. Yet almost no one said so. Why not?

The most plausible reason is that the 9/11 attacks reduced the capacity of most Americans – citizens, journalists and public officials alike – to feel sympathy for the suffering of others, especially for those living on the peripheries of the advanced industrial world. The plotters, perhaps deliberately flashing their cruel equivalent to a matador's cape, excited a desire in the United States not to help but to hurt the weak. The suffering periphery was no longer a distant object for Western almsgiving and rescue. It turned overnight into a target, a place where America could get even, a free-fire zone in which to show that Americans would not take it lying down. Violence from the world's ghetto had crashed through the gates of the wealthy. It tore down more than simply buildings. It dismantled the pillars of humanitarian sympathy, raised high in the 1990s, leaving ruins still smoldering with vindictive desires.

Inaction in the Face of Atrocity

Samantha Power did not set out to explain why liberal protests against the Iraq war inside the United States remained so tame and equivocal for so long. She did not intend to answer the question: Why did the keenest protests against Bush's strategically unnecessary unilateralism come from the internationalist wing of the Republican Party (for example, Brent Scowcroft and James Baker) rather than from the Democrats or the left? But her book, *"A Problem from Hell": America and the Age of Genocide*, has unintentionally provided an important part of the answer.[6]

Power was motivated to study the history of disappointing U.S. responses to genocide by her indignation at the Clinton Administration's belated reaction to mass killings in Bosnia, where she worked in the early 1990s as a young freelance reporter. She was understandably appalled by what happened after the carnage began in 1992: "Despite unprecedented public outcry about foreign brutality, for the next three and a half years the United States, Europe and the United Nations stood by while some 200,000 Bosnians were killed."[7] The book's bitterly ironic title distils her feelings about this period of inaction. It was Warren Christopher, the Clinton Administration's Secretary of State (1993–1997), who called genocide "a problem from hell," implying basically that butchery in the Balkans was a public relations fiasco for the Administration. Callous or not, the West sat on its hands, refusing to undertake even relatively costless gestures, such as knocking out the emplacements around Sarajevo. This particular lapse reminds Power of the Allies' refusal to bomb the rail lines leading into Auschwitz during the Second World War. The analogy is meant to sting. The Western countries that did nothing between 1992 and 1995 were the same ones that, with great solemnity, had opened museum after museum to memorialize the Holocaust and had repeatedly vowed "never again."

To get some distance on the Bosnian catastrophe and to comprehend the dynamics underlying American nonintervention, Power decided to study the history of U.S. responses to atrocities abroad. She returned from her historical quest with a tale of cowardice and mendacity, stretching from the massacre of the Armenians in 1915 to the slaughter of the Tutsi in 1994. Her basic theme is "America's toleration of unspeakable atrocities, often committed in clear view."[8] It turned out that "the United States had never in its history intervened to stop genocide and had in fact rarely even made a point of condemning it as it occurred."[9] She hammers home the coldly calculating nature of U.S. policy with instructive studies of America's passivity in the face of mass murder in Rwanda, Cambodia, and Iraq, as well as Bosnia.

Here is a typical passage: "The Rwandan genocide would prove to be the fastest, most efficient killing spree of the 20th century. In a hundred days, some 800,000 Tutsi and politically moderate Hutu were murdered. The United States did almost nothing to try to stop it."[10] No U.S. troops were dispatched. No UN reinforcements were authorized. No high-level U.S. government meetings were held to discuss nonmilitary options, such as jamming Hutu radio broadcasts. No public condemnations were uttered, and no attempt was made to expel the genocidal government's representative from the UN Security Council, where Rwanda held a rotating seat at the time.

Endeavoring to keep some scintilla of hope alive even while detailing America's refusals to rescue foreign victims of mass slaughter, Power reassures us (and herself) that pessimism of the intellect leaves ample room for optimism of the will. The historical picture she paints is dark almost to the point of misanthropy, however. Basically, one U.S. administration after another stood idly by, feigning ignorance and impotence, while preventable genocide occurred. She freely reports this finding even though it considerably blunts her indictment of the Clinton Administration, whose reluctance to intervene militarily on humanitarian grounds comes across, in the end, as exactly what one would expect.

Not the United States alone, we are also given to understand, but every powerful nation looks first to its economic and strategic interests, embarking on missions of mercy only rarely and unreliably. All responses to injustice are selective, and the principles of selection are invariably tainted with the partiality of power-wielders towards themselves and their friends. During the Cold War, for instance, America eagerly dwelt on Soviet violations of human rights. Today, by contrast, the United States pays scant attention to Moscow's behavior in Chechnya, perhaps out of respect for the two countries' shared confrontation with Islamic terrorism. Power is not the first to discover it, but, in international affairs, the political distinction between "them" and "us" trumps, not to say buries, the moral distinction between just and unjust.

Although quite well known, another example of this shameful but enduring pattern bears retelling. President George H.W. Bush's largesse toward Iraq outdid President Ronald Reagan's, even after Saddam Hussein's murder of a hundred thousand Iraqi Kurds had been amply documented. The credits provided by the first President Bush "freed up currency for Hussein to fortify and modernize his more cherished military assets, including his stockpile of deadly chemicals."[11] In 1989–90, Bush Sr. gave financial support to the bloody-minded dictator in Baghdad not only in order to curry favor with American farmers, eager to peddle their crops abroad, but also because he was thinking of Tehran, that is, because he accepted the platitude that the enemies of his enemies were his friends.

Homicidal autocrats are sometimes toppled, it is true, but rarely by good Samaritans. Power summarizes her dispiriting conclusion this way: "Unless another country acts for self-interested reasons, as was the case when Vietnam invaded Cambodia in 1979, or armed members of the victim group manage to fight back and win, as Tutsi rebels did in Rwanda in 1994, the perpetrators of genocide have usually retained power."[12] What about the decision of the United States and its allies to intervene belatedly in Bosnia and, more rapidly, in Kosovo? According to Power, these are simply the exceptions that prove the rule.

The eventual decision to intervene militarily to halt the Balkan atrocities was the product of a coincidence of factors very unlikely to be repeated. For one thing, might does not even listen to right unless the latter occupies a fashionable address in Washington, D.C. In this case, according to Power, the influential American Jewish lobby, galvanized by televized images of emaciated white men behind barbed wire, set to work and put irresistible domestic pressure on the White House. Not universal morality but group politics cut the ice: "Jewish survivors and organizations put aside Israel's feud with Muslims in the Middle East and were particularly forceful in their criticism of U.S. idleness."[13] The apparent reason why "American Jewish leaders pressed for military action" was that "[t]he Bosnian war brought both a coincidence of European geography and imagery."[14] To emphasize the decisive role played by ethnic particularism, despite all talk of moral universalism, Power adds that the similarity between the images of Bosnia and the images of the Holocaust was an important factor in the creation of the UN war crimes tribunal for the former Yugoslavia.

Apparently, Clinton's desire not to appear weak also influenced his ultimate decision to intervene in the Balkans: "This was the first time in the 20th century that allowing genocide came to feel politically costly for an American President."[15] NATO's dread of losing its raison d'être and Europe's anxieties about refugees combined with such domestic U.S. factors to provide the necessary boost for a policy of humanitarian intervention. Such concerns gave the intervening states, or their leaders at the time, their own nonhumanitarian rationale for supporting military action. Moral conscience had been demanding intervention for several years, to no avail. Only when political pressure built up simultaneously on several fronts did forcible intervention occur.

The Secret Tribalism of the Genocide Convention

Before turning to her gruesomely detailed case studies, Power devotes three peculiarly upbeat chapters to the story of the Convention on the Prevention and Punishment of the Crime of Genocide. Here, she temporarily discards her usual tough-mindedness and preference for action over words to extol the good intentions of Raphael Lemkin, the indefatigable Polish-Jewish activist who crafted the Convention and lobbied for its passage. She eulogizes Lemkin as a hero of liberal internationalism, devoted to ending atrocities everywhere, if not to ensuring perpetual peace, by means of laws and treaties and international courts. She pays little attention, at this point, to the sheer improbability of Lemkin's utopian project, in light of the unforgiving realities of international politics, but her uncritical approach to such idealism provides her with a towering moral pulpit from which to observe and condemn the indescribable savageries she is about to recount. Just how rickety this utopian platform turns out to be is left for the reader to discover.

Approved by the UN General Assembly in 1948, the Genocide Convention came into force in 1951, and was guardedly ratified by the United States in 1988. Ratifying states are required to adopt legislation making genocide a criminal offense, even for heads of state. Trials for genocide must be held either in the country where the genocide occurred or at an international penal tribunal, if such a court is ever established. These and accompanying provisions at first sound anodyne and easy to implement. But in fact the Genocide Convention represents an improbable attempt to modify several basic principles that have dominated international law since the Treaty of Westphalia. It aims, above all, to curb the sovereign right of national governments to decide, without being second-guessed by foreigners, what domestic threats they face and what responses, on their own territory, are available to meet such real or imaginary threats.

Before the Convention was ratified, the Western powers had intervened episodically to protect coreligionists in the Ottoman Empire, China, and elsewhere. Yet international law did not expressly recognize any remedy for atrocities committed by a government against its own citizens within its own borders. Because there is no unambiguous right without a reliable remedy, it follows that, under traditional international law, citizens had no right *not* to be brutally murdered by their governments within their state's sovereign frontiers. Every government was master in its own house, and mass murder was an internal affair. As Power points out, this was a morally repulsive and even "maddening"[16] conception, although it accurately reflected heartless political realities.

This "maddening" doctrine, surprisingly enough, prevailed even at Nuremberg. Although the tribunal there prosecuted German officials for crimes against Germans inside Germany, the proceedings did not satisfy Lemkin. The Nazis were charged first of all with the crime of aggressive war. They were held responsible for atrocities against German citizens only when these crimes occurred after German armies crossed international borders. In other words, the Nuremberg precedent still assumed that borders were in some sense sacrosanct. Like the UN Charter, the Nuremberg tribunals still accepted the principle that national sovereignty formed the basis of a minimally moral international order.

That Lemkin's hopes of upending this traditional order and imposing humanitarian norms on powerful international actors have not been fulfilled is amply documented by the 1990s, a decade when talk of universal human rights flowed copiously against a backdrop of brazen crimes against humanity. The road to hell, it seems, is paved with good conventions. The decision to declare genocide a crime, against the older tradition of international law that exempted a state's treatment of its own citizens within its own borders from the jurisdiction of international tribunals, has had little or no noticeable effect on the behavior of homicidal maniacs in power. There are various reasons for this failure.

For one thing, the leaders of large and internationally powerful states such as China and Russia remain confident that, however they behave in, say, Tibet or Chechnya, they will not be dragged before the kind of international penal tribunal reserved for fallen tin-pot dictators such as the late Slobodan Milosevic. For another thing, although cruel leaders of lesser states, faced with the threat of prosecution for genocide, may, it is true, be deterred, they are just as likely to cling ferociously to power whatever the cost in human lives. Stimulated to think ahead, for example, inveterate adventurers may plot to eliminate witnesses who might testify against them. Power herself suggests that anticipation of future trials and fear of incriminating testimony may have encouraged Hutu officials to widen the circle of their killings. This implies that the effect of the Genocide Convention on the behavior of bloodthirsty leaders is not only observably weak and erratic, but is also indeterminate in principle.

These chapters of *"A Problem from Hell"* also reveal that the Genocide Convention defines mass murder from a unique and even morally contestable point of view. The Convention's departure from Enlightenment universalism is already suggested by the origins of the idea of genocide in attempts to criminalize the massacre of Armenians: "Most Europeans identified with the Armenians' suffering because they were fellow Christians. But when the Russians suggested condemning 'crimes against Christianity,' it seemed too parochial, and the phrase 'crimes against humanity and civilization' was chosen instead."[17] Since partiality may hide its face without losing its grip, this change in wording did not necessarily signal a shift in attitudes. Whatever international law stipulates on paper, crimes against whites and Christians still receive greater attention from Western powers than crimes against nonwhites and non-Christians. Samuel Huntington would presumably applaud such unprincipled tribalism; but Power does not.

The Genocide Convention has been implemented in a one-sided and selective fashion, but it was also one-sided and selective in its very conception. First of all, the Soviets succeeded in excluding mass murder undertaken for political reasons from the definition of genocide: "The law did not protect political groups. The Soviet delegation and its supporters, mainly Communist countries in Eastern Europe as well as some Latin American countries, had argued that including political groups in the convention would inhibit states that were attempting to suppress internal armed revolt."[18] As a consequence, Power bitterly observes, not even the death of ten million Africans between 1880 and 1920 as a direct result of Belgian colonialism would have counted as genocide: "Leopold's crimes were mammoth, but . . . they were not aimed at wiping out one particular ethnic group. Any and every African slave was vulnerable."[19] Because the victims were of mixed ethnicity, their killings may have added up to mass murder, but not to genocide, as Lemkin explicitly conceived it.

As legally defined, in effect, genocide refers to the massacre only of certain communities. It is a crime committed not against members of ethnically or racially or religiously mixed groups but only against members of ethnically or racially or religiously homogeneous groups. For this reason, Power admits, the mass murder of two million Cambodians by the Khmer Rouge does not fit Lemkin's definition perfectly, even though she, for her own reasons, includes that case here. According to the Convention Lemkin drafted and shepherded into existence, "If the perpetrator did not target a national, ethnic or religious group *as such*, then killings would constitute mass homicide, not genocide."[20] This point often gets lost in discussions among nonspecialists. The Genocide Convention does not criminalize attempts to destroy a multicultural community such as Sarajevo. It was not meant to cover a mass-casualty attack on ethnic, racial, and religious patchworks such as London or New York City. It was explicitly drafted to protect homogeneous, not heterogeneous, groups.

Lemkin himself seems to have believed that killing a hundred thousand people of a single ethnicity was different in morally significant ways from killing a hundred thousand people of mixed ethnicities. Just like Huntington's hero, Oswald Spengler, Lemkin was convinced that each cultural group had its own "genius" that should be preserved. To destroy, or attempt to destroy, a culture is a special kind of crime because culture is the unit of collective memory, whereby the legacies of the dead can be kept alive. To kill a culture is to cast its individual members into everlasting oblivion, their memories buried with their mortal remains. The idea that killing a culture is "irreversible" in a way that killing an individual is not reveals the strangeness of Lemkin's conception of genocide from a liberal-individualist point of view.

This archaic-sounding conception has other illiberal implications as well. For one thing, it means that the murder of a poet is morally worse than the murder of a janitor, because the poet is the "brain" without which the "body" cannot function. This revival of medieval organic imagery is central to Lemkin's idea of genocide as a special crime. It also implies that the rape of a woman by a man of another ethnic background is *essentially* distinct from the rape of a woman by a man of her own ethnic group. The very idea of "genocide," in other words, implicitly views the female body instrumentally, as a vessel designed by some higher power to perpetuate into the future an unalloyed racial stock.

Did Humanitarian Interventionism Ease the Path to Iraq?

All this is fascinating and disturbing, but the most politically consequential feature of *"A Problem from Hell"* is Power's palpable frustration with

multilateralism and legalism. An important clue to this aspect of her thinking is the marked approval with which she cites two unilateralist hawks
closely associated with the Bush Administration's decision to invade Iraq:
Paul Wolfowitz and Richard Perle. During the 1990s, both of them urged
U.S. military intervention in Bosnia and Kosovo outside the framework
of the UN and contrary to its Charter. As a result, Power heartily wel-
comes them into the humanitarian fold. And one of the things that she
admires most about them is their refusal to make a fetish of multilateral
institutions. This is where things become interesting.

The Rwanda debacle was, at least to some extent, a product of dysfunctional multilateralism, a rotten fruit of UN dithering and incoherence.
The UN's credibility had already been severely damaged on the streets of
Mogadishu. During the 1990s, as a consequence, human rights advocates
did not speak deferentially about the UN – quite the contrary. Uncertain
of their mandate in Rwanda and focused on self-protection, the hapless
Blue Helmets allowed themselves to be disarmed before ten of them
were brutally murdered. Referring to the passivity of the United States
as the catastrophe unfolded in Rwanda, Power remarks: "The United
States could also have acted without the UN's blessing, as it would do
five years later in Kosovo."[21] Acting promptly and effectively sometimes
requires a great power with a moral conscience to extricate itself from
international decision-making forums easily paralyzed by discord among
multiple veto-wielders with petty and conflicting agendas.

After UN inspectors turned out to have been better informed than
the CIA about Iraqi weapons of mass destruction (the issue that ostensibly triggered the war), liberal attitudes toward multilateralism began to
change. His liberal critics now lambaste Bush for *failing* to act through
multilateral institutions and in accord with international law. He thereby
gratuitously alienates potential partners from America's just antiterror-
ist cause, they explain. That is not necessarily the way liberals felt in the
1990s, however. In those days, liberals were the ones disparaging multilateralism as a formula for paralysis and inaction. They pointed out, for
example, that the exquisitely multilateral European Union was pitifully
unable to mount a serious operation in the Balkans. When Morocco tried
to seize a tiny uninhabited Spanish island in July 2002, the EU proved
unable to act decisively for the simple reason that its member states could
not agree among themselves. (Colin Powell resolved the crisis by phone.)
On the question of Iraq, the leading member-states in the EU took dramatically inconsistent positions. One could even argue that the United
State's fatal turn to unilateralism is a natural consequence of Europe's

embrace of dysfunctional multilateralism. For how can Washington act in concert with allies who, although fused at the hip, cannot settle internal differences in a timely fashion? How wrong was Bush when he suggested to the General Assembly in September 2002 that, without U.S. leadership and law enforcement capacity, the UN risks becoming another League of Nations?

The crucial historical point to make here is that, in the 1990s, the proponents of humanitarian intervention were among multilateralism's least forgiving critics. Power's book brilliantly exemplifies this interlude between the fall of the wall and the collapse of the towers in the evolution of liberal internationalism. Whenever Clinton preached "consultation," she tells us, it meant that his Administration lacked a clear policy of its own. A proclivity to endless discussion and negotiation is just another dismaying sign of multilateralism's inadequacy from a moral point of view. When it came to confronting atrocities, she implies, America should have made up its own mind, and then tersely apprized its allies of what it was going to do. There is nothing wrong with "our way or the highway" so long as "our way" is morally obligatory and right. From the same perspective, Power also comments unflatteringly on the Yugoslav war crimes tribunal. The tribunal was initially established, she correctly explains, as a sop to pacify public outrage, thereby allowing the Western powers to avoid taking serious military action. In emergencies, legalism can prove as debilitating as multilateralism. The law's delay, including the devotion of professional lawyers to meeting the lofty standards of due process, can prevent a timely response to genocide. We need to move swiftly and flexibly against the worst international villains, Power insists, even if this means unleashing lethal force on the basis of hearsay testimony and circumstantial evidence: "an authoritative diagnosis of genocide would be impossible to make during the Serb campaign of terror."[22] Indeed, pre-emptive deployment of troops on the basis of clues collected by operatives in the field might be the only way to stave off a Rwanda-style massacre. The very idea of a war against genocide also implies a relaxed attitude towards *mens rea*: "Proving intent to exterminate an entire people would usually be impossible until the bulk of the group had already been wiped out."[23] Careful observance of procedural niceties will impede any speedy response, and that means any response with a chance for success, to an unfolding massacre.

Deference to public opinion may be another unaffordable luxury, Power adds, especially when the electorate is self-absorbed, parochial, and fixated on body bags. One cannot help wondering if her failure to sympathize with public aversion to military casualties might have anything to do with the infrequent human contact between human rights activists and the families of the grunts who are asked to die to uphold vaguely worded international laws. Be this as it may, Power also suggests that a chronically reticent military should be rolled over by morally attuned civilian leaders in order to confront wicked forces in the world. Faced with humanitarian atrocities in distant lands, any American official or citizen who claims to see shades of grey or two sides of the story, or who claims not to know exactly what is happening in the interior of a distant country, is probably feigning ignorance to deflect calls for action and to get the United States off the hook. Some of those who declare murderous situations inside closed societies to be indecipherable by distant foreign observers are simply liars, whereas others are culpable accomplices to genocide. If Power does not put her point exactly this way, she comes close.

Needless to say, 1990s advocates of humanitarian intervention, whose moral sensibility Power vividly displays and defends, are marginal actors on today's political scene, with little or no influence on current policy, but that does not mean that their way of thinking has been inconsequential. They have, on the contrary, unwittingly muffled the voices of Bush's critics. This is the principal relevance of *"A Problem from Hell"* to post-9/11 political debates. Power helps us understand a neglected reason for the near paralysis of the American left in the face of the preemptive and unilateralist turn in American foreign policy. The Democrats' embarrassingly weak grasp of the differences between al Qaeda and Saddam Hussein and their perpetual fear of being branded unpatriotic are not the only pertinent factors. Having supported unilateralist intervention outside the UN framework during the 1990s, liberals and progressives were simply unable to make a credible case against Bush.

Formulated differently, 1990s advocates of humanitarian intervention have unintentionally bequeathed a risky legacy to George W. Bush. They have helped rescue from the ashes of Vietnam the ideal of America as a global policeman, undaunted by other countries' borders, defending civilization against the forces of "evil." By denouncing the United States primarily for standing idly by when an atrocity abroad occurs, these well-meaning liberal interventionists have helped repopularize the idea of America as a potentially benign imperial power. They have breathed new life into messianic fantasies, and they have suggested strongly that America is shirking its moral responsibility when it refuses to venture abroad in pursuit of monsters to destroy. By focusing relentlessly on grievous harms caused by American inaction, finally, they have unintentionally clouded public memory of grievous harms caused by American action.

To be sure, Power discusses the many petty complicities of the United States with various wicked regimes. The generous aid that Bush père provided to Iraq has already been mentioned. For similar reasons, to please China and displease Vietnam, "Carter sided with the dislodged Khmer Rouge regime,"[24] orchestrating a vote in its favor in the UN credentials committee. She also mentions other cases in which, for geopolitical and economic reasons, America cynically consorted with the perpetrators of mass killing, including Nigeria in 1968 (one million Christian Ibo killed) and Pakistan in 1971 (almost two million Bengalis killed). But her principal stress throughout is on the immorality of the bystander who does nothing to prevent other peoples' crimes. In 1975, for example, "when its ally, the oil-producing, anti-Communist Indonesia, invaded East Timor, killing between 100,000 and 200,000 civilians, the United States looked away."[25] It is typical that she gives greater attention to this "looking away" than to the weaponry and other active support that the United States supplied, say, to Suharto ten years earlier, when he killed perhaps a million people in his campaign against the Communist Party of Indonesia.

Every revealing is a concealing. The natural result of focusing intently on atrocities that the United States did nothing to prevent is to press other forms of wrongdoing and miscalculation into the background. Above all, the humanitarian interventionists helped the Bush Administration achieve one of its principal ideological goals – namely, to erase from public memory the chastening lesson of Vietnam. In a footnote, to be fair, Power recollects the United States' own crimes at Mai Lai: "Although not one villager fired on the U.S. troops, the Americans burnt down all the houses, scalped or disemboweled villagers, and raped women and girls or, if they were pregnant, slashed open their stomachs."[26] The overall effect of her gripping book is to blur such memories, however, to obscure how the use of U.S. military force abroad, perhaps admirable in its original purpose, sometimes mires America in local struggles that it cannot master, radically weakens the democratic oversight that a chronically parochial public can exercise over a secretive military operation, involves our own soldiers in savage acts, and undermines the country's capacity to deliver some modest help to distressed peoples elsewhere in the world.

If we are responsible for our incredulity, as Power claims, are we not also responsible for the credulity that our good intentions create in others? If human rights activists push an interventionist policy that cannot be politically sustained, what have they done? If the international community coaxes the Bosnian Muslims to sit unarmed in a "safe area," but then sits back impassively when Srebrenica turns into a shooting gallery, who is responsible for abandoning those in whom unrealistic dreams of rescue have been nurtured? Are we responsible when we awaken false expectations by earnest talk? Are human rights advocates responsible when they initiate a policy that they know cannot be sustained politically, given domestic indifference to foreign affairs and the paralyzing array of political forces back home? Power acknowledges this problem, explaining that, because the West had promised bombing, the Muslims of Srebrenica did not reclaim the tanks and antiaircraft guns that they had turned over to the UN in 1993 as part of a demilitarization agreement. But she does not draw out the implications of this appalling bait-and-switch story for her overall depiction of humanitarian intervention. Can a cause so politically dubious really be morally obligatory?

In a battle with palpable "evil," no means and methods seem impermissible. In the midst of a humanitarian catastrophe, the downstream consequences of short-term strategies will never occupy the center of attention. Even in photographs, mutilated corpses disinterred from mass graves overwhelm the senses and the mind, because the visual is visceral enough. Witnessing the immediate aftermath of an atrocity will drive out calculations of opportunity costs and tradeoffs and induce a false feeling of moral clarity. Choices will seem simple, black versus white, good versus evil. Max Weber called it the ethics of conscience. But a sickened heart does not necessarily exempt us from taking responsibility for what happens *after* we intervene. What if the side on whose behalf we bomb urban areas subsequently commits ethnic cleansing under our military protection? Even if it begins with moral clarity, in other words, humanitarian intervention may gutter into moral ambiguity once the interveners find themselves, as in Kosovo, on the side of ethnic cleansers or propping up an unseemly local "elite" infested with drug smugglers, arms smugglers, human traffickers, and brutal gangsters.

Putting a quietus to atrocities is a moral victory. But if the partisans of humanitarian intervention are incapable of maintaining support back home for the next phase, for reconstructing what they have shattered, the morality of intervention is ephemeral at best. If political stability could be achieved simply by toppling a rotten dictator, or if nations could be forged at gunpoint, this problem would not be so pressing, but human rights cannot be reliably protected unless a moderate, coherent, and locally sustained political authority is in place.

The only reliable human rights organization is the liberal state. As it turns out, the United States was completely unprepared for building a domestically supported liberal political order in Iraq, where a multiethnic and multisectarian society had been glued together by a regime of fear administered by a basically monoethnic and unidenominational tribal grouping. A functioning and moderately decent state can be created only with the active cooperation of well-organized civilian constituencies. An occupying military force cannot import it. Where were such constituencies in Iraq when America invaded? Where are they now? A stable democracy cannot easily be created out of hostile paramilitary groupings. If the constituent subgroups of a society are themselves internally incoherent, split by rivalries and conflicts, then these subgroups cannot even successfully negotiate and seal a stable power-sharing agreement with each other.

Did anyone involved in planning the Iraq war give any thought to these issues? Did the liberals who supported the Iraq war on humanitarian grounds believe that militarily powerful outsiders with minimal understanding of Iraqi society would conjure well-organized prodemocratic groupings out of thin air? The failure to think through, in advance, cogent answers to such questions is part of the dubious legacy bequeathed by genuinely well-meaning humanitarian interventionists to the considerably less well-meaning nonhumanitarian interventionists who may have disastrously changed the course of Western history – and world history – in March 2003.

The Antiwar Generation Goes to War

Replete with colorful anecdotes, David Halberstam's *War in a Time of Peace* nicely complements Power's *A Problem from Hell*. Halberstam's main story concerns U.S. military interventions after the Cold War, with special focus on Clinton's reluctant use of force in the Balkans. He says he wants to help us understand "the contradictions and the ambivalence of America as a post-Cold War superpower."[27] He therefore describes how the sudden collapse of the U.S.S.R. and the 1990s economic boom led to "an era of consummate self-indulgence,"[28] luring Americans into lowering their collective defenses. Foreign policy, he explains, loses its focus in a time of peace.

The entertainment culture, we are also told, has gobbled up the American broadcast media, rewarding "journalistic feather merchants"[29] and sidelining the kind of serious reporting of foreign news that could help the United States exercise responsibly its unparalleled global power. The flattering and teasing portraits Halberstam paints of personal friends, such as Richard Holbrooke, reveal the extent to which this is an insider's tale, a story recounted by someone with enviable access to the Washington political scene. Based on long private conversations with the powerful, the book is meant to make readers feel that they understand the way Washington thinks.

Halberstam catapulted to fame in the early 1970s with *The Best and the Brightest*, his account of the United States' catastrophic involvement in Vietnam. He has written many other books in the interim, but it is not surprising that here, returning to foreign affairs, he still has a great deal to say about "the ghosts of Vietnam."[30] He writes very well, for instance, about the military's lingering fear of being lured into an impossible quagmire and then being abandoned by a sauve-qui-peut civilian leadership. He is also eloquent about the psychological torment of Tony Lake and other onetime antiwar activists who came to power under Clinton and, compelled to respond in some way to foreign genocide, learned to jettison their youthful doubts about American military interventions abroad.

This brings us to the principal reason for reading Halberstam alongside Power. *War in a Time of Peace* inadvertently reveals the story of the author's own dramatic metamorphosis. A beacon to the antiwar generation, Halberstam, too, re-emerged in the 1990s having shed his distrust of American power. He has gone so far in this direction that he seems genuinely dazzled by the high-tech weaponry he describes. The reason for this about-turn is important to notice. For he, along with many others, sees in humanitarian intervention an irresistible moral cause that authorizes the use of what he had once considered forbidden means. This same change of heart, incidentally, prepared him to compose a patriotic preface to his book after September 11. He swaggers there about the "muscularity and flex in American society" and informs the world that "our strengths, when summoned and focused, when the body politic is aroused and connects to the political process, are never to be underestimated."[31]

The Washington, D.C., we discover in these pages, however, is not exactly the self-assured capital of a global empire. Muscularity and flex are not much in evidence. Instead, Halberstam's Washington seems like a small town racked by palace intrigue, grandstanding, back-stabbing, information hoarding, careerism, cronyism, bureaucratic inertia, lack of focus, and supine inattention. Sometimes decision makers are excessively cautious, at other times they are maddeningly reckless. We also hear of scandal mongering, vested interests, tunnel-vision NGOs, obsolete mindsets,

CNN-driven policymaking, and corrosive envy of exceptionally talented individuals. In election years, politicians thrash around blindly in an attempt to humor or captivate public opinion. Overstretched policymakers feign knowledgeableness and control when they are actually flying by the seat of their pants. Cabinet members appearing on Sunday morning talk shows are apprized of their own Administration's policies only after placing frantic Saturday-night phone calls.

Incoherence and strife, too, are ubiquitous. Tensions between civilians and the military run so deep that they seem cultural rather than merely a matter of turf. Political parties, Congress, the executive branch and the military are all internally divided as well as at war with each other. Halberstam's ruminations on the ideological or normative basis of paralysis in U.S. foreign policy remain relevant today. Oversized egos are not the only sources of confusion and immobility. Even more important is the war of analogies: namely, the battle between conflicting narratives or interpretative frameworks. Which image will dominate American foreign policy over the next decade: Munich or Vietnam? What should we fear most: appeasing dictators in Iran and North Korea who may eventually strike us or our allies without warning, or being dragged into still another quagmire? In this ongoing struggle, there is something to be said on both sides. That it cannot be reduced to a battle between reckless warmongers and spineless appeasers is one of Halberstam's wisest claims.

Dampened or disciplined by the Cold War, such conflicts flowered luxuriantly after 1991. Flummoxed by an illusion of peace, the United States lost its foreign policy bearings. No one managed to formulate a comprehensive doctrine to replace containment and deterrence. Clinton's unsleeping critics attributed the confusion to a leadership vacuum, to the inability of a domestically oriented president to frame foreign policy issues forcefully, but this problem cannot be laid exclusively at Clinton's feet. In 2000, just as in 1992, an electorate profoundly uninterested in the rest of the world elected a former governor with no foreign policy experience to the presidency. Intervention in the Balkans came so late for a perfectly democratic reason: "There was little in the way of a constituency, either in or outside the Government, for taking military action against the Serbs."[32] Parochial voters get the inward-looking leaders they want rather than the worldly leaders they presumably need.

Revealingly, Halberstam's book illustrates several of the shortcomings it purports to dissect. It is a Washington-centered study, for one thing, in which voices from Europe or the Balkans are almost never heard. This is not necessarily Halberstam's doing. He spoke to everyone who is any-one in Washington and apparently no one ever mentioned that people elsewhere in the world do not necessarily see things the way Americans see them. In his concluding remarks, he rather defensively explains: "This book was always premised to be about America, not about the Balkans or any other foreign country."[33] To study the use of U.S. military force abroad, intimate knowledge of our allies or even of the countries in which American forces are deployed is apparently optional. Why should the student of American intervention know more about the rest of the world than those who plan and carry out the action?

This insular attitude may explain why Halberstam leaves unmentioned various interpretations of NATO's Kosovo operation that are widely diffused in the region itself: for instance, that NATO did exactly what Milosevic wanted and that the latter's only mistake was to underestimate the exasperation of the Serbian population that would afterwards drive him from office. The claim that NATO was reading from a script written by Milosevic builds on the premise that, before the war, Kosovo presented Belgrade with an irresolvable dilemma. As a poor Albanian province where few Serbs wished to live, it could not be integrated into Yugoslavia. Milosevic could not simply grant independence to Kosovo, however, because of the province's critical role in Serbian national mythology. The ideal solution, from his point of view, was to have Kosovo ripped away by Serbia's overwhelmingly powerful foreign enemies, allowing him to cut loose the province while appearing to be an unwavering defender of national honor. My point is not that this interpretation of events is accurate or even plausible, merely that it is a commonplace in the Balkans. Halberstam's failure to mention it suggests that what is commonplace in the rest of the world can be totally unheard of in Washington, D.C.

During the writing of Halberstam's book, the United States was steadily cutting back its commitment of troops and treasure to the Balkans, despite the unsettled situation in Macedonia, and handing over responsibility to the uncertainly prepared Europeans. Here again, Halberstam follows Washington's lead. He, too, turns away from the region, revealing scant interest in the aftermath of military intervention. His few remarks on Bosnia today, for example, indicate a shaky grasp of what it means for international authorities to try to impose a multiethnic democracy on three peoples who, after the horrors of 1992–95, have no stomach for knitting together a common life. Having canvassed the opinions of America's foreign policy elite, Halberstam has nothing to say about managing the consequences of U.S. intervention in the Balkans. His book therefore helps us see the world from the Bush Administration's point of view. That is to say, it provides a window onto the mindset of those for whom "regime change" means destroying a wicked system, full stop, rather than replacing a rotten government with a moderately better one that has a sporting chance to endure.

8 | THE WAR OF THE LIBERALS

Even if they had no influence on the decision to topple the Baathist regime in Baghdad, prowar liberals contributed significantly to the stifling of national debate about the wisdom of the war in the run-up to the invasion. Paul Berman, considered by some to be "the leading liberal hawk,"[1] wants us to understand America's war in Iraq as part of the long twentieth-century conflict between liberalism and totalitarianism. All good antifascists and anti-Stalinists, he suggests, should have known where to line up. Berman's (unsuccessful) demonstration that Saddam Hussein and Osama bin Laden represent two wings of a single hostile Islamo-fascist formation was obviously designed to support the Bush Administration's eccentric claim that tyrants and terrorists, oppressors and rebels, are one and the same. Berman's insinuation that critics of the plan to invade Iraq were somehow accomplices in atrocity seems to have been part of a largely successful campaign to set the house of liberalism against itself, playing hostility to tyranny against hostility to war, leaving liberals with essentially no voice. Berman's belief that a military invasion of an oil-rich Arab country would drain the anti-Semitic extremism out of the Middle East does not comport well with the still-valid truism that violence breeds violence. Yet casting the war against terror, including the war in Iraq, as a confrontation with absolute "evil" does relieve the forces of relative good of any duty to think carefully about the instruments they employ, the opportunities they forego, and the hidden interests of those with whom they are riding into battle.

This chapter also discusses David Rieff, one of the least forgiving critics, in the 1990s, of antiwar liberals. At the time, he eloquently denounced the exaggerated hatred of American power, inherited from the Vietnam era, which led some American liberals to tolerate avoidable genocides in Rwanda and elsewhere. Rieff's subsequent visits to American-occupied

Iraq made him see the complicity of interventionists as just as morally dubious as the complicity of noninterventionists. At his most intemperate, he accuses humanitarian interventionists, such as Samantha Power, of being ideologues of American empire as well as fomenters of endless do-gooder wars. With such statements Rieff vastly exaggerates the role of moral idealism in the actual conduct of U.S. affairs abroad. He is on more solid ground when arguing that liberal hawks fail morally when they do not examine the motives and capacities of the political actors who will actually be in charge of conducting the humanitarian interventions they support. Is there any chance that the people who will determine the outcome will behave in a decent and competent way? If not, then liberals clamoring for intervention have turned themselves into unwitting pawns in a political process that they certainly do not control and probably do not understand.

More instructive than the speechlessness of the Democratic Party, still unable to react coherently to the relentlessly downward spiral in Iraq, is the debate among progressive writers about the justice of the invasion. To penetrate the thinking of the prowar liberals, whose zeal for toppling a malignant dictatorship split the left and therefore eased the slog to disaster, we need to cast our eyes back to the 1990s one more time. Two highly personal books written by thoughtful observers of the current crisis help us understand the gestation of liberal hawks in the dozen years between the fall of the wall and the fall of the towers. Images of Rwanda and Kosovo were not especially poignant for the principal Bush Administration insiders who made the decision to invade Iraq. At the outset, for them, humanitarianism was not even a pretext for war. But, as Chapter Seven should have made clear, the appalling failures and modest successes of humanitarian intervention during the 1990s did shape the thinking of certain sparkling liberal intellects. Their heady support for war played little or no role in the decision to invade Iraq, but it did diminish and isolate voices of dissent, helping insure that Bush's ill-fated war was set afoot with little national debate, even in the high-circulation liberal press.

The Antitotalitarian Left

The tenor of Paul Berman's recent book, *Power and the Idealists: Or, The Passion of Joschka Fischer, and its Aftermath*, is suggested by the word "tragedy" in the title to his concluding chapter, "The '68ers and the Tragedy of Iraq." He freely acknowledges "the scale and gravity of America's blunders in Iraq."[2] But he can find nothing especially critical to say about the handful of former '68ers who, invoking humanitarian commitments, clambered aboard the wagons of war. They should be judged for their good intentions alone, he implies.

The seeds of this forgiving – and self-forgiving – attitude are sown in chapter one. The book opens with a lengthy essay on the tribulations of Joschka Fischer, the popular Green politician and German foreign minister from 1998 to 2005, who had been embarrassed by the publication of some old photos that showed him as a young man beating a policeman. Originally published in the Sept. 3, 2001, edition of *The New Republic*, Berman's reflections on Fischer open a window onto his own pre-9/11 mindset. His preoccupation, at that time, was to show "the evolution of the leading '68ers from revolutionary leftism to liberal internationalism."[3] He traced the path by which Fischer, the young antibourgeois street fighter in blue jeans who flirted discreetly with lethal vandalism, came to endorse German participation in the Kosovo war. Berman's theme was "how someone with an extremely radical New Left orientation could have ended up, in the fullness of time, a friend of NATO."[4]

Foreign-policy realists would never have backed the Kosovo intervention, Berman contends, because "realism is never genocide's enemy."[5] "The veterans of the student uprisings circa 1968" kept the lofty principles that inspired the Kosovo action alive, he speculates.[6] These idealists hated genocide with a passionate intensity and "put matters of conscience at the heart of their thinking."[7] Thus, Berman concludes, "NATO's intervention could just as easily be described as the '68ers' War."[8]

The shift from skirmishing with the police to bombing the *génocidaires* was "a generational trajectory,"[9] not limited to Fischer's swapping of blue jeans for a three-piece suit. It was the story, according to Berman, of how the New Left, beginning in France in the 1970s, shed its antimilitarist, anticapitalist, antibourgeois, and anticolonialist stances and became, instead, fiercely antitotalitarian. The Cambodian genocide had been an earsplitting wake-up call, forcing open-minded leftists to admit that cruelty and oppression do not stem exclusively from Western imperialism. By the mid-1990s, some had come to believe that American power could be a, even the, force for good in the world.

The Imaginary Unity of Tyranny and Terror

Under the impact of the terrorist attack on New York City, Berman put aside his chronicle of the New Left's coming of age and produced, in short order, *Terror and Liberalism*, a passionately written and widely heralded interpretation of the meaning of 9/11. The book's thesis was intentionally provocative. The consensus at the time was that a diffuse and mobile enemy such as al Qaeda presented a radically new threat, impossible to compare with Nazi Germany or the U.S.S.R. Berman belittled such differences, declaring that the "war on terror" was really nothing new. It was certainly not part of Huntington's alleged clash of civilizations. It was, instead, just one more battle in the ongoing twentieth-century confrontation between liberalism and totalitarianism.

Modeling himself roughly on Hannah Arendt, who exposed the deep but underappreciated similarity between German Nazism and Soviet Communism, Berman drew attention to what he considered the underlying identity of state tyranny and nonstate terrorism. Or, rather, he set out to justify two farfetched analogies, both essential to defending the Bush Administration's response to 9/11. He first tried to convince us that the Israeli-Palestinian conflict, far from being a tribal war over scarce land and water, is part of the wider spiritual war between liberalism and apocalyptic irrationalism, not worth distinguishing too sharply from the conflict between America and al Qaeda. He then attempted to show that Saddam Hussein and Osama bin Laden represented two "branches" of an essentially homogeneous Muslim extremism. By hammering away at this second parallel, he echoed Bush's contention that the invasion of Iraq was both a fitting reply to 9/11 and a shrewd way to protect America from 9/11-style attacks.

True enough, Berman hurled an occasional jeer Bush's way. After all, the president's entourage did not disguise its contempt for "the Vietnam generation." Nevertheless, by enlisting antifascism to support the Administration's "war on terror," Berman made Bush into a steely *résistant* fighting the new totalitarian evil. Less explicitly but more worryingly, he implied that Bush's antiwar critics were, in some unwitting fashion, collaborators with violent extremism. They were playing into Saddam's hands, abandoning Saddam's victims and of course flirting with anti-Semitism.

Having secured his reputation as a liberal hawk and withering critic of Bush's critics, Berman has returned to his earlier project, adding to his original essay on Fischer four lively chapters that trace the way certain former New Leftists (though not Fischer) went beyond their support for the Kosovo war and endorsed Bush's invasion of Iraq. His heroes are all highly cultured Europeans. They intuitively grasp, the way Bush's antiwar critics supposedly do not, "the dangers posed by the extremist currents in the Arab world."[10] In their youth, curiously enough, some of them had thought the spirit of "absolute evil" (namely, Nazism) had survived

World War II and mysteriously migrated to postwar bourgeois society and to Israel. Berman resurrects this idea, breathing new life into the metaphor of itinerant malevolence by varying the destination. The spirit of absolute evil (apocalyptic totalitarianism) has survived the Cold War, he writes, and has now migrated to the Middle East, transmogrified into Arab and Muslim extremism.

Although he sneers at Richard Perle ("Pangloss on the Potomac"[11]), Berman ultimately allows little daylight between himself and the neoconservatives. He accepts their interpretation of antiwar liberals as quaking pacifists who live in denial, inventing a picture of the world that requires no military action, presumably because they are afraid to stand up and fight. It comes as no surprise, therefore, that he writes deferentially of "some people" around Bush who had a "strategic overview" and "entertained large geopolitical ambitions."[12] He basically agrees with them that "something ambitious had to be done, not just in Iraq but with an eye to transforming the entire region"[13] and setting off "a broader revolution for liberal values in the Arab world."[14] Military defeat had forced German extremists to abandon their apocalyptic anti-Semitism. So why couldn't military defeat force Muslim extremists to abandon their apocalyptic anti-Semitism?

This is how Berman formulates the neoconservative case for war, to which he subscribes:

> The American strategists noticed that terrorism had begun to flourish across a wide swath of the Arab and Muslim world. And they argued that something had to be done about the political culture across the whole of that wide swath. The American strategists saw in Saddam's Iraq a main center of that political culture, yet also a place where the political culture could be redressed and transformed.[15]

Something had to be done "to bring about the downfall of extremist currents throughout the region," and that something would be war, "a human-rights intervention that was also going to be a national-security intervention."[16] A side benefit would be the destruction of the one army in the region "large enough to worry the Israelis."[17]

A Morally Pure Case for War

Although making common cause with right-wing supporters of Bush's militarized response to 9/11, Berman apparently feels little cultural affinity for such prowar conservatives as Charles Krauthammer and William

Kristol. For more agreeable companionship, he seeks out European writers like the ex-Maoist French philosopher André Glucksmann and Polish dissident Adam Michnik. He honors them for their belief that American tenacity alone can dislodge brutal tyrants from power. He admires Glucksmann as "an enemy of extreme suffering"[18] who early abandoned anticapitalism and embraced hostility to tyranny in every form and who, in blessing Bush's war, memorably remarked that Iraqis, too, deserve their D-Day. And Berman is also pleased to inform us that prominent Eastern European dissidents, among them Václav Havel and Michnik, claim that "people all over the world needed America to lead a resistance against the new totalitarianism of the Muslim world."[19]

Yet the principal hero of Berman's story is Bernard Kouchner, a founder of Doctors Without Borders and head of the United Nations administration in Kosovo from July 1999 to January 2001. For Berman, "nobody in Europe was more heroic"[20] than this "fearless humanitarian doctor"[21] who always seemed to be "on a mission against injustice."[22] The basic principle underlying Kouchner's political activism was that "the supremely oppressed had a right to be rescued, no matter what the theorists of anti-imperialism or the defenders of the inviolability of borders might say."[23] Kouchner supported the war because he knew that Iraq was studded with Srebrenicas. If you hate genocide, place matters of conscience at the heart of your thinking, and appreciate the larger grandeur of the interventionist idea (in Kouchner's terms, the *droit d'ingérence*, or right of interference), then you can only applaud the American invasion of Iraq. Never mind that most ex-'68ers, including Daniel Cohn-Bendit and Joschka Fischer, opposed the war as an expression of the Bush Administration's revolutionary hubris. Kouchner's example reassures Berman that an ex-'68er could join the war party and preserve his "left-wing soul."[24]

Like Kouchner, Berman was "furious that Bush didn't make the pure humanitarian case" for war.[25] Instead of stressing the morally lofty *casus belli* advanced by Kouchner and other prowar European liberals, Administration spokesmen implied that the war in Iraq had purposes other than rescuing the oppressed and rolling back Islamic extremism. They emphasized the same short-run objectives that had rallied public support behind the early phase of the Afghan campaign, namely revenge for 9/11 and self-defense against weapons of mass destruction. That these were the "most widely publicized presentations to the general public,"[26] Berman remarks, indicated the Administration's deplorable lack of strategic vision.

"Why didn't the Bush administration, in trying to drum up a few European allies, look to these people and their arguments – to the dissident heroes and the admired humanitarians?" he asks.[27] This question is presumably rhetorical. That Bush could have mobilized significant support from Europe by drawing on Kouchner's "moral prestige"[28] defies belief. And Berman certainly knows that Bush had little to gain domestically by embracing Europe's chastened '68ers, who favored giving war a chance on purely moral grounds. As he says, most Republicans had "sunk into nationalist isolation"[29] and were "contemptuous of the Western Europeans."[30] To rally his base, moreover, Bush regularly flaunts his indifference to the patronizing morality of lesser and weaker nations. For that reason alone, Kouchner's high-minded endorsement of Bush's war was destined to be just as inconsequential as Berman's.

Snubbed by the prowar party in Washington, Kouchner was forced to observe the invasion's disastrous aftermath from the sidelines. But the catastrophic bungling of the American occupation proved almost too painful to watch. According to Berman, at least, "Kouchner was beside himself,"[31] especially when Paul Bremer disbanded the Iraqi army. When he was faced with such delirious incompetence, his "Gallic nostrils flared."[32] As things went *de mal en pis*, "Kouchner fumed,"[33] "Kouchner was dumbfounded,"[34] "Kouchner was amazed,"[35] "Kouchner was apoplectic,"[36] "Kouchner was astonished"[37] and "Kouchner was dumbfounded yet again."[38] But these droll reminders of how prowar idealists became disillusioned when tyranny was replaced by anarchy seem oddly flippant. True, today's Iraq can be labeled "a tragedy," but this does not exculpate those who worked tirelessly to beautify the garbled motives behind Bush's war. Their surprise does not lift responsibility from their shoulders, for they could easily have taken more seriously the widely predicted possibility of a tragic outcome. Fischer did, and if he was sickened when things went badly, he was not "dumbfounded." For he understood, even before the invasion was launched, that the Bush Administration was probably incapable, in such a dauntingly complex environment, of accomplishing the lofty goals it had publicly proclaimed.

Some Fallacies in the Pure Case for War

Where exactly does Berman's theoretical analysis go wrong? Five deficiencies in his argument stand out.

His analogies, first of all, are tendentious to an extreme. Islamist murderousness resembles Bolshevik and Nazi murderousness. The planetary battle against terrorism (World War IV) resembles the planetary battle against communism. Baath dictatorship resembles Islamic militancy. The problem with such comparisons is not only that they are strained; they are also transparently calculated to serve a partisan political program. Analogies that challenge the Bush Administration (such as Palestinian violence and anticolonial violence) are filtered out, not because they are unrevealing but because they introduce a dissonant note.

Take, for instance, Berman's peculiar claim that "on the plane of anti-American propaganda, the Iraqi Baath and al Qaeda were already allied"[39] because Saddam's press had celebrated the September 11 attacks. The nature of this purported alliance between religious insurgents and a secular oppressor is never explained. In other passages, moreover, Berman concedes that Islamic radicalism has arisen in opposition to authoritarian secular regimes, but he is much less interested in possible causal connections between the two than in their metaphysical identity. His false moral clarity rests entirely on his assertion that spiritually they are one and the same. The Administration's attempts to associate Iraq and al Qaeda logistically came to naught. Berman's cultural and philosophical approach, by contrast, raises the identification of Saddam and Osama, the tyrant and the terrorist, to a level of blurry abstraction that no facts can possibly refute.

A second weakness appears in Berman's repeated assertion that anti-war liberals are naïve optimists, oblivious to the deep roots of irrational violence in human nature and therefore unable to take the true measure of our fanatical enemies. Such dismissive comments suggest an obvious question: Should someone who speculated that an American invasion of Iraq would force Islamic extremists to give up their paranoid conspiracy theories about the Jews accuse others of facile optimism? Berman classifies Saddam's Iraq as "totalitarian" because "there was no sign of democratic opposition at all."[40] Did this absence not suggest that an occupying army would find no well-organized constituencies for a reconstruction of Iraqi politics along liberal lines? What kind of political system did Berman imagine would emerge in Iraq after the toppling of Saddam? Was it going to be a democracy, namely a system in which a well-organized incumbent party loses elections to a well-organized opposition party and voluntarily leaves office knowing that it will not be harmed once out of power? Is that what he, with his understanding of human irrationality, expected for Iraq?

Additionally, how good a job does Berman himself do at identifying and understanding the gravest threats to American national security? Here lies the third flaw in Berman's framework. He uncritically endorses Bush's repeated claim that 9/11 was not a crime of mass murder but rather an act of war against America. Putting his own thoughts, as he often does, in the mouth of his subject, he writes: "Fischer rejected the policeman's view of

Islamist terror – the idea that, with a handful of well-chosen arrests or the dismantling of a small number of underground cells, the problem could be solved."[41] Terrorism is not a police problem, because policemen cannot redraw the political map of the Middle East, spread freedom, or compel extremists to abandon their extremism. Only soldiers, apparently, can do these things.

We are dealing, as already discussed, with off-the-shelf categories, because neither the war paradigm nor the crime paradigm fits perfectly the battle against transnational Islamic terrorism, which involves political violence by nonstate actors. But Berman, like Bush, prefers the war model to the crime model, because the former seems to signal a more serious approach, a willingness to send young men to die in large numbers, for example.

Yet this suggestion of greater realism and seriousness is deceptive. The war paradigm not only inflates all too conveniently the unsupervised powers of the executive branch, as we will see in Chapter Thirteen, it also assumes that America's unrivaled military superiority guarantees its success in the current struggle. It suggests that our enemy will eventually surrender and that we will be able to put the nightmare behind us. The crime paradigm has less rosy implications. It assumes that our government can no more stop the importing of a nuclear weapon into a major urban center than it can stop the clandestine flow of contraband drugs. That is to say, the crime paradigm, when applied to terrorism, has chilling implications precisely because it denies that "the problem can be solved." To turn from the crime paradigm to the war paradigm, therefore, does not bespeak a greater willingness to face the enemy. On the contrary, it is a classic case of sticking one's head in the sand (of Iraq).

A fourth and closely related objection concerns Berman's insistence that our real enemy is Muslim extremism. This idea, too, appears confrontational but is actually escapist. The gravest threat to American national security today is no longer the Soviet nuclear arsenal, obviously, but neither can it be identified exclusively with Muslim extremism. American national security is threatened most seriously by those laxly regulated markets in lethal materiel and know-how that, in the aftermath of the Cold War, have emerged alongside the global communication, transportation, and banking systems created largely by the West. Terrorist groups have a global reach, as mentioned previously, only because we have supplied it to them on computer discs, via the Internet and ATMs and so forth. These are not the West's only contributions. The petrodollars that we are now pumping at an unprecedented rate into politically unstable parts of the world may make it easier for a private group to acquire, without detection, a compact weapon of unspeakable destructiveness – a weapon, of course, originally created by Western science.

It may be disheartening to realize that the dangers we face, because they are deeply intertwined with American power and prosperity, cannot be eliminated. Candor in this respect, however, can at least help us avoid the temptation to tie down a vast proportion of our scarce national-security assets in distant and territorially localized conflicts. Heightened self-awareness can also help us avoid identifying the ultimate source of danger, erroneously, with an odious enemy whom we can definitively defeat in war. Berman's construct has the opposite effect. By encouraging us to focus obsessively on Islamic extremism, it fosters a cavalier attitude toward other threats, such as nuclear proliferation from Russia, Pakistan, and North Korea. It also leads us to ignore the extent to which our economically open and technically advanced way of life, and not a replaceable network of zealots intoxicated by an amalgam of religious and revolutionary slogans, is the frighteningly enduring problem with which we have to cope.

A fifth obscurity in Berman's thinking concerns the way faith has influenced both sides in the war on terror. He wants us to believe that we are witnessing a confrontation of freedom versus tyranny. Europeans, by contrast, are much more likely to code the conflict as a struggle of secularism versus religion. The second polarity, needless to say, is embarrassing to an administration that is no more eager to blame proselytizing religion and rogue religious charities for revolutionary violence aimed at the United States than it is to lay any responsibility on unregulated markets and geysers of petrodollars. A rogue state is a much more convenient scapegoat, distracting public attention from nonstate sponsors of terrorism (including rogue religious charities) that hit too close to home. The reader will not be surprised, therefore, when Berman labors to muffle the role of religion in 9/11, claiming that Islamic fundamentalism is really "a modern ideological temptation, familiar to Europeans."[42] He is particularly certain that "jihadi suicide" is "the height of modernity."[43]

In the Muslim world, over the past few decades, an obvious alternative to the God That Failed has been, well, God. Totalitarian ideologies – as Berman, too, learned in college – contained secularized eschatologies. Totalitarianism rejected the religious answers but retained the religious questions, re-creating a worldview that contained heretics and orthodoxy, sacred texts and martyrs, banishment and anathema, contamination and purity. So why is Berman so sure, when he sees these ideas resurface among Islamists, that they derive from the secularized religion of totalitarianism rather than from religion itself, which lent them to totalitarianism in the first place? After all, antiliberalism did not begin with twentieth-century totalitarianism. Nor is apocalypse a twentieth-century idea. Monotheism can itself be deeply antiliberal, to the extent that it makes a self-appointed vanguard of the faithful so certain of what God wants that it feels free to use coercion to force the rest of society to submit to God's ostensible will. There is nothing "entirely modern" about such an outlook, nor about a "system of oppression that reaches into the coziest and most private corners of life."[44]

Berman's decision to turn "totalitarian" into a catchall term, covering Osama bin Laden as well as Hitler and Stalin, also encourages Americans to cling unthinkingly to their Cold War habits of mind. Why make any profound readjustments if we are still fighting totalitarianism? One stimulus to radically refashioning the country's approach to national security is the striking fact that an antireligious enemy has been displaced by a religious enemy. Berman's conceptual scheme blunts the impact of this obvious truth. It also helps conceal a deep perversity of the current war of good versus evil. The U.S. president apparently believes that he has been personally assigned to punish the enemies of God. This fantasy is disquieting because we are now facing enemies who believe that they have been personally assigned to punish the enemies of God. By drawing such a clear-cut contrast between liberals and totalitarians, Berman throws a veil over this unsettling coincidence of self-images.

Interestingly enough, Berman admits, "Fantasy role-playing" – the Bush Administration comes to mind – "lies at the heart of a good deal of modern history."[45] It is so pervasive, it turns out, that Berman indulges in it too. He poses as a modern-day Orwell, standing up to tyranny, however insufferable to the literati such a daring posture may prove to be. This is not the book's most pernicious analogy, to be sure. It may be the most revealing, however, designed as it is to preemptively swat away Berman's future critics by associating them with weakly conventional minds unable to recognize authentic moral courage when they see it. Readers should not be put off by this modest conceit. They should instead savor this colorful book for what it is: the last testament of an exotic species, the 1990s liberal hawk, by no means destined to survive the blast furnace of Iraq.

A Disillusioned Interventionist

That David Rieff, too, aims to explore the relation between idealism and power is evident from the very title of his recent book. He is a more widely traveled observer of reality than Berman, however. Having spent years studying what he once called "the political instrumentalization of humanitarianism,"[46] Rieff is well poised to help us understand how, in the Iraq war, human rights talk lent an illusory aura of legitimacy to an initially dubious and ultimately ruinous military adventure.

The first half of *At the Point of a Gun* consists of articles written over the past dozen years about genocide, sundry failings of the UN, Rwanda, Kosovo, and liberal imperialism. The second half, to which the first is merely a prelude, is devoted to Iraq. Rieff appends a brief comment to each essay, informing us how his views have or have not evolved in the interim. Although Rieff "began the decade in Sarajevo a convinced interventionist,"[47] today he is "no longer an interventionist,"[48] having returned from Iraq with grave "doubts about the entire project of human-itarian intervention."[49]

Back in the 1990s Rieff denounced in scorching language "a left that would prefer to see genocide in Bosnia and the mass deportation of the Kosovars rather than strengthen, however marginally, the hegemony of the United States."[50] This accusation was meant to shame liberals into shedding their Vietnam-era distrust of U.S. military actions abroad. At this period, then, Rieff was "at least partly of Wolfowitz's party,"[51] favoring "a recolonization of part of the world."[52] He wrote that "liberal imperi-alism may be the best we are going to do in these callous and sentimental times,"[53] adding that "the real task" was not to destroy but rather to "humanize this new imperial order"[54] and to correct its excesses where possible.

Rieff's tenderness, a decade back, for American hegemony arose from the perceived absence of feasible alternatives. Who, if not the United States, could take effective action during humanitarian crises? Certainly not the pitiful UN – a "broken instrument"[55] and "little more than a waste of hope,"[56] as he put it. Passivity, servility, conformism, complacency, cowardice, and indolence made a mockery of the UN's implicit claim to be "the bureaucratic arm of the world's transcendental values."[57] The Secretariat, because of "its wish not to raise problems, which the Permanent Five prefer to ignore,"[58] stood by and watched massacres unfold without even making an effort to publicize or mobilize a response to the horror.

Contributing little to world peace and security, the UN has failed to live up to the hopes of its founders. The best that can be said for it is that it remains "the world's leading humanitarian relief organization,"[59] a kind of giant Red Cross. Absent U.S. backing, the UN is unable to enforce the most basic human rights norms. It was almost inevitable, therefore, that the UN would become "a de facto colonial office to US power."[60] As a result, Rieff "could see no other alternative to western military power."[61] He therefore argued, quite forcefully, "The deployment of US power is to be preferred to the alternatives on offer."[62]

And today? Faced with the "appalling and degrading"[63] conditions in postwar Iraq, where things were "worse than anything I was able to write about it,"[64] Rieff has felt compelled to reconsider his advocacy of U.S.-led humanitarian intervention. What he discovered on his visits to Iraq was a collapsed state, not a liberated country. Those who fervently embrace American power, it turns out, are also condemning people to death. Rieff shifts his emphasis, therefore, from the complicity of noninterventionists to the complicity of interventionists. He begins to write persuasively about "the responsibility one has in advocating war when one will have little or no responsibility or say in how it is waged."[65] Idealists who trumpeted a purely humanitarian case for invading Iraq should have known that their benevolent motives were not sufficient to trigger the war and were not going to govern the way the war and the occupation unfolded.

Human Rights as Imperial Ideology

Rieff's analysis is appealing in many ways. Yet it, too, has a few critical shortcomings. Some of his most debatable claims appear in a chapter titled "The Specter of Imperialism: The Marriage of the Human Rights Left and the New Imperialist Right." There he argues that "human rights has become, however inconsistently applied, the official ideology of the American empire – something conservatives have understood, even if most activists themselves have not."[66] In the Cold War, admittedly, "the American human rights movement collaborated intimately with Washington in its activism within the Soviet empire."[67] But is devotion to human rights now, or has it ever been, the ideology of American empire?

Rieff's chief exemplar of the humanitarian left is Samantha Power, whom he takes to be "emblematic of the historic compromise between the human rights movement and the American empire."[68] Rieff calls her book *"A Problem From Hell"*, discussed in Chapter Seven, "a breviary for this new military humanism."[69] In it, he says, she "has made the case for legal imperialism more elegantly and fastidiously than any other advocate on the American scene today."[70]

According to Rieff, Power wraps herself in the antiseptic sheets of international law, not admitting that her ideals can be defended only if the American empire expands unilaterally, without excessive regard for international law. In his own words: "For activists to now, after a decade of calling for the U.S. to unleash its power, lament the demise of multilateralism and regimes of international law is grotesque and unseemly."[71] Here Rieff makes an interesting point: If you call for a war crimes tribunal you are implicitly calling for invasion and conquest, for there is no "Nuremberg-style justice without a Nuremberg-style military occupation."[72] From this reasonable premise he concludes, more contentiously, that liberals who both advocate human rights and distrust the military imperialism of a conservative, arrogant, and secretive Administration are morally incoherent. After all: "These human rights regimes will be imposed by force of arms or they will not be imposed at all, and it is disingenuous of a human rights movement that, wittingly or unwittingly over the course of the 1990s, set the moral table for the new imperial mood in America, to suddenly recoil from the Bush Administration Captain Reynault-style because, shock, horror, they're unilateralist, Bible-thumping, gun-loving, anti-civil liberties reactionaries."[73] Neoconservatives like Robert Kagan and Max Boot are much more clearheaded than Power, Rieff concludes. They sleep perfectly soundly after running with the hounds.

One might have thought that Rieff's attitude toward the humanitarian left would mellow as he became disenchanted with America's imperialist project. But that is not what we find here. He dissociates himself further from Kagan and Boot, of course. Yet in this collection, at least, he reserves his most biting criticisms, again, for Samantha Power, this time for her "hubristic altruism,"[74] which he interprets as an invitation to endless do-gooder wars. She wants to pledge America to righting the world's wrongs, he claims, but she does not realize that this unleashing of self-righteous violence will end up corrupting the would-be saviors of mankind. An uncompromising absolutist, she is "on the same millenarian kick as the administration,"[75] inadvertently corroborating the good-versus-evil simplicities that excited and misled Bush in his bungled response to 9/11. And arguments like hers, he suggests, have provided "a recipe for a recapitulation in the twenty-first century of the horrors of nineteenth-century colonialism."[76]

After lambasting the humanitarian left first for its legalism and then for its millenarianism, Rieff launches a third line of attack. He explains that Power, Michael Ignatieff, Aryeh Neier, Kenneth Roth, and other human rights activists ended up objecting to the Iraq War only because of their East Coast snobbery. They would have favored the war, or supported it much longer, if Clinton had launched it, because their "real objections" to the invasion were "aesthetic rather than political."[77] Bush is simply too uncouth for such classy types to follow him into battle, even against an appalling violator of human rights. Their antiwar sentiments, therefore, were mostly an expression of elitist bias and a "loathsome" narcissism of small differences.[78] This passage may seem intemperate. But it illustrates the emotional depth of Rieff's alienation from the human rights community, whose imagined influence on U.S. foreign policy he evidently regrets.

The Morality of Ambivalence

Why Rieff chooses to pick this particular fight remains obscure, however. He sometimes attacks human rights militants for willing the end without willing the means. They want to prevent genocide, but they do not feel comfortable handing a blank check to the U.S. military, particularly under Bush's control, to fight oppression abroad. I suppose someone could clobber Power and the others with this sort of objection. But it cannot be Rieff, whose book is basically a defense of this very stance.

Rieff's scorn for "the vacillations of the humanitarian left"[79] seems unwarranted, in the end, because he is such a flagrant vacillator himself. He criticizes action and nonaction, imperialism and anti-imperialism, hope and hopelessness, taking sides and neutrality, too much caution and too little caution. He assumes these contrary stances simultaneously, not sequentially, moreover. He blames liberals for addressing effects, not causes, and at the same time advocates a modest approach to the world's woes, alleviating wrongs rather than righting them, which boils down to addressing effects rather than causes. With one eye trained on Rwanda and the other on Falluja, he can neither renounce nor embrace "the selective recolonization of the world."[80] He identifies wholeheartedly with "the victims" and then feels sick when he sees how easily victims become perpetrators. He aims to be skeptical but not paralyzed, even though he recognizes that militant antiutopianism will demoralize well-meaning reformers.

Although he excoriates the humanitarian left for its incapacity to make up its mind, Rieff cannot decide what he thinks about humanitarian intervention. He confesses it quite explicitly: "I am of two minds."[81] He does not like the Iraq War, but he cannot bring himself to criticize those who called for military intervention in Bosnia and Rwanda on moral grounds. And even about Iraq, his stance is hard to pin down. In a book review published after *At the Point of a Gun* appeared, he berated Larry Diamond and others for criticizing the execution of the war rather than denouncing the war itself.[82] But in the book itself, he catalogues all the usual failures of execution, especially the unforgivable neglect of policing after the regime fell and the arrogant refusal to take advantage of available expertise, domestic and foreign, that could have improved the performance of the occupying power. The disaster was not fated. Opportunities were squandered. No serious planning was undertaken for the postconflict phase. Thus, the calamity in Iraq is "a self-inflicted wound, a morass of our own making."[83] In other words, under better management, things could have turned out much better than they did.

What we have before us, then, is a co-authored work – in effect, a debate between Rieff's interventionist self and his anti-interventionist self. In this very personal back-and-forth, both parties are exceptionally courteous and forbearing. Neither side accuses the other of abetting genocide or promoting futile wars, for example. The errors Rieff acknowledges are few and relatively minor, moreover, but the unresolved disagreement is no less serious for that.

Rieff valiantly presents his inner dissonance as intellectual and moral virtue: "If this book argues for anything, I suppose it is against consistency, against ideology and utopia."[84] This candid admission of incoherence is meant to be, and is, disarming. Nor can we dismiss it as the fruit of laziness or sloppy thinking. It reflects, instead, a genuine moral dilemma. Powerful considerations point simultaneously in contrary directions. Anguished memories of Rwanda make it hard to renounce humanitarian intervention in principle, while sickening reports from Iraq make one hesitate to embrace the idea outright. Rieff's book vividly documents this apparent moral dilemma. That is its most valuable contribution.

Idealism as Pretext and Obfuscation

On the other hand, his renunciation of consistency, ideology, and utopia raises some serious questions, especially concerning his understanding of the origins of the Iraq war. By publicly renouncing utopianism, ideology, and dogmatic humanitarianism, he seems to be implying that these factors influenced the calamitous decision to invade Iraq. But is this true? Doesn't Paul Berman, champion of the very idealism that Rieff now scorns, have a more realistic understanding of the influence of intellectuals when he laments the negligible role played by Kouchner's humanitarian considerations in shaping America's Iraq policy?

During the 1990s, according to Rieff, the "human rights revolution" provided "an over-arching moral context for the exercise of power by Western countries."[85] A new international consensus emerged around the idea that "certain conduct by nations within their borders should not be tolerated."[86] What happened, allegedly, was that "half a century of campaigning by human rights activists" had "a profound effect on the conduct of international affairs."[87] Indeed, human rights activism produced nothing less than a "post-Cold War moralization of international politics."[88] The willingness of the West to intervene in Kosovo signaled "a radical change in international affairs."[89] And this was all a direct result of "people's faith in the idea of armed intervention in the name of democracy, human rights, and humanitarian need."[90]

But Rieff's account of a human rights revolution is more fantasy than reality. Not even in the 1990s was the moral duty "to right the world's wrongs"[91] an especially powerful driver of American foreign policy. Rieff is therefore exaggerating when he says, "Human rights became an organizing principle for action in the 1990s the way anticommunism had been throughout the Cold War."[92] During the Cold War, anticommunism virtually was America's public philosophy. It was an irresistibly powerful force, reorganizing government, commandeering vast resources, sanctioning brutalities committed by U.S. allies in Africa, Latin America, and Asia, and even provoking suppression of domestic dissent. Nothing similar could be said during the 1990s about human rights. The dignity of all people everywhere may have been celebrated from podiums, but in the field human rights were defended only fitfully and selectively. They filled a rhetorical gap but did not mobilize the community the way lethal enmity did during the Cold War and has done again to some extent during the war on terror. After 9/11, rescue missions became even more of a luxury than before, making it difficult, even impossible, to believe that the Iraq War sprang from a "hypermoralization of international political action."[93]

Here we return to the theme of Chapter Seven. Did the Kosovo campaign, undertaken outside the UN system to rescue potential victims of genocide, set the table for the invasion of Iraq? As mentioned, Republican publicists such as William Kristol shrewdly played the genocide card in the run-up to the Iraq War to embarrass antiwar liberals and split the left. But did a utopian desire to rescue the oppressed have any influence on the actual decision to invade Iraq? Does it make sense, when discussing the war party inside the Administration, to speak of the "Carterization" of the American right? The fact that a majority of Republicans strongly opposed an active military role for the United States in the Balkan wars suggests not. Genocide in distant lands, these Republicans argued, had nothing to do with American national security. The existence of a handful of advocates of the Iraq War who had earlier favored the Kosovo campaign, such as Paul Wolfowitz, is not decisive here. The questions that must be asked are: Did such thinking have much influence in the inner circles of the Administration? Did Dick Cheney and Donald Rumsfeld lose sleep over Rwanda? Had their closest Republican allies supported the dispatch of American troops to protect Kosovar Albanians on moral grounds? Was their principal objective in toppling Saddam to create a decent society for Iraqis? These questions bear directly on what Rieff considers the central revelation of his book, namely the marriage of the human rights left and the imperialist right. And the answer to every one of them is a resounding no.

The ruses and stratagems of the current Administration are well known to Rieff, but he has not quite absorbed their corrosive significance. The human rights advocates who initially supported the invasion lent moral legitimacy to a right-wing war undertaken for reasons having little or nothing to do with human rights. There was no "marriage" of left humanitarianism and the imperialist right, however. The affair was never consummated, except in words. The consensus between right and left that Rieff claims to have identified was a false one – a sham agreement without a genuine meeting of minds. By revealing the Administration's cavalier indifference to the fate of ordinary Iraqis, the grievously botched occupation was bound to unravel the bogus accord and drive most of the humanitarian left (with notable exceptions, such as Paul Berman) back into opposition.

The critical point here is that the Iraq war was not a humanitarian intervention, as Kenneth Roth of Human Rights Watch, among others, has argued in an official paper.[94] Why Rieff fails to clarify this elementary point is uncertain. Because humanitarian considerations had a negligible influence on the decision to invade, he should not have felt compelled, after visiting Iraq, radically to revise his thinking about interventions on humanitarian grounds. He dimly intuits this truth, it should be said, which is why he assures us that he would still support military action in Rwanda even after knowing everything he knows about Iraq. So why does he retreat into a pose of unprincipled inconsistency? He could have said, quite coherently, that the Iraq debacle teaches us less about the dangers of humanitarian intervention than about the appalling consequences of what he had earlier called "the political instrumentalization of humanitarianism." Having advocated a military response to genocide in the 1990s, Rieff now confesses to a sore conscience about the Iraq war. That is what makes his book so absorbing. *At the Point of a Gun* documents better than any other printed source the inner torment of humanitarian interventionists who, without forgetting Rwanda and Bosnia, have gazed into the Iraqi abyss. *Power and the Idealists* is equally riveting, but for the opposite reason. As intelligent as he obviously is, Berman has yet to pry open his eyes. His stubborn unwillingness to acknowledge that high ideals have been hijacked for nonideal ends, although not especially admirable, is a perfectly human reaction to a disastrous war launched and conducted under deceitful pretenses. The two books, in the end, leave us with one and the same question, namely: How is the left to regain its moral bearings in a world where the right has brazenly stolen progressive ideals (human rights, liberation, democracy, relief of suffering) and marched the country into a bloody calamity under a false flag of liberty? That this vital question remains unanswered is shocking and sobering. To have focused our minds on the challenge ahead is the shared achievement of these tortured and illuminating works.

9 | THE NEOCONSERVATIVE INTIFADA

> "No idea holds greater sway in the mind of educated Americans than the belief that it is possible to democratize governments anytime, anywhere, under any circumstances."
>
> – Jeanne Kirkpatrick (1979)

The clearest evidence that the urge to democratize the Middle East played no role in the decision to invade Iraq is the Cheney-Rumsfeld group's shocking lack of preparation for, or interest in, post-Saddam Iraq (where democratization would presumably be taking place). When the invasion was launched, plans for building Iraqi democracy had not gotten beyond the stage of posturing and sloganeering. Nonetheless the "forward strategy of freedom," as applied to Iraq and proposed for the entire Middle East, is worth examining for what it tells us about the war party's overall approach to counterterrorism. No one in the U.S. government has any clue about how to promote democracy, in the Middle East or elsewhere, so we are talking theory here, not practice. Yet even theory can be revealing. Some influential neoconservative thinkers have written that the root cause of anti-American terrorism is a democratic deficit in the Arab world. Autocratic regimes in Egypt, Saudi Arabia, and other Arab countries provide no outlet for political protest and dissent. One consequence, these neoconservatives claim, is that festering anger at the corrupt and odious oligarchs who rule such lands inevitably flows into the mosques, wrapping itself in the idiom of radical Islam. When young religious militants, whose antiregime views have incubated among radical Islamists, start causing trouble, they are viciously repressed by the authorities, imprisoned, tortured, and sometimes exiled. This is what it means to say that, on 9/11, the United States was visited by someone else's civil war or by someone else's crushed rebellion. The angry protest movements that are repressed in the Arab Middle East spill promiscuously across international borders. Unable to attack their local autocrats successfully, local militants sometimes adopt an indirect strategy, assailing their rulers' distant sponsor, namely the United States. To stave off such attacks, America must therefore make a major effort to promote political reform in the Middle East. The point here is not to judge the validity of this neoconservative argument, but rather to focus attention on the startling premise behind it. The argument presumes that jihadists conspiring to attack America, despite their evident hostility toward religious toleration, are not driven to violence by their hatred of American-style freedom. What tips their frustration into political rage, and what lures angry new recruits to their cause, is fury at their own lack of freedom. They do not hate America's principles. Instead, they hate what they see as America's unprincipled support for Arab tyrants. These assertions are not excerpted from some radical jihadist website or the essays of Noam Chomsky. They form the very core and basis of President Bush's own "forward strategy of freedom." This strategy assumes, extraordinarily, that the jihadist cause is basically just, even if the cruel means that the jihadists choose to employ are savagely criminal. It assumes that the jihadists hate us for what we do (support Arab autocracies), not for what we are. It also implies that terrorism can be stripped of its appeal only by political reform, by opening up channels for domestic political participation in the Arab world. The entire democratization agenda, admittedly, has been recently set back by the electoral successes of radical anti-American parties in the Middle East and elsewhere. Nevertheless, exposing the premises underlying Bush's "freedom agenda" can still cast considerable light on the inner incoherence of the Administration's counterterrorism policy. To deny that Cheney and Rumsfeld are neoconservatives is to emphasize their commitment to a half truth, namely their visceral conviction that violence breeds compliance. This dubious principle led them to predict that American ferocity would, by sheer intimidation, produce moderation in the Middle East. They apparently imagined that "legitimacy" can be delivered on the back of an Abrams tank. The neoconservatives who support democratization, by contrast, mitigate their still recognizably hawkish worship of force with a somewhat incongrous appeal to noble ideals, especially the end of tyranny and the spread of liberty. Such idealistic talk apparently appealed greatly to President Bush himself. It must have satisfied his need, not shared by Cheney or Rumsfeld, to inject "the vision thing" into his Administration's response to 9/11. The neoconservative democratization agenda, however, is deeply incompatible with the Cheney-Rumsfeld intimidation agenda. Rather than flatly refusing to negotiate with "evil," democracy promoters are more concessive, implicitly acknowledging the legitimacy of at least some of the smoldering grievances that fuel jihad. Democratizers, as democratizers, look past the immediate enemy to discover the problem that gives rise to anti-American enmity itself. What they discover, roughly speaking, is the old verity that violence breeds violence. This may not seem like news, but in the mental world of Bush's war cabinet it is. The cruelty of Egyptian jailers gives rise to antiregime terrorism, and antiregime terrorism provokes more jailhouse torture, in an endless cycle. Democratization is meant to lead the way out of this trap. In neoconservative thought, essentially, democratization responds to violence not by using overwhelming force but by undermining violence's appeal, offering a "political horizon" for the expression and remedy of social frustrations. Just as Woodrow Wilson hoped to end all wars by eliminating the conditions that produced war, so the neoconservatives propose to end terrorism by eliminating the conditions that engender it. Admittedly, the Administration's democratization agenda is now basically defunct, partly because the Iraq debacle has associated American-imposed democracy with sectarian slaughter, criminalization, and economic collapse. That voting rituals cannot reconcile bitterly hostile armed factions is now self-evident. Political power in Iraq depends less on the purple fingers of voters, in any case, than on the trigger fingers of armed foreigners and Shiite militias. Electoral competition among political parties with paramilitary wings might be called death-squad democracy. That such a system is clamorously undemocratic is the least that might be said. The electoral success of virulently anti-American Islamist parties in Egypt and Palestine as well as Iraq has further discredited the hopes of happy democratizers. After Guantánamo and Abu Ghraib disclosed America's indiscriminate mistreatment of Muslims, it seems, Muslim electorates are unlikely to vote the way the neoconservatives hoped. But neoconservative theory is nevertheless well worth revisiting, not as a blueprint for political reform in the Middle East, but for its implicit and persuasive criticism of the simplistic Cheney-Rumsfeld view that military force, ferociously applied, will effectively dry up the wellsprings of terror.

In the immediate aftermath of 9/11, neoconservative Francis
Fukuyama signed an open letter arguing that the overthrow of Saddam
Hussein was essential to "the eradication of terrorism," even if Saddam
were revealed to have had no connection to al Qaeda and no hand in the
attack.[1] At that time, in other words, and alongside neo-con celebrities
such as Charles Krauthammer and William Kristol, Fukuyama was beating
the drum for a "shift in focus from al Qaeda to Iraq."[2] He now expresses
qualms about the killing of "tens of thousands" of innocent Iraqis who
had done nothing to harm America or its inhabitants: "These casualties in
a country we were seeking to help represent an enormous human cost."[3]
Such guarded words of regret will strike most readers as welcome and
overdue. To unrepentant apologists of the war, by contrast, they have the
feel of apostasy and betrayal.

The question is: Does Fukuyama tell us anything that we don't already
know? Can he explain how "the irresponsible exercise of American power"
became "one of the chief problems in contemporary politics"?[4] Can he
help us understand how "so experienced a foreign policy team" could
make "such elementary blunders"?[5] Can he indeed tell us why the Administration decided to do what he and his former allies had encouraged them
to do: namely, to transform Saddam's isolated dictatorship into a central
battlefront in the global war on terror? This is the essential issue because,
as Fukuyama himself admits, the Iraq war has "unleashed a maelstrom,"[6]
inflaming the anti-American extremism it was ostensibly launched to
quell.

As it turns out, Fukuyama's book sheds considerable light on the cognitive biases and intellectual incoherence behind America's catastrophic
response to 9/11. Above all, it deepens our understanding of the Administration's twisted interpretation of the terrorist threat. From Fukuyama's
analysis of Bush's foreign policy, we can distill five debatable but stimu-
lating propositions. First, the fatal decision to invade Iraq was based on a
genuine, not merely contrived, "conflation" of the threat posed by rogue
states with the threat posed by nuclear terrorists. Second, Cold War habits
of mind and a misunderstanding of the causes of the collapse of the Soviet
Union contributed to the Administration's blurred reading of the new
enemy and therefore to its decision to launch an ineffectual, misdirected,
and self-defeating counterattack. Third, the neoconservative democratization project, having become a widely publicized justification for the
invasion after the fact, makes assumptions about the nature of the threat
that clash with the basic theoretical framework of the Administration's
war on terror. Fourth, nonmilitary counterterrorism policies in Europe

(multilateral police operations and proposed social programs designed to aid the integration of Europe's alienated Islamic youth) reflect a much clearer understanding of the terrorist threat than unilateral military intervention in the Middle East. And finally, the Administration's visceral hostility to multilateralism has led it to play down threats to U.S. national security that can be managed only cooperatively.

I will limit myself in this chapter to discussing two propositions that I have not explored in much depth elsewhere in this volume: first, that Cold War habits of mind are alive and well in the Bush Administration; and second, that the chimerical neoconservative "democratization" project clashes with the assumptions of Bush's war cabinet about the terrorist threat and what to do about it.

Cold War Legacies

Although he is fiercely critical of contemporary neoconservatives such as Kristol and Krauthammer, Fukuyama has little negative to say about neoconservatism during the Cold War. After the break-up of the U.S.S.R., however, the neoconservatives, and especially the younger generation, proved unable, intellectually and emotionally, to adapt to the radically altered security environment. Having created a formidable war machine to oppose Soviet power, the United States suddenly found itself dominating the globe, its military power not merely unrivaled but seemingly irresistible. Nevertheless, "many neo-conservatives continued to see the world as populated by dangerous and underappreciated threats."[7] They simply could not dial down their inherited alarmism. The context had shifted radically, but their reflexes remained the same. This failure to adapt may have been to some extent self-serving. So long as America appeared seriously endangered, the neoconservatives could continue to inflate their own importance, admiring and advertising themselves as the only Americans capable of understanding the formidable dimensions of the threat. Whatever their motives, they tended "to overestimate the level of threat facing the United States."[8] They also resorted impulsively to old tropes, excoriating liberals for a spineless unwillingness to confront the enemy, and even for being soft on terrorism, just as an earlier generation had accused its liberal cohort of being soft on Communism.

The Soviet Union collapsed because of "its internal moral weaknesses and contradictions,"[9] Fukuyama tells us. But the neoconservatives credited President Reagan with ending the evil empire by forcing the Russians into an economically unsustainable arms race. As we know from the case of bin Laden and the Afghan Arabs, the illusion of having brought down the U.S.S.R. can reinforce latent psychological tendencies to megalomania. Fukuyama does not highlight this parallel, but his account suggests that many neoconservatives, like many of the jihadists, experienced a high when the Soviet Union came crashing down in 1991, for somewhat analogous reasons and with distressingly analogous results.

It is also important to remember that during the Cold War neoconservatives had adamantly opposed détente. Scorning containment, they preached rollback instead. They did not believe that the United States should learn to coexist with the Soviet Union, in short, insisting rather that it could win an uncontested victory. Coexistence, they argued, implied accommodation, which would turn into appeasement, which would soon dissolve into capitulation. After the Soviet Union unexpectedly fell apart, they did not revisit or apologize for their overestimation of the Communist system's resilience and strength. On the contrary, they felt totally vindicated. Although they had been spectacularly blind-sided, they concluded that they had been brilliantly prescient. As a result, according to Fukuyama, they were unwilling to admit that their eccentric intuitions of impending danger might ever prove to be false alarms. This is why "so experienced a foreign policy team" came to make "such elementary blunders."[10] They committed fundamental errors because their guiding principles, distilled from the Cold War stand-off, had become obsolete.

Excessively pleased with themselves, the neoconservatives drew two lessons from the collapse of Communism. First, threats should be eliminated, not managed. Second, American security is invariably enhanced by the transformation of autocracies into democracies. That the democratic transformation of Eastern Europe was triggered not by an invasion but by the withdrawal of a foreign army apparently made little impression on them. All they knew was that the threat to America from the Communist bloc had been eliminated by the more or less successful transformation of its former members into democracies or, at the very least, democracies in the making.

That an anxious electorate would prefer to eliminate a lethal threat, rather than live under its ominous shadow, goes without saying. However, when applied to the current terrorist threat, this impetuous desire "to end evil," as Richard Perle defines the neoconservative project, has deeply pathological consequences. The danger posed by radical Islamic anti-Western terrorists armed with weapons of unimaginable destructiveness cannot be dismantled overnight. The conditions that make Islamic radicalism dangerous to the West are ineradicable features of the modern world. They include global systems of transportation, communication, and banking, rivers of petrodollars coursing through politically unstable Muslim countries, and the gradual spread of nuclear know-how. Under such conditions, a counterterrorism policy that aims at extirpating the terrorist threat is bound to be delusional. Promoted by an unsound analogy with the end of the Soviet Union, such utopian impatience can also be profoundly self-defeating, especially if it prompts policymakers to focus irrationally on the wrong part of the threat – for example, on a minor danger that happens to lend itself to definitive obliteration. Saddam Hussein comes to mind.

The Freedom Agenda

As for the neoconservative democratization project, Fukuyama writes that the disgraceful failure of the war party around Cheney and Rumsfeld "to think through the requirements of post-conflict security and nation-building"[11] reveals the emptiness of their feigned interest in the fate of post-Saddam Iraq. For the Vice President and Secretary of Defense, the suggestion that the invasion would bring about "Iraqi democracy" was merely an "ex-post effort to justify a preventive war in idealistic terms."[12] Their cavalier attitude to the sovereignty of other nations was the flip-side of their unapologetic commitment to America's globally unlimited freedom of action. True, they agreed that it would periodically be "necessary to reach inside states"[13] to create conditions favorable to U.S. interests. But this does not mean that Cheney or Rumsfeld shared the democratizing hopes of those self-described idealists in and around the administration who stress "the importance to world order of what goes on inside states."[14] For a start, the willingness of Cheney and Rumsfeld to intervene in the internal affairs of other nations was not and is not humanitarian. And they have not extrapolated from American efforts in postwar Germany and Japan to suggest that democratization serves U.S. security interests everywhere and always. They understand perfectly well the tactical benefits of cloaking narrow American interests, as they define them, in the language of do-gooder morality. But this doesn't make them eager to spread electoral democracy, with all its unpredictable consequences, into politically unstable and strategically vital regions of the world.

As argued above, the desire to demonstrate America's unrivaled military power, after the country's vulnerability was exposed on 9/11, played a much more important role in the decision to invade Iraq than the desire to establish a model democracy there, but the illusion of democratization nevertheless deserves special examination. Why did Paul Wolfowitz and a few others argue, with reported sincerity, that a democratic Iraq was vital to America's national-security interests? True, they did not anticipate the exorbitant costs of the war, in lives and money, but they did assert that Iraqi democracy had become especially important to America after 9/11. Why?

The neoconservative answer to this question is fairly simple: Lack of democracy in the Middle East is, as Charles Krauthammer put it, "the monster behind 9/11."[15] The United States had to deploy its military might to Iraq because American national security was (and is) threatened by the absence of democracy throughout the Arab world. The premise behind this allegation is not the much-debated notion that democracies seldom go to war with one another and, therefore, that democratization makes an important contribution to the pacification of the globe. The neoconservative argument is less concerned with relations among potentially warring states than with class or group dynamics within a single state that may spill over and affect other countries adversely.

Their thesis is that democracy is the most effective antidote to the kind of Islamic radicalism that hit the United States on 9/11. According to Krauthammer, again, "the root of the problem" is "the cauldron of political oppression, religious intolerance and social ruin in the Arab-Islamic world – oppression transmuted and deflected by regimes with no legitimacy into the virulent, murderous anti-Americanism that exploded upon us on 9/11."[16] The exponents of this view begin with the premise that tyranny cannot tolerate the public expression of social resentment that its abuses naturally produce. To preserve its grip, tyranny must therefore crush even modest stirrings of opposition, repressing dissidents and critics with unstinting ferocity if need be. In the age of globalization, however, repressed rebellions do not simply die out. They splash uncontrollably across international borders and have violent repercussions abroad. Middle Eastern rebellions have been so savagely and effectively repressed that rebels have been driven to experiment with an indirect strategy to overthrow local tyrannies and seize power. They have traveled abroad and targeted those they see as the global sponsors of their local autocrats.

On 9/11, this argument implies, the United States woke up in the middle of someone else's savage civil war. The World Trade Center was destroyed by foreign insurgents whose original targets lay in the Middle East. The explosive energy behind the attack came from Saudi and Egyptian rebels unable to oust local autocrats and lashing out in anger at those autocrats' global protectors. Thus, the rationale for reaching "inside states" is not the traditional need to replace hostile or uncooperative rulers with more compliant successors (of the type Ahmed Chalabi was apparently slated to become), but rather to "create political conditions that would prevent terrorism."[17] The political condition most likely to prevent anti-American terrorism from arising, so the neoconservatives allege, is democracy.

Their reasoning at this point becomes exasperatingly obscure and confused, but their guiding assumption is clear enough: Democratic governments channel social frustrations inside the system instead of allowing discontent and anger to fester outside. Violent methods for redressing grievances will lose their appeal if peaceful methods for redressing grievances become available. In Bush's own words, "Citizens who can join a peaceful political party are less likely to join a terrorist organization."[18] This offhand comment may seem somewhat pollyannish, but it does reflect a widely held belief about the recent history of the Middle East, namely that "The lack of any avenue for legal dissent forced political opposition to the margins, almost ensuring that it would become extreme."[19] Autocratic governments in the Arab world have shown themselves capable of retaining power by sheer coercive force, but their counterrevolutionary efforts, under contemporary conditions, have serious "externalities," especially the export of murderous jihad to the West. America's security challenge is to shut down this export industry. To do so, the United States must find a way to democratize the Middle East.

This convoluted and debatable argument played only a marginal role in the Administration's original decision to invade Iraq. It played a more substantial role in the post-invasion presentation of America's "mission" in Iraq, however. It is also a central focus of Fukuyama's book. So how should we evaluate the idea? Is a democratic deficit in the Middle East the principal cause of anti-Western jihadism? Is democratization a plausible strategy for preventing the export of political violence?

Democracy's Preconditions

The first thing to say is that fighting terror by promoting democracy makes little sense as a justification of the American invasion and occupation of Iraq. Although the lack of democracy in Saudi Arabia and Egypt may be indirectly fueling anti-Western jihad, it has never done so in Iraq. In nondemocratic countries with which the United States is allied (such as Saudi Arabia and Egypt), antiregime violence inevitably escalates or swerves into anti-American violence. The idea that a lack of democracy in countries overtly hostile to the United States (such as Saddam's Iraq or contemporary Iran) will have such an effect is logically implausible and unsupported by historical evidence.

To argue that creating democracy in Iraq will help defeat Islamic terrorism is to bank on a multi-stage process by which democracy, once established in Iraq, will spread to Egypt, Saudi Arabia, and so on, by force of its inspiring example. Only then, after neighboring dominoes (including governments allied with the United States) begin to fall, would the democratization of Iraq contribute seriously to draining the terrorists' proverbial recruitment pool. Of course, such political revolutions, in the unlikely event that they actually erupted, would be wholly impossible to control or steer. That is reason enough to doubt that Cheney or Rumsfeld, for example, ever took seriously this frivolous bit of neo-con futurology.

The idea of a democratic cure for terrorism assumes that there are two separate causes of anti-American jihad: Middle Eastern autocracy and unprincipled or opportunistic American backing for it. Anti-American jihad would subside, the theory implies, if either condition could be eliminated. Thus, the neoconservative rationale for regime change in the Middle East seemingly justifies something much less radical, and presumably less difficult, than creating stable multiparty democracies in Mesopotamia: the gradual withdrawal of American support from the region's corrupt oligarchies and oppressive autocracies. Putting daylight between the United States and abusive Middle Eastern regimes should be enough to insulate America from the violent backlash such tyrannies produce.

Unfortunately, this pathway is blocked. America cannot simply disengage from a region in which so many of its vital interests, including the steady flow of oil and the tracking down of terrorists, are at stake. Yet the paradox remains. From the impossibility of disengaging and the perils of engaging with autocrats, the neoconservatives conclude that American interests require engagement with a democratic Middle East. The logic sounds impeccable at first, but it is based on the unfounded assumption that periodically elected governments in the region will necessarily be stable, moderate, and legitimate, not to mention pro-American.

An even more fundamental argument against fighting terrorism by promoting democracy, as already discussed in Chapter Four, is that no one in the U.S. government has any idea how to promote democracy. Fukuyama accuses the neoconservatives of chatting offhandedly about democratization while failing to study or even leaf through the "huge academic and practitioner-based literature on democratic transitions."[20] Their lack of serious attention to the subject had an astonishing justification: "There was a tendency among promoters of the war to believe that democracy was a default condition to which societies would revert once liberated from dictators."[21] Democracy obviously has many social, economic, cultural, and psychological preconditions, but those who thought America had a mission to democratize Iraq gave no thought to them, much less to helping create them. For their delicate task of social engineering, the only instrument they thought to bring along was a wrecking ball.

One might have thought that this "remove the lid and out leaps democracy" approach was too preposterous ever to have been taken seriously. However, it is the position that Fukuyama, with some evidence, attributes to neoconservatives in and around the Administration. They assumed, he writes, that the only necessary precondition for the emergence and consolidation of democracy is the "amorphous longing for freedom"[22] which President Bush, that penetrating student of human nature, detects in "every mind and every soul."[23] Their sociology of democracy boils down to the universal and eternal human desire not to be oppressed. If this were democracy's only precondition, then Iraq would have no trouble making a speedy transition from clan-based savagery and untrammeled despotism to civilized self-restraint and collective self-rule. Skeptics, such as James Kurth,[24] who harp on the impossibility of creating a government that would be both coherent and representative in a multiethnic, multisectarian, and tribally fragmented country simply fail to appreciate the love of freedom in every human heart.

Cavalierly designed by midlevel bureaucrats who were both historically and theoretically illiterate, the Administration's half-baked plans backfired badly. Bullets obviously play a much greater role than ballots in post-Saddam Iraq. This should have come as no surprise. Prospects for political reform in the wider Middle East, moreover, have not been improved by the perception that democratization in the region, at least when promoted by the West, spells violent destabilization, civil strife, separatism, criminalization, and a collapse of minimally acceptable standards of living.

Neoconservatives, Fukuyama implies, seldom do the hard work required to learn about the evolving political and social dynamics of specific societies. Instead, they over-personalize any "regime" that they dream of destabilizing, identifying it with an individual ruler who can, in principle, be killed with an air strike or hanged after a show trial. Here again they walk into a serious self-contradiction. One of their principal claims is that a bad regime will have long-lasting negative effects on the society it abuses. A cruel autocracy puts down "social roots"[25] and reshapes "informal habits."[26] Thus, "Saddam Hussein's tyranny bred passivity and fatalism – not to mention vices of cruelty and violence."[27] It is very likely, in other words, that Saddam unfitted the Iraqi people for democracy, for a time at least. This is what Machiavelli had in mind in Book I, Chapter Sixteen of his *Discourses on Livy*, where he argued that a people who have been living under an autocratic government will find it almost impossible to hold onto freedom when their tyrant is suddenly removed by an external shock. It is also, more relevantly, a logical implication of the neoconservatives' own theory of "regimes" as shapers of character, but not one that they considered in this context, presumably because it would have knocked the legs out from under their idealistic case for war.

The Core Contradictions

These fallacies and contradictions are not even the most egregious of those associated with the democratization rationale; not when you consider that the basic justification for helping spread democracy in the Middle East flatly contradicts the claim that Islamic radicals are apocalyptic nihilists who love death and hate freedom. No one would contend that al Qaeda is at war with the House of Saud and Mubarak because those regimes are democratic. Indeed, the observation that Islamic radicals hate tyranny, not freedom, is the central premise of the argument for promoting democracy.

In Administration rhetoric, terrorism (a method for waging asymmetrical war) is routinely opposed to liberty (a principle for organizing a modern society). The antithesis of liberty, however, is not terrorism but tyranny. So, when the Administration tries to place jihadism in the space vacated by Communism, turning it into the new global enemy of liberty, it confuses both itself and others.

Tacitly, the neoconservative advocates of Middle Eastern democracy are siding with the young men who might be tempted to join terrorist conspiracies against their clientalistic, kleptocratic, and nondemocratic governments, which are officially allied with the United States. Al Qaeda is less similar to the KGB than to the KGB's implacable foe, the Afghan mujahideen, "freedom fighters" supported by Ronald Reagan, among others. The jihadists rail against the impiety of Middle Eastern autocracies; but their fury would lose its gusto were it not supplemented by a perfectly secular rage against corruption and lack of freedom. Today's neoconservatives no longer want to imitate Reagan by helping resentful young Muslim men regain their dignity through violent insurgency. Instead, they want to give them an alternative path to dignity: namely, liberal democracy. Yet the basic reason for supporting frustrated Muslim youth, that they deserve American support in their noble search for liberation, is the same.

It is worth dwelling for a moment on this massive contradiction. Although obvious in a way, it is seldom discussed; Fukuyama himself doesn't seem to notice it. The neoconservatives defend two diametrically opposed propositions: first, that the jihadists hate freedom and, second, that they hate their own lack of freedom. On the one hand, neoconservatives assert that Islamic radicals despise American values (such as religious toleration), not American policies (such as support for Israel), and deny that America's past behavior has in any way provoked anti-American violence. On the other hand, they imply that the 9/11 plot was inspired and implemented by terrorists radicalized by Arab autocracies allied with or sponsored by the United States. This suggests precisely that 9/11-style terrorists hate American policies (backing the oppressors of Muslim peoples), not American values. They hate not the principles of American liberty but, rather, America's unprincipled support for tyranny. Jihadist rage against the impiety of Muslim leaders and their Western backers would be much less virulent, and would attract much less popular sympathy, were it not fueled by rage against the corruption, cruelty and unfreedom of the ostensibly apostate regimes America flagrantly supports. That is to say, jihadism, however repugnant, is not simply "evil" but has a perfectly comprehensible rationale. If we do not grapple honestly with this rationale, we will not be able to reduce the jihadist appeal.

Paradoxically, then, the neoconservatives agree with bin Laden himself when, rejecting "Bush's claim that we hate freedom," he declares that "we fight because we are free men who don't sleep under oppression." Embracing bin Laden's analysis, presumably unconsciously, the neoconservatives argue that democratization will prevent the majority of Arabs and Muslims from drawing the terrible conclusion that bin Laden himself draws, namely: "We want to restore freedom to our nation, just as you lay waste to our nation. So shall we lay waste to yours."[28] To prevent oppressed Arabs and Muslims from turning their rage against America, we need to help these peoples escape from oppression. To promote democracy in the Middle East is therefore to admit, implicitly, that jihadist rage is not only understandable but even in good measure just.

The proposal to increase American security by such means logically presupposes that America's problem is not terrorism but Islamic radicalism, initially turned militant and subsequently turned outward. Terrorism is not the enemy. It is a tactic that Islamic radicals have found exceptionally effective. To recognize that America's fundamental problem is Islamic radicalism, and that terrorism is only a symptom, is to invite a political solution. Promoting democracy is just such a political solution. It assumes that the United States is ready to take seriously Muslim grievances, including grievances against America. Although publicly invoked to support a military invasion, the goal of a democratic Middle East implies that terrorism must be stripped of its appeal by political reform precisely because it cannot be crushed by overwhelming military force. The radical incompatibility of this perspective with the Cheney-Rumsfeld approach to counterterrorism, aiming to make America feared rather than loved, should be self-evident. The "forward strategy of freedom," however unrealistic, assumes that the United States must address the root cause of terrorism (that is, the lack of democracy in Muslim countries), rather than trying to repress anti-American violence, which is only a symptom, by overwhelming force. It assumes that America is in some degree culpable for having, in the past, supported nondemocratic regimes in the Middle East. For Cheney and Rumsfeld, by contrast, the very idea that America might commit grave moral wrongs against foreign peoples is incomprehensible. And for Bush himself, 9/11 was all the proof he needed that "infinite justice," not mere human and partial justice, was on the American side.

And that is not all. Fukuyama himself stresses a completely different contradiction afflicting the neoconservatives. The proposal to pull Mesopotamia into the modern world, he says, is based on a facile optimism reminiscent of 1960s liberalism and publicly rebutted by the original neoconservatives. Progressive dreams are bound to be dashed on the hard realities of social habit. One of the fundamental goals of neoconservatism, in its formative period, was to show that "efforts to seek social justice" invariably leave societies "worse off than before."[29] They were especially "focused on the corroding effects of welfare on the character of the poor."[30] All distribution from the rich to the poor and from whites to blacks is allegedly counterproductive. Progressive attempts to reduce poverty and inequality, although well-intentioned, have "disrupted organic social relations,"[31] such as residential segregation, triggering a violent backlash and failing to lift up the downtrodden. According to the neoconservatives, it is wiser to concentrate on the symptoms, using police power and incarceration to discourage violent behavior and protect civilized values.

The neoconservatives, according to Fukuyama, never explored the relevance of such warnings to U.S. foreign policy. Proponents of the Iraq war, very much like old-style liberal advocates of welfare, "sought worthy ends but undermined themselves by failing to recognize the limits of political voluntarism."[32] Their failure in Iraq was just as predictable as the failure of American liberals to improve the lives of poor American blacks. In short, the plans of today's idealistic hawks for creating Iraqi democracy show how utterly they have betrayed the neoconservative legacy. Perhaps the deepest irony is that their enthusiasm for destroying the status quo and overthrowing the powers that be (without giving much thought to how to replace them) recalls the institution-bashing antics of 1960s student radicals more than the counterrevolutionary posture of the founding fathers of neoconservatism.

Democratization and Organized Interests

Addressing the possibility that the United States can still play a positive role in bringing democracy to the Middle East, Fukuyama is surprisingly optimistic. In fact, he continues to endorse what he calls "the perfectly fine agenda of democracy promotion."[33] Going beyond the bland liberal assumption that, on balance, less autocracy is better than more, he argues, "There is an imperative to liberate people from tyranny and promote democracy around the world by reaching inside states and shaping their basic institutions."[34] Without wincing, he still advocates "a revolutionary American foreign policy agenda."[35] One of his principal reasons for sticking with this agenda is that it allegedly has history on its side: "There is a broad, centuries-long trend towards the spread of liberal democracy."[36] Sweeping generalizations of this sort are meant to remind the reader of Fukuyama's first book, *The End of History and the Last Man* (1992). For good or ill, he has never fully repudiated the ostentatious idea, which made him world famous as a young man, that human history is moving inevitably towards a "culmination" that closely resembles Americanization.

Fortunately, Fukuyama's reluctance to disagree with himself does not extend to his former colleagues among the neoconservatives. He argues, for example, that the United States should promote democracy abroad only for its own sake, not for its imagined usefulness in combating terrorism. He also dissents from present neo-cons on the proper methods for promoting democracy and "the time frame"[37] within which democratic change can be expected. America can accelerate its inevitable arrival by training, advice, funding, and election monitoring, not to mention by good example, but it cannot do so by military invasion and conquest. This is why Fukuyama pleads for "a dramatic demilitarization of American foreign policy and re-emphasis on other types of policy instruments."[38] The Pentagon, alongside its other deficiencies, is poorly positioned and incorrectly staffed for fostering democratic transitions. American "experts" who write laws and design institutions for countries making the transition to democracy must be "immersed in the habits, mores and traditions of the people for whom they are legislating."[39] Such culturally informed Americans may or may not exist, but they don't work for the Department of Defense.

Promoting democracy requires a sophisticated understanding not only of specific cultures but also of the relation between institutions and organized interests. Institutional reform frequently fails, Fukuyama says, because it "threatens entrenched interests."[40] Institutional reform is "almost always more of a political than a technocratic problem,"[41] because "certain powerful actors have a strong self-interest in the status quo."[42] As a result, "strong, unified indigenous groups willing to resist the former regime"[43] must exist within a society in order to overcome the resistance of entrenched spoiler elites. The amorphous love of liberty in every human heart is neither here nor there. The key is to strengthen proreform forces and weaken antireform ones.

For Fukuyama, this means, for example, "developing a local constituency in favor of fiscal reform, or otherwise eliminating the political support for recalcitrant political groups."[44] His plausible conclusion here is that "institutions will not be created unless there is a strong internal demand for them."[45] Strong external demand, coming, say, from the United States, is not a sufficient condition for successful institution building or institutional reform. The Administration's plans for swiftly democratizing Iraq were doomed from the outset, he persuasively argues, because America had "no organized local allies"[46] there. The planners and managers of the invasion paid no attention to this fatal lack. They were taken aback by the invasion's chaotic aftermath because of their appalling ignorance of the elementary preconditions of political stability. That formal institutions function properly only when supported by informal social networks seems to have occurred to none of those assigned to manage the postwar process of reform.

Such grave misapprehensions diminish not only the legitimacy but the effectiveness of U.S. efforts in the war on terror. Fukuyama's unnervingly persuasive claim is that they have also undermined the decency and even the sanity of America's response to 9/11. Administration dead-enders are unlikely to appreciate his final suggestion that "a new team," with "new policies,"[47] would be able to free itself from this spider's web of fallacies and fixations. Less partisan readers will be grateful for the random rays of hope, justified or not, with which Fukuyama lightens his bleak but informative account of an American foreign policy that has completely lost its bearings, with consequences grievous, and perhaps irreparable, that we have only begun to see.

PART IV

WAIVING
THE RULES

10 | LIBERALISM STRANGLED BY WAR

> Safety from external danger is the most powerful director of national conduct. Even the ardent love of liberty will, after a time, give way to its dictates.
>
> — *The Federalist Papers*, No. 8.

What can students of the war on terror learn from the wartime measures of previous presidents? Several lessons stand out. First, the executive discretion necessary in wartime has, more than once, opened the door to poor judgment and factional agendas. Unprincipled motives have periodically stolen into public policy under the carte blanche of wartime security. Foreign dangers, moreover, have regularly been perceived through the prism of partisan politics. Nor is it uncommon for war, hot or cold, to be accompanied by a degeneration of partisan mudslinging into outright charges of treason by both sides. Easy resort to allegations of disloyalty and lack of patriotism, however, make learning through public disagreement and the use of evidence and argument to compel revision of failed policies difficult if not impossible. Geoffrey Stone's history of freedom of speech in wartime, *Perilous Times: Free Speech in Wartime From the Sedition Act of 1798 to the War on Terrorism*, discussed in this chapter, reveals the shallowness of the platitude that security can be automatically increased by curtailing liberty. One liberty that presidents are especially tempted to curb in wartime, when embarrassing missteps are inevitable, is freedom of speech. At times, the U.S. government has even used the criminal law to punish citizens simply for disagreeing publicly about the justice and wisdom of a particular war. Freedom of speech is as much a

public as a private right, however. It is part and parcel of the citizens'
freedom to examine their government, and includes the right to contest
the government's claim that a war being launched or already underway is
truly necessary. What sense does it make to sacrifice the right to inspect
and question the government for the sake of national security? It seems
unlikely that an unexamined government, sheltered from all criticism, will
perform satisfactorily or defend national security with skill and honesty.
At first glance, the civil liberties record of the Bush Administration seems
to hold up well when compared to Lincoln's suspensions of habeas corpus, Wilson's Sedition Act, and Roosevelt's internments. These flattering
comparisons are somewhat misleading, however. For example, Lincoln's
suspension of habeas corpus in April 1861 without prior Congressional
approval was driven by serious considerations of urgency (Congress could
not be convened so quickly) and judicial capacity (the Maryland courts
could not handle appeals from all those detained in the Baltimore riots).
The Bush Administration's effective suspension of habeas corpus in the
case of one individual, José Padilla, for a period of two years cannot possibly be justified by invoking white-hot urgency or the limited capacity of
the civilian courts. In general, anti-American Salafi terrorism is an enduring threat, not a sudden or unexpected event. As a result, it requires
not unchecked discretionary power in the hands of the president and
his immediate entourage, locked in a partisan bunker, but long-term,
rule-governed cooperation among specialized executive agencies, with
important functions assigned to the legislative and judicial branches, to
reduce the probability of fatal errors. It is true that the Bush Administration has not infringed on civil liberties as badly as some previous
wartime presidents. But this is largely because those who have suffered
most grievously from the Administration's malfeasance have been foreigners abroad. Traditional reasons for reliably protecting the rights of
American citizens while treating aliens overseas as if they possessed no
rights at all may have become obsolete in an age when resentful foreigners,
burning with a sense of grievance, are only one cheap air ticket away from
U.S. shores. The possible benefits of extending minimal legal protections
to aliens overseas are unlikely to sway most Americans, admittedly. Spared
the burden of the draft, the American public seems unfazed by the tens
and perhaps hundreds of thousands of Iraqis who have died because
of the U.S. invasion. So why would the U.S. political system display
any greater sensitivity to the rights of foreigners imprisoned in offshore
prisons by American authorities without a chance to contest the reasons

alleged for their confinement? It is true that the Supreme Court, in *Rasul v. Bush* and *Hamdan v. Rumsfeld*, has stood up to the Administration on the issue of executive detention, but this is not necessarily a sign that today's Court is much braver than the earlier Courts criticized by Stone. It probably signals something else, namely the current majority's awareness that, whatever President Bush's lawyers pretend, a potentially endless war against invisible micro-armies plotting to provoke visceral fear that outstrips their actual capacity to inflict harm, is not the kind of "war" that justifies unchecked and unwatched executive authority. If the executive branch is able unilaterally to inflate its own authority by invoking threats that no other branch has the opportunity to verify, our constitutional system of mutually correcting powers will be fundamentally and perhaps irreversibly altered, damaging the country's capacity to adapt intelligently, effectively and creatively to ever-evolving threats.

To help us grope our way through the perilous present, Geoffrey Stone, a leading authority on the First Amendment, has produced a rich and readable overview of America's curtailment of civil liberties in wartime. He focuses primarily, but not exclusively, on restrictions of freedom of speech, examining in engrossing detail six historical episodes: the Sedition Act of 1798, the Civil War, World War I, World War II, the Cold War, and the Vietnam War. He appends a brief discussion of civil liberties after September 11, but his real contribution to the study of the war on terror is his book as a whole. Each episode, as Stone retells it, speaks in one way or another to painful issues of the present day. His general conclusion is that "the United States has a long and unfortunate history of overreacting to the perceived dangers of wartime."[1] He hopes that a bit of self-knowledge will inspire us to do better this time around. Political dissent has been criminalized in the United States only when foreign powers have threatened our national security. This exception implies, disturbingly yet understandably, that the United States has two constitutions, one for peace and one for war. Since our enemies will not always fight by the book, it would be suicidal to insist that our leaders adhere punctiliously to preestablished rules when reacting to foreign threats: The executive's discretionary power to respond flexibly to unpredictable attacks is justified, but it is also dangerous. The loosening of existing rules and the bypassing of established procedures for making decisions opens the door even wider than usual to poor judgment and factional agendas.

The Sedition Trap

The possibility that emergency powers, however necessary, will also be abused became apparent as early as the sedition trials at the end of the eighteenth century, which is where Stone begins his story. The incumbent Federalist Party used the threat of war with France as a pretext to discredit its Republican rival in the run-up to the election of 1800. Trumping up an alarm of danger, as their adversaries vividly charged, the ruling Federalists treated pungent criticisms of President John Adams as if they were treasonable assaults on the very nation.

Historical precedents for wartime abuse of executive power are simultaneously reassuring and unsettling. On the one hand, they suggest that we have survived bouts of unconstitutionality before. On the other hand, they imply that deviations from the Constitution are simply what we should expect. Writing as a historian, Stone aims to explain how legal doctrines and practices have buckled under the pressure of violent political events. But he never lets post-September 11 America drift far out of sight. In his first chapter, for instance, he reminds us that the incumbent Federalists, between 1798 and 1800, relentlessly accused their partisan rivals of underestimating the foremost foreign menace and even, as closet Jacobins, of being ready to hand their country over to the French. At the time, admittedly, the judiciary was stacked with judges belonging to the president's party, and they cooperated readily in the campaign to shut down opposition newspapers and to choke off criticisms of the Administration and its policies. So the intriguing analogy to the present remains to some extent imperfect.

Imperfect, but still illuminating, The Alien and Sedition Crisis is not our crisis, but it reminds us helpfully that we are far from being the first Americans to interpret foreign dangers through the distorting prism of party politics. Indeed, this politicization of national security seems to be the rule rather than the exception. When severely criticized by partisan rivals, previous incumbents, too, have inflated foreign threats and invoked the honor of the troops in the field in order to squelch embarrassing criticisms of Administration policy. Not war only, but even the threat of war, may entice a sitting president into slurring opposition politicians with intimations of disloyalty. Citing foreign dangers as a pretext to silence domestic competitors may have unfortunate consequences for the nation – not only may an alleged threat, upon inspection, prove to be exaggerated or imaginary, but, as rudimentary First Amendment theory instructs, censorship also stupefies the citizenry. Albert Gallatin, leader of the House Republicans at the time, repeatedly stressed the point. In response to the sedition trials, he remarked that clampdowns on freedom of speech and the press "prevent the diffusion of knowledge," cramp the productive exchange of views, and "throw a veil on the folly" and the "crimes" of the government.[2] The outlawing of dissent, whatever the excuse, undercuts public reason as well as private rights.

More specifically, the curtailment of freedom of speech and the press under the threat of foreign war weakens the country by depriving citizens of their inalienable right to examine and to judge their government. A more grievous injury to the Constitution is difficult to imagine, for this political right is the guardian of all private rights. The issues involved here are immensely complex, but already in his first chapter Stone dispels a basic confusion afflicting contemporary discussions. Others have expressed discomfort with the notion that the war on terror requires us to sacrifice liberty for security. The alleged causal relation between reduced liberty and increased security seems highly speculative, for one thing. But Stone, because he is focusing on the First Amendment, takes this objection a step further. How much sense does it make, he implicitly asks, to sacrifice the critical understanding of government action for the sake of security? To redescribe the proposed trade-off in these striking terms is to draw much-needed attention to the potential, not to say actual, conflict between the interest of today's incumbents in hiding mistakes and the interest of the country as a whole in correcting mistakes.

To Preserve the Union

Only after the Civil War, in the celebrated case of *Ex parte Milligan* in 1866, did the Supreme Court deny that the government could resort to military commissions on American territory to try alleged civilian conspirators during war or rebellion when the ordinary courts were open and functioning. Writing for the majority, Justice David Davis famously declared that the Constitution is the law of the land "equally in war and in peace," and that "the great exigencies of government" do not free the executive branch from "any of its provisions." The Bill of Rights, in other words, is not "silent among arms."

This is an inspiring piece of idealism, often cited by opponents of the Bush Administration's resort to military tribunals. As Stone shows, however, it is somewhat misleading as a statement of fact. Lincoln's suspension of habeas corpus, for instance, carried out in open defiance of Chief Justice Roger Taney, would have been unthinkable in peacetime. It was one of the principal measures his partisan opponents cited when accusing him of trying to dismantle traditional American liberties. Additionally, Lincoln, for his part, manifestly believed that the letter of the Constitution could be violated in a state of emergency, though not in ordinary times, to preserve the Union and the safety of the people. Among the practices that he explicitly approved was trial by military commissions of civilians accused of "discouraging voluntary enlistments," that is, of seriously weakening the Union's capacity to preserve itself militarily.

The most rabid conflicts over freedom of expression in American history, Stone suggests, arose in the context of drafting soldiers for dangerous service in controversial wars. This is perfectly natural, because military conscription tests the outer limits of liberalism. There is nothing remotely "consensual" about conscripts in rival armies trying to kill each other. The liberalism of individual rights and due process of law is invariably weakened by the collective discipline and discretionary authority of wartime mobilization. Today's insipid talk about "balancing" liberty and security seems quite remote from these harsh and brutal realities. War allows the government to sacrifice not only the liberties but also the lives of individual conscripts for the sake of group security as defined by the party that happens to be wielding political power. After a war is declared, those who do not believe that the alleged threat is sufficiently grave and imminent to warrant the deployment of military force are not granted footloose freedom to withhold their participation. They are instead compelled to bend their private wills not to the demands of national security defined by a national debate, but to the incumbent's perhaps gratuitous and unilateral interpretation of the danger at hand.

This potentially fatal subordination of individual lives to collective purposes, defined by the officeholders of the moment, has deep, even primordial origins. The drill and discipline of its military, that is, the "constitution" of the force that protects inhabitants from foreign predators and marauders, is fundamental to the survival of any society. The first rule of such an Ur-constitution was long thought to be the right of the military leadership to execute deserters. Without such a power, it was traditionally believed, no army could be maintained in the field; and whoever wills the end must will the means.

Thus, a constitutional and democratic state can deprive citizens of life and liberty by drafting them into the military, against their individual wishes, in time of war. But is censorship of political speech a necessary and permissible means to raising armies and keeping them afoot? Communications between Lincoln and his distant military commanders were slow and sporadic. Therefore, as Stone emphasizes, Lincoln's officers sometimes acted on their own initiative without the president's foreknowledge.

At various points, they forced opposition newspapers to close, and they inflicted criminal punishments on critics of the president and the war. Attempting to justify the silencing of antidraft publicists, a repressive measure of which he did not necessarily approve, Lincoln asked memorably: "Must I shoot the simple-minded soldier boy who deserts, while I must not touch a hair of a wily agitator who induces him to desert?"[3] The underlying logic here draws attention to the tight connection, which resurfaces in Stone's accounts of World War I and Vietnam, between restrictions on freedom of speech and the greatest of all "infringements" of civilian liberty, namely, the coercively enforced consignment of young male citizens to the slaughterhouse of battle.

As the Civil War's death toll soared, enrollment officers were harassed and even murdered, and antidraft riots spread across the North. All this cried out for a forceful response. Even before the Emancipation Proclamation, antiwar sentiment was closely associated with racism. Opponents of the draft acrimoniously inquired: Why should white boys be forced to die for the freedom of blacks who will afterward move north to steal white jobs? Thousands of allegedly disloyal individuals residing within the Union were taken briefly into military custody for inciting rebellion and expressing sympathy with the Confederacy. At stake, however, was not merely freedom of speech or the government's authority to silence those who publicly cast doubt on the justice of the Union cause. The issue was more basic and cut deeper. What sort of constitutional limits can and should be placed on the incumbent president's right to decide that a given threat is so grave and imminent that thousands of conscripts must lose their lives to beat it back? Are there no limits to the government's power to decide when and where collective security demands the sacrifice of individual liberty? Can the government quash debate about these matters by criminalizing the speech of citizens who dare challenge its claim that the sacrifice of individual liberty is actually serving collective security as opposed to benefiting some illicit factional interest?

An additional point should be made here about habeas corpus. That Lincoln suspended the writ is less interesting, from today's perspective, than his reasons for doing so. The Union cause was seriously jeopardized, Stone explains, by disorder and opposition in the border states abutting the nation's capital, especially in Maryland. The Constitution provides for the right, during invasions or rebellions, to suspend the writ of habeas corpus, whereby the executive branch is ordinarily compelled to explain before an independent judge its grounds for holding a prisoner. (Whether the right to suspend the writ belongs to the president or to Congress has been a matter of dispute.) Insurrectionary activity in Maryland, including bridge-burning, was putting at risk transportation links between Washington, D.C., and the North. After murderous clashes between Union troops and Baltimore mobs, Lincoln suspended habeas corpus, reasoning that the government was faced not with hundreds of ordinary crimes, but rather with mass rebellion. As Stone paraphrases the position of Lincoln's supporters: "The rebellion involved treasonable activity on so vast a scale that the ordinary criminal process was simply inadequate to deal with the situation."[4]

Yes, the courts were still open; but they would not have been able to handle large numbers of rioters. Moreover, conditions of rebellion did not lend themselves to the gathering of evidence or the taking of testimony, let alone conviction by a jury drawn from the accused's own state and district as the Sixth Amendment requires. If rioters were brought before civilian judges, they would in all likelihood have been released, only to replenish the rebellion. Lincoln justified his decision, therefore, by arguing, "men may be held in custody whom the courts, acting on ordinary rules, would discharge,"[5] especially if they are going to be freed a few months later when the momentary danger has passed.

It is again worth stepping back to ask what light this historical episode might cast upon the current war on terror. Lincoln's thinking differs instructively from the reasoning of Bush's apologists and lawyers. The latter have argued that ordinary due-process rules could be suspended in cases such as that of José Padilla, the alleged dirty bomber, originally arrested at Chicago's O'Hare airport in May 2002. (In November 2005, after having been held in military detention for more than two years, he was transferred to civilian jurisdiction and charged with aiding terrorists and conspiracy to murder U.S. nationals overseas.) Government officials initially insisted that Padilla was no ordinary criminal, but rather an unlawful combatant in an unprecedented global conflict.

Lincoln, it should be noticed, contrasted ordinary crime not to a clandestine war but to an open rebellion. This makes a difference. In a technical legal sense, not worth discussing here, Bush did not actually suspend habeas corpus in Padilla's case; but he did so for all practical purposes. In any case, Bush's attorneys worked hard to deny Padilla his constitutional right to due process. Unlike Lincoln, however, they could not claim that the sheer number of potentially treasonous offenders was soon likely to exceed what ordinary courts could process. They could not honestly cite as a precedent Lincoln's suspension of habeas corpus to safeguard the transport of Union troops through territory verging on rebellion. Rioters taken into custody during (in Lincoln's words) "sudden and extensive uprisings against the Government"[6] could easily have overtaxed the criminal justice system. The same cannot be said about the one or two American suspects kept by Bush out of ordinary civilian courts.

Disagreement as Disloyalty

Stone labels the Sedition Act of 1918 "the most repressive legislation in American history."[7] It outlawed "conspiracy to publish disloyal material intended to obstruct the war and cause contempt for the government of the United States."[8] This draconian legislation was a product of war and the intense emotional identifications spawned by life-and-death struggles between political communities. President Woodrow Wilson dealt harshly with what he called "the poison of disloyalty." Because they were allegedly promoting contempt for the government and disaffection among the troops, antiwar groups had to be silenced. Healthy or harmless in peacetime, political disagreements among Americans had to be quashed lest they boost the morale of foreign foes.

Censorship may be a perfectly sincere expression of respect. To gag speakers is to acknowledge that speech is potent, that a single word may kindle an all-engulfing flame. Calls for a general strike might conceivably have been taken up, disabling the American war machine. With such apprehensions in mind, the government prosecuted and convicted Eugene V. Debs for publicly stating, among other things, that the rich were shipping poor soldiers to their deaths for crass commercial gain. One unfortunate filmmaker was sentenced to ten years in prison for accurately portraying British brutality toward Americans during the Revolutionary War and thereby presumably jeopardizing America's World War I alliance with Great Britain. The bare mention of war profiteering was considered tantamount to treason. Many of the Americans who denied that Germany's submarine warfare against England posed a grave threat to U.S. security were of German or Irish ancestry. That is to say, political disagreements about the imminence and the gravity of a foreign threat expressed underlying ethnic cleavages. This dispute was resolved in the usual manner: The holders of public office prevailed.

Judges, including two of the most distinguished justices on the Supreme Court, Oliver Wendell Holmes and Louis D. Brandeis, at first acquiesced to Wilson's personal intolerance for criticism and proclivity for repressive solutions. They produced, in their wartime decisions, what Stone calls "dismal precedents that took the nation half a century to overcome."[9] In one famous case, on behalf of a unanimous Supreme Court, Holmes wrote that the First Amendment creates no constitutional right to say anything that encourages mutiny, hinders the war effort, or impedes the raising of armies. Such holdings were not exactly monuments to liberalism.

Yet, neither were they gross anomalies. In wartime, judges have a hard time balancing individual rights against government interests. They are unfavorably positioned to second-guess the executive's diagnosis of government interests under emergency conditions. They lack independent sources of information to help them verify or falsify the executive's assessment of foreign threats. How can they possibly decide if allegations of military necessity are valid or not? Moreover, as William O. Douglas later wrote of the American judiciary, "Its members are very much a part of the community and know the fears, anxieties, craving and wishes of their neighbors."[10] Stone clearly disapproves of this dim view of judges, even though nothing in his book suggests that it is especially inaccurate.

At the Great War's end, the fears and the anxieties of ordinary Americans abated, and, presumably as a result, the Supreme Court slowly began to shift course. After the storm had passed, Holmes and Brandeis caught their breaths and, in influential dissents, laid the foundations for the robustly liberal First Amendment jurisprudence that Stone himself celebrates. The "clear and present danger" test, associated with Holmes, eventually made it more difficult for the government to silence political speech. Stone's behind-the-scenes account of how this standard developed is one of the highlights of the book and, indeed, one of the most intriguing tales of unintended innovation in American legal history.

If judges failed to moderate the executive branch's oppressive reflexes while World War I was still ongoing, the public at large proved less honorable still. When youngsters are dying in war, as Stone explains, many people back home are emotionally compelled to believe that the sacrifice must be worth it. They favor restrictions on freedom of speech not so much because they think that antiwar agitation is actually impeding the war effort, but simply because, in such a stressful period, they cannot tolerate, for psychological reasons, the grating sound of dissonant and doubting voices.

In peacetime, democracy encourages law-abiding behavior not by coercively suppressing frustrations but rather by guiding them into officially sponsored channels, allowing citizens to campaign for the repeal of unpopular laws. Wartime is different. In the stress of wartime, ordinary citizens may fail to distinguish attempts to overturn laws meant to support the war effort from disruptive violations of these same laws. During World War I, Stone contends, jury members, with sons perhaps at the front, had little patience for the distinction between antiwar speech calling for legislative change and antiwar speech calling for disobeying the law. Aflame with nationalist zeal, juries regularly found antiwar agitators who had called for a perfectly legal change of policy guilty of sedition, that is, of acting with malicious intent and with the likely effect of obstructing the raising of armies and the defense of the nation. During an existential conflict with a lethal enemy, in other words, ordinary citizens may be no more likely than robed judges to act as reliable guardians of the Constitution. Civil society is no less bigoted than officialdom. That explains why the right to criticize incumbents and agitate for change has always proved easy to abridge in times of war.

Politicizing Executive Detention

Francis Biddle thought along similar lines. In an arresting phrase, he wrote, "the Constitution has never greatly bothered any wartime President."[11] As Roosevelt's attorney general between 1941 and 1945, Biddle was in a good position to know. The most glaring violation of constitutional principles under FDR was undoubtedly the mass internment of more than one hundred thousand ethnic Japanese, citizens as well as resident aliens, undertaken (similar to the recent internments in Guantánamo) without any individualized findings of guilt. What was the official justification for such a sweeping measure? It was that the United States must relocate all persons of Japanese origin away from the West Coast, an area where certain defense industries were located, because government officials did not possess sufficient linguistic or cultural knowledge to discriminate accurately between innocent and guilty members of the group. This is the same logic with which we are regaled today. The government's failure to make a serious investment in the linguistic and cultural knowledge of public officials was invoked to justify a minority community's loss of rights.

According to Stone, political and even partisan factors played a considerable role in Roosevelt's decision to approve the wholesale evacuation against the advice of J. Edgar Hoover, among others, who insisted that his agents had the situation fully under control. Roosevelt wanted to focus early American war efforts on Europe, and may have therefore allowed what Justice Frank Murphy (one of Stone's judicial heroes) called a "legalization of racism"[12] in order to vent anti-Japanese feeling without diverting military resources to the Pacific. Similarly, the numbers and the political clout of Italian-Americans and German-Americans, and not merely their geographical dispersal away from a militarily vulnerable coast-line, help explain why they, in turn, were not relocated en masse. Japanese-Americans may have been singled out less because they were dangerous than because they were weak. Their appalling internment, Stone adds, received some measure of public support on racist grounds, because the internees were nonwhite.

The implicit comparisons between this episode during World War II and certain notorious events in the contemporary war on terror are again eye-catching; so much so that Stone feels little need to dwell on them or even to discuss them explicitly. In any war or emergency situation, the executive branch has a strong incentive to represent itself to the public as highly effective. Incumbents can even convince themselves that exaggerations in this respect are selflessly patriotic, because the mere reputation of effectiveness may dishearten the enemy and embolden one's own forces. One consequence of this need to appear effectual is that innocent detainees, interned by mistake, may not be released promptly when the government discovers that it has erred. Their exculpation and discharge, after all, would expose the incompetence and the slipshod screening procedures of the arresting authority. For the sake of appearances, therefore, wrongfully detained individuals may well be held in custody until a politically opportune moment (until, say, presidential elections are over).

This, Stone indicates, may have been what happened to the interned Japanese-Americans. Roosevelt was advised already in 1943 that these detentions did nothing to increase America's security. But he did not release the detainees until after the election of 1944. If Franklin Delano Roosevelt behaved this way, what can we expect from George W. Bush? Has the current Administration, too, unconscionably prolonged the incarceration of guiltless captives simply to shield itself from public embarrassment? The very possibility reminds us that appallingly unprincipled motives can easily steal into public policy under the carte blanche of wartime secrecy.

The Enemy Within

Although it comes late in Stone's story, the Cold War turns out to be, in his account, "perhaps the most repressive period in American history."[13] Such a recent violation of the basic liberties of American citizens, it should be said, challenges the "Whiggish" belief that our constitutional liberties are somehow destined to expand. This expectation of progress is so strong that it even appears fleetingly in Stone's own account. But the past that he surveys provides liberals with no ironclad assurances about the resiliency of the American constitutional order in the face of danger, real or alleged, from abroad.

During the early 1950s, the beliefs and the associations of American citizens were monitored by a network of domestic spies and informers. The roots of this nightmarish development remain mysterious to some extent. Popular support for repressive government, at the time, may have derived in part from an intense psychological stress, similar to today's, caused by the stark incongruity between immense American power and inescapable American vulnerability. After World War II, nuclear weapons and long-distance missile technology obliterated America's comforting geographical isolation from the world's violence and turmoil. The end of insularity, we might speculate, could have been sufficiently disorienting, psychologically and emotionally, to excite a popular yearning for scape-goats. And stoking the climate of anxiety was a fear – not a baseless one – that America's principal foreign enemy had domestic followers and fellow travelers. Many suspicions of Soviet espionage and subversion were illusory, even hallucinatory, but by no means all; some have since been confirmed.

The interesting point here is that the early 1950s witnessed a much more thorough and pernicious blurring of the homefront and the foreign front than anything we have seen since September 11. Stone's recounting of the early Cold War period, therefore, provides an important reality check for fearful liberals today. At that time, progressives were not accused simply of being weak on defense. They were also charged, very much like the Republicans during the Alien and Sedition Crisis, with being treasonous collaborators with the country's mortal enemy. Even by today's uncivil standards, the levels of vituperation at the time were extraordinary. So, why the difference?

American territory today may host a handful of sleeper cells, but our party politics has not yet been poisoned by a generalized fear of a "fifth column" or an "enemy within" of the sort exploited by red-baiters during the Cold War era. The partisan hijacking of the current war on terror is inexcusable. And the rhetorical smearing of some Democratic candidates in 2004 and 2006 was at times unbelievable. But none of this, as Stone's history reminds us, has yet reached the self-destructive and fanatical extremes of the McCarthyite exploitation of America's confrontation with Communism.

No Antiwar Movement without an Antidraft Movement

Stone turns finally to the Vietnam War, a period that he experienced first-hand. Parallels to the present again swarm through his account. Examples include the American government's confident predictions of an American "victory" in a distant counterinsurgency and American plans to strengthen the South Vietnamese military and then withdraw. Lyndon Johnson and Richard Nixon both invoked national security to limit the right of the electorate to know what was being done in its name. Both coded criticism as enmity, craved unswerving loyalty, and careened forward without a plan. Nixon even presided over a secret government within the government. Among their other antics, members of his inner circle placed backroom pressure on news executives to toe the Administration line. Setting an example for subsequent public-private partnerships in this domain, they had the FBI recruit right-wing newspapers to smear critics of the war. As Stone remarks, "If direct censorship was no longer available to silence critics, secrecy, deceit and half-truths still remained effective weapons in the government's propaganda arsenal."[14]

So much for the government. What about the opposition? The most striking thing about the antiwar movement, as Stone suggests, is how long it took to get under way, that is to say, how difficult it was to make the general public bring into focus the hellish violence that the American military was perpetrating abroad, in a war launched on a dubious theory and conducted on the basis of shoddy intelligence. As Justice Brandeis said, in a passage cited elsewhere by Stone, "an inert people"[15] is the greatest enemy of freedom.

The debatable but intriguing analogy between the Vietnam War and the Iraq war raises the following question: Why has the American public not been more concerned with what our troops have wrought at Abu Ghraib or in Fallujah? We hear grumblings about the "backdoor draft" affecting fellow Americans, but popular attitudes toward Iraqi suffering, with some exceptions, seem characterized by dimmed awareness if not denial. Government infringements of freedom of speech cannot be blamed for this numbness. How do we account for public passivity and inertness in the face of the bruising toll of death and destruction that American military power has doled out to thousands of Iraqi civilians who never did America any palpable harm? This passivity has barely fluttered, even after it became obvious that the invasion of Iraq could be justified neither as revenge for September 11 nor as self-defense against weapons of mass destruction. How can it be explained?

Civic quiescence may be temporary, of course. In time, antiwar effervescence, the growth of which Stone traces in his chapter on Vietnam, may emerge. Or it may not. According to classical "republican" theory, the public is goaded into keeping a close watch on its elected government by taxation and conscription. These two coercively enforced forms of extraction from society by the state create zones of contention and conflict where, as Charles Tilly has argued, democratic citizenship is forged. To obtain a degree of voluntary compliance with taxation and conscription, the government must provide the affected citizens with plausible sounding reasons for the sacrifices they are being asked to make.

As mentioned in Chapter Four, Bush's war cabinet learned from the Vietnam War that the best way to "put to sleep" domestic questioning of foreign military adventures was to eliminate the draft, create an all-volunteer force equipped with high-tech weaponry, reduce taxes, and take large loans from (among other sources) the Chinese Central Bank, to be repaid by future generations who cannot vote because they are not yet born. Without the energy provided by draft resistance and tax revolts, the Administration correctly calculated, antiwar protests are bound to be anemic and easy to ignore. This crafty scheme for circumventing democratic accountability eventually produced, among other disasters, the troop shortages that made it impossible for the United States to halt the looting and the wildcat violence that surged after the fall of Saddam. It has also immunized President Bush, at least so far, from an antiwar movement of the sort that tormented Lincoln, Wilson, and Nixon.

Another reason to doubt that the American public will soon awaken to the realities of Bush's war in Iraq also emerges from Stone's account. During the Vietnam War, the antiwar movement drew strength from the public's fear that nuclear annihilation might be triggered by the reckless and bellicose party in power. In the war on terror, by contrast, the fear that New York and other American cities could experience their own "Hiroshimas" tends to mute criticism of the government by a public hoping desperately to be saved from an invisible but grave and purportedly gathering threat.

The American Tradition and the War on Terror

Has Bush simply been acting in the tradition of Lincoln, Wilson, and Roosevelt, predictably infringing civil liberties under the extraordinary conditions of war? To say so would amount to praising the current Administration with faint damns, which hardly seems to be Stone's intention.

How, then, can a historian of America's wartime excesses avoid normalizing the Bush presidency? To dissociate Bush's unconstitutional behavior from that of his illustrious predecessors, we might simply deny that the so-called war on terror should even be included in a study of wartime liberties under siege. After all, the war on terror is not a full-scale military confrontation in the sense of the Civil War, World War I, or World War II. Stone does not quite choose to draw the distinction this way, however. The war on terror might not be a war in any traditional sense – but a successful act of nuclear terrorism against, say, Washington, D.C., would have incalculable consequences for the American system of government. Dismissing this threat as basically unserious compared to previous dangers would not be wise.

An alternative, more compatible with Stone's approach, would be to accept that Bush is just as much a wartime president as Lincoln, Wilson, and Roosevelt, but then to scour the historical record in order to identify something unprecedented about Bush's "overreaction to perceived dangers," some cavalier treatment of the Constitution that sets him apart from his predecessors. Certainly the Iraq war seems like one of the worst (and least comprehensible) blunders in the history of American foreign policy. Saddam Hussein may have once posed some sort of a threat to the United States, but the exact nature of this threat has never been coherently explained. He certainly did not pose the threat that the Bush Administration said he did. The Administration's war aims and its criteria of success remain hazy to this day even after Saddam has been put to death. So the very strangeness of the Iraq war suggests that Bush is doing something never done before rather than simply following in illustrious footsteps.

The genuine novelty of Bush's behavior in "wartime," in fact, emerges directly from Stone's story. Neither the Iraq war nor the wider war on terror to which it allegedly belongs has involved any criminalization of dissent. True, dissenters inside the executive branch have been fired. If you speak truth to power, in this Administration, you lose your security clearance. But there have been no sedition trials, unlike the earlier episodes studied by Stone. Why not? The absence of conscription is one obvious reason. Without a draft, there will be no antidraft movement; and without an antidraft movement, an antiwar movement may of course exist, but it will be erratic and uncertain. Only presidents who have to deal with draft resistance are tempted to flout the First Amendment directly, repressing speech that urges draft resistance.

If Bush has behaved unconstitutionally, he has not behaved unconstitutionally in the manner of Lincoln or Wilson, or even in the manner of Roosevelt. True, hundreds of innocent American citizens have been caught up for a time in panicky counterterrorism investigations, and at least two American citizens, perhaps culpable of serious offenses, were held incommunicado for almost two years without access to an attorney. Yet the most morally abhorrent acts of this Administration have involved the mistreatment of foreign nationals outside the United States and cannot therefore be easily classified as violations of the Bill of Rights.

Lincoln, Wilson, and Roosevelt, whether justifiably or not, violated the constitutional rights of American citizens on American territory. Bush has done this too; but he has been much more active in violating the human rights of aliens abroad. Because he has asserted (in the original Padilla case, for example) his authority to deny fundamental due process to American citizens, there is no reason to relax our vigilance on this front. Bush, however, at least so far, has violated the Bill of Rights only episodically. Most of the abuses that he has condoned have involved non-Americans overseas, and, despite some complications and unsettled law in this area, the Bill of Rights, in its crucial aspects, has never applied to foreigners extraterritorially. The behavior of some prison guards and interrogators at Abu Ghraib and Guantánamo is sickening. The mind-boggling toll of death and destruction unloaded on Iraqi civilians who never did the United States any palpable harm is morally repugnant. Neither constitutes a clear-cut wartime violation of civil liberties, however, not in the ordinary sense.

This is not to deny that, in its conduct of the so-called war on terror, the Bush Administration has violated important and long-standing constitutional norms. At his most radical, Bush has claimed that Congress has no right whatsoever to interfere with the way he chooses to conduct his war on terror. This historically unprecedented inflation of the Commander-in-Chief power, to be discussed in Chapter 13, is a radical assault on our constitutional system of checks and balances. It flies in the face of the text of the Constitution, which grants a series of concomitant war powers to Congress, including the power to define offenses against the law of nations. Brushing aside original intent and two hundred years of constitutional practice, Bush Administration lawyers have audaciously and irresponsibly argued that Congress has no right to turn international law prohibitions on torture and war crimes into enforceable federal law if the latter in any way restricts the president's total discretion to treat foreign captives overseas however he wishes. This overreaching is truly flagrant, even by the lax standards governing the wartime presidencies examined by Stone.

This deliberate dismantling of checks and balances, it could be argued, also infringes on civil liberties, at least indirectly. This is what Stone is getting at when he mentions "the Bush Administration's obsession with secrecy."[16] It has not criminalized dissent, but the Administration has overclassified documents, restricted Freedom of Information Act access, hounded executive-branch leakers, and blacklisted nettlesome journalists. It has thereby eroded, to some extent, the freedom of information that gives freedom of speech its political bite. It has abridged the inalienable right of citizens to examine and to judge their government. Serious and across-the-board censorship has proved unnecessary for maintaining popular support despite a catastrophic foreign policy blunder. The absence of a draft and the strategic reduction of taxes seem once again to provide the key to this puzzling development, though we should not neglect the contribution to public confusion made by powerful broadcast media in the hands of partisan supporters of the Administration.

Even if the extraterritorial torture or inhumane treatment of detained foreign suspects does not involve any violation of the Bill of Rights as it has traditionally been understood, it does involve a spectacular challenge to Congress's constitutional authority. It also involves a violation of several international treaties ratified by the Senate. Bush has sinned more often against international human rights than against domestic civil liberties. That, unfortunately, is a further reason why political protests in the United States have remained relatively meek. No vocal domestic constituency is directly injured when the Administration flouts the Geneva Conventions and other rules that have previously moderated American behavior overseas. The Supreme Court initially asserted jurisdiction over the Guantánamo detainees in *Rasul v. Bush* (2004) and subsequently imposed limits on the Administration's unfettered power over aliens abroad in *Hamdan v. Rumsfeld* (2006). But Congress, under executive-branch pressure and perhaps in sync with public opinion, pushed back, largely overruling the Supreme Court. At this point, it seems at least possible that Bush will succeed in his grab for unfettered power over aliens abroad. It is therefore worth reminding ourselves that he has rashly claimed this new freedom from civilizing restraints in an age of globalization when the kith and kin of those individuals whom American forces humiliate, injure, and kill abroad now have a historically unprecedented capacity to target Americans anywhere in the world, including here at home.

Freedom as Vulnerability and Resilience

It is sometimes said that the September 11 hijackers exploited our generous liberties in order to attack us. If this were true, we would have to become a less liberal society in order to become a better-defended one. But is the premise true?

Not necessarily. What if, to infiltrate the United States and to evade our defenses, the al Qaeda terrorists took greater advantage of our technology and our complacency than of our liberties? What if ignorance of foreign languages and cultures inside America's national-security bureaucracies opened the door to 9/11? What if judicial interference with executive discretion was a negligible problem compared to turf wars and information hoarding between rival executive agencies?

What remedies would such diagnoses demand? Would weakening the constitutional system of checks and balances, for example, help the executive become more focused and less reckless? That is unlikely. Indeed, the Administration's desire to circumvent traditional checks and balances patently weakened its capacity for critical thought and self-correction, preparing the way for its gratuitous decision to invade Iraq. To defend ourselves against our most dangerous enemies, we do not need unrestricted government. We need intelligent government. And no Administration that shields itself compulsively from criticism has a prayer of being even sporadically intelligent.

Governments will always be less transparent in wartime than in peacetime, and justifiably so. The rights of citizens to pry into government secrets cannot possibly be as expansive in war as in peace. Still, emergency conditions do not suspend the laws of human fallibility. Wartime leaders, too, need some form of adversarial process to protect them from cognitive biases and false certainties. Excessive secrecy may breed disconnection from reality. Panic may spread inside the bunker, and illicit private interests may colonize public policy if decision making is monopolized by a few like-minded individuals who never listen attentively to alternative points of view. One-party and single-branch government weakens incentives for decision makers to acknowledge errors and make midstream readjustments. The consequences cannot possibly be favorable.

Stone's admirable history strongly suggests that, in practice, the United States does indeed have one constitution for peace and another for war. This is a disquieting revelation. It is unsettling for an often-cited reason: The high-priority manhunt for anti-American terrorists, which Bush has styled a "war," promises to endure so long as weapons of mass destruction remain available to crazed conspirators – that is, for the foreseeable future. As we have now discovered, a largely unchecked executive has a tendency to gallop off on wild-goose chases, paying little heed to opportunity costs, tying down our troops in the wrong places, and failing to husband the resources that we are undoubtedly going to need to defend ourselves in an increasingly dangerous world. True, in the war on terror, as in previous wars, domestic criticisms of the Administration may sometimes give heart to the enemy. Allowing a small clique within the government to continue making momentous choices behind a veil of secrecy, on the basis of publicly unexamined evidence, and oblivious to contrary views, however, will surely debilitate the country and abet the enemy even more.

The constitutional right of American citizens to examine their government has invariably faded in times of violent conflict. This is an ominous precedent because we are now embroiled in a potentially endless battle, whether or not it qualifies as a war. By chronicling the most serious historical deviations from our ordinary constitutional order, therefore, Geoffrey Stone's outstanding book alarms as much as it clarifies. As the current Administration flouts the Constitution in genuinely groundbreaking ways, it is also exposing the rest of us to dangers hitherto unknown.

11 | THE UNILATERALIST CURSE

This chapter joins the debate about the Bush Administration's so-called unilateralism and its alleged effects on the war on terror. Multilateral institutions are often dysfunctional to the point of paralysis, but it remains true that the United States cannot deal effectively with many important problems, including terrorism and proliferation, without voluntary cooperation from other countries. Unilateralist tendencies will seriously endanger U.S. national security only if an exaggerated attachment to unilateral methods dissuades the country's national-security agencies from paying sufficient attention to threats that must be dealt with cooperatively. Many executive-branch agencies specializing in counterterrorism, including the FBI and the CIA, have good cooperative relations, mostly bilateral but also multilateral, with counterpart agencies abroad. (Some of these are "dark side" relations that cannot be publicly acknowledged by either party.) But American counterterrorism, in the broadest sense, still suffers to some extent from a unilateralist bias because the most unilateral of the country's national-security agencies, namely the Pentagon, has exercised disproportionate influence over the way priorities have been set in the war on terror. The Department of Defense has little or no experience in collaborating with law-enforcement and intelligence establishments around the world where most of the professionals knowledgeable about radical Salafi terrorism work. The accurate intelligence on which effective counterterrorism depends, moreover, assumes deep cultural and political knowledge about remote lands and peoples and a sophisticated capacity to work with, not to say "work," foreign colleagues without being duped and used. The Pentagon does not have inside its own bureaucracy anything like the skills and level of knowledge necessary to design and implement an innovative, flexible, and effective counterterrorism strategy.

Other U.S. government agencies have shortcomings of their own, but none is hobbled by the Pentagon's aloof view of foreign peoples and undue impatience with indecisive international negotiations. A unilateralist bias may also explain why the nightmare scenario of a suitcase nuke brought by stealth into an American city has not persuaded Administration officials to put more effort into trying to reduce the threat of nuclear proliferation. Cheney and Rumsfeld presumably realized that strong-arming (if not bombing) Iran and North Korea did not constitute a comprehensive approach to the proliferation problem and that the overall threat could be managed, if at all, only by strengthening international treaties on arms control and nonproliferation, agreements that Cold War hawks of their breed were, for ideological reasons, devoted to dismantling. So long as the Pentagon sops up the lion's share of America's national-security budget, in any case, efforts to track down elusive and scattered Salafi terrorists and to interdict illicit sales of nuclear weapons and materiel will probably remain under-resourced. The neoconservative slogan, "multilateralism when possible, unilateralism when necessary" admittedly sounds reasonable at first. What it implies, however, is that the United States can, when push comes to shove, defend its national security without much help from allies – or rather with help only from those countries that are frightened of U.S. power or drawn into the slipstream of U.S. success. The implausibility of these assumptions has been dramatically demonstrated by the Iraq debacle and, more particularly, by the scandal of the missing Iraqi weapons of mass destruction. The European leaders who warned America against the invasion of Iraq turn out to have been right. The international inspection teams affiliated with the United Nations had a more accurate picture of the Iraqi weapons program than did the CIA. What these facts bring to our attention is that allies have interests, yes, but they also have ideas, insight, information, imagination, and skill. To gratuitously deprive ourselves of these assets is shortsighted at any time, but most especially at a time when the United States, as the principal target nation, cannot easily bring the evolving terrorist threat into focus, much less counter it, without substantial foreign help.

September 11 forced both the stewards and the diagnosticians of U.S. foreign policy to revisit some of their deepest assumptions, but it is important to remember that there was wisdom also before September 11, in many contributions to the debate about America's international role that appeared before the world was turned upside down. G. John Ikenberry's *After Victory* is such a work. Written before the attacks, the book helps us understand the deep sources and disturbing consequences of the Bush Administration's seemingly unilateral approach to foreign affairs, starting with its decision to withdraw unilaterally from the Antiballistic Missile Treaty. To understand why the Administration reacted the way it did to 9/11, we have to understand the mindset with which Bush's foreign policy team came into office. The key to their thinking can be found in their cavalier attitude toward multilateral institutions already visible during the initial nine months of Bush's first term, in serial rebuffs of the International Criminal Court, the International Treaty to Ban Land Mines, the Biological Weapons Protocol, and the Kyoto Protocol, the Comprehensive Test Ban Treaty, and the Small-Arms Control Pact. The rationale behind such gestures has been clearly articulated by conservative columnist Charles Krauthammer. The whole point of multilateralism, Krauthammer writes, is "to reduce America's freedom of action by making it subservient to, dependent on, constricted by the will – and interests – of other nations. To tie down Gulliver with a thousand strings."[1] Because America does not want its freedom of action reduced, it must flex its muscles and break the strings with which other, weaker nations would craftily seek to tie it down.

In the confusing aftermath of the attacks, the Administration seemed to flirt for a moment with a return to multilateralism. Rumsfeld and Cheney soon sidelined Colin Powell, however, making sure that a haughty unilateralism, dripping with contempt for capable allies, remained the Administration's public posture. The theory behind this stance seems to have been that negotiations and alliances make a superpower look weak. No one would contend that Cheney and Rumsfeld favored the invasion of Iraq simply because some of America's traditional allies opposed it; but the Vice President and Secretary of Defense certainly agreed that "the United States must not be perceived as being constrained by alliances."[2]

Viewed institutionally, as discussed in earlier chapters, American unilateralism represents the paramountcy of Defense over State. The upshot of this victory in an interagency power struggle by a partnership of the Office of the Vice President (OVP) and the Office of the Secretary of Defense (OSD) was that military force became a more important tool than diplomacy in the struggle against terrorism. Formulated the other way round, the American military's capacity to act (more or less) alone guaranteed that U.S. counterterrorism strategy, once militarized, would be effectively unilateral.

The Americanization of International Law

Before September 11, American unilateralists regularly asked: If the European Union and Japan fight us through trade, why should we foot the bill for their security? Why should foreign powers, which naturally prefer their own interests to America's interests, have a veto over our initiatives? Is not military spending a more sensible way to conduct foreign policy than consulting dubious allies? To such September 10th questions, Ikenberry offers the following heartfelt reply: "If American policy makers want to perpetuate America's preeminent position, they will need to continue to find ways to operate within international institutions, and by so doing restrain that power and make it acceptable to other states."[3] The Administration's contempt for this sort of thinking was not moderated by 9/11. So, who is right?

Ikenberry reaches his very reasonable-sounding conclusion by way of a long march through history and theory. After three analytically shrewd chapters on "the sources of order" in international affairs, he wades into three dense case studies, comparing postwar settlements after 1815, 1919, and 1945 with an eye to teasing out their commonalities and differences. He claims to have discovered some sort of teleology or learning process tying these cases together: "Settlements have moved in the direction of an institutionalized order."[4] When pointing out "the increasing use of institutional strategies"[5] among Western peacemakers after 1815, he means to identify the post-1945 settlement as the ideal end-point toward which earlier generations of diplomats were, in some sense, unconsciously groping.

What the post–World War II peacemakers achieved, in Ikenberry's account, was nothing less than "history's most sweeping reorganization of international order."[6] The reorganization was not merely far-reaching, it was also unique – although foreshadowed to some degree. What made it exceptional was the success of the United States, by far the most powerful of the victorious nations, in designing, building, and maintaining multilateral institutions of collective governance. World affairs are still dominated today either by the institutions forged after the war or by their lineal descendants, namely NATO, the International Monetary Fund, the United Nations, the World Trade Organization, and the European Union.

This extraordinary flurry of institution-building after 1945 needs explaining. As the Iraq war distressingly illustrates, triumphant powers often behave otherwise in the wake of knockout victories. Indeed, "never has there been a great power that has sought to institutionalize the postwar order so thoroughly."[7] Ikenberry formulates his basic explanatory puzzle is follows: "Why would the United States, emerging from World War II as the most powerful country the world had yet seen, agree to spin a dense web of international institutions and place itself squarely within them?"[8] Why did the homeland of nonentanglement not revert to isolationism or unilateralism after the war, turning its back on the rest of the world and abandoning former allies and enemies alike to the law of the jungle?

Stripped to its essentials, Ikenberry's answer is that "the institutional model of order building" underlying the postwar settlement reflected a "sophisticated power game."[9] The strategy was sophisticated because it was based on the paradoxical insight that less is more – in this case, that less power is more power. The United States allegedly agreed to rein in its own ascendancy, to make its behavior more predictable (sacrificing the advantages of ad hoc, arbitrary decision-making), in order to obtain useful cooperation from potential allies and partners.

This is Ikenberry's implicit retort to the two most common, and mutually inconsistent, attacks on multilateralism. For the American right, multilateral institutions are essentially forums for humiliating if not paralyzing the United States. (The August 29-September 7, 2001 United Nations conference on racism, held in Durban, comes to mind.) The international left, by contrast, excoriates multilateral institutions as front organizations artfully designed to work and disguise America's will (the G-7 and the IMF). Ikenberry counters these two clashing forms of anti-multilateralism by weaving them deftly together. The United States has made its power more durable and more extensive, he argues, precisely by sacrificing unsupervised mastery, voluntarily curbing its capacity to act unilaterally and unpredictably.

Although leftists throughout the world are correct to see international law and international institutions as serving U.S. interests, the American right is also correct to accuse international law and international institutions of hamstringing American power. To reconcile these dueling criticisms, and to convert them into praise, Ikenberry only has to defend the following two-part claim: Powerful actors can achieve more of their aims and solve more of their problems, and do both more effectively and more quickly, if they manage to mobilize the voluntary cooperation of the relatively weak; and powerful actors who obey their own laws, thereby becoming predictable to others, are more likely to elicit voluntary cooperation than powerful actors who work their will through erratic intimidation and threats.

Not even those inclined to accept Ikenberry's sunny assessment of postwar American foreign policy would claim that its theoretical premise is especially novel. The strongest is never strong enough to rule without some degree of voluntary compliance. To become sustainable, might must be turned into right. The ideal liberal solution, approximated in domestic settings, is to make power acceptable to most citizens, and thereby to enhance its stability, by subjecting it to constitutional limits. On this uncontroversial foundation Ikenberry builds his arresting thesis: The United States, in the aftermath of World War II, was the first global power successfully to apply the liberal legitimacy formula to the international domain. Thanks to the wise framers of postwar American foreign policy, he tells us, the world order now has "constitutional characteristics."[10]

Obligatory Consultations

By building and agreeing to work through multilateral institutions, the United States not only signaled restraint, it also made a credible commitment to protect its allies, to work with them, and to treat them fairly. It mobilized cooperation by binding itself. Admittedly, "self-binding" is a somewhat strained and awkward metaphor. For one thing, it implies a kind of inflexibility, or resistance to midstream adjustments, incompatible with effective governance in a world of kaleidoscopically evolving challenges and threats. However ironclad they appear, a state's commitments must not prevent timely adaptation to shifting opportunities and dangers, interests and purposes, resources and problems, partners and adversaries. This is why Ikenberry, when illustrating his point, focuses on a commitment that is eminently compatible with the need to react to unforeseen events, namely, obligatory, fixed-calendar consultations.

The history of Western liberalism suggests the centrality of regularly convened deliberative councils and semipublic negotiations about policy for the evolution of modern constitutional government. After World War II, says Ikenberry, the United States consciously transplanted precisely this robust but flexible aspect of domestic constitutionalism into the international arena. In so doing, the United States was building on the efforts of Britain in the aftermath of 1815. That was the period when great-power multilateralism was born. The Vienna system, established at the time, already amounted to "permanent diplomacy by conference."[11] Britain's "breakthrough" lay "in its appreciation of the potential role of ongoing consultative mechanisms as institutional devices to maintain order and manage potential adversaries."[12] Later, the United States took up the torch, giving its allies after 1945 "institutionalized 'voice opportunities'"[13] – not equal influence, of course, but a genuine say in making policy, especially when the distribution of burdens and collectively produced benefits were involved, as well as a chance to air grievances and seek redress when frustrations arose, as they inevitably did and do. More concretely: "The acceptability of American hegemony was facilitated by the ability of the Europeans and Japanese to maneuver within it."[14]

Liberal theories of international order usually build hopes for peaceful coexistence among armed states on three factors: interdependencies of trade; agreements on norms of international behavior; and democratization. Ikenberry mentions these, of course, but his principal point is the one just noted: that power can become more effective by becoming more responsive to the ideas and wishes of those whose help it needs. Because it refused to follow this internationalist strategy, we might conclude, the Bush Administration has ended up seriously eroding America's global power. If it accommodates the legitimate demands and viewpoints of potential partners, by contrast, a dominant state can mobilize the cooperation it needs to solve collective problems and to achieve its own aims, so long as it manages to maintain its basic coherence in the face of a cacophony of aspirations and interests.

Frequent parleys and congresses among allies increase chances of coming up with imaginative formulas for reconciling interests that might initially appear to be conflicting. Interest groups within a liberal democracy have knowledge and imagination as well as interests. This is an important reason for listening to what they have to say. The same is true about allies in an international coalition. The leading state in an alliance will be better informed, learn of dangerous developments before they get out of hand, and have a more comprehensive understanding of its own options if it opens itself to periodic consultations. Or so says this version of liberal internationalism.

What Does "Self-Binding" Explain?

Ikenberry's leading idea – that the United States stabilized and increased its power after 1945 by a strategy of self-binding – is paradoxical and provocative. Even though it opens up an interesting perspective, however, it is not entirely convincing. He admits as much when he describes it as a "stylization" or an "ideal type."[15] The dim light of political science illuminates historical events by devising "models." Striving for generality valid across space and time, models necessarily homogenize reality, blotting out contextual or historically specific factors such as the illness and the death of key actors, their venomous jealousies and their clueless stupidities, their skill and their initiative, their brilliant timing and their dogged persistence, their murky ideologies and their bitter memories, their lack of imagination and their hunger for attention. Because they leave out such decisive factors, the parsimonious models of political science have a difficult time explaining actual historical events.

For his part, Ikenberry avails himself freely of such difficult-to-model factors in his discussion of the spectacular failure of liberal internationalism after World War I. He is too much of a historian, in other words, to be a consistent modeler. Yet he nevertheless insists that the "remarkable durability of the 1945 order among the industrial democracies despite the end of the Cold War"[16] can be explained in large measure by a single mechanism called "credible commitment." Standard international relations theory instructs us that victories usually weaken or terminate alliances. Why have the multilateral organizations built by the United States and its allies after World War II proved to be an exception to this generally valid rule? Why, after the collapse of bipolarity and despite disagreements about the transnational terrorist threat, have America and its Cold War allies continued to work together harmoniously inside the multilateral institutions set up after 1945? Why did the financial architecture established after World War II successfully weather a crisis in the security architecture of the Cold War? Why, despite periodic outbursts of anti-Americanism, has no serious political movement arisen in allied countries proposing withdrawal from the intergovernmental organizations that the United States still dominates? Ikenberry's explanation is straightforward: "These institutions continue to persist because they are part of the system of mutual commitments and reassurances whose logic predated and was at least partly independent of the Cold War."[17] But how cogent is such an explanation?

One problem is that not enough time has passed, not even in the years since he put forward this analysis, to judge if Ikenberry is right or wrong. The "remarkable stability"[18] that he aims to explain has not lasted long enough to be called genuinely enduring. That the end of bipolarity destabilized the preceding world order is undeniable. We still do not know how far this unraveling will go, however. Already in the early 1990s, fretful Atlanticists were warning that Europe was souring on America just as America was losing interest in Europe. Their warnings may have been overstated, or perhaps not. (Trends point both ways: the Iraq war divides

Americans and Europeans, and the targeting of "the West" by radicalized Muslim youth brings Americans and Europeans together.) So far, in any case, the basic institutions designed for trans-Atlantic partnership have survived. Yet why invoke "credible commitment" to explain the perpetuation, after the end of the Cold War, of Cold War patterns of cooperation? Do not vested interests, the absence of feasible alternatives, sheer inertia, and the relatively low costs (so far) of maintaining current arrangements explain the staying power of inherited institutions just as well? Not that Ikenberry ignores such factors. Indeed, he emphasizes them voluminously. The problem is that he redescribes them as something that they are manifestly not, namely, as instruments in a successful strategy of constitutional self-binding adopted by America's sophisticated foreign policy elite in the wake of World War II.

Is it really illuminating to invoke the "binding power" of old agreements to explain why states cooperate when they grapple with problems that can be solved only cooperatively? No single country, not even the mighty United States, can take on single-handedly the problems of nuclear proliferation, drug trafficking, arms smuggling, global organized crime, environmental degradation, energy conservation, global financial instability, tax evasion by multinational corporations, and of course transnational terrorism with radical Salafi affiliations. All such problems cry out for multilateral initiatives. Joint decision making and the pooling of resources are palpably in the interest of all parties. This does not mean that multilateralism will occur or persist, only that an existing framework for international cooperation is unlikely to be jettisoned overnight. So here again, why bring up "self-binding" if the (temporary) perpetuation of multilateralism can be explained in simpler ways?

It seems odd, moreover, to describe the decision to rebuild Germany after WWII as an expression of American self-restraint. For its part, Germany joined the West not because it trusted America's "credible commitments" and "signals of restraint," but because it was forced to do so. It is not even accurate to depict the emergence of the European Union as an example of "self-binding." The denationalizing of European politics, as Ikenberry himself reconstructs it, was to some extent an American initiative, designed in Washington to dampen Franco-German antagonisms and to prevent a rerun of the post-Versailles sequence of events, as well as to create a market large enough to sustain capitalism, thereby commercializing Germany, destroying its militaristic ethos, and preventing it from being drawn into the Soviet orbit. Although eager to box in the seemingly suicidal Europeans, the militarily and economically ascendant

United States never ceased being a judge in its own case. It always retained the option to use or not use the institutions, such as the United Nations, that it helped to create.

Opportunism or Restraint?

Depending on your ideological inclinations, Ikenberry's image of a fettered and rule-bound United States is either rosy or dreary. Yet it is at best only partly correct. Opportunistic multilateralism, in particular, was not invented by the Bush Administration. Administrations of both parties have regularly indulged in forum shopping, seeking out, on an ad hoc basis, the regional association most compliant to shifting American interests.

Self-restraint is a faulty metaphor, in this context, also for another reason. It assumes that the dominant power forgoes doing something that it otherwise wants and would be perfectly capable of doing. As Ikenberry recognizes, however, the British did not *renounce* territorial ambitions on the Continent after 1815 for the simple reason that they never entertained such ambitions. The same is true of the United States after World War II. It makes no sense to say that the United States restrained its ravenous desire to wield arbitrary control over the vast regional domains orphaned by the simultaneous collapse of German, Japanese, and British power. It did not sacrifice this ambition because it did not possess this ambition. This lack of American ambition was due not only to its presumably virtuous dislike of foreign entanglements, but also to the scarcity of its resources. That explains why, outside the Western hemisphere, the United States sought disengagement as much as power. World domination takes too many evenings, and no one needs reminding today that entanglements in violent conflicts on the other side of the globe are not necessarily glamorous or rewarding.

To squeeze so many unruly facts into his minimalist theory, Ikenberry has to say that the United States "restrained" its desire to disengage from Europe, a play on words that is wilier than it is illuminating. He cites a memo by George Kennan, head of policy planning after the war, written in October 1947: "It should be the cardinal point of our policy to see to it that other elements of independent power are developed on the Eurasian land mass as rapidly as possible in order to take off our shoulders some of the burden of 'bi-polarity.'"[19] The desire to get Europe back on its feet and off American backs was undoubtedly an important motive of U.S. foreign policy in the immediate aftermath of World War II, even before the clear emergence of the Soviet threat. The aim was to shift burdens and to cut costs. As it turned out, American troops remained stuck in Europe for decades. One reason was that Eisenhower could not contrive a way to withdraw the troops without, in turn, supplying nuclear weapons to a German people who had only recently flirted with Götterdämmerung. It is possible to call this "self-binding," I suppose, and to see it as a "signaling of restraint"; but it would be more straightforward to understand it as the failure to off-load a burden in inherently difficult circumstances.

Ikenberry's treatment of "permeability,"[20] too, is somewhat rickety. He argues that American power was accepted because "the American post-war order was an open or penetrated hegemony,"[21] that is to say, our allies could speak back to us, communicate, remonstrate, and influence our decision making. His argument here refuses to sit still, however. At times, he claims that "postwar institutions created conduits into the American policy making system,"[22] implying that the postwar peacemakers substantially increased the openness of the American policymaking process by committing America to multilateral institutions. At other times, he simply invokes the United States' "distinctively open domestic political system," meaning that the "open American polity," rather than the new-modeled postwar institutions, "created opportunities for allies to lobby actively and engage American officials and influence the policy process."[23]

Any country where decision making involves many different agencies and individuals will have a hard time keeping secrets. Multiparty competition and a free press also make the United States relatively easy for outsiders to monitor. Pluralism also means that diverse actors with divergent perspectives can be played against each other by skillful foreign emissaries. This is true for embittered enemies as well as for allies, and it has nothing to do with a sophisticated power game played by the framers of the postwar order. Foreign powers, including adversaries, could keep tabs on the United States, and perhaps alleviate unwarranted suspicions, "because its domestic democratic institutions created openness and access."[24] Yet this benefit was not the fruit of strategic self-restraint. It was merely a by-product of democracy and the open-door policy that the United States adopted on other grounds.

The Need for Cooperation

Ikenberry traces the moderation of the powerful, when it occurs, to their perceived need for ongoing cooperation, not to their fear of one-shot retaliation for unpopular decisions. This focus on the palpable and present-day benefits of international cooperation, not naïve hopes about the normative supremacy and binding power of international law, is what makes Ikenberry more of a liberal than a realist. In the absence of a higher-level enforcer, what "binds" the United States is not a temporally prior commitment, but (as in the current struggles against proliferation and terrorism) a present and ongoing need for voluntary collaboration, or rather the belief of its key policymakers that such voluntary collaboration is indispensable. The United States made concessions to its relatively weak allies after World War II because it required their concert and cooperation. It needed their help to counter the Soviet threat and to avoid the kinds of financial turbulence that directly threatened American economic interests, but it also aimed, as Ikenberry says, to rebuild the German economy without spooking France and Great Britain. This required not military bullying alone, but also considerable diplomatic tact.

If a powerful state makes concessions to its weaker allies only when it needs their voluntary agreement to pursue important purposes, then its concessions are likely to cease, or to be substantially modified, when its goals change or when it no longer needs extensive international cooperation to achieve them. Before September 11, the Bush Administration seems already to have concluded that there was nothing any country, whether ally or adversary, could do to stop the United States from acting in whatever way it liked. That is why it was more interested in managing allied objections than in taking them seriously. Its gratuitously insulting attitude toward some of America's principal European allies survived 9/11 because the Administration quickly (and unwisely) concluded that these allies had little or nothing to contribute to the war on terror that had just begun.

This brings us to a curious inconsistency between Ikenberry's idealistic recommendations and his realistic descriptions. He pleads with the pre-9/11 Bush Administration to avoid the pitfalls of unilateralism. Above all, he says, the United States should not replace a consultative style with an imperious style. In issuing such a plea, however, he implicitly acknowledges that there is *nothing inevitable* about multilateralism. It does not emerge according to some inescapable law of social science. It is, at least to some extent, a political choice. American domestic institutions had not suddenly lost their "permeability," yet the Bush Administration was already tilting aggressively toward unilateralism. The institutions of global governance had not become mysteriously less "sticky" than before, but the unilateralist turn had already begun. In other words, permeability and stickiness do not bear the explanatory weight that Ikenberry places upon them.

How should we explain the Administration's embrace of unilateralism before 9/11? The simplest explanation invokes the Administration's failure, already at the time, to appreciate the present and future need of the United States for international cooperation to protect its most vital interests. Excited by America's unprecedented lack of peer competitors, the Administration failed to recognize the extent to which the sole remaining superpower needs voluntary cooperation from its allies – to pressure Iran and North Korea, for instance, or to base radar and tracking equipment for the fantasized missile shield.

Ikenberry's hope is apparently to resuscitate multilateralism by convincing the country's foreign policy elite that the United States' fundamental interests cannot be protected without extensive voluntary cooperation from allies, but this is where he walks into a contradiction. His entreaty makes sense because America's behavior on the international scene is restrained, if at all, by the plausible and implausible convictions of its policymakers. And this implies that America's foreign policy is restrained, if at all, by its leaders' beliefs; it is not really "institutionally restrained," at least not to the degree and in the way that Ikenberry's theory would lead us to expect.

A further ambiguity involves the ostensibly pro-American bias built into the multilateral institutions constructed after the war. Ikenberry's argument is that the United States committed itself to a consultative style of global governance, agreeing to restrain its own arbitrary discretion and to take into account the interests and the concerns of its allies (as these evolved over time) in order to obtain vital cooperation. The purpose of this cooperation was not only to oppose the Soviet threat, but also to avoid self-defeating conflicts inside the allied camp. But this thesis, worth disputing on its merits, loses its clear contours because Ikenberry combines it with a very different – indeed, a contrary – proposition: that during the years of postwar chaos, when American power was at its zenith, American policymakers skewed the rules of multilateral governance in America's favor, "locking in" an otherwise ephemeral ascendancy, and immunizing the country's strategic dominance against an inevitable waning of American power and an equally inevitable growth of the power of its allies. This may be true or false, but it is a very different claim than the one so far discussed. Which is it? Did the United States cagily shortchange its allies or did it design multilateral institutions to cater to their legitimate and shifting demands? Both stories, admittedly, may capture aspects of the truth; but Ikenberry does not help us to think through the obvious tension between them.

Stickiness or Sclerosis?

Whether or not they will retain a vise-grip on the consciences of future statesmen, present-day agreements can create well-organized vested interests wedded to predictable procedures and routines. To explain how one generation can "bind" the next in practice, therefore, Ikenberry draws our attention to the way treaties can inaugurate the reorganization of bureaucracy. Evidence that international agreements can populate institutions with careerists who have a strong incentive to keep their agencies in business is provided by NATO, which continues to exist and even to expand after its original purpose abruptly disappeared. Owing to the strong incentive for self-perpetuation, institutions "raise the costs of sharp reversals in policy and create vested political interests and organizational inertia that reinforce stable and continuous relations."[25]

This is true enough, but it does not fit as smoothly into Ikenberry's thesis as he seems to assume. What he calls "the stickiness"[26] of institutions may just as well be labeled sclerosis. (Max Weber might have spoken of an "iron cage.") Ikenberry downplays the obvious disadvantages of institutional rigidity because, once again, he interprets it as a contrivance in a sophisticated power game – in this case as an unshakable real-world guarantee that promises will be kept, even when they are made by sovereign states. As a consequence, he does not even bother to distinguish between predictability and paralysis.

True, vested interests may obstruct change. Irreversible processes can be set in motion. Fluid situations will calcify. Facts on the ground can block once feasible avenues of escape. But, although interesting and important, such factors do not lend themselves as easily as he suggests to strategic use. Is policy viscosity always good? Do fossilized commitments always produce the effects that their makers anticipate? If international bureaucracies, owing no loyalty to any national constituency, develop their own stubborn corporate interests, what makes us expect that they will act for the good of the wider world community? America's "imperial presidency" (Chapter Thirteen) was consolidated during the global standoff between liberalism and communism. Perhaps the "stickiness" of this institutional form helps explain why it has survived the Cold War to become even more unbridled after 9/11. Whether such an explanation makes sense, the example suggests that institutional holdovers provide no guarantee of political stability, sobriety, or sanity.

Framers and founders may deserve their acclaim; but one generation cannot really control the next. No matter how sophisticated, the designers of institutions, domestic or international, lack the foresight and the skill to choreograph in detail the behavior of their successors. One important reason for this incapacity is that institutional rigidity increases behavioral unpredictability. This is true because stringent rules and inflexible decision-making bodies can be shattered by the unexpected crises that a more loosely constructed and flexible framework might easily have survived.

Ikenberry's implicit contention, that American foreign policy is restrained not by fluctuating beliefs but by sturdy institutions, brings him, in the end, to "an optimistic view of the future stability of the Western order."[27] The problem with optimism is its tendency to dissolve into complacency. And in fact the very structure of Ikenberry's argument leads him to understate the degree to which the collapse of bipolarity continues to rattle American foreign policy. One problem is that the disappearance of our Soviet adversary affected the United States directly, rather than merely eating away at the coherence of the alliance it leads. Public understanding of American interests abroad, never impressive, was further diluted by the disappearance of an easy-to-identify Cold War enemy. For similar reasons, the coherence and the purposiveness of American foreign policy itself was seriously compromised. This affected not only our ability to sort out priorities and to discipline domestic constituencies, but also our ability to keep foreign allies and partners on board. If we cannot explain clearly what we want and how we plan to achieve it, we are much less likely to secure necessary cooperation, however well-designed our international institutions or tenacious our commitments to them. This is even more true if we do not know what we want or how to achieve it.

The Multilateralist Trap

In his zeal to highlight the advantages of multilateralism, finally, Ikenberry neglects the other side of the coin. He makes antimultilateralism seem wholly unmotivated and incomprehensible. Why would anyone complain about the false promise of multilateral institutions when they deliver such bounty? Why would realists pour scorn on "the multilateral mishmash" if multilateralism solves problems without creating more? Doubts about multilateralism, however, although sometimes overwrought, are not altogether unfounded.

Without intensive cooperation by intelligence apparatuses around the world, from Islamic and non-Islamic countries alike, our military today would not even be able to put together a reliable list of bomb-worthy targets. Nevertheless, many of our most useful allies in the antiterrorism coalition have interests palpably at odds with our own. Countries that have Islamic insurgencies within their borders, such as India and Russia, are likely to define "terrorist" in a way that increases rather than decreases the appeal of transnational Islamic radicalism. Similarly, by associating ourselves too closely with politically unaccountable "moderate Islamic states," we make it painfully easy for radical Islamists to stoke anti-American passions. America is a crudely hypocritical power, they will say, a power addicted to double standards, spouting democratic ideals while supporting undemocratic regimes.

Srebrenica is another example, already available to Ikenberry, of the way multilateral initiatives can end badly. The molasses of international bureaucracies can impede flexible response. Ikenberry himself assumes as much in his interesting discussion of the Russian withdrawal from Eastern Europe. Gorbachev effectively accepted the absorption of a reunified Germany into NATO because he correctly believed that a Germany snared in a multilateral web would be perfectly harmless to Russian interests and generally unable to act in unexpected ways. Slobodan Milosevic had a similar perspective and was proved wrong in part, though no one would argue that the Western alliance, immobilized by multilateralism, intervened in the former Yugoslavia in a timely manner. It is no surprise, then, that the Western alliance during the past decade has been repeatedly flummoxed by swiftly unfolding events, in the Balkans and elsewhere, because, before an alliance swings into action, dozens of semi-independent states, with slightly different interests and maps of the world, must be coaxed into consensus. Nature intervenes most dramatically in politics in the form of time, swiftly moving and always scarce. The need to respond to dangerous situations under the pressure of a ticking clock makes it imprudent to subject the power to conduct foreign policy to a tangle of procedural checks. Even obligatory consultations can interfere perilously with timely action.

Multilateral institutions are most effective, therefore, when a small handful of core states, with common goals and good working relations, take the initiative, canvass the alternatives, rally the troops, and follow through. This is not to argue that the United States should turn its back on multilateral institutions. It is only to observe that multilateralism tends to fail when, as in 1919, participating states are divided by beliefs as contrary as Wilson's and Clemenceau's. Multilateral institutions function best when a few states, with an agreed-upon set of priorities, assume a strong leadership role.

There is no principled reason why the United States could not reform existing multilateral institutions or create new ones to serve its national-security interests in the twenty-first century. But the Bush Administration is very unlikely to undertake such a project, committed as it remains to America's unlimited freedom of action. In speech after speech, Bush has tellingly declared that he will accept no outcome, either in Iraq or in the general war on terror, except "total victory" or "complete victory." How he envisages such a victory is by no means clear. The way things are going, ultimate success will never be celebrated, but we already have a fairly good idea how Bush would behave "after victory," if he ever managed to get that far. Creating international institutions, much like the heroes of Ikenberry's story, would not be his first priority. Rather than establishing frameworks of cooperation and consultation, where the diverse viewpoints of able allies might be listened to and taken into account, he would surely hold another political rally on an aircraft carrier where nothing but shouts of partisan approval could be heard.

Postscript

"Unilateralism," admittedly, works better as a damning reproach or idle boast than as an accurate description of American behavior in the world. Unilateral counterterrorism and unilateral antiproliferation refer to no known or conceivable policies of the current or any other administration. Moreover, international police and intelligence cooperation in the war on terror has indisputably flourished since 9/11. Until massive space-based weapons platforms are up and running, which will not occur anytime soon, America's capacity to project its military power, too, will hinge on basing rights and over-flight rights that must be obtained by diplomatically negotiated agreements.

The myth of "unilateralism" would not be so widespread, however, if it did not resonate politically. Both Democrats and Republicans seem to find it a useful term to help differentiate the two parties' approaches to foreign policy. The Democrats advocate "working with allies" and the Republicans favor "going it alone." In reality, whenever they are in power, Republicans negotiate and compromise ceaselessly with long-term and short-term allies. Yet their electoral strategists seem to have calculated that a Republican candidate can excite an important voting bloc by publicly declaring that, as president, he will never take the interests and opinions of other countries into account when defending U.S. national security.

Another reason why the Administration may exaggerate its unilateralism is to hide, after 9/11, America's "'dark side' alliances with perilous regimes that now acted like friends."[28] Fighting terrorism sometimes requires American officials to sup with the devil, showering luxuries on admitted mass murderers for their vital cooperation in tracking down terrorists and shutting down clandestine networks of nuclear proliferation.[29] This may be ethically repulsive, but it is also inevitable.

To describe U.S. counterterrorism policy under the Bush Administration as "unilateral" is not wholly mistaken, obviously, but it misstates the essential problem. What is wrong with Bush's counterterrorism policy is not that it is excessively unilateral but that it is excessively unidimensional. Instead of bringing all of America's national-security assets, to whatever agency they belong, to bear as needed on the terrorist threat, the Administration has promoted an arbitrary and unbalanced approach. This unfortunate skewing can be traced, as is widely acknowledged, to Bush's decision to give OSD excessive power to shape priorities in the war on terror.

As we saw in Chapter Two, OSD naturally assigns priority to certain kinds of problems, namely problems that can be solved best by the Pentagon and that allow the Pentagon to strut its stuff. This "agency bias" in the perception of threats is captured nicely in the classical principle that bureaucracies do not solve problems, rather they redescribe problems in order to make them seem amenable to off-the-shelf solutions. This mechanism does not fully explain the debacle of postwar Iraq, but it helps. As detailed accounts by Ron Suskind, James Risen, Bob Woodward, Thomas Ricks, and others have now shown, although OSD took total control of the invasion and occupation, it focused almost all of its energies on the invasion. Stabilization was not a priority. This was not because stabilization was objectively unimportant but seemingly because, in Rumsfeld's mind, the Pentagon did not "do" peacekeeping. In general, tasks that required cooperation from other executive-branch agencies were given a lower priority than tasks that the Pentagon could accomplish alone. Tasks that required international cooperation were placed even lower on OSD's list of priorities.

Instead of denouncing the "unilateralism" of U.S. counterterrorism policy, therefore, it is more helpful to focus on the Administration's skewed ranking of priorities. Smaller threats were given more attention than larger threats for the wholly gratuitous reason that the former required less and the latter required more cooperation from international partners as well as from other U.S. government agencies. Earlier chapters detailed OVP/OSD reluctance to consult and cooperate with other executive-branch agencies. We will therefore restrict ourselves here to the Administration's parallel reluctance to consult and cooperate with capable allies. The fact that the Pentagon is the national-security agency most capable of acting without substantial international cooperation is probably the main cause of anomalies in the way the U.S. government, after 9/11, ranked its national-security priorities. Equally influential was the intellectual background of many Republican defense intellectuals in Bush's first term, especially their inherited hostility to détente, arms control, containment, and coexistence with the enemy. These reflexes became largely obsolete when the Soviet Union collapsed. Few human beings are psychologically flexible enough to shed acquired habits as soon as the threat environment changes, however. Hence, the Administration's foreign policy team carried with them, into a wholly new kind of war against a wholly new kind of enemy, a state-centered view of serious national-security threats, a proclivity to alarmism or threat-inflation, and a taste for tougher-than-thou confrontationalism.

(Another legacy of the Cold War, visceral hostility to the United Nations, is particularly ironic given the extreme animus against the United Nations expressed by America's most virulent enemies. In fact, John Bolton's dislike of the United Nations pales in comparison to the contempt expressed by Sheikh Omar Abdel Rahman who encouraged young jihadists to blow up the entire building. Similarly, Osama bin Laden's mentor, Abdullah Azzam, made "no negotiations, no conferences, and no dialogues" into a motto.[30] Not even Donald Rumsfeld would have gone that far.)

That this intellectual baggage was a hindrance to rational policymaking was made clear by the Administration's approach to proliferation. Its fundamental mistake in this area, besides its neglect of the urgent need to secure Russia's stockpiles of highly enriched uranium (HEU), was its incoherent attempt to combine disarmament with regime change. The United States sent two messages to Iran and North Korea. First, America wanted them to stop their drive to acquire nuclear weapons. Second, America was committed to overthrowing their governments. This one-two punch was like telling emotionally riled-up and perhaps paranoid dictators to put down their weapons so that we could kill them more easily. It was an offer that they were guaranteed to refuse. That the certainty of rejection is exactly what made the offer appealing to some of the more bellicose members of Bush's foreign policy team is a disturbing thought indeed.

In essence, the Administration plays up its unilateralism and plays down its multilateralism because its multilateralism contradicts its politically crafted self-presentation, especially in the war on terror. To understand what is at stake here, it helps to compare the war on terror to the battle against contagious diseases, such as SARS, avian flu, and hemorrhagic viruses. International cooperation in this area is not free of problems, but it works fairly smoothly because there exists a baseline consensus that contagious disease is a threat to all mankind. No one says that "one man's pathogen-fighter is another man's pathogen." Even within the World Health Organization, politics may still affect threat assessment to some extent, but political considerations obviously weigh much less in the fight against disease than in the fight against terrorism.

The reason is that the very category of "terrorism" has a political connotation. Those who use the term implicitly declare that the political cause advocated by those employing violence against civilians is "unjust" or insufficiently important to justify cruel and indiscriminate methods. The problem is, countries and groups disagree about what is just and unjust. We may not like this, but we cannot change it either. Such differences of opinion, which occasionally create a serious obstacle to multilateral counterterrorism, are an ineradicable feature of human plurality. That many Americans do not see the firebombing of Tokyo and the nuclear attacks on Hiroshima and Nagasaki as "state terrorism," despite the blatant targeting of civilians, has everything to do with their belief in the ultimate justice of the American cause. Multilateral attempts at neutral definitions of "terror" cannot create political consensus; they can only disguise it. Differences of political perspective guarantee that one man's terrorist will be another man's freedom fighter. Today we honor as heroes those that the Nazis called "terrorists" in occupied Europe. Some call Hezbollah a terrorist organization and others call it a national resistance movement. Such conflicting classifications are founded on mankind's irrepressible partiality, that is, a primordial preference for me and mine over thee and thine.

Ironically, it would have been somewhat easier to gain international consensus about terrorism if the Administration had stuck to the crime paradigm. It is much easier to get international agreement that drug smugglers are criminals than to obtain a consensus that Hezbollah fighters are terrorists. One strong argument in favor of the law enforcement model for counterterrorism is that those who think of terrorism as a criminal matter, namely policemen throughout the world, tend to work extremely well

together, multilaterally and bilaterally, in the attempt to take down terrorist cells. Because it chose to see terrorism as more akin to war than crime,
the Bush Administration has implicitly and perhaps eagerly accepted, from
the very beginning, that no worldwide consensus about "the enemy"
would ever be achieved. Or rather, it has accepted that this consensus cannot be voluntary and must be created by the application of irresistible force.
This expectation of a universal coerced consensus on what is just/unjust
is unrealistic, however, and can lead only to disappointment, frustration,
and failure.

A more general point, first raised in Chapter Two, is worth reiterating
here. The spread of English as the world's language has had a paradoxical effect on American national security. It has made the United States
transparent to people around the world (including aspiring terrorist infiltrators and saboteurs), while making the rest of the world increasingly
opaque to Americans, who have fewer and fewer incentives to invest in
the acquisition of linguistic skills and cultural knowledge. It would be an
exaggeration to say that the United States is surrounded by a one-way
mirror, but the metaphor captures a frightening asymmetry. Foreigners
have an easier time learning about us than we have learning about them.
American parochialism would simply be mildly embarrassing in a less turbulent time. What makes it dangerous is anti-America terrorism. Among
the outsiders who are invited to peer into our house of glass, a handful
no doubt wish us ill, inspired by real or imagined injuries inflicted by
Americans on themselves, their friends, their nations, or their religious
community.

The United States cannot easily reduce its transparency to outsiders,
but it can improve its ability to read and interpret the rest of the world.
This is a strong argument for opposing the Administration's fondness for
unilateral posturing and public scorn for able allies, especially in Europe.
Frustration with allies is perfectly understandable. They have interests and
agendas that do not always mesh easily with American interests and agendas. Allies have ideas and information as well as interests, however. They
have knowledge and viewpoints that may actually merit attention. Elementary human psychology teaches that individuals who shun contact with
others have a weak grasp of reality. Individuals who are never criticized by
companions they trust have a hard time remaining mentally balanced. The
same is true of nations. Even allies that are relatively weak militarily can
contribute in a substantial way to the effectiveness of U.S. foreign policy.
They can do this by providing a sanity check. This is the point that some
American liberals were trying to make by invoking a "global test." There

is nothing unpatriotic about this idea, contrary to what the Republicans insinuated in their spoofs of John Kerry, who used the phrase in his 2004 presidential debates with Bush. Alexander Hamilton summarized the basic liberal point in *Federalist Papers*, No. 63:

> An attention to the judgment of other nations is important to every government for two reasons: the one is, that, independently of the merits of any particular plan or measure, it is desirable, on various accounts, that it should appear to other nations as the offspring of a wise and honorable policy; the second is, that in doubtful cases, particularly where the national councils may be warped by some strong passion or momentary interest, the presumed or known opinion of the impartial world may be the best guide that can be followed. What has not America lost by her want of character with foreign nations; and how many errors and follies would she not have avoided, if the justice and propriety of her measures had, in every instance, been previously tried by the light in which they would probably appear to the unbiased part of mankind?

It is not necessary to believe that an important part of mankind is wholly "unbiased" to accept the basic logic of Hamilton's argument here. U.S. counterterrorism policy is likely, on occasion, to be warped by strong interests and passions inside American policymaking bodies. A truly useful alliance is not one in which 60 countries do whatever the American president tells them to do. What makes allies indispensable to an effective national-security policy is the ability of like-minded nations to provide the reality checks without which a fallible superpower will be unable, as we have regretfully seen, to keep its balance on swiftly evolving and treacherous international terrain.

12 | BATTLING LAWLESSNESS WITH LAWLESSNESS

American treatment of terrorist suspects has included "interrogation" unto death. As a result, no discussion of the legality and wisdom of questioning detainees held in U.S. custody with "unconventional methods" can skip lightly over the issue of torture. Sympathizers with the Administration ordinarily defend harsh interrogation, beyond anything we would allow to be performed on suspects in criminal cases, by alleging that unorthodox procedures are "necessary" to extract information vital for protecting American lives. They accuse Administration critics of being human-rights fundamentalists or bleeding-heart liberals who do not understand the overwhelming, pragmatic need to bend the rules in conditions of extreme danger. The argument for harsh interrogation is weaker than it defenders admit or realize, however, for the simple reason that "necessity" is much easier to allege than to prove. To show that harsh interrogation is "necessary," the government must demonstrate that the interrogators could not have obtained the same information in other, less coercive ways. Given the truly immense resources available to the U.S. government, a lack of feasible, less violent alternatives would very often be difficult to prove before an impartial tribunal. In some rare cases, harsh interrogation may actually be necessary. Yet the difficulty of proving or disproving the claim of "necessity," and a general awareness that abusive officials have an endless capacity to invent unfalsifiable excuses for their misbehavior, should make us worry that something else is going on in the Administration's only half-veiled embrace of harsh interrogation. Can we be certain that the rush to harsh interrogation does not have as much to do with emotional release as with instrumental rationality? Might it not have as much to do with communicating "resolve" in the war on terror (a message that does not necessarily require a scrupulous attention to the difference between the innocent and the guilty) as with extracting actionable intelligence? Might the nightshift at Abu Ghraib not have been acting on the same impulse that drove the Administration to invade Iraq, namely, the all-too-human desire of many people, after being confronted with their own mortality, to demonstrate and contemplate their God-like power by inflicting pain on the weak?

Lawyers for Torture

The displacement of the Cold War by the war on terror has had an ironic consequence. The most infamous penal colony in a Communist country is now located at Guantánamo Bay Naval Base. We have come a long way since Solzhenitsyn. To Cuba, it turns out, the United States has spread not the blessings of liberty but the rule of manacles, stress positions, cages, and hoods. And Guantánamo is merely one internment facility, and by no means the worst, in what is presumably still a worldwide archipelago of U.S.-administered detention centers where terrorists, real and alleged, are incarcerated with little or no access to the outside world. Legal responsibility for what has gone on in these camps remains uncertain, but inside them detainees have been, and in some cases continue to be, interrogated in a cruel, inhumane and degrading manner. We know that at least twenty or thirty prisoners have died in captivity, apparently from wounds inflicted by their American jailers. The sordid details have been widely publicized. Less evident are the reasons why the U.S. government has created such a system. The most flagrantly paradoxical justification for what would otherwise be an odious violation of America's system of values is that such behavior alone makes it possible to protect America's system of values.

To inflict what amounts to punishment on suspects before establishing their guilt through some sort of minimally fair judicial process seems contrary to the basic principles of the rule of law. Yet it is perfectly in tune with the general counterterrorism policy of the Administration, especially its seeming indifference to the morally fundamental distinction between innocent and guilty detainees. Cruel interrogation techniques may be incompatible with ordinary principles of legality, but not moreso, say, than extrajudicial executions. Today, U.S. officers, operating clandestinely around the world, are apparently licensed to kill suspected al Qaeda members (and others in their vicinity) on the basis of fragmentary evidence and uncorroborated hearsay. If U.S. agents, without a finding of criminal liability, can *kill* possibly innocent suspects in cold blood, then it is not surprising that U.S agents can also, shielded from judicial scrutiny, subject possibly innocent suspects, detained on the say-so of bounty hunters, to "extreme interrogation," verging on torture.

True, neither policy seems particularly compatible with "liberty and justice for all." To explain why such deviations from liberal practice are permitted, or even required, the Administration has put its lawyers to work. Their job has been to lend such policies a patina of respectability. This is nothing new. Since ancient times, legal experts have made themselves available, for a fee, to provide technically refined justifications for the carefully dosed infliction of pain as a method for extracting information.[1] Legal experts and consultants may or may not have played a decisive role in introducing torture, but the amoralism of hired-gun lawyers has certainly helped deflect human compassion from victims of the practice. In late medieval and early modern Europe, doctors of law seem universally to have endorsed excruciating inquisitorial procedures as but one more versatile tool inherited from Roman Law.[2] Legal experts and scholars praised interlocutory torture, not only as an efficacious technique for compelling confession but also as a hard-to-resist way of coaxing suspects into betraying the identity of accomplices. Evidence elicited by water torture, simulating the feeling of drowning up to the moment when the subject loses consciousness, was long said to be especially suitable for use in court to demonstrate guilt. But lawyers have not always been satisfied with their role as unprincipled servants of power, concocting ingenious justifications to lend an aroma of decorum to the schemes of the powerful. They have therefore occasionally added, with a flash of conscience, that torture, although legitimate in principle, should be applied only "as the due measure of well-regulated reason requires."[3]

What exactly does "reason" require in this domain of screams and spasms? Attempting to establish when torture should and should not be used, Western legal thinkers have devoted themselves through the centuries to manufacturing subtle distinctions. According to Edward Gibbon, the selective embrace of the practice in Rome reflected an implicit disquiet: "The deceitful and dangerous experiment of the criminal *question*, as it is emphatically styled, was admitted rather than approved, in the jurisprudence of the Romans. They applied this sanguinary mode of examination only to servile bodies, whose sufferings were seldom weighed by those haughty republicans in the scale of justice or humanity; but they would never consent to violate the sacred person of a citizen till they possessed the clearest evidence of his guilt."[4] Slaves could be tortured regularly, but not citizens. Lawyers codified and rationalized this all-important distinction.

Visceral disgust at the practice of torture could be reduced, easing the task of torturing authorities, if the ruling element in society could be reasonably sure that such methods would be used exclusively on others. This particular method for making torture acceptable is very much alive in the American war on terror.

Already in antiquity, in any case, the law laid down boundaries between people who could be tortured, without any qualms, and others, the privileged, who were ordinarily exempt from judicially inflicted torments. Above all, aliens were treated more brutally than citizens. Cruelties are easier to accept when ordinarily reserved for "the other." In ancient Athens, for instance, inquiry by torture (*basanos*) was used, under specified conditions, to extort evidence from slaves, but applied to citizens, if at all, only in cases of high treason. The Roman practice discussed by Gibbon was similar. From the outset, therefore, interlocutory torture was applied in a "republican" manner, with proper respect for the sensibilities and solidarities of citizens. It was also a rule-governed activity. The rules in question were many and also evolved over time. A common maxim was that torturers should not pose leading questions to those being tortured. Such guidelines were presumably set forth because spontaneous abuses, such as suggestive questioning, endangered the reliability of coerced confessions. Did apologists for torture, however, really believe that truth could be extracted, like a rotten tooth, with a pair of pliers?

Reliability on Trial

Throughout history the powerful seemed to have enjoyed inflicting pain on the weak, sometimes instrumentally, sometimes gratuitously. Yet the lawyers who decorated such cruelty with plausible-sounding excuses were not operating in an intellectual vacuum. They were confronted with a growing chorus of legal philosophers who decried the practice and exposed its unreliability. What were the principal arguments that the legal apologists for torture, throughout the centuries, were obliged to ignore?

Although no rebel against Greek legal practice, Aristotle set forth very clearly what were to become the standard criticisms of a practice that was commonly condoned: "Those under compulsion are as likely to give false evidence as true, some being ready to endure everything rather than tell the truth, while others are equally ready to make false charges against others, in the hope of being sooner released from torture." [5] The unreliability of testimony extracted under duress, even today, remains one of the most commonly invoked arguments against torture. Allegations of false confessions at Guantánamo Bay and elsewhere, some now definitively confirmed, make it interesting to consider how Aristotle spelled out his hesitations: "It may also be said that evidence given under torture is not true; for many thick-witted and thick-skinned persons, and those who are stout-hearted, heroically hold out under sufferings, while the cowardly and cautious, before they see the sufferings before them, are bold enough." Once they are actually facing torture, some subset of prisoners would lose their audacity and choose to confess to crimes they did not actually commit. "Wherefore," Aristotle concludes, "evidence from torture may be considered utterly untrustworthy."[6]

Torture's willing advocates, needless to say, took a much more "optimistic" line. They argued that extreme physical pain, artfully applied, will take away the examinee's freedom to keep secrets and withhold the truth. This "deliberation" (or removal of free will) no doubt bears fruit some of the time. Yet the implicit theory that truth can be wrested from an individual by bodily violence was never without serious critics. One of them was Cicero, whose doubts about torture seem to build directly upon Aristotle's: "The course of examination under torture is steered by pain, is controlled by individual qualities of mind and body, is directed by the president of the court, is diverted by caprice, tainted by hope, invalidated by fear, and the result is that in all these straits there is no room left for the truth."[7] The turbulence and numbness injected into an addled consciousness by intense bodily agony, combined with the inevitable private agendas of the all-too-human administrators of pain, may easily obscure rather than illuminate the facts of the case under examination.

Roman jurist Ulpian (d. 228), as a servant of the law, also accepted the admission at trial of evidence extracted by torture. But he could not entirely ignore such compelling doubts: "It is stated in constitutions that reliance should not always be placed on torture . . . for it is a chancy and risky business and one which may be deceptive. For there are a number of people who, by their endurance and their toughness under torture, are so contemptuous of it that the truth can in no way be squeezed out of them. Others have so little endurance that they would rather tell any kind of lie than suffer torture; so it happens that they confess in various ways, incriminating not only themselves but others also."[8] So here again torture is presented as a trustworthy technique for probing endurance, but an unreliable method for establishing veracity.

Two centuries later, this time with a religious twist, Augustine recited these same doubts. He acknowledged, "The accused are often overcome by the pain of torture and so make false confessions and are punished, though innocent." In a vein that is distressingly pertinent to U.S. interrogation practice today, he went on to say, "although not condemned to death, they often die under torture or as a consequence of torture." True justice would be possible only if judges could peer directly into the minds of both accusers and accused to see who was lying and who was telling the truth – but judges are no more clairvoyant than other men. The truth of any criminal accusation, therefore, remains ultimately inscrutable even to the most discerning judge. Because human justice will always involve a fumbling in the dark, the city of man will never resemble the city of God.

Human law, nevertheless, instructs judges to try to ferret out the hidden truth by inflicting painful torments on witnesses as well as on the accused. But, Augustine laments, the rude means provided are wholly inadequate to the ideal end being pursued. Torture does not give the judge a privileged access to the innermost thoughts of those being tortured, for all of the reasons cited above, but especially because people will generally recount all manner of untruth to make the unbearable torment stop. As a result, "the ignorance of the judge generally results in the calamity of the innocent." Christian judges must therefore pray to God to deliver them from the burdens of this miserable life, which obliges them to engage in torture, a calamitous practice that inevitably confounds the innocent with the guilty. Judicial torture is not technically a "sin," he concludes, but it is sickening enough to make any honorable judge feel morally unworthy and even to pray to escape from this vale of tears.[9]

By the sixteenth century these classical doubts about the reliability of testimony extracted via torture began to coalesce into a straightforward, unambivalent rejection of the practice. A fine example is Montaigne, who repeated the ancient themes but this time from the point of view of someone fully expecting the practice to be abolished: "Torture is a dangerous innovation; it would appear that it is an assay not of truth but of a man's endurance. The man who can endure it hides the truth, so does he who cannot. For why should pain make me confess what is true rather than force me to say what is not true?"[10] In the seventeenth century, with even more bitter irony, La Bruyère reiterated that torture tests stamina, not truthfulness: "The rack is a marvelous invention, and an unfailing method of ruining an innocent weakly man and saving one who is robust and guilty."[11] And, finally, in the eighteenth century, Blackstone expressed a growing scorn for interlocutory torture, accusing its advocates of "rating a man's virtue by the hardiness of his constitution, and his guilt by the sensibility of his nerves!"[12]

Cesare Beccaria transformed these perennial dissatisfactions with interlocutory torture into a morally self-assured assault on the practice in his immensely influential treatise *On Crimes and Punishments* (1764). Beccaria's principal moral concern, which had been Augustine's and which remains alive today, is "the risk of torturing an innocent person."[13] Torture is randomly applied punishment, Beccaria argued. Such inflicting of penalties on mere suspects, before they are convicted of any crime, can be justified only by the corrosively antilegal principle that might is right.

It is absurd to make physical pain into "the crucible of truth," Beccaria explained.[14] The reason is simple: "the impression of pain may become so great that, filling the entire sensory capacity of the tortured person, it leaves him free only to choose what for the moment is the shortest way to escape from pain."[15] This is why, in all countries and in all ages, innocent people have confessed to crimes they did not commit. Beccaria's argument continues in a familiar vein. Far from being a reliable method for distinguishing the guilty from the innocent, he says, torture is better suited for exculpating the strong and inculpating the weak. In practice, torture undermines the interrogator's capacity to distinguish between guilt and innocence, one proof being the plentiful (false) confessions to witchcraft extracted, in early modern Europe, by ingenious torments. The very same dynamic makes Beccaria doubt the veracity of testimony about accomplices extracted under torture: "As if a man who accuses himself would not more readily accuse others."[16]

Beccaria also mentions, more originally, the way in which interlocutory torture made telltale body language unintentionally illegible. Intelligent interrogators who are prohibited from inflicting physical anguish during interrogation can sometimes read the body language of suspects to determine if they are lying or telling the truth. This is why physical torments ordinarily result in a loss of information. Subtle signals disappear when a torture victim writhes in agony, "if this truth is difficult to discover in the air, gesture, and countenance of a man at ease, much more difficult will its discovery be when the convulsions of pain have distorted all the signs by which truth reveals itself in spite of themselves in the countenances of the majority of men."[17]

Legal acceptance of torture, finally, creates a perverse incentive for interrogators. This is why a policy of torture tends to weaken the system of criminal justice in the long run, even if single acts of torture can occasionaly disgorge useful bits of evidence. If they are *not* allowed to torture witnesses and suspects, interrogators have an incentive to search for evidence elsewhere or to develop alternative information-extracting skills. (In the case of U.S. interrogators at Guantánamo Bay and elsewhere, such useful skills might include, for example, mastery of relevant foreign languages.) If torture is allowed, by contrast, interrogators will have less motivation to develop more refined and conceivably more effective methods of seeking and establishing the truth.

Legalization effectively creates a self-justifying and self-perpetuating system of interlocutory torture. It discourages interrogators from seeking better evidence and honing their skills and dissuades supervisors from increasing the size and talent of their staff. Interrogators who have failed to acquire nonviolent skills can then "justify" their resort to torture by alleging, with superficial plausibility, that torture is the only method available to them for wringing information out of noncooperating detainees. Although logically and morally worthless, this justification is apparently both rhetorically effective and psychologically comforting.

The Necessity Defense

Most defenses of torture, in the war on terror, boil down to a claim of necessity. Torture is intrinsically odious, its advocates say, but the government is forced to engage in a repugnant practice in order to save innocent lives. The ticking bomb scenario, to be discussed later, fits here; but I want to begin at a more general level.

In his infamous August 1, 2002, "torture memo," John Yoo (whose controversial theory of unlimited presidential power will occupy us in the next chapter) makes an explicit analogy between justifiable or excusable torture and justifiable or excusable homicide, arguing, for example, that "self-defense can be an appropriate defense to an allegation of torture."[18] Even if an interrogation method would clearly violate the federal anti-torture statute, he says, "necessity or self-defense could provide justifications that would eliminate any criminal liability."[19]

Such justifications are anything but straightforward, however. For one thing, the necessity defense is easy to abuse. This is why law typically regards claims of necessity with extreme skepticism, as possible fabrications designed to deceive. In the Anglo-American tradition, the law of self-defense places at least some burden on an individual who claims to have killed in self-defense to prove that his act was genuinely necessary, in other words, that he had no other readily available options, such as running away. As William Blackstone formulated this traditional principle: "to excuse homicide by the plea of self-defence, it must appear that the slayer had no other possible means of escaping from his assailant."[20] Moreover, deadly force is excusable only when such force is reasonably necessary to prevent grave bodily injury or death to oneself or others. If the user of deadly force unreasonably believes that deadly force is necessary, the homicide he commits in alleged defense of self or others is not excusable but negligent.

John Yoo is perfectly aware of this reasonableness standard and, citing a criminal law casebook, he explains that "if A kills B reasonably believing it to be necessary to save C and D, he is not guilty of murder even though, unknown to A, C and D could have been rescued without the necessity of killing B."[21] To understand what Yoo is implying here, we should apply his conceptual scheme to torture. If a government interrogator tortures a detainee to death reasonably believing that doing so was necessary to save many innocent lives, then he is not guilty of a crime even if, unbeknownst to him, the detainee possessed no actionable intelligence and innocent lives were not actually in danger.

To be psychologically and not merely legally persuasive, a defense of torture must dull any feelings of compassion toward the individual being tortured. There is no reason to suspect that Yoo has deliberately contrived his rationalizations to simultaneously stoke public fears and increase public willingness to accede to a policy of torturing suspects in detention. His justifications for torture happen to work that way, however. They effectively blunt compassion for the victims of abuse by heightening the public's sense of alarm. A detainee in U.S. custody, Yoo explains, "may possess information"[22] that could help the government prevent a nuclear attack on America. Since the suspect "may" possess actionable intelligence, the authorities, charged with protecting the country, are morally obliged to do whatever it takes to get him to talk. Who would not accept the sacrifice of one detainee's human dignity to avoid having masses of innocent citizens incinerated in the middle of the night along with their children? Only civil liberties fundamentalists, defenders of torture allege, would object to such a tradeoff. Opponents of torture may whine about the violation of the terrorist suspect's human rights and human dignity, but that is because they have lost all sense of perspective and proportion. They do not grasp, in Yoo's words, the simple truth that "any harm that might occur during an interrogation would pale to insignificance compared to the harm avoided by preventing such an attack, which could take hundreds or thousands of lives."[23]

It would be wrong to dismiss this argument out of hand. It is not perfectly reasonable, but it contains a strand of truth that needs to be taken seriously. What makes it seem sinister is the way it is introduced – with deadpan nonchalance, as if worries were wholly misplaced and nothing serious was at stake. That there is something unbalanced in Yoo's analysis appears most clearly in his statement, citing "leading scholarly commentators," that "terrorists may be hurt in an interrogation because they are part of the mechanism that has set the attack in motion."[24] What is alarming here, of course, is his unspoken assumption that the individual we are hurting in our savage little interrogation is actually a terrorist.

The war on terror is so difficult, it is often remarked, because we cannot easily identify the enemy. We cannot distinguish clearly between the innocent and the guilty. That is one of the principal reasons why, according to the Administration's paid and unpaid defenders, we have to subject terrorists to harsh interrogation, so they will divulge the names, whereabouts, and plans of their accomplices. The glaring defect in this line of reasoning leaps from the page: If we cannot clearly discriminate terrorists from non-terrorists, how do we know if we are torturing the right individual? Above all, how do we avoid what Beccaria begged us to avoid, namely "the risk of torturing an innocent person"? The answer provided by the legal apologists for torture seems to be that we cannot avoid cases of mistaken identity. This is "war," and the presumption of innocence is a luxury we cannot afford. Every war involves collateral damage. The collateral damage of the war on terror will include innocent detainees tortured to extract information that they do not, in fact, possess. Counterterrorism is not beanbag. Torturing the innocent is regrettable but unavoidable, especially given our dismal understanding of the communities from which terrorists emerge and where they often hide. That, at least, is what the torture lawyers want us to believe.

I will return in a moment to the predictable political fallout of a decision to "regretfully accept" the torture of innocents in the name of national security, but I want first to deepen our discussion of the necessity defense.

What if an interrogator were to justify his resort to torture by saying that he had to do it because he was too lazy to walk across the hall and ask a colleague who already knew the piece of actionable intelligence that he, the interrogator, had subsequently extracted by inflicting intense bodily pain on a detainee? What if we could have learned virtually everything that the tortured prisoner confessed, simply by asking a U.S. official from a different agency who was sitting in an office elsewhere in the same facility? This is not such a far-fetched hypothetical, after all. When policemen are allowed to beat confessions out of suspects, they have much weaker incentives to go out and find reliable evidence about who actually committed the crime. Yet laziness is obviously not a moral justification. An interrogator cannot say that torture was "necessary" because he simply did not feel like discovering the vital information in any other way.

The concept of "necessity" is not self-explicating. Those who invoke it may be hiding more than they reveal, therefore. This is even truer when a government rather than an individual invokes the necessity defense. It is much harder for a government than for an individual to prove necessity, because a government commands many more resources and therefore has many more feasible options than a solitary pedestrian accosted after midnight in Central Park.

It would be scandalous if an interrogator claimed that it was necessary to torture a certain detainee because the interrogator's Arabic was too poor to read the local Yemeni newspaper where the information being sought was printed on page three. If it would be scandalous for an individual to invoke this sort of defense, it would be utterly grotesque for a state to allege that it had to torture a detainee because it had not hired or trained enough Arabic speakers to interrogate him in less coercive ways.

My own lack of skills is a poor excuse for depriving someone else of his or her basic rights. As we saw in Chapter Ten, admittedly, this justification has been alleged at various times, including in the case of the Japanese internments during WWII. Because the government could not distinguish between the loyal and the disloyal, it chose to intern them all indiscriminately. That this is not an honorable precedent to follow in the war on terror, unfortunately, seems more obvious to the Administration's critics than to its defenders.

Can a state claim that torture is necessary because it has too few Arabic speakers to coax information from detainees in less coercive ways? This is morally dubious, because, as mentioned, a government as powerful and well-endowed as the United States has many options about how best to allocate its national-security assets. If it had wanted to have more Arabic-speaking interrogators, it could have allocated funding to such a purpose. In other words, the "necessity" that is alleged to justify torture is often a man-made necessity, and therefore a necessity only in a qualified sense. The government's own voluntary decisions, based partly on its refusal to take seriously the absolute prohibition on torture, have put it in a position where less coercive options are (temporarily) unavailable. If it had believed that it would have been unable to engage in torture, it would surely have scrambled to find interrogating personnel with the skills and training appropriate to eliciting information without physical abuse.

I do not introduce these considerations to close the debate about the justifiability of torture in the context of the war on terror. My aim is simply to cast doubt on one of the central claims of the advocates of harsh interrogation. A hidden circularity compromises the necessity defense for torture when alleged by governments, because the necessity that governments allege is frequently a direct result of personnel decisions that these governments have made on the basis of the perceived legality or permissibility of torture. This flaw in the necessity defense comes on top of the more general problem that governments, like individuals, lie for expediency, claiming that they "had" to do something that they did not in fact have to do but simply wished to do.

To summarize: The most common justification of torture is that it might possibly result in actionable intelligence that could save innocent lives, but this justification is seriously flawed. To justify torture, it is not enough to show that the information extracted by applying it was reliable and saved lives. One must also demonstrate that there was no other, less brutal and inhumane method for acquiring the very same information. This is very hard to prove, especially for a government with significant resources at its disposal. In a case of seemingly "successful" torture, we always have to ask: Could we have obtained the information we needed by other means, not involving physical torture of a defenseless detainee? Could we have acquired the same information by less cruel methods, for example, by developing a rapport with the prisoner or offering him modest inducements? If it turns out that alternative techniques are just as effective as torture and just as easily available, then we cannot confidently say that the torture was justifiable even if, viewed in isolation, it "worked."

The assertion that torture is necessary in a particular case deserves a hearing. What it does not deserve is acceptance on faith. Miscreants, public and private, are always scheming to duck responsibility for their misdeeds, and their claim that they "had no other choice" is as common as lying. When the citizens of a democracy hear their government alleging "necessity," are they supposed to put all their critical faculties to sleep? Government lawyers laboring to justify torture seem to think so, but they are by no means a model and inspiration for the rest of us.

Montesquieu was one of the first to attack the necessity defense alleged by lawyers who were hired to make torture seem eminently justifiable. Proof that torture is not a necessary institution, he wrote, was provided by England, where criminal justice functioned perfectly well even though torture there was virtually unknown: "We have before us the example of a nation blessed with an excellent civil government, where without any inconvenience the practice of racking criminals is rejected. It is not, therefore, in its own nature necessary." If the benefits ascribed to torture can be obtained without torture, then torture's sophistical defenders have been engaging in an intellectual sleight-of-hand. If judicial inquiry without torture works just as well as judicial inquiry with torture, then the observed utility of torture, to which its legal advocates point with pride, does not suffice to prove that it is legitimate or desirable. That was how Montesquieu, an important source of the wisdom of the American Founders, swished aside the torture-justifying lawyers of his time.

Even if the practice of inquisitorial torture occasionally bears fruit, we must also examine its predictable side effects. Today, for example, we can ask: What will be the long-term effects on American political sensibilities, of normalizing torture as a means for increasing national security? What does it mean for America's attempt to spread "liberty" throughout the world that the United States is curtailing "liberty," at home and abroad, to increase security and defeat the enemy? Is the United States spreading liberty or curtailing it? How are the two projects related to each other? This mixed message is certainly confusing. Those concerned with American public diplomacy might wish to discover which part of it has been more forcefully conveyed.

Torture's effect on individuals is more concrete and less controversial. The searing psychic wounds and physical disabilities of individuals who have survived torture are difficult to heal. The scars of humiliation left by torture tend to endure for years, because it may be impossible to remember the experience of being tortured without *reliving* the degradation. The moral-emotional effect on the individuals who do the torturing, must also be taken into account. These breakers of men have triumphed over captives, making defenseless individuals hostages to their own excruciating pain. The latent sadism of the captors is no doubt awakened by their freedom to abuse the helpless. Although they may learn to compartmentalize, their capacity for human sympathy and compassion for the weak will necessarily shrink. Unlike soldiers on the battlefield, they did not expose themselves to any physical danger in order to confront their purported enemy, now *hors de combat*. What is the likely result? Perhaps their sense of personal power will become pathologically inflated. Perhaps they will return home depraved and disturbed. All this is uncertain, but it is interesting to note that America's jailors and interrogators in the war on terror were assured by their superiors that torture (that is, treating captives as less than human) was not only permissible but was noble and patriotic.

Finally, we need to consider the effect of America's embrace of cruel and inhuman interrogation techniques on the country's reputation abroad. We might recall, in this context, that one of the charges leveled against the Nazi war criminals at Nuremberg was that "civilians of occupied countries were subjected systematically to 'protective arrests' whereby they were arrested and imprisoned without any trial and any of the ordinary protections of law."[25] While imprisoned without trial, the indictment continues, "Civilians were systematically subjected to tortures of all kinds, *with the object of obtaining information*" (my emphasis).[26] One does not have to accept a wildly implausible comparison of Bush Administration policy to the policy of the Nazis to realize that a public embrace of imprisonment without due process and highly coercive interrogation will further erode America's dying good name in the world. What are the concrete and practical consequences of this blemished reputation? How will it affect the number and quality of detainees that come into U.S. custody? How will it affect the inquisitorial practice of other nations? How will it affect the treatment of captured U.S. troops (including special forces who travel in combat zones without distinguishing military insignia)? Has the Administration made the rest of the world more or less hospitable to American interests by advertising loudly that the United States has no intention of complying with rules previously thought applicable to all? It may well be that if we add up all of the negative side-effects of a policy of interlocutory torture, we will discover that, yes, torture occasionally "works," but that any short-term gain is nevertheless far outweighed by long-term losses.

It is remarkable that the handful of U.S. lawyers and law professors who, perhaps from partisan passion, justify the practice of torture point triumphantly to the claim that "it works," as if this consideration sufficed to put an end to the debate. Their failure to explore either the available alternatives to torture or torture's likely side effects is disturbing. Their assurance that inhumane and degrading interrogation will pacify potential enemies rather than radicalize them is presumptuous and wrong. So how can the untroubled consciences of torture's legal apologists be explained?

An Emergency Power

Classical arguments against resort to torture, even during national emergencies, are not ironclad. But they are so strong that overcoming them is by no means assured. Some false confessions under torture are inevitable because "the sensitive innocent man will . . . confess himself guilty when he believes that, by so doing, he can put an end to his torment."[27] Keeping open the torture option encourages underinvestment in skills that might prove more effective in the long run. Closing down the torture option, contrariwise, creates a positive incentive to develop valuable skills. This logic can perhaps be observed in the American criminal justice system where "the elimination of police inquisitions and the third degree," at least according to Leonard Levy, "led to a better educated and better trained police force."[28] Moreover, a reputation for torture makes it less likely that investigators will get useful informants into their custody, and so forth. Many of these objections have been well known for over two millennia, but they seem to have made little or no impression on the legal defenders of current U.S. policy concerning coercive interrogation. Why not?

Why is the United States continuing to send detainees to countries where they are certain to be tortured? Why are our military and intelligence officers presiding over grave-like "dungeons" across the globe where captives can disappear without a trace? Why is the United States engaged in interrogation practices designed to destroy the dignity and dismantle the personality of possibly innocent prisoners? Why have twenty or thirty individuals, of unknown culpability, expired under U.S. interrogation? Are we really involved in such an unsavory business because we *have* to be? Are such despicable practices truly necessary? Would a refusal to do these things, which are repugnant and dishonorable, make the country measurably less safe?

Lawyers have abetted these controversial policies in a number of ways. They have pored over treaties and legislation, looking for loopholes, in an attempt to make highly coercive and sexually humiliating interrogation seem less patently illegal than had previously been believed. They have tried to develop defenses against criminal and civil liability for supervisors and perpetrators involved in harsh and demeaning treatment of detainees. Above all, they have stressed the way national security, the unprecedented threat of terrorism and the Commander-in-Chief power can be woven together into an all-purpose excuse for executive-branch activities, including inhumane interrogation, which would ordinarily be banned and forbidden.

Although they have justified and rationalized brutally coercive questioning techniques, including near suffocation, the lawyers did not initiate such policies. If the excuses were legal, the decisions were political. Nor can the political motivation for the policy be inferred from the legal justifications set forth. This is apparent from the famous torture memos themselves. The principal "legal" argument for highly coercive interrogation has been that, in some settings, law simply does not apply. The lawyers who advanced this claim, in other words, accepted the liberal view that torture is completely incompatible with the American system of criminal justice. From this they concluded not that torture must be banned but rather that the American system of criminal justice must be, for some purposes, set aside. In the current crisis, that is to say, ordinary restrictions on executive-branch discretion must be temporarily lifted. This is a very old story. Historically, even the most fastidious adherents of the rule of law have excused, or at least understood, its breach in times of grave crisis. In the late 16th century, for instance, England was faced with a serious foreign threat from Spain. In this situation, even Blackstone acknowledged that the "rack for torture," otherwise alien to English traditions, "was occasionally used as an engine of state, not of law."[29]

This is a telling phrase. *Torture is an engine of state, not of law.* It is a "naked" exercise of state power, whose victims, strangely enough, are often naked in a nonmetaphorical sense. Harsh interrogation is an extra-legal tool, wielded by political rulers, outside the ordinary system of legality, without the involvement of judges and courts, to defend the political order from lethal enemies conspiring to destroy it. Public safety trumps legalism and even constitutionality. This is essentially the position taken by most of the legal professionals who continue to defend the use of highly coercive interrogation in the war on terror. In this conflict, they say, the executive branch cannot afford to fight with one hand tied behind its back. It must therefore shed all ordinary restrictions, domestic and international, upon the way it behaves, including especially the way it treats foreign prisoners held overseas. To gain the flexibility it needs to meet the lethal threat of transnational terrorism, the executive branch needs to suspend the rule of law whenever it thinks that it is an obstacle, so long as the conflict endures.

This view is debatable, but it is not without some basis in reality. For instance, the legalistic requirement to ask permission of a judge is said to have prevented the FBI from examining Zaccarias Moussaui's computer. If they had examined the computer, FBI agents might allegedly have been able to foil the 9/11 conspiracy. Indirectly, therefore, judicial oversight of executive action increased the country's vulnerability to terrorism. Whatever the merits of this particular story, it exemplifies the way in which law and legalism can conceivably interfere with national security.

Do such incidents imply that the United States can successfully fight the war on terror only by abandoning due process? The Administration's defenders believe so; but its critics disagree. To illustrate the way enemy prisoners can be given due process without compromising U.S. security, these critics sometimes mention the way America treated the Nazis at Nuremberg. As one reporter put it at the time: "In the courtroom at Nuremberg something more important is happening than the trial of a few captured prisoners. The inhuman is being confronted with the humane, ruthlessness with equity, lawlessness with patient justice, and barbarism with civilization."[30] This sounds noble enough. Yet those today who deny that the Bill of Rights and international covenants against torture are appropriate tools for confronting terrorism have a ready reply. The Nuremberg Trials occurred *after* World War II, they remind us, when the Nazi threat was already a thing of the past. We are not in that position today. The attack of 9/11 was only one episode in an ongoing war. We must therefore behave not like we did at Nuremberg, but rather as we did (around the same time) at Nagasaki. To respond to the savages who want to kill us, we must cast off our Christian-liberal meekness and embrace a "healthy savagery" of our own. We must confront ruthlessness with ruthlessness, it is alleged. We must pull out all the stops. There is no place for squeamishness in wartime. To defeat a ruthless enemy, we must accept the inevitability of collateral damage. It is tragic, but innocent civilians will have to die. After victory, we will have plenty of time for civility, guilt feelings, and the rule of law.

This line of argument may not be very convincing. (Indeed, the suggestion that the United States should conduct the war on terror according to Hiroshima principles is horrifying.) It nevertheless reveals why legal apologists for torture find the "war model" for counterterrorism so irresistibly appealing.

The Secret of the Ticking Bomb

Academic commentaries on this controversy operate at a higher level of abstraction. They stress the way in which ordinary moral and legal prohibitions must sometimes be cast aside in order to meet a looming threat. The question of how to treat a prisoner who knows the whereabouts of a ticking time bomb is commonly debated in this context. Imagining that the bomb is a nuclear device easily escalates the stakes in the case. Although neither realistic nor representative, the hypothetical is nevertheless revealing. For one thing, the idea that the authorities might get a nuclear terrorist into their custody, after he has planned an attack but before he has executed it, is a utopian fantasy. The elusiveness of al Qaeda conspirators is immensely frustrating and naturally gives rise, among counterterrorism officials and Hollywood scriptwriters, to daydreams of superman-style rescues. To set policies on the basis of such far-fetched scenarios would be folly.

The ticking bomb parable is also interesting for another reason. It makes the legitimacy of torture depend wholly on its future consequences, namely, on the prevention of grave harm. In this way, it tracks perfectly the thinking of Administration lawyers and apologists. With its focus on the future, the hypothetical reveals the limited relevance of most historical debates about torture, which assumed that torture was justified or not depending on how useful it proved in uncovering reliable evidence of guilt for past crimes. The ground has now thoroughly shifted. Torture is morally justifiable, or will at least be publicly accepted, if it helps save a major urban center from Armageddon.

The ticking time-bomb fable also suggests the quiet heroism of those who, defying moral norms and legal conventions, choose torture. They sacrifice their scruples for the greater good. They come close to being martyrs for their country, sacrificing moral conscience on the altar of political responsibility. This seems to be what Judge Richard Posner has in mind when he suggests that torture, even though legally prohibited, should be politically applauded, when thousands of lives are at stake, as a morally obligatory act of civil disobedience by public officials.[31]

Those who torture, or approve the torture of, prisoners, according to the implicit storyline, are protecting their fellow Americans from mass death by nuclear incineration. No causal chain need be demonstrated in any particular case. Instead, the ticking time bomb parable creates a presumption. What seemed illegitimate because it yielded dubious confessions now seems legitimate because it provides a ray of hope in a dark and dangerous world. The once-scorned torturer now appears as a potential savior. This torturer/savior fusion does not seem all that remote from the self-image of those who support current U.S. policies of harsh interrogation. This heroic self-image seems pervasive even though none of the prisoner-abuse in Abu Ghraib, for example, could have contributed in any way to the safety of Americans back home. (This heroic American self-image, incidentally, was obliterated by the Abu Ghraib photographs. These nauseating images also dramatically rebutted the Administration's boast that it was bringing the benefits of American-style democracy to Iraq, confirming instead the radical Islamic message that Americans are sexual perverts.)

What is the most important implication of the ticking time-bomb parable? It is, quite simply, the insinuation, without evidence or argument, of an intimate connection between torture and terrorism. In the imaginary scenario, in fact, torture is the *only possible response* to terrorism. The suggestion is subliminal, to some extent. No *reasons* are given to explain why, faced with terrorism, the United States should resort to torture, but the correlation comes through loud and clear. What should we make of such associational thinking?

To understand why torture might be thought to be an appropriate response to terrorism, it helps to look briefly at how the Bush Administration understands terrorism. The main points to stress are these: First, terrorism is an attack upon symbolic targets, aimed at displaying the attackers' power and the victims' impotence. Second, terrorism kills innocent civilians for the purpose of intimidation and to send a political message. Third, terrorism is completely inexcusable.

Let us begin with this last point. Colin Powell wanted to speak for everyone when he said: "There can be no political justification [for terrorism]. There is no religious justification." And "the kind of evil and terror that we saw perpetrated against us three years ago on 9/11 . . . must be fought. It must be resisted. There can be no compromise in this battle."[32] What is most interesting about the *absolutist* claim that terrorism admits of no justification is the way it is echoed, in international law, by the *absolutist* claim that torture admits of no justification. For instance: "No exceptional circumstances whatsoever, whether a state of war or a threat of war, internal instability or any other public emergency, may be invoked as a justification of torture."[33]

Mirror-Imaging

According to the consensus view of international law, neither terrorism nor torture can be justified, no matter how extreme the circumstances or how desperate the cause. The prohibition on both terrorism and torture is equally absolute, unambiguous, and final. Excuses and exceptions are not allowed. The parallelism here may provide a clue to the unexplained choice of inhumane interrogation techniques by the American government and its approval after the fact by American voters. One of the greatest shocks to American liberals was that "The system of torture has, after all, survived its disclosure."[34] Yet why has the American public not been mortified or disillusioned by the revelations from Abu Ghraib? Historically, torture has sometimes turned a public violently against the policies of their government. For instance, "it was the very use of torture that in the end convinced most French people that the cause of Algérie-Française was not worth the enormous strain that it was placing on the societal fabric."[35] This has not (or not yet) occurred in the United States. Why not? One possible answer is that the American public is prepared to accept any conceivable treatment of Arabs, including the torture of innocents unto death, so long as such behavior is presented to them as a response to 9/11. We are facing a "new enemy" and must toss the old rules and scruples overboard.

Abuse of prisoners has proven politically acceptable in the United States, according to this theory, not because, although shameful, it is especially useful in the war on terror. The absence of any metrics of success or failure in the war on terror is by now a commonplace. The utility of torture is very difficult to prove, for all the reasons discussed above. Thus, the most plausible reason for the public to embrace harsh and humiliating interrogation is that abuse of detainees is an "appropriate" response to terror. The 9/11 hijackers violated an absolute prohibition. What possible reaction could be adequate to what they did? Only a response that trespasses on equally sacred ground.

The absolute prohibition against torture, according to this line of argument, was not a legalistic obstacle to be swept aside to achieve important strategic aims (such as the extraction of timely information about future threats). On the contrary, the absolute prohibition provides an independent reason for resorting to torture. Because it violates an absolute prohibition, torture sends a message that there is nothing the United States is unwilling to do. This is fairly close to the message sent by the 9/11 attack itself. Osama bin Laden, imagining himself at war with a military superpower, scorns the no-terrorism absolutism of international human rights covenants as an implicit request for his side's unilateral disarmament. This stance is explicitly mirrored, on the American side, by Charles Krauthammer who sniffs at "no-torture absolutism" as "a form of moral foolishness."[36]

To respond in kind to 9/11, America had to engage in behavior that was just as universally condemned as terrorism against civilians. Overthrowing the Taliban was widely approved and therefore could not serve to convey America's audacity, ferocity, and readiness to feed the rulebook into the shredder. Invading Iraq, a country that had nothing to do with 9/11, was a good start. But the inhumane and degrading treatment of randomly assembled prisoners was also very well suited to send this message. That many of those who are physically abused are perfectly innocent makes torture a more appropriate, not less appropriate, response to 9/11, for the 9/11 hijackers killed perfectly innocent people themselves.

Rules for the humane treatment of prisoners during wartime are based on expectations of reciprocity. One side treats its enemy captives humanely in the expectation or hope that the enemy will treat its captive soldiers in the same way. This sort of reciprocity cannot be expected in the war on terror. Not only is al Qaeda not a "state party" to any of the international conventions concerning POWs, but al Qaeda was always as much a network as an organization. Today, it seems to have liquefied even further, becoming an untraceable ideology or movement (if not a "brand" or "franchise") that is very unlikely to have sufficient command-and-control powers to enforce any rules upon its far-flung, unruly, and self-appointed operatives.

If we cannot have civilized reciprocity with our new global enemy, what sort of reciprocity can we have? The answer is *uncivilized* reciprocity, and that means a return to the original form of reciprocity, namely revenge against the offender's family and friends. We can respond to their lawlessness with our own lawlessness. This decision to return to a primitive lex talionis is sometimes quite explicit. According to James Risen, for instance: "Supporters of the use of harsh or even abusive interrogation techniques have argued that they are necessary in a new and unconventional war against suicide terrorists who don't abide by the traditional rules of war themselves."[37]

If our enemies have renounced the laws of civilization, so will we. If they organized a sneak attack, then we will respond with a dirty war. If they terrorized us, we will terrorize them. If they desecrated our skyline, we will desecrate theirs. If they gloated about our dead, we will smile over their cadavers packed in ice. If they killed randomly assembled civilians, we will do the same in response. If they symbolically humiliated us, we will symbolically humiliate them. This last form of primitive reciprocity, incidentally, was explicitly recommended by Henry Kissinger, who said that Arab terrorists had humiliated us, and therefore "we need to humiliate them."[38] The precise identities of the "they" and the "them" in Kissinger's proposal are disturbingly obscure.

In any event, the attempt to explain America's anomalous torture policy by invoking primitive reciprocity is obviously speculative. The suggestion that torture has proved publicly acceptable because it is widely seen as a form of primitive reciprocity or "equivalent" response is no doubt difficult to prove, but it nevertheless seems a profitable line of research. A similar hypothesis about the motives behind Administration policy is advanced by William Pfaff. He claims that "the Bush administration is not torturing prisoners because it is useful but because of symbolism,"[39] not because of the information that torture reveals, but because of the message that torture sends. Twenty years ago, Elaine Scarry provided a slightly different, but eerily compatible, view of the subject, arguing that "torture is a grotesque piece of compensatory drama,"[40] meaning that the brutal treatment of defenseless prisoners is common not because it provides vital clues but rather because it allows the torturing individuals or groups to see their own power mirrored in the torment of those they torture. Custodial torture might still be "instrumentally rational" even if it does not produce actionable intelligence. It could simply be a savage strategy for delivering a warning to potential adversaries not yet in custody, reducing their willingness to engage in violent resistance by filling them with fear. To the extent that Scarry is right, however, custodial torture escapes the logic of instrumental rationality. It is expressive and consummatory, not instrumental. It gives vent to bottled-up rage and provides soldiers, who see friends dying without victory coming nearer, with a chance to re-imagine themselves as the irresistible power they were supposed to be. Prisoner abuse, according to this line of argument, is exactly the kind of behavior to be expected when people need to reassure themselves about their dominance after it has been called into question: "It is, of course, precisely because the reality of that power is so highly contestable, the regime is so unstable, that torture is being used."[41]

The claim that torture is meant to intimidate the victims' community and reassure the community of the perpetrators cannot be easily verified or falsified. But it certainly makes more sense of the observable facts than the principal alternative, namely that torture was employed and has proved acceptable because of its utility in extracting information necessary to prevent future calamities. The rational and instrumental explanation of American torture policy shipwrecks on the fact that most of the prisoner abuse perpetrated by Americans in the war on terror has occurred in the Iraqi theater and had nothing whatsoever to do with gathering intelligence. The kind of treatment in question includes strapping captives across the hoods of vehicles like slain deer, urinating on detainees, sodomizing them with sticks, and forcing them to bark like dogs. None of this has the feel of instrumentally rational behavior. An American infantry leader submitted the following testimony about the mistreatment of detainees in Iraq in September 2003.

> Beating prisoners until they passed out or collapsed quickly became routine at his outpost near Fallujah, Forward Operating Base Mercury, he said. "To 'fuck a PUC' [for person under control, and pronounced "puck"] means to beat him up," he recalled. "We would give them blows to the head, chest, legs, and stomach, pull them down, kick dirt

on them. This happened every day." These attacks weren't inflicted to collect intelligence but simply to blow off steam. "Everyone in camp knew if you wanted to work out your frustration you show up at the PUC tent. In a way it was sport." One day in the fall of 2003, a cook came by, ordered a prisoner to hold a metal pole, and "broke the guy's leg with a mini Louisville Slugger that was a metal bat."[42]

This method of "blowing off steam" seems to confirm the Scarry thesis. Harsh interrogations, in the American war on terror, have not been conducted in a context that was otherwise lawful or even rational. Torture to extract information has occurred side by side with torture as a sick kind of sport, with outrages that have an emotionally disturbed quality and that, if we follow Scarry, serve to reassure the emotionally roiled abusers of their own evanescent superiority. This suggests that we ought to be extremely skeptical when plausible-sounding pretexts for torture are alleged. How can we be sure that these excuses are not forms of deception and self-deception? A strong case can be made that torture is less a tactic to defeat the enemy than a grotesque piece of compensatory drama, designed to reassure the psychologically disoriented community of abusers. Can defenders of torture be sure that this allegation is off the mark?

Defiance of Law as a Proof of Success

One reason the Administration's defenders remain unmoved by the numerous powerful arguments against the utility of coercive interrogation might be that they are not really focused on the information extracted by these methods. (Compared to the French in Algeria or the Israelis in the West Bank and Gaza, the Americans at Abu Ghraib and Guantánamo Bay may have too little background knowledge to make much sense of the fragmentary information disgorged during harsh interrogations.) They may prize the cruel, inhumane, and degrading treatment of prisoners precisely *because* it violates international norms and the rules of war. Psychologically persuasive evidence that a medicine is effective is that it tastes unbearably foul. This analogy is disquieting because it, too, suggests that torture may be more of a magical-emotional than a rational-strategic response to 9/11.

The debate between the opponents and defenders of U.S. torture policy, in fact, may be much more subtle, and psychologically twisted, than meets the eye. Those who oppose torture say that torture is illegal and does not work. Those who defend torture imply that torture is valuable, even if it does not work, *precisely because it defies the law*. Such magical thinking would help explain the otherwise inexplicable indifference of torture's apologists to the practice's less brutal alternatives and undesirable side-effects. As the violation of an absolute prohibition, torture sends a message about American determination, ruthlessness, and willingness to act without asking permission or making excuses. By defying civilized conventions, the torturing authority shows its public, in an eye-catching way, that it is leaving no stone unturned. How else could it get this message across? The underlying logic may even be less rational than this makes it seem. It is at least conceivable that the defenders of torture embrace the practice because they themselves have no other way to measure success in the war on terror. They may not know what works, but they know that torture shocks the conscience of mankind and may *therefore* infer that it is a fitting response to 9/11, a "proof" that we are doing everything that we possibly can.

If this interpretation has any validity, then torture is not undertaken and accepted because it prevents specific harms. It is undertaken and accepted, rather, because it mirrors the harm that was done to us, thereby certifying that we are adequate to the dangers ahead. Torture is both payback and promissory note. It repays a blood debt and conveys a readiness to fight. An extreme injury requires an extreme remedy. George W. Bush may have been reelected in 2004, in part, because he was widely perceived as having fewer scruples than his opponent and therefore as being more willing to give the terrorists a taste of their own medicine. With their brows furrowed over Vietnam, so say the Administration's defenders, self-flagellating Democrats risk making Americans feel guilty about defending themselves ferociously in an increasingly dangerous world. Not so the Republicans. They are uninhibited and single-minded. They know how a sheriff must behave in the lawless frontier. They will not be hamstrung by legalisms or the opinion of other nations. Critics of the Administration, of course, have ceaselessly asserted that torture is counterproductive as well as illegal. One reason this argument has had so little political purchase may be that the supporters of prisoner abuse in Guantánamo Bay and Abu Ghraib are not thinking clearly about consequences. They applaud torture for the same reason that most human beings do most of the things they do – because of the way it makes them feel. They want to respond with appropriate ferocity to 9/11. They interpret illegality, by an obscure associational logic, as a symptom of gloves-off ferocity. The thrill of "giving as good as we get" apparently blocks their realization that the vast majority of those being mistreated, sometimes savagely, by the United States had nothing whatsoever to do with the 9/11 attacks.

Torture is an emotionally satisfying (not useful) form of counterterrorism because it holds up a mirror to terrorism itself. On the most primitive level, it is meant to terrorize. This primitive reciprocity has many disturbing implications. One is the way the United States, in the war on terror, mimics Osama bin Laden's "holy war." According to Judith Shklar, "no form of arrogance is more obnoxious than the claim that some of us are God's agents, his deputies on earth charged with punishing God's enemies."[43] In the war on terror, America has carbon-copied the venomous arrogance of the jihadists with a venomous arrogance of its own. To say that the United States, too, has a divine mission to punish God's enemies is to say that we are at war with "evil." It is to believe, with General William Boykin, Deputy Undersecretary of Defense for Intelligence, that the Christian God is "bigger" than the Muslim God.[44] Evil calls for exorcism, not for a rational assessment of priorities. When faced with evil, moreover, we are allowed to employ any possible means to help us prevail, including methods that would otherwise be forbidden. Defeating evil is such an absolute moral obligation, moreover, that it frees us from thinking about the possibly negative downstream consequences of our actions, such as the collapse of America's moral standing in the world.

On 9/11, al Qaeda gave Americans a burning inferno, a taste of hell. In the torture chambers of Guantánamo Bay and Abu Ghraib, the United States returned the favor. These sick and sickening facilities are not merely lawless zones, they are imitation hells. In one manual, written to prevent the abuse of detainees, we read: "Placing a detainee on the ground or putting a foot on him implies that you are God. This is one of the worst things we can do."[45] That the jailers did this and worse is now a matter of public record.

Beccaria traces the roots of late medieval and early modern torture to Christian mythology. We torture a prisoner "to purge him of infamy in some metaphysical and incomprehensible way."[46] Torturers imitate the torments God inflicts upon sinners in Purgatory and Hell. Strangely enough, the photos of the Abu Ghraib prison abuse resemble nothing so much as Giotto's Last Judgment in the Scrovegni Chapel in Padova. Here, too, we see naked bodies piled up in painful mock promiscuity, naked limbs attacked by sharp-toothed beasts, naked men wearing hoods, manhandled, flagellated, in stress positions, and dragged on leashes.

Could torture be a blasphemous attempt to imitate God? Could American torture of Islamic detainees contain a distant echo of ecclesiastic torture of Christian heretics in the Middle Ages? That it is a perverted religious answer to a religiously inspired attack on America is strongly suggested by the following story. "One detainee, named in the report as Ameen Saeed al-Sheik, said he was asked by a soldier whether he believed in anything. 'I said to him, "I believe in Allah." So he said, "But I believe in torture and I will torture you."' He said one soldier struck his broken leg and ordered him to curse Islam. 'Because they started to hit my broken leg, I curse my religion,' the paper quoted him as saying. 'They ordered me to thank Jesus I'm alive.'"[47] Such random stories prove nothing, of course, but they do associate torture, plausibly, with self-divinization, the purging of heretics, and an absurd belief that the laws of human fallibility do not apply to the U.S. side in the war on terror.

In explaining the greatest danger of anti-Communism, George Kennan wrote, in an often cited passage, that: "something may occur in our own minds and souls which will make us no longer like the persons by whose efforts this republic was founded and held together, but rather like representatives of that very power we are trying to combat: intolerant, secretive, suspicious, cruel, and terrified of internal dissension because we have lost our own belief in ourselves and in the power of our ideals. The worst thing that our Communists could do to us, and the thing we have most to fear from their activities, is that we should become like them."[48]

Should not the United States, in conducting its war on terror, refuse to model itself on its mortal foes? What makes the danger loom so large today is well explained by the Israeli military historian and theorist, Martin van Creveld: "War being among the most imitative of all human activities, the very process of combating low-intensity conflict will cause both sides to become alike, unless it can be brought to a quick end."[49] Wartime's logic of imitation should perhaps make the United States rethink its hasty description of 9/11 as an act of war rather than a particularly atrocious crime in a serial crime spree.

By making counterterrorism resemble terrorism, by answering terrorism with torture, the American government and electorate may experience a temporary feeling of adequacy to an obscure and unparalleled threat, yet the ultimate effect on American political culture may resemble defeat more than victory. As Nietzsche wrote: "When you are looking into an abyss, the abyss also looks into you."[50] Torture can corrupt the torturing community even if the United States, by some miracle, prevails in the war on terror. The story of the 9/11 hijackers reveals how a powerful psychological bond can be created among people who act together to commit an appalling crime. It would not be surprising if U.S. interrogators in Abu Ghraib and Guantánamo Bay felt linked by a similar emotional bond. America will certainly lose the moral dimension of its war on terror if it continues to build its sense of national solidarity around pride and pleasure at flouting the civilized norms that limit the way jailers treat defenseless prisoners, of unknown guilt, who fall by chance into their hands.

Postscript

The "rule of law" is a complicated concept with a convoluted history. Many of the principles and practices that we commonly associate with the rule of law, however, stem from the truism that violence breeds violence. To interrupt the cycles of retaliation characteristic of vendetta cultures, organized political communities do not prohibit revenge but rather organize and rationalize it. If an individual from one group kills or injures grievously an individual from another group, the rule of law forbids self-help (the revenge killing of a member of the first group by a member of the second) and channels the irrepressible craving for revenge into the criminal justice system. Inside that system, culpability is attached solely to the individual perpetrator or perpetrators, not to their clan or kin group. This individualized culpability, moreover, has to be proved before a neutral tribunal in the presence of the accused who has a right to dispute or refute the evidence presented against him. The criminal punishment that is inflicted in the case of a guilty verdict is indeed "violent," but it is regularized, disciplined, and targeted violence, and therefore violence that is much less likely to spiral out of control than eye-for-an-eye retaliation between groups in the absence of the rule of law.

This is a highly stylized story, but it contains enough of the truth to help make an important point about the Bush Administration's casual and dismissive attitude toward the rule of law in the context of the war on terror. Antilegalism remains difficult to understand until we look behind it to discover its source. The basis for the Administration's cavalier attitude toward venerable legal principles is an unexamined conviction that violence, for the most part, quells violence or, alternatively, that violence breeds compliance, docility, resignation, fatalism, and submission. It may seem unfair to accuse the Cheney-Rumsfeld circle of ignoring the possibility that violence may breed violence. But how else can their reckless policies be explained? Such blindness provides as good an explanation as any for the Administration's self-defeating tendency to flout the rule of law. If they had any idea that such behavior might end up harming national security or undermining American power, they would surely have renounced the lawless violence that they have, in fact, boastingly embraced.

Take torture, the subject of this chapter. Cheney seems to have made it his personal mission to insure that American officials can savagely mistreat suspects in U.S. custody.[51] He obvious believes that freedom to engage is such lawless behavior will never come back to haunt the United States. Is he right?

The very existence of suicide missions, as mentioned in Chapter One, suggests that he may well be wrong. One of the principal reasons why suicide missions have emerged and survived as a popular method for weak groups to inflict serious damage on organized states is the expectation of torture. Any savvy resistance group will want to minimize the chance that its captured operatives will divulge the entire network of accomplices, including the topmost leadership of the group. The danger is increased, of course, if the state being attacked regularly tortures captives to extract actionable intelligence. How can this acute danger be reduced? The simplest way is to replace hit-and-run operatives with suicide operatives, for they will not be around, after the attack, to divulge any secrets in the torture chambers of the authorities.

This is only one illustration of the old rule that violence can breed violence. A more general observation is that torture engenders terrorism. The violence of torture is designed to break the will, but it may easily have the opposite effect, hardening and animating the will. We see this pattern repeatedly. In his rambling treatise, *Knights Under the Prophet's Banner,* for example, Ayman al-Zawahiri speaks bitterly of his comrades and "brothers" who were "killed by acts of torture" or "killed under torture."[52] He explicitly justified jihad as "retribution for . . . the souls of the tortured people throughout the land of Islam."[53] This is the context in which to understand *takfir*, Arabic for the denunciation of other Muslims for apostasy, a kind of freelance excommunication that permits the assassination of public officials. About Muslim radicals, particularly those influenced by Sayyid Qutb, it has been said: "Their belief in *takfir* has also been influenced by their ordeals in prisons. These ordeals made it possible for them to conclude that those who inflicted ruthless torture could not be Muslims."[54] Incidentally, such an inference shows once again why it is so difficult to disentangle jihadist rage at the impiety of Middle Eastern regimes from jihadist rage at the cruelty, autocracy and unfreedom of these regimes.

The idea that torture breeds terrorism mirrors the claim that terrorism breeds torture, not as a strategic countermeasure but as an emotional reflex. Both processes exemplify the basic rule that violence breeds violence unless humans are creative and nimble enough to discipline their collective emotions.

Pierre Hassner has formulated the suggestion that terrorists and torturers are making the same mistake in a provocative manner:

> it may be that this error was committed both by the authors of the attacks against America and Israel, thinking they would make their bourgeois adversaries buckle, and by the latter, thinking they could break the will of the terrorists by punishment alone, neglecting the humiliation and craving for vengeance that punishment excites.[55]

Hassner may not be correct about the thinking behind the 9/11 attacks, since Osama, Zawahiri and KSM seem to have assumed that violence breeds violence and to have calculated that the ensuing chaos would weaken their American adversaries. About the Bush Administration, however, he is surely right. Unaware that cruelty can fuel violent resistance, the Cheney-Rumsfeld group appears to have been clueless about the strategic benefits to the stronger party of following the rule of law.

To "go around the law" when combating terrorism is to regress into collective punishment. High tolerance for mistaken identity and the abandonment of the presumption of innocence are characteristic of Bush's "war on terror." The predictable result has been not only increased flexibility for counterterrorism officials. It has also been a reversion into a preliberal order where individual findings of culpability are no longer deemed essential. Going around the law permits forms of collective punishment, including mass detention of individuals caught up in police sweeps conducted on the basis of religion and ethnicity. Waiving the rules will do the work of the terrorists in this sense: it will recreate a world where violence breeds violence – where terrorism breeds torture and torture breeds terrorism. This will not be a safer world.

13 | THE INFALLIBILITY TRAP

Vice President Cheney saw in 9/11 a chance to remake the constitutional balance of powers. His experience in the Nixon and Ford
Administrations had convinced him that excessive Congressional power
makes it difficult for America to exercise its rightfully dominant role in
the world. He did not necessarily want or need a dignified historical
pedigree for his belief, rooted in ideology and experience, that the
executive branch should be freed from interference by the other
branches of government. But John Yoo tried to provide him such a
pedigree anyway, working tirelessly to unearth authorizing antecedents
for unlimited executive authority even before the war on terror began.
Yoo's historical claims are doubtful, however. It is true that, for good
or ill, the declare-war clause of the Constitution no longer serves as
a serious check on the president's power to start wars on his own
initiative. Yet to assert, as Yoo does, that the Founders never dreamed
that it might serve as such a check is to distort history in an attempt
to claim ancestral authority for an unfettering of presidential discretion
that none of the Founders, acquainted as they were with the dark
impulses of the human heart and the cognitive imperfections of the
human mind, could have possibly defended. In fact, Yoo's claim that the
Founders themselves shared the extreme views about unilateral executive
power later advanced by Cheney is so contrary to the historical record
that it begs to be explained on psychological, political, or other grounds.
The Founder's Constitution is based on three basic principles: all
people, including rulers, are prone to make serious mistakes; all people,
especially rulers, are loathe to admit their mistakes even when midstream
readjustments would serve the public interest; and most people are
delighted to point out the mistakes of their rivals. The separation of

powers is basically a system that assigns the right to make mistakes to one branch and the right to correct mistakes to the other two branches, as well as to the free press and to the electorate at large. The Constitution imagined by Cheney and theorized by Yoo is quite different. It is founded on the empirically untenable principle of presidential inerrancy. It assumes that the executive branch will perform better, especially when faced with a wholly unprecedented threat, if it is able to operate in total secrecy, with no input from meddling outsiders, and no critics to point out avoidable errors. This theory has been tested in practice over the last half-dozen years. It turns out that an executive branch that never has to give reasons for its actions soon stops having plausible reasons for its actions. Surrounded by yes-men and sheltered from seriously informed criticism, such a pampered and unchecked executive becomes dangerously disconnected from reality. This irrational result is certainly not what the Founders intended. Legacy disputes aside, the anomalous Cheney-Yoo doctrine that neither Congress nor the courts can set any limits to presidential discretion to launch or conduct wars has never seemed less persuasive than it does today. If we have learned anything from the Bush debacle, it is that the counterterrorism agenda and the imperial-executive agenda are two different, unrelated, and even contradictory agendas. Concentrating excessive authority in the executive does not increase effectiveness in time of danger for the simple reason that an all-powerful president becomes impervious to bad news. This is the true lesson of an administration that made disastrous and self-defeating use of artificially swollen powers in a conflict with Salafi terrorism that, however serious it is, will inevitably be mismanaged if conducted as a "war."

As one of the "fiercely conservative lawyers in the Justice Department" between 2001 and 2003, John Yoo was "pushing the envelope."[1] He demonstrated his radicalism, as we saw in Chapter Twelve, by crafting a series of legal opinions in which he spelled out the fundamentals of a secret emergency Constitution under which the president's inherent powers in the "war on terror" are essentially unlimited. In the wake of 9/11, Yoo argued, the United States was at war in a constitutional sense, and consequently Congress and the courts could no longer purport to second-guess or interfere with or even learn about the president's national-security decisions, however momentous. Supposedly vital for fighting mass-casualty terrorism, Yoo's presidential Constitution was never publicly discussed or debated. Instead, it began to leak out, one memo at a time, only after important policy choices had been made on the basis of its presumed authority. The memos claimed to provide legal grounds for a whole range of now hotly contested decisions concerning indefinite executive detention without access to counsel, harsh interrogation techniques, rendition to countries known for torture, the establishment of clandestine prisons for "ghost detainees," the assassination of terrorist suspects by U.S. hit squads worldwide, and warrantless surveillance of telephone and e-mail communications between the United States and overseas.

Many and perhaps most constitutional scholars viewed these policies, to the extent that they knew about them, as legally dubious acts of executive-branch overreaching, but Yoo's carte blanche constitutionalism suited the ambitions of Dick Cheney and the other architects of Bush's gloves-off response to 9/11. Adherence to legal principles or procedural requirements, they believed, would have forced them to fight ruthless terrorists with one arm tied behind their backs. Legalistic niceties – such as the presumption of innocence and squeamishness about mistaken identity – only played into the hands of the enemy.

Addressing himself to impatient officials bridling at statutory and other restrictions, the 35-year-old government lawyer proved obliging. Laws that cramp the executive, including requirements of transparency and oversight associated with checks and balances, are unconstitutional infringements of the president's authority, he made clear. The Commander-in-Chief can confidently dispense with rules that had previously governed the intelligence community. Indeed, he should be freed from all constraints that might conceivably cripple the U.S. side in the battle against transnational terror. The president's ultimate duty to protect and defend the nation, the memos collectively advised, gives him the right, if he so wishes, not only to ignore Congress and the courts but also deliberately to deceive them, and the public at large, for the sake of national security.

As a government lawyer, in other words, Yoo focused on the powers of the Commander-in-Chief during wartime, whether these powers derived from the Constitution or from Congress's authorization of the use of military force against al Qaeda, Afghanistan, and later Iraq. What Cheney and company wanted was unbridled authority to do whatever they deemed necessary in the course of these wars. Yoo worked unstintingly to meet their needs.

A Constitutionally Unlimited War-Making Power

As a fledgling scholar, by contrast, Yoo had a different obsession, stemming from older controversies over Vietnam and the 1973 War Powers

Resolution. In his pre-9/11 academic writings, he was less interested in the president's powers during wartime (the subject of his subsequent memos) than in the president's authority, on his own initiative, to set the country on the path to war. Echoing various Cold War hawks, the young law professor insisted on the power of the president to deploy offensive force on his own authority and, more radical still, in the face of Congressional opposition.

Elaborated before 9/11, Yoo's grandiose view of the president's war-making power was in no way novel. Bold claims of executive authority to use military force unilaterally can be traced back at least to FDR and Truman. In 1966, for example, President Johnson's State Department issued a famous memo alleging considerable historical precedent to justify the president's independent war powers in the absence of Congressional approval. The memo contended that "since the Constitution was adopted there have been at least 125 instances in which the President has ordered the armed forces to take action or maintain positions abroad without obtaining prior Congressional authorization, starting with the 'undeclared war' with France (1798–1800)." To such historically debatable accounts of unchecked presidential discretion in military affairs, Yoo adds little. His thinking seems to have been shaped even more definitively by Nixon's lawyers, especially by their defense of the president's plenary power to launch covert military operations despite explicit statutory prohibitions. On all basic points, Yoo was "pushing the envelope," in other words, by dusting off and re-presenting the most radical positions of Nixon-era advocates of executive power.

What makes Yoo original, therefore, is not the radicalism of his belief in presidential authority. His claims to originality rest entirely on the assertions he makes about the intellectual origins of that authority. He developed his unusual stance in a series of law journal articles, composed before Bush came to power and expanded into a book, *The Powers of War and Peace*. Although he was already associated in the 1990s with important conservative figures like Orrin Hatch and Clarence Thomas, Yoo could only have dreamed that his idiosyncratic historical argument would soon be invoked to justify a bold new presidential grab for power.

To understand what Yoo is arguing for, we must first understand what he is arguing against. The leading students of presidential war powers, as he freely admits, agree that the Framers wanted to apportion the government's war powers between the legislature and the executive, vesting the power to initiate offensive war, along with other war powers, in Congress, and assigning to the president, as chief commanding officer of military and naval forces, only two powers: the power to conduct an authorized war and the power to repel surprise attacks.

This allocation of war powers, as the Framers envisaged it, proved politically unstable for various reasons. The most decisive factors included the executive's superior capacity for secrecy, dispatch, and information gathering, and America's increasing entanglement with the rest of the world. Equally important was the inescapable elasticity of the idea of national self-defense, capable of being stretched from repelling actual attacks on U.S. territory to preventing anticipated attacks on American lives, property, and allies around the world. The eventual routine maintenance of large peacetime standing armies was also critical, as were the provincial focus, internal dissension, and chronic shirking of Congress. The eventual realization that the Atlantic and Pacific oceans would be useless as moats against a nuclear first strike contributed to the same development. For these and other reasons, the power to commence declared and undeclared wars has gradually shifted, against the Framers' wishes, to the executive branch.

While Congress has debated, the president has acted. That is the nub of a historical development that the Framers neither intended nor foresaw. The president's role as supreme foreign policy maker, including considerable executive discretion in the initiation of war, has become the American default mode at least since Truman. After the Korean War, admittedly, Congress has formally authorized all major U.S. conflicts, including the Vietnam War (the Gulf of Tonkin Resolution) and the two Iraq wars. Legislative complicity, in practice, has proved more useful to the president than to Congress, however. By exaggerating and even fabricating lethal threats that Congress has limited capacity to verify, the executive branch has been able to ensnare the national legislature into approving its military adventures abroad. Senators and Representatives who originally voted to approve a war on false pretenses have subsequently hesitated to criticize it, no matter how calamitous the outcome, because after-the-fact dissent embarrassingly reveals their own prior gullibility and lack of foresight.

Fictionalizing the Founding

Yoo does not merely breathe new life into the most extreme claims of Nixon-era executive hawks. He also claims unique insight into "the mindset of the Framers," disowning the "conventional academic wisdom" according to which the emergence of unilateral executive powers involved a marked departure from original intent. The Framers' Constitution, as he oddly reconceives it, wholly endorses "the practice of unilateral presidential warmaking."[2]

In the past, those who hoped to increase Congress's role in war making were the ones who invoked the intent of the Framers. Aiming to run the reel backward and reduce presidential war powers to the dimensions that the Founders intended, they sought, unsuccessfully, to transform a policy debate into a legacy dispute. With whimsical eccentricity, Yoo has devoted much of his short career to swapping places with these defenders of frayed tradition, claiming that original intent supports not Congressional but presidential prerogative, not only during wartime but also in the run-up to war.

The Framers charged the president with protecting the nation, he tells us, "even if that meant fighting with the legislature to enforce the desires of the people."[3] True to their British heritage, Yoo also asserts, the Framers modeled the president's war powers on those of King George III. They therefore refused to grant Congress even a concurrent power to commence war. At its core, the Constitution embodies the Framers' intention to prohibit Congress from "encroaching"[4] on the executive's power to initiate as well as conduct war.

To make his contrarian claim ring true, Yoo whites out contrary evidence and draws dubious conclusions on the basis of fragmentary and carefully selected facts. He disregards the main thrust of the historical record and misrepresents the parts he acknowledges. He ferrets out (and exaggerates the importance of) scattered shreds of evidence that, at first glance, seem to back up his predetermined narrative. This cherry-picking of the sources may explain why he fits so comfortably into an administration known for politicizing intelligence, smothering doubts, silencing critical voices, and fixing the facts around the policy.

Yet why would an aspiring legal scholar labor for years to develop and defend a historical thesis that is manifestly untrue? What is the point and what is the payoff? That is the principal mystery of Yoo's singular book. Characteristic of *The Powers of War and Peace* is the anemic relation between the evidence adduced and the inferences drawn. The footnotes and citations teem with ambiguity and complexity, whereas the summary statements snap dogmatic simplicities. For instance, in a section devoted to the powers of war and peace in various state Constitutions, between independence and the ratification of the Constitution, Yoo uses selective citation to convey the impression that state executives not only possessed substantial foreign-policy powers but were also, when commanding the state militias, freed from any obligation to act according to laws passed by state legislatures. That his case is wobbly on both counts is the least that might be said. What makes his misleading account additionally baffling, however, is that he cites without comment the very provisions in several state Constitutions that deny the executive branch any power to act except "under the laws" passed by the legislative branch.[5]

In a stray footnote, to take another example, Yoo reproduces Madison's assertion that "executive powers ex vi termini, do not include the Rights of war & peace."[6] And other Framers, too, classified the powers of war and peace as "legislative." But Yoo is convinced that the powers of war and peace must necessarily be classified as "executive." Faced with statements to the contrary, he buries or ignores them. The nimbleness with which, on several occasions, he simply inverts the manifest significance of historical texts that contradict his preset beliefs can only be called athletic.

Yoo's fictionalizing of the founding period is best exemplified by his lengthy discussion of the Aug. 17, 1787, debate at the Constitutional Convention in Philadelphia. The surviving notes of this debate are admittedly garbled, cryptic, and open to interpretation, but two things come through with ringing clarity. First, the word "declare," as the Framers used it, had a loose and fluctuating meaning. Second, most participants in the discussion agreed on the importance of limiting the president's war powers by granting important war powers to Congress. This consensus stemmed from a conviction that war is the nurse of executive aggrandizement and that the president, whose powers balloon unnaturally in wartime, has a dangerous incentive to contrive and publicize bogus pretexts for war.

Yoo is no doubt right to emphasize the idea, central to *The Federalist Papers*, that "exigency justified the expansion of government authority in war and peace."[7] But when Hamilton and Madison referred to "government authority," they were thinking of the authority of the executive and legislative branches together, not of the executive alone. Because the ruses, stratagems, and timing of the enemy cannot be known in advance, it would be folly to tie down the nation's defensive power to a set of rigid rules. This does not mean that the Framers wished to make war powers an executive monopoly. In *The Federalist*, No. 30, for instance, Hamilton asserted that no constitutional limits can be placed on the power to tax, precisely because future necessities admit not of calculation. This broad constitutional grant of emergency power to the government, made with an eye to providing for the common defense, in no way swells executive power vis-à-vis the legislature or implies any curtailment of Congress's exclusive power of the purse.

Determined to "prove" a thesis that is shaky at best, Yoo cannot bring himself to write straightforwardly. Some of the book's cloudiest passages are devoted to the counterintuitive claim that, for the Framers, "the President's authority under the Constitution did not differ in important measure from that of the king."[8] He has to make this case against plentiful counterevidence, including Hamilton's lengthy analysis in *The Federalist*, No. 69, of the "total dissimilitude" of the American president and the British king. One reason why Hamilton thought that the president's authority under the Constitution differed in important measure from that of the king was that, in the U.K., according to the standard account, "the law ascribes to the king the attribute of *sovereignty*."[9] Exactly where the U.S. Constitution places "sovereignty," or if it places it anywhere, is debatable. But the Constitution certainly does not lodge sovereignty in the president. To underscore what is at stake here, it is useful to cite another comment by Blackstone on the British monarchy: "Besides the attribute of sovereignty, the law also ascribes to the king, in his political capacity, absolute *perfection*. The king can do no wrong."[10] The inerrancy here ascribed to the British monarch has a specific and subtle legal meaning, to be sure. Yet to the presidency created by the American Constitution such pompous terminology, however qualified or metaphorical, cannot be applied.

Equally frustrating for the careful reader is Yoo's repeated claim that Madison inherited from Montesquieu "a pure separation of powers scheme, one in which each governmental function was classified as either legislative, executive, or judicial, and then allocated to that branch."[11] In fact, in *The Federalist*, No. 47, Madison went to great lengths to repudiate the pure separation of powers scheme, arguing that Montesquieu had defended a system in which the legislative, executive, and judicial departments "are by no means totally separate and distinct from each other."[12]

Yoo repeatedly asserts that the Framers gave Congress only two checks on the executive's foreign-policy powers: namely, the power to impeach and the power to cut off supplies. This is prima facie implausible, given the impressive arsenal of foreign-policy powers assigned to Congress by the Constitution, including the powers to define violations of the law of nations, to issue letters of marque and reprisal, to make rules concerning captures on land and water, to raise and support an army and navy, to make rules for their governance and to regulate international commerce – not to mention the Senate's powers to accept or reject ambassadorial appointments and to approve or reject treaties, and, of course, Congress's power to declare war.

Yoo's assertion that the power to defund an ongoing military campaign "can easily forestall hostilities"[13] is also unconvincing. In practice, it has turned out, power over supplies is worth little, because sitting legislators are highly unlikely, for political reasons, to pull the plug on American troops already engaged in combat on executive authority. To the extent that it makes sense, moreover, Yoo's claim is largely antiquarian. In the founding era, when standing armies were still viewed with deep suspicion, Congress could forestall executive adventurism by denying the president the funds necessary to fight a war. Today, when large peacetime standing armies have become routine, the funding power cannot possibly have the checking force that the Framers intended it to have.

It hardly follows, in any case, that by reserving to Congress one method for blocking unilateral executive war making, the Framers intended to withhold from Congress all other means. Indeed, the Framers' fear of executive adventurism – reflected in their emphasis on the power to appropriate money for the common defense – also led them to grant Congress the lion's share of powers pertaining to war, with the notable exception of the executive command function. Congress could deny funding, but it could also refuse to raise an army or navy, deny the president the right to employ privateers, deny privateers the right to earn prize money, and even decline to call forth the militia. Congress could also refuse to declare war – its most direct method of achieving the aim that its other powers would allow it to accomplish only indirectly. Yoo characteristically fails to ask why the Framers vested in Congress so many powers over war, nor does he pay any attention to the political theory that underlies their constitutional thinking on this point. His "originalism," or pretended fidelity to the intent of the Framers and the ratifying conventions, is highly selective. He pores over the documentary evidence, it sometimes seems, only to discover, and exaggerate the importance of tiny technical loopholes that appear to subvert the Framers' fundamental design.

For presidentialists, obviously, the most embarrassing passage in the Constitution is the one that unequivocally vests in Congress the power to declare war. Yoo's bold but futile attempt to explain away this provision makes up the heart of his book. His first ploy is belittlement. He contends, against the evidence, that "declare" had a narrow technical meaning at the time and that the power to declare war, having nothing to do with the power to commence war, was therefore a paltry power merely to "recognize an existing state of hostilities"[14] and to clarify legal relations among belligerents and between belligerents and neutrals.

That even prolonged and serious wars took place without formal declarations was no secret at the time of the founding. And the Framers knew that an attack from abroad, with or without a declaration of war by the aggressor, could thrust the United States into a state of hostilities. It would therefore have been absurd for them to imply that the United States could never find itself in a state of hostilities unless Congress had previously declared war. And of course they neither said nor thought any such thing.

Eager to encourage foreign trade but wary of foreign entanglements, the Framers wanted to make it difficult for the government to initiate war, but they made sure not to abolish or overly restrict the power to repel surprise attacks. This latter power they implicitly placed in the federal executive but also, and more explicitly, in the state governments, on the assumption that foreign aggression might require a hair-trigger response before any consultation with Congress, perhaps out of session or sitting far away from the point of incursion, was possible. Eventually, the federal executive did something the state governments could not do: It expanded its originally limited constitutional permission to repel surprise attacks, without Congressional approval, into an "inherent power" to unleash military force in response to actual injuries or imagined threats to American interests, as the president unilaterally defines them, anywhere in the world. One result of this gradual magnification of presidential power has been the atrophy of the declare-war clause as a realistic check on executive war making.

How does Yoo expunge the extensive textual evidence demonstrating beyond any doubt that the Framers and ratifiers wished to make offensive war difficult to initiate? He adopts a double strategy. When a statement is too flagrant to interpret away, he concedes the point and asserts that the view expressed in the offending passage is wholly unrepresentative. This is how he disposes of Madison's perfectly clear notes, taken at the Convention, according to which James Wilson "did not consider the Prerogatives of the British Monarch as a proper guide in defining the Executive powers. Some of these prerogatives were of a Legislative nature. Among others that of war & peace &c."[15] Faced with such unambiguous counterevidence, Yoo dismisses it as exceptional and atypical, classifying Wilson as "a dissenter from the prevailing Federalist view on war powers."[16] He concedes that "Wilson was a leading Federalist who relied on the Declare War Clause as a limitation on the war power" of the president. But "history will show," he authoritatively instructs, that Wilson "was the only one."[17] In fact, as Yoo well knows, other Framers made identical or nearly identical claims.

To deflect the plain meaning of their words, he suggests that they were try-ing to say something subtly different from what all previous constitutional historians have understood. Whenever the Framers discussed Congress's power to inhibit the initiation of offensive war, Yoo claims, they did not have in mind generic war but only a specific subvariety, "total war." This deft footwork allows Yoo to assert with spurious confidence that, apart from Wilson, the Framers agreed that Congress's power to declare war in no way limits the president's war powers.

Note the radical concession that Yoo is inadvertently making, however. He admits that the declare war clause was not such a trifle, after all, since it "limited the executive's ability to plunge the nation into a total war."[18] Congressional powers over war and peace are not limited to impeachment and appropriations, since "the executive branch cannot wage a total war without Congress's declaration of war."[19] After feverishly insisting that the declare war clause, as originally understood, gave Congress no authority whatsoever to restrict presidential war making, and that Congress par-ticipates in foreign affairs only via the appropriation and impeachment powers, Yoo suddenly pirouettes and admits that the declare war clause did give Congress significant authority to limit the president's war powers.

In an attempt to extricate himself from the transparent inconsistency in his argument, Yoo distinguishes sharply between war and "total war," but this improvised escape craft is not seaworthy. His imaginative construct shipwrecks on the unambiguous constitutional provision, in Article I, Section 8, which assigns to Congress, not to the president, the power to issue letters of marque and reprisal, which happens to be a power to engage in hostilities short of all-out war that might easily escalate into all-out war.

The Legal Nullity of the Treaty Power

After devoting the first half of his book to the president's power to launch wars on his own say-so, Yoo turns to his second fixation. This is his pet idea, shared by other conservative scholars, that treaties, even after being ratified by the Senate, are not the supreme law of the land. Here again, he projects current-day conservative policy preferences, including an exag-gerated abhorrence of international agreements, back into the minds of the Framers. The authors and ratifiers of the Constitution, Yoo explains, agreed that "no treaty could have direct legislative effect without the par-ticipation of Congress."[20] He again bolsters his case by twisting the plain sense of words. For example, he cites Madison's claim that the House's "approbation and co-operation *may often* be necessary in carrying treaties into full effect" to prove that "any significant treaty *would require* an implementing statute that must come from Congress" (my emphasis).[21] Similarly, when one of the Framers states unambiguously that treaties "have the force of law," Yoo tells us that this did not mean what naïve readers might think it did. The Framers simply wanted to establish that treaties possess the vanishingly weak, almost metaphorical, "force of law" characteristic of agreements "between sovereign nations under international law."[22]

It follows, then, that treaties, domestically, are legal nullities. If this was common knowledge in the founding period, why did some anti-Federalists worry, as Yoo amply documents, that "the treaty-power, because of the Supremacy Clause, had become tantamount to the power to legislate"?[23] The ratification-period debates about the treaty power – particularly the frequently expressed apprehension that the treaty power shared by the president and the Senate would not only undermine residual state power but would also marginalize the House's lawmaking authority – would make no sense if everyone had agreed, as Yoo ardently claims they did, that treaties had zero domestic validity without additional legislation by Congress. Yoo writes that his deep skepticism about international agreements stems from his concern for Congress's constitutional role. It is a curious claim, coming from someone who expresses scant concern that Congress's constitutional role might be undermined by secretive presidential decision-making. Why in the world is the treaty power harder to reconcile with "the standards of democracy and accountability established by our constitutional system" than unilateral commander-in-chief powers?

Fear Mongering and Ancestor Worship

Yoo's mutually contradictory postures and beliefs are as striking as his exaggerations. At times he pretends to be the quintessential fair-and-balanced moderate. At other times, he poses as a paradigm-shattering revolutionary. Yoo's understanding of the implications of 9/11 is similarly contradictory – and telling. On the one hand, the terrorist attacks changed everything. On the other hand, we need to adhere strictly to the original intent of our eighteenth-century Framers. How can Yoo's national-security paradigm be both venerably perennial and shatteringly new?

The liberal plan to involve multiple veto actors in the formulation of foreign policy and especially to share war powers between the executive and the legislature, he tells us, "might have been more appropriate at the end of the Cold War, when conventional warfare between nation-states remained the chief focus of concern and few threats seemed to challenge American national security."[24] He believes, however, that the liberal bias against the massive deployment of American troops overseas, an after effect of the Vietnam War, was made obsolete by 9/11. Our reflexive impulse today, at first glimmer of danger, must be toward all-out military attack on enemies far and wide, not toward peaceful diplomacy and negotiation. Since the emergence of the terrorist threat, "it certainly is no longer clear that the constitutional system ought to be fixed so as to make it difficult to use force."[25] He summarizes his position as follows: "These *new* threats to American national security, driven by *changes* in the international environment, should *change* the way we think about the relationship between the process and substance of the warmaking system" (my emphasis).[26]

In such passages, Yoo's justification for presidentialism seems to be wholly contextual, contingent, and contemporary. If that is true, however, why has he buried himself in the library to prove that the Framers themselves intended unchecked presidentialism to be the basic system for conducting American foreign policy? Why has he argued, against a mountain of contrary evidence, that Madison, Hamilton, and the others wished to make unilateral presidential war making "as easy as lying," and that they were already and miraculously imbued with a post-9/11 mindset?

The "pestilential breath of faction," warns *The Federalist Papers*, "may poison the foundations of justice."[27] John Yoo, as is well known, belongs to the Federalist Society, an association that Madison and Hamilton would perhaps have classified as a mischievous domestic faction. Its members are conservative Republican lawyers who claim to be committed to recovering the original understanding of the Constitution. In 2000 they watched their preferred candidate accede to the presidency. They were naturally eager to exploit this window of opportunity and were therefore driven by the logic of incumbency to argue for an expansion of executive authority. Because of their commitment to "originalism," however, they were also compelled to cloak their momentary ambitions as pious adherence to the intent of the Framers. This is the immediate intellectual context in which to make sense of *The Powers of War and Peace*.

More substantively, the book's unstable mixture of contextualism and originalism stems from Yoo's decision to yoke two distinct rhetorical ploys for winning public support for presidential power: fear mongering and ancestor worship. By highlighting the unprecedented dangers of the present, he encourages people to entrust their own and their families' lives to a savior-president. By claiming that the Framers themselves would have been perfectly happy with unchecked presidential power, he encourages people to believe in the deep fidelity of a constitutionally unleashed president to an ideal America that was always meant to be. Although it is not particularly coherent, this fusion has a certain emotional appeal.

Somewhat less exasperating, though equally perplexing, is the relation between Yoo's exaltation of presidential power and his denigration of the treaty power. This is a strange coupling, for one thing, because the treaty power obviously increases executive authority, by giving the president a hand in lawmaking that he would otherwise lack. Having insisted that the Framers modeled the American presidency on the British monarchy, Yoo seems not to have fully absorbed the significance of Madison's commentary, in *Federalist Papers*, No. 47, on the British king: "He alone has the prerogative of making treaties with foreign sovereigns, which, when made, have, under certain limitations, the force of legislative acts." In addition, presidents of both parties have claimed that treaties, even in the absence of implementing legislation by Congress, provide sufficient authority to deploy U.S. troops overseas. And like it or not, international organizations created by treaties are frequently used by executive officials, in virtually every democratic country, to do an end run around their national legislatures. Both Truman in the Korean War and Clinton in Kosovo claimed that U.S. military action, without Congressional approval, had been authorized by the United Nations.

Needless to say, Yoo would denounce this search for authorization from foreign sources, believing that the president has the inherent authority to go to war whenever and wherever he wants. His way of thinking, however, whatever else we may want to say about it, makes it impossible to understand the actual political dynamics by which the executive branch has gradually weakened Congress's checking power, a process in which, as an empirical matter, the making, interpretation, and implementation of treaties (not to mention the increasing importance of international organizations) have played an important role. Of course, Yoo has no interest in helping us understand how we have traveled from there to here. Constitutional change holds no mysteries for him because from his perspective America is blessed with an imperishable Constitution, and presidential powers today, even after 9/11, remain pretty much what they were meant to be more than two centuries ago.

Enabling Restraints

Yoo's legal theory, it should be said, is as dubious as his historical scholarship. For starters, he has a zero-sum conception of the government's foreign-policy powers. He expresses bafflement at James Wilson, who both favored a strong executive and gave a major role in foreign affairs to Congress. Wilson's support for Congressional war powers, Yoo says, "does not square perfectly with his broad thoughts in favor of a strong executive expressed during the ratification debates."[28] But the enigma dissolves if power-sharing can actually increase the capacity of the executive to achieve its aims. Executive power hinges upon the president's capacity to mobilize support and voluntary cooperation for its projects. That such power might be increased by accepting Congressional oversight and input is self-evident, although apparently incomprehensible to Yoo.

Power-sharing can increase overall power in another way as well. Human beings do not always perform best when unwatched and uncorrected. Cheney has repeatedly argued that the Administration can get "unvarnished" advice only under conditions of the strictest confidentiality, and there is something to this argument. It is equally obvious, however, that secrecy has its own pathologies, including a tendency to perpetuate mistaken policies long after they could have been profitably corrected. Hence, an executive branch under serious scrutiny by a well-informed legislature with real power to push back will not necessarily perform more poorly than an executive branch sheltered from criticism and control.

If the executive is not compelled by Congress and the courts to give plausible reasons for its actions, it may end up having no plausible reasons for its actions. It will lash out violently in the "war on terror," but its choices will feel distressingly arbitrary. It will not establish an intelligent list of priorities, keep its powder dry, or allocate scarce resources in a prudent and effective manner. Administration spokesmen have repeatedly explained that since 9/11 "the risks of inaction have become far greater than the risks of action."[29] And Yoo agrees: "The costs of inaction can be extremely high – the possibility of a direct attack on the United States and the deaths of thousands of civilians."[30] Fixation on the potential costs of inaction is patently one-sided, however.

The leap from inaction to action cannot possibly, on its own, guarantee a reduction of risk. Precipitate action may well produce deep commitments from which it will prove impossible or immensely costly to extricate ourselves. In a world of scarce resources and opportunity costs, moreover, every decision to act is a decision not to act. To commit Arabic speakers to the Iraqi theater, for example, is to withdraw them from other tasks, such as the manhunt for Osama bin Laden. To act more forcefully in one arena is to act less forcefully in another. Such trade-offs are seldom desirable, but they are often inevitable. As a result, the relative costs of action and inaction cannot be declared ahead of time, by fiat, but must be estimated, using the best information available, on a case-by-case basis. Suppressing embarrassing information to build support for bold action is not a recipe for success.

By dismantling checks and balances, along the lines idealized and celebrated by Yoo, the Administration has certainly gained flexibility in the "war in terror." It has gained the flexibility, in particular, to shoot first and aim afterward. It has acted on disinformation, crackpot theories, theological certainties, and utopian expectations that could perhaps have been corrected or mitigated if traditional decision-making protocols had been respected and key policymakers had not "spoken power to truth," silencing dissident voices and sequestering themselves in an echo chamber. Yoo sees no danger in allowing a poorly educated and sketchily briefed president, perhaps surrounded by yes-men and fed picked-over intelligence, to define unilaterally the principal threats facing the country. He is not disturbed by the thought that an amateurish president might be so "divorced from the actual policy apparatus"[31] that he has little idea about the implications of the policies he is, in effect, rubber-stamping. It has not occurred to him that excessive executive-branch secrecy can prevent the timely correction of potentially fatal mistakes. He cannot imagine that giving a blank check to the executive would be equivalent to giving "soft budget constraints" to the legislature, encouraging reckless behavior undisciplined by an understanding of opportunity costs. He does not worry about irreversible decisions taken impetuously, without eliciting a second opinion, and outside the statutory policy-making process designed "to weed out really stupid or dangerous ideas."[32] Yet if the misbegotten Iraq war proves anything, it is the foolhardiness of allowing an autistic clique that reads its own newspapers and watches its own cable news channel to decide, without outsider input, where to expend American blood and treasure – that is, to decide which looming threats to stress and which to downplay or ignore.

Yoo begins with the premise that the Constitution gives the president virtually unchecked power over foreign affairs. This is an alarming thesis, for all the reasons addressed, but it becomes especially counterproductive in the post-9/11 context. It makes nonsense, for one thing, of the Administration's push for political reform in the Middle East. Why do Middle Eastern political systems need reforming? According to the United Nations' *Arab Human Development Report 2002*, the central flaw in these systems is the following: "In most cases, the governance pattern is characterized by a powerful executive branch that exerts significant control over all other branches of the state, being in some cases free from institutional checks and balances."[33] Instead of working with Bush to export democracy to the Middle East, it seems, Yoo has been working with Cheney to Egyptianize the United States.

In the war on terror, finally, the foreign front and the home front have become harder to distinguish. Infiltrators and saboteurs are no longer minor and peripheral to the war effort. They are the main enemy, and the battlefield on which we meet them emphatically includes U.S. soil. As a result, the president's war powers, if grotesquely distended and freed from oversight as Yoo would like, threaten to overwhelm and submerge the Constitution, not just abroad but also domestically. Only if our rulers were infallibly clairvoyant would it be safe to gamble in this reckless way not merely with our personal liberties but also, and perhaps more importantly, with our country's national security in an age of multiple, unfamiliar and – we have every reason to fear – still metastasizing threats.

CONCLUSION

After the temporary destruction of al Qaeda's sanctuary in Afghanistan, it is now generally agreed, something went terribly wrong with America's response to 9/11. Opinions differ, however, about exactly what went wrong and why. Some who supported the Iraq war say that the invasion and occupation of Iraq, the most visible and therefore easiest-to-criticize part of the proclaimed war on terror, was executed badly. The problem lies deeper than faulty execution, however. Things went so calamitously wrong because of a mistaken way of seeing, and setting priorities among, the threats to American national security disclosed by 9/11.

All of the major errors of the Administration discussed in this book – the misbegotten war itself, the bungled occupation, the abuse of detainees who were not given a serious chance to challenge the alleged reasons for their confinement, and the concentration of unaccountable power in the hands of woefully unprepared executive officials – reflected a fundamental misreading of the terrorist threat. The prism was defective and, as a consequence, very real dangers were misperceived or grasped only obliquely, hazily, and selectively. For various reasons, some obvious and others less so, the key decision makers placed excessive emphasis on enemies who could be unilaterally and definitively defeated, and devoted insufficient attention to threats that require patient management over time, in cooperation with allies, without any expectation of triumphant finality. This concluding chapter, as a consequence, summarizes an argument, implicit in the foregoing chapters, against the war party's psychologically understandable but strategically mistaken focus on a conquerable "enemy." It argues instead for a more complex and pluralistic conception of strategic threats.

Why did the Cheney-Rumsfeld group have such a hard time defining both the enemy it faced and the conflict in which it was engaged? One possibility to be explored is that 9/11 had such a traumatic impact on the thinking of key actors that momentary feelings of confusion and defenselessness became frozen into long-term policy. Be that as it may, the biographies of the central policymakers – alongside bureaucratic politics, ideology, and electoral considerations – conspired to make an invasion of Iraq seem almost irresistibly appealing. That answering the 9/11 provocations by gearing up for war in the Middle East was a fateful blunder is dismayingly obvious in retrospect. It is patently impossible to eliminate, or even substantially reduce the appeal of, transnational Salafi terrorism by militarily crushing a secular Arab dictatorship. It follows that the United States should begin to do now what it should have done from the very beginning, namely, refocus its efforts on "incapacitation," and that means reducing the capacities of anti-American terrorists to inflict grievous harm. U.S. counterterrorism policy should concentrate scarce resources on securing fissile material, interdicting nuclear smuggling, and reducing the flow of petrodollars to politically unstable parts of the world, not on a psychologically alluring but ultimately futile attempt to smash a far-flung and elusive enemy on a geographically concentrated battlefield.

Double Exposure

Two clues strongly suggest that the post-9/11 disaster stems from an elementary misreading of the threat. The first is the Administration's blurred image of the enemy, and the second is its farfetched metaphor of "war."

Usually, as wars unfold, each side gradually gains a clearer picture of its adversary. Not so in the "war on terror." Ask who is America's enemy in this war, and the Administration, even today, replies with a garbled tongue. It flounders awkwardly among overbroad labels – ranging from "terrorism" to "violent extremism" to "Islamo-fascism" – for the hostile force it aspires to vanquish. A mysterious need to balloon the enemy into a shapeless monstrosity rather than zeroing-in on the actually culpable conspirators was already in evidence on 9/11 when President Bush famously announced that the country had been attacked "by evil."[1] Commenting on the phantasmagoric imprecision of the image of the enemy in America's war on terror, a French scholar of Islamic radicalism dryly comments: "The 'us or them' battle cry is not supported by a clear-cut conceptual definition of the 'them'."[2]

Other critics have denounced what George Orwell would have called "the sheer cloudy vagueness"[3] of the Administration's political language as a ruse to gull the public, and slippery talk after 9/11 did seem gauged to parlay the public anger and fear generated by 9/11 into support for the Iraq war. A clearer definition of the "them" would have spoiled the rhetorically effective slogan: We are fighting "them" over there so that we do not have to fight "them" in America. This merging of two distinct "thems" conveyed the subliminal message that invading Iraq was the most effective way to avenge 9/11 and prevent a follow-up al Qaeda attack.

Admittedly, no commentator without a partisan agenda would have described Saddam Hussein and Osama bin Laden as two faces of a single Arab-Islamic threat to American national security. Because the Administration's attempt to meld them together was manifestly self-serving, it has been widely dismissed by knowledgeable experts as nothing but a shrewd ploy to mobilize public support for an invasion of Iraq undertaken for reasons unrelated to 9/11. From notes jotted down in the war room of the Pentagon on the afternoon of September 11, for instance, we know that Donald Rumsfeld was already thinking, while the Pentagon was still smoldering, of how to exploit the terrorist attacks as a pretext for overthrowing Saddam Hussein.

James Bamford cites and summarizes Rumsfeld's by-now notorious comments as follows: "Despite the fact that there was absolutely no evidence implicating the Iraqi leader, Rumsfeld wanted to 'hit S.H. [Saddam Hussein] at the same time.' The idea was to 'sweep' him up, whether 'related' to 9/11 or 'not.'"[4] Later that evening, Richard Clarke attended a White House meeting that he reasonably assumed would be focused on al Qaeda. But he soon "realized with almost a sharp physical pain that Rumsfeld and Wolfowitz were going to try to take advantage of this national tragedy to promote their agenda about Iraq."[5]

A good case has been made by reliable commentators, in other words, that the blurred image of the enemy that began surfacing in Administration talking points immediately after 9/11 should be viewed as little more than a scam to fool the public. According to Max Rodenbeck, "the Bush administration willfully blended al Qaeda into a peculiar amalgam including other, far less urgent threats to concoct a perceived global enemy."[6] Summarizing and sharpening this view, Frank Rich writes that "the White House's biggest lie" was "conflating Saddam's regime with the international threat of radical Islam, fusing the war of choice in Iraq with the war of necessity that began on 9/11."[7] To prepare the public for a "counterstrike" against a wholly unrelated and preselected target, allegedly, the Cheney-Rumsfeld group peddled a badly out-of-focus picture of the enemy, suggesting illogically but apparently persuasively that the United States had been attacked by generic "terrorism." Any country or group that could plausibly be tarred with that wide brush was fair game. According to the president himself, "On September the 11th, we resolved that we would go on the offense against our enemies, and we would not distinguish between the terrorists and those who harbor or support them."[8] Bush also famously said "you can't distinguish between al Qaeda and Saddam when you talk about the war on terror."[9] This deliberate refusal to draw elementary distinctions made it easy to associate Iraq, a country that had neither harbored nor supported the 9/11 terrorists, with Afghanistan, a country that had. Rather than engaging politically alert citizens in a reasoned debate about how to respond to 9/11, the Administration lured a traumatized public into a gratuitous war by the power of suggestion, making two unrelated threats seem to be emanations of a single dark and fiendish force.

The assumption underlying such plausible sounding analyses is that the Administration's response to 9/11 was controlled by hidden agendas. Cheney wanted to expand executive power and weaken Congressional oversight. Rumsfeld wanted to field-test his theory that, in modern warfare, speed is more important than mass. Both wanted to overcome the legacy of Vietnam. Some of their advisors wanted to improve the security situation of Israel. Others were thinking ahead to the collapse of the Saudi monarchy and the eventual need to have troops in the region to protect the world's oil supply, and so forth. The destruction of al Qaeda's Afghan sanctuary was not adequate to any of these aims.

That such political ambitions and hidden agendas played a role in motivating the Iraq war cannot reasonably be disputed. So why should we not conclude that the Administration's blurred picture of the enemy, Osama-the-tyrant-slayer fading into Saddam-the-crusher-of-rebels, was a subterfuge, concocted to bring the public along? The Cheney-Rumsfeld group's ability to act on such hidden agendas would certainly have been reduced if politically active Americans had quickly grasped that al Qaeda, acting alone, was wholly responsible for 9/11. The need to maintain residual public support for a war that was growing increasingly unpopular might even be invoked to explain why the Administration delayed the trial, by military commission, of Khalid Sheikh Mohammed (KSM), the principal organizer of the 9/11 plot. KSM was taken into custody in March 2003, two weeks before the invasion of Iraq. Three-and-a-half years later, in the run-up to the 2006 midterm elections, he was unexpectedly plucked from his secret dungeon and transferred to Guantánamo, presumably to distract public attention from the bloody disintegration of Iraq and to remind voters of 9/11. Before this well-timed campaign commercial was aired, it was commonly assumed that KSM would never be tried. The fact that he had been tortured in captivity was sure to emerge at trial, making prosecution difficult and embarrassing the Administration. Current talk of scheduling a trial sometime in 2008 raises the possibility of a different explanation. A motive for waiting five years to bring KSM "to justice" might be that almost any kind of trial would reveal, through a riveting narrative, that Saddam Hussein had nothing whatsoever to do with 9/11. That was a revelation that the Administration, scrambling to justify retrospectively its impetuous rush to war, had powerful political reasons to postpone.

If it was a hoax, the Administration's slurring of "thems" boomeranged badly. For one thing, it meant that some of the troops sent to Iraq in the first wave believed, disgracefully, "that they were avenging the 3,000 dead from September 11."[10] That misapprehension was not only shameful; it was also consequential. According to Thomas Ricks, "The strategic confusion about why the United States was in Iraq, such as the Bush Administration's insistence that the war was part of the counterattack against al Qaeda-style terrorism and so was somehow a response to the 9/11 attacks, may have led some American soldiers to treat ordinary Iraqis as if they were terrorists."[11] Cruel and arbitrary behavior by some U.S. forces helped stoke the violent insurgency that followed. That is to say, the fogged-up picture of the enemy that launched the war, by demonizing ordinary Iraqis in the eyes of American troops and sowing confusion in the government's own ranks, contributed seriously to the war's spiraling wickedly out of control.

Alchemy of the Mind

Precisely because it successfully generated public support for a gratuitous invasion and occupation of a Middle Eastern country, the Administration's attempt to link Osama and Saddam miscarried fatally. Was this commingling of portraits really as cynical, however, as the above account makes it sound? Do hidden agendas and political ambitions provide a comprehensive explanation for the decision to invade Iraq? That is what many, indeed most, of the recent bestsellers about the Bush Administration suggest. But a focus on secret schemes to promote unspoken interests is not necessarily the best way to understand what has gone wrong since 9/11.

In general, eagerness to deceive others does not guarantee freedom from illusions of one's own. That is why we should consider looking at the Administration's curiously murky picture of the enemy not just as a clever ploy, but also as a window onto the Cheney-Rumsfeld group's own hopelessly blurred thinking. We should view it not only as a trick, that is to say, but also as a clue.

The suggestion that Saddam Hussein was responsible for 9/11 seems preposterous today, but how did it seem at the time, for example, to Deputy Secretary of Defense, Paul Wolfowitz? Long before 9/11, Wolfowitz (who apparently sees himself as some sort of amateur sleuth or clairvoyant connector of dots) had come to believe that Saddam was behind the 1993 attempt to demolish the World Trade Center. As Bob Woodward's accounts make clear, moreover, Bush himself, at the outset, suspected that Iraq had been involved in 9/11. Vice President Cheney's widely reported visits to the CIA – that is, his unrelenting efforts to pressure analysts to unearth evidence supporting his hunch of a furtive Iraq-al Qaeda conspiracy – also belie the hypothesis that the war party's failure to distinguish sharply between Osama and Saddam was nothing but a cynical ploy.

They may have deliberately misled the public to some extent, but key figures in the Administration were not thinking very clearly themselves. This is not entirely surprising, given the shock of the attacks. What their stunned amazement does not explain is their insistence, despite ample historical evidence that terrorists strike at tyrants and tyrants crack down on terrorists, that terrorism and tyranny were two facets of one and the same depravity. They were not simply eliding two threats in order to fool the public; they were able to promote the illusory necessity of the Iraq invasion with such palpable sincerity because, at some level, they perceived the two threats as inextricably intertwined. That they have not disentangled the two, even today, is conveyed by the 2006 *National Security Strategy*, where we read, "Democracy is the opposite of terrorist tyranny."[12] What exactly is this exotic two-headed monster, "terrorist tyranny"? It is the Administration's own radically out-of-focus picture of the enemy in the war on terror. Bush's national-security team accepts this smudged image of the enemy, a mysterious double-exposure, implicitly. It symbolizes the Administration's chronic inability to keep itself patiently focused on al Qaeda. It gives visual expression to the Administration's seemingly uncontrollable impulse to drift away from the actual threat posed by terrorists and to rivet its attention instead on the largely imaginary threat posed by a cruel tyrant in Baghdad.

Bush and Cheney have repeatedly emphasized that 9/11 represented a turning point in their thinking about national security. The Administration's critics tend to deny this, asserting or insinuating that 9/11 simply provided a pretext for carrying out preconceived plans.[13] There is a great deal to be said for this sort of skepticism, but criticism of the dominant players in the Administration can actually be deepened if we accept their claim that 9/11 changed the way they saw the world. Much of what has gone awry since the al Qaeda attacks, including the ruinous invasion and occupation of Iraq, may spring from a view of the threat environment enduringly distorted by what can only be called the trauma of 9/11.

Skeptics are especially keen to cast doubt about the claim that, after al Qaeda struck, the war party suddenly saw Saddam as more dangerous than before. Daniel Benjamin and Steve Simon succinctly summarize these widely shared qualms: "Did Saddam's weapons pose a greater threat after September 11 than before? Did al Qaeda's attack tell us something new about Saddam Hussein's behavior? The answer to these questions is the same: no."[14]

This curt dismissal of the suggestion that 9/11 conveyed any new information about the Iraqi threat sounds perfectly plausible at first. Yet the psychologically irresistible reply to a question may be "yes" even when the logically and empirically defensible reply is "no." Bush himself, as has often been noted, seems to have been personally changed by 9/11. Cheney, for his part, consistently refers to 9/11 as a "watershed." Both routinely insist that the attacks fundamentally transformed the way all Americans interpreted the world, and this includes, of course, the way those around the White House and Pentagon saw the Iraqi threat. Their track record of shading the truth does not mean that they can never be taken at their word. That 9/11 really did change their motives, not merely their opportunities, seems at least possible. So what could they have seen in 9/11 that could have affected them so profoundly?

What They Saw in 9/11

In the minds of Cheney, Rumsfeld, and the others, the 9/11 attacks summoned up a mental picture. It was a picture of Washington, D.C. incinerated without warning by an untraceable nuclear sneak attack. The end of deterrence had been theorized before, but on 9/11 it became, for the first time, easy to imagine. And the threat was deadly serious, touching on the physical survival of the leadership itself.

The merest hint that such an attack might occur was paradigm shattering. The possibility of "an American Hiroshima" in the nation's capital was presumably unnerving enough to cloud the thinking of political operatives who were skillful at confusing the thinking of others. It may even have been shocking enough to make them shelve temporarily some of their political agendas. Above all, it demolished the dream, cherished by many

Administration insiders, of surviving the end of deterrence by constructing an impenetrable missile shield. That hope was never especially realistic. It was a doomed attempt to resurrect old ideas of perimeter defense and fortified borders that had long been rendered obsolete by air power and, in the United States' case, by intercontinental ballistic missiles. The attacks of 9/11 brought this fond illusion crashing to earth. Terrorist infiltrators could do an end-run around any conceivable missile shield.

After the attacks, Bush's national-security team began to focus obsessively on unverifiable warnings of nuclear, chemical, or bio-pathogenic materials in the hands of unspecified al Qaeda operatives. Why did Bush, in his January 29, 2002 State of the Union address, claim that rogue states such as Iraq posed an existential threat to the United States? The answer is simple: "States like these, and their terrorist allies, constitute an axis of evil, arming to threaten the peace of the world. By seeking weapons of mass destruction, these regimes pose a grave and growing danger. They could provide these arms to terrorists, giving them the means to match their hatred."[15]

In his descriptions of the terrorist enemy, Vice President Cheney elaborated on the same theme: "And they know no restraint. There's no reason in the world why they would hold back and not use something like that [chemical, biological or nuclear weapons] if they could get their hands on it. So the biggest threat we face today is the possibility of a terrorist cell setting up shop inside one of our own cities, with one of those truly deadly weapons – a biological agent of some kind, say, or even a nuclear weapon that [would] cost perhaps hundreds of thousands of lives, not just 3,000, if they were to launch such an attack. It's a whole different scale of threat, a different kind of problem than we've had to deal with in the past."[16] Many lesser figures orbiting around the war party argued along the same lines. John Bolton, for instance, wrote that "The attacks of September 11 reinforced with blinding clarity" that "our greatest threat" comes from "transnational terrorist cells that will strike without warning using weapons of mass destruction."[17]

And this is only a sampling. Innumerable pronouncements by many, if not most, of the Iraq war's architects, strongly suggest that they saw 9/11 as a decapitation strike aimed at the collective assassination of the nation's leaders. (They knew about decapitation strikes, having planned one for Iraq.) This would explain why they took the 9/11 attacks so personally. In the days and weeks that followed, Cheney, Rumsfeld and the others were reminded of their mortality at every morning briefing. They were repeatedly informed that Washington, D.C. (where they worked and lived with their families) could be attacked, and, at the extreme, even erased from the map, with zero lead time. Their intelligence analysts presumably explained, in the words of the 9/11 Commission Report, that "Bin Laden had reportedly been heard to speak of wanting a Hiroshima."[18] The anthrax mailings to the Congress and Supreme Court reinforced the same harrowing message. All of them, along with much of the federal government, might soon be targeted for thermonuclear obliteration. With this all-too-personal warning unsettling their minds, President Bush's principal aides and advisors deliberated about how best to respond to 9/11.

By arousing awe and anxiety and undermining the target population's sense of security and self-control, according to one prominent scholar, terrorism provokes "infantile apprehensions."[19] The prospect of nuclear terrorism would presumably have a similar effect, even on seasoned officials. It would not be wholly surprising if, under these unprecedented conditions, high officials, closeted in their bunkers and looking desperately for some way to react, chose to lash out almost at random and reached for exorbitant powers without thinking through the consequences.

According to Cass Sunstein, the American public overestimated the risks of terrorism after 9/11 because emotionally-charged risks, especially ones that are easy to visualize, tend to "crowd out" the realization that the probability of a subsequent disaster on the same scale is actually quite small.[20] There is no reason to think that a handful of officials, closeted inside a partisan echo chamber and isolated from external sanity checks, would not exhibit the same semi-rational "probability neglect" as the wider public. The 9/11 catastrophe made it easy for Cheney, Rumsfeld and their commingled entourages to visualize a nuclear follow-up attack. The salience of the imagery may have induced a kind of phobia, meaning fear out of proportion to the danger at hand. If so, they were deluding themselves, not only the public, when they announced that "today terrorists can strike at any place, any time, with virtually any weapon."[21]

Especially if armed with thermonuclear weapons, nonstate terrorists present a threat difficult, if not impossible, to contemplate in tranquility. Because they are geographically dispersed, elusive, protean, mobile, and unafraid of death, as commentators were universally quick to point out, such transnational murder gangs cannot be deterred. Openly to admit this, however, is to admit that the greatest military superpower in history is essentially defenseless against a small group of homicidal zealots. To confess to America's defenselessness, however, must be extremely difficult psychologically, especially for individuals emotionally invested in, not to say exhilarated by, America's global military supremacy. So, what strategies were available, after 9/11, for denying or covering up this indigestible truth?

The simplest was mental alchemy, the "reconceiving" of an impalpable enemy as a palpable enemy. To reassure the public and itself, the hawks around Cheney and Rumsfeld must have felt a powerful urge to link the shadowy and elusive enemy that had perpetrated the 9/11 attacks to a sun-lit and tangible enemy against whom a terminal blow could be struck. The claim that self-deception was at work is obviously speculative and probably indemonstrable. Yet, is it really so implausible? After all, as a loose-knit terrorist network, al Qaeda presented a frustratingly insubstantial target. If it could be grafted, in fantasy, onto Iraq, it would immediately become a much more vulnerable target and a much less frightening enemy, the kind of enemy that America knows how to defeat. This at least is the implict claim of those who argue that "in the minds of the administration, the inability to engage Al Qaeda effectively left no alternative but to invade Iraq."[22]

In the war on terror, there is no battlefront where the elusive enemy can be confronted and crushed. This suggests that Vice President Cheney, when he asserts that Iraq is "the geographical base of the terrorists" who attacked the United States on 9/11,[23] is indulging some kind of battle-front nostalgia. The same is true for President Bush who continues to call Iraq, which is now widely acknowledged to have been a distraction and a diversion, "the central front in our fight against terrorism."[24] How can there be a central front in a war without fronts of any kind? It might seem farfetched to ascribe a craving for psychic comfort to ostensibly tough-minded individuals, but what if wishful thinking were the only alternative to a candid admission that the United States had become an essentially defenseless superpower?

The war party's blurred image of the enemy, Osama superimposed on Saddam, may have been a ruse to lure the public into supporting the war, but it is also more than that. It is an indicator, a symptom, a window onto the Administration's muddled conception of the threat that came to light on 9/11. This misapprehension of the threat was partly cognitive, but it also had an emotional basis. The thought that America, including Washington, D.C., had become indefensible was psychologically intolerable. It cannot be demonstrated, of course, but the speculation is suggestive: To repress feelings of defenselessness associated with an unfamiliar threat, the decision makers' gaze slid uncontrollably away from al Qaeda and fixated on a recognizable threat that was unquestionably susceptible to being broken into bits.

The Administration may also have intuitively foreseen what turned out to be the case, that it would be much easier to locate Saddam than to track down Osama. Moreover, as a head of state, Saddam had statues that could be pulled down. As the leader of a nonstate conspiracy, by contrast, Osama had yet to be immortalized in public statuary. In compensation, his image was emblazoned on millions of T-shirts throughout the Muslim world. The problem for the war party was obvious. The United States could topple a statue, but it could not topple millions of T-shirts. It cannot be proved, but the need to knock over something, visibly and dramatically, after great American icons had been ignominiously brought down, may actually have provided a potent reason, in some agitated minds, for invading Iraq. That is essentially the position of Olivier Roy, who argues, with a characteristically ironic reference to political "logic," that "After 9/11, quite logically, Washington tried to target states because a state can be punished, toppled, and replaced through military action."[25] If we wished to extend this analysis in an even more speculative, not to say psychiatric, direction, we might also want to consider a hypothesis offered, in a different context, by René Girard: "When unappeased, violence seeks and always finds a surrogate victim. The creature that excited its fury is abruptly replaced by another, chosen only because it is vulnerable and close at hand."[26] Such psychological-emotional speculations are worth taking seriously only because, from all reports, the expectation of a "cakewalk" played a genuinely important role in convincing the war party to launch the invasion of Iraq.

A Nebulous War

A second clue to the Cheney-Rumsfeld group's serial misperceptions, deceptions, and blunders after 9/11 can be found in their misuse, in describing the armed struggle with al Qaeda, of the metaphor of "war." To some extent, "war talk" was just that – talk. "War" was a rhetorical flourish. To describe the surprise attack as an act of war was to express shock and horror. To say "this means war" was not only to acknowledge the deadly serious situation but also to promise merciless retaliation. This was far from the end of the story, however.

On many occasions, the president has expressed himself as follows: "I was affected very deeply by the effects of September 11th. It became clear to me that day that we were at war. I know that we are at war."[27] But why were Bush and those around him so quick to infer that "this is war"? Answering this question will cast further light on the hazy thinking of those responsible for the Administration's reckless response to 9/11. The place to start is the generally accepted polarity of crime versus war. To say that the armed struggle against al Qaeda is a "war" is to deny that it is a "law-enforcement matter." As Bush said in his Jan. 20, 2004, State of the Union address: "After the chaos and carnage of September the 11th, it is not enough to serve our enemies with legal papers." We should kill these people, he implied, not read them their Miranda rights or permit them to chat privately with their civil liberties attorneys.

The 9/11 attack by a transnational terrorist group cannot be accurately depicted as either crime or war. It was not a crime, in any ordinary sense, because it was only the latest in a series of al Qaeda strikes on symbolic American targets. The entire string of attacks, including the ones that were promised to follow, was essentially political. Bank robbers break into vaults to abscond with the funds, not to deliver a political message. Because sending a message is the principal purpose of terrorism, by contrast, terrorists sometimes do what no bank robber would do, namely, voluntarily kill themselves in committing the act. Terrorists are sometimes willing to do this because their principal aims are political: To publicize a cause, inspire recruits, expose the vulnerability of the enemy, extract concessions, or trigger an overreaction. Apprehending terrorists is less conclusive than apprehending criminals because the former, unlike the latter, aim to redress widely perceived grievances and will quickly be replaced by new recruits committed to the same cause. These factors distinguish terrorism from ordinary criminality.

Because it is not launched by a hostile state, on the other hand, 9/11-style terrorism is nothing like a traditional act of war. The 9/11 attack was neither crime nor war. So what exactly was it?

Viewed from a distance, 9/11-style terrorism defies conventional categories. It is *sui generis,* neither a criminal act nor an act of war. But this is not the way the Administration acted or spoke. Instead, it kept asserting that "this is war," even after it had had ample time to regain its footing after the initial shock. This labeling decision needs to be explained because an informal declaration of war inadvertently honors the homicidal maniacs who attacked the United States on 9/11, validating their lunatic pretension to be "warriors" in God's army, a phalanx of wholly innocent men willing to die for their (imaginary) country. To denigrate them as a criminal gang that planned and carried out mass murder in cold blood, which is everywhere considered a heinous crime, would have been no less accurate and would have more pungently expressed moral revulsion and a refusal to negotiate.

Why then did the Administration prefer the "war model" to the "crime model?" Cumbersome due-process constraints are not the only reason why the Administration so publicly renounced the law-enforcement paradigm for counterterrorism. One of its tacit motives for refusing to describe 9/11-style terrorism as monstrous criminality was probably that, even though crime rates go up and down, crime itself never disappears. Drug smuggling can be managed, re-routed, and disrupted, but it cannot be stopped. Wars, by contrast, come to an end, often with tickertape parades. To describe counterterrorism as a "war" is implicitly to promise that it will end. This promise was unrealistic, but clinging to the mirage of closure and finality makes psychological sense in light of the unnerving truth that the threat of nuclear terrorism by nonstate actors, once it appears, will never vanish.

Incidentally the Administration's policies (as opposed to its pronouncements) implicitly deny that the current conflict can be classified as a "war." Bush's principal justification for refusing to assign Prisoner of War status to captured al Qaeda operatives is that al Qaeda is a loose-knit network of maniacal extremists who could never be expected to offer reciprocity to captured American soldiers. The reason that the United States refuses to grant Prisoner of War status to captured enemies in the war on terror, in other words, is that the war on terror is not actually a "war" – it is not, that is to say, an armed struggle between organized states. Because the enemy is not a well-organized state, it cannot offer reciprocity. For the very same reason, it cannot surrender or sign a peace treaty. Because our terrorist enemies will never lay down their weapons and desist, the Administration declares that the laws of war do not apply. It then turns around and brazenly shouts, "this is war!"

What Scare Tactics Presuppose

Even some of the Administration's defenders admit that what Bush's national-security cabinet saw in 9/11 was the end of deterrence; but they then go on to claim that the invasion of Iraq, far from being an act of escapism or denial, was a perfectly rational response to this dramatic change in America's security environment. They usually field, in this context, two distinct justifications for the invasion. The first involves a "handoff scenario" and the second a "scare the Muslims" strategy.

The handoff scenario seems rational enough on the surface. Rather than blurring Saddam and Osama together into a mysterious "terrorist tyranny," it treats them as distinct agents able to cooperate on an ad hoc basis against a common enemy despite their clashing ideologies and aspirations.

The logic of the handoff scenario is this. A hostile rogue state, such as Iraq, could attack the United States with a nuclear weapon and nevertheless avoid retaliation if it could successfully manage to cover its tracks. It could do this by clandestinely providing an anti-American terrorist group, whose operatives were willing to die for God, with a ready-to-use device that could be smuggled into a U.S. city and detonated without warning. Such an attack, because untraceable to a state, would be impossible to deter. The question that this doomsday fantasy thrust upon those charged with defending the country was how to pre-empt any such nuclear hand-off from occurring in the first place. Their proposal was to "take out" a string of rogue states before they got to the point of transferring any such weapon to crazed fanatics. This is the rationale behind the war party's radical, and radically destabilizing, idea of disarmament by regime change.

The "scare the Muslims" strategy has a different but complementary logic. It starts with the entirely plausible assumption that the Administration felt blind-sided by 9/11. It did not see the attack coming and it had no clue from which direction a follow-up attack might arrive. What could be done to defend against an enemy able to lurk in the shadows until the moment of attack? One answer was to find a place, any place, to display to the world America's immense capacity for destructive violence. In one reporter's words: "The primary impetus for invading Iraq, according to those attending NSC briefings on the Gulf in this period, was to make an example of Hussein, to create a demonstration model to guide the behavior of anyone with the temerity to acquire destructive weapons or, in any way, flout the authority of the United States."[28] Similarly, "One of the reasons the United States had invaded Iraq was to demonstrate the effectiveness and ferocity of the United States military."[29] Following these accounts, the war party viewed Iraq less as a threat than as a showcase. The purpose of unleashing American firepower in Iraq was not so much to remove a cruel but puny dictator but rather to advertise the folly of defying the United States. The proximate aim of this blood-curdling advertisement was to persuade Muslim leaders who had been helping terrorists to stop doing so and to persuade Muslim leaders who had been tolerant of terrorists to start cracking down.

Each of these narratives seems to capture something important about the thinking of the policymakers around Cheney and Rumsfeld in the run-up to war. When examined carefully, however, both turn out to be based implicitly on a narrowly state-centered view of America's threat environment. As a consequence, neither turns out to be as rational as it initially seems. Both the "handoff scenario" and the "scare the Muslims" strategy assume that we are still back in the good old days when deterrence reliably worked, when territorial states were the only dangerous actors in the international environment, and when "homeland security" could be maintained by threatening or defeating hostile states. In other words, these two attempts to justify the turn from al Qaeda to Iraq inadvertently confirm what they strive to deny, namely the degree to which even the Administration's most plausible rationales for the Iraq war are tainted by wishful thinking, in particular by the denial that nonstate actors can ever pose a serious strategic threat to American national security.[30]

It was at least possible, though not probable, that the United States could have measurably reduced the threat of anti-American terrorism by toppling Saddam and thereby intimidating various Arab and Muslim leaders in the region and around the world. What made the decision to invade Iraq seem so hopelessly irrational, even before its calamitous consequences came into view, was not the total implausibility of any connection between Iraq and anti-American violence. Rather, what the rush to war showed was the war party's failure to establish national-security priorities in a serious, thoughtful, and reasonable way. In what possible universe did the Iraqi threat deserve hundreds of times more attention and resources than the threats posed by a mentally unhinged dictator in North Korea and unsecured highly enriched uranium (HEU) in a semi-anarchical Russia? The Administration might reply, with some embarrassment, that it never imagined that so many of America's scarce national-security assets would end up being burnt to ashes in the Iraqi incinerator. This does not answer the prior question, however: Why did Iraq come first?

No professional survey of the threats facing the United States after 9/11 would have placed a disproportionate emphasis on Iraq. The motivations for that disproportionate emphasis must therefore be sought elsewhere. This is the point at which various hidden agenda are usually pulled from the drawer: expanding executive power, streamlining military tactics, eliminating an enemy of Israel, stationing forces within striking distance of the Saudi oil fields, and so forth. All of these objectives arguably played a part in the decision to invade Iraq. The contributing factor that, in my opinion, has been least appreciated so far, however, is the one on which I have been focusing, namely, the need of the war's advocates, which was as much psychological as political, to deny that they were helpless to protect the country from the ominous threat that, by implication, was made manifest on 9/11.

At the very root of the Administration's counterterrorism strategy we can discover the following thought. When deciding how to behave in a post-9/11 security environment, one must multiply the probability of the threat by the gravity of the threat. Thus, even a very small chance of a catastrophic event (for instance, the detonation of a smuggled nuclear weapon in the nation's capital) requires immediate aggressive action by the United States. We cannot wait until we are sure that the threat is real. We must "prespond," not merely respond. We must "deal with threats before they materialize," as Bush likes cryptically to suggest.[31] Solid and convincing evidence of an upcoming attack on an American city with a nuclear device might be impossible to obtain or might be obtained too late. The smoking gun (our first serious clue) might turn out to be a mushroom cloud (the last thing we know). To protect the public, therefore, the Administration granted itself carte blanche to unleash lethal force against vaguely suspicious targets on the basis of hearsay and circumstantial evidence.

A one percent chance of a mass casualty event provides greater reason for unleashing lethal force than a 99 percent chance of a modestly harmful event.[32] Worst-case reasoning suggested that Saddam Hussein had to be eliminated soon because he might possibly have WMD, or might possibly be able to acquire them, and might possibly hand such devastating weapons over to a terrorist group that, in turn, might possibly use them on the United States. This is an exceedingly roundabout and tenuous justification for the use of lethal force. In domestic law, for example, an individual accused of intentional homicide cannot successfully invoke a right to self-defense by claiming that he was only defending himself when he killed someone because the victim, in the future, might possibly have sold a gun to someone else who, in turn, might at some unspecified time have murdered the accused. Rather than pleading "necessity," after acting on such reasoning, a preemptive self-defender would be better off pleading insanity. But analogous reasoning, if we want to call it that, seems to have played a serious role in the decision to invade Iraq.

The problem with the "logic" of preventive war is that there existed, in 2002, a minuscule possibility of a catastrophic event in several world hotspots. Worst-case reasoning, in other words, does not help establish priorities (why Iraq before North Korea?) or dictate where to apply scarce resources most effectively. Worst-case reasoning reinforces tunnel vision and mental fixation. That is how it becomes a Trojan Horse for "probability neglect" and a variety of pre-rational commitments, immunizing them from rational examination.

If our enemy is dispersed and the gravest threats we face can come from any direction at any time, it cannot possibly be rational for the United States to tie down 70 percent of its national-security assets in one place. We cannot know in advance where the next danger may emerge. Therefore, we must always keep some of our powder dry and have a considerable reserve force at the ready. The doctrine of preemption obliterates such prudential considerations. Leaping at the first hint of danger means devoting scarce resources – such as Arabic speakers, surveillance satellites, or the limited attention span of senior policy makers – to one remote and hypothetical threat instead of another. This is why "we can't afford to wait" gives no guidance to those trying to establish priorities among a multiplicity of merely potential threats that have yet fully to emerge. The possibility of catastrophic terrorism does not abolish the laws of scarcity. It is unwise to shoot first and aim afterwards, which is what preemption in effect requires, for the simple reason that our supply of ammunition is never unlimited. Giving the executive a blank check to respond in any way it wishes to any possible national-security threat will, as mentioned, have the same effect as institutionalizing soft-budget constraints. It will encourage irrational, excessive and misplaced spending. The Iraq war has shown how an unrivaled military can be overstretched and, indeed, almost broken. This is why the danger of acting may sometimes be greater than the danger of not acting, especially in an age when nuclear terrorism may soon become a real possibility.

Preemption may even encourage the transfer of scarce resources to relatively minor threats, such as Saddam, simply because military force offers a readily available method for preventing a known enemy from doing future harm. Threats which are relatively difficult to preempt, such as a future attack by elusive terrorist networks, will take a backseat to threats which are relatively easy to preempt, such as nuclear blackmail by a sickeningly cruel dictator. Arguably, this is exactly what happened. A psychological and political need to act without delay gave emotions, fixations, and random hunches undesirably dominant roles in setting the country's national-security priorities. The fatal result was the bloody undoing of Iraq in a war that also consumed massive American resources desperately needed to confront more dangerous and imminent threats.

It is at least conceivable that the Administration's need to deny its own helplessness explains why it judged the remote Iraqi threat to be more urgent than the serious proliferation threats posed by North Korea and

Russia. Unlike those two countries, Iraq presented a target that the United States could effectively destroy. It was a well-lit stage for propaganda by deed. While shattering the Baghdad regime, America could make a show of its military might. The advocates of the Iraq war may also have expected the demonstration of U.S. power to be inherently pleasurable. If so, they lobbied for an invasion not only as a means to intimidate potential trouble makers, but also as an expression of U.S. supremacy, to be savored as such. In any case, the Iraq war allowed the Administration to convey to the public something comforting but only partly true, that it was capable of defending the country against its most malign enemies. It may also have allowed the security hawks in Bush's war council to reassure themselves, contrary to expert opinion, that they really were capable of warding off a follow-up nuclear sneak attack.

The al Qaeda attack may or may not have been a watershed in the thinking of Cheney and the others. If it changed the way they saw the Iraqi threat, then it probably did so through an emotional and irrational process of the sort I have hypothesized, driving them to grab hold of a tangible target because the intangible enemy poured through their fingers like sand. On the other hand, they may have deceitfully exaggerated the impact of 9/11 on their perception of strategic threats. It is probably impossible to know, one way or the other. What we can say, nevertheless, as a matter of empirical observation, is that the swivel of the cannon from Osama to Saddam was accompanied by the blurred image of the enemy as a terrorist-tyrant. The shift of focus was also strongly encouraged by a whole series of other factors – personal, bureaucratic, ideological, and electoral. It is to these auxiliary factors that we now turn.

Distorting Optics

Let us briefly review the dramatis personae, since America responded the way it did to 9/11 because of who did and who did not catch the president's ear. Framing the armed struggle with al Qaeda as a "war" jibed perfectly with the bureaucratic interests and personal ambitions of the two leading figures in the Administration. Because it triggered the president's war powers, as described in Chapter Thirteen, "war" justified a significant expansion of executive authority – exactly what Vice President Cheney had ardently desired since Watergate and Vietnam. For then Secretary of Defense Rumsfeld, in turn, "war" meant that the Office of the Secretary of Defense (OSD) became the lead agency in designing and carrying out America's response to 9/11.

If Al Gore had been president, Rumsfeld would not have been in command of America's military bureaucracy. Nor is it likely that a Gore White House would have assigned to OSD such a dominant role in the war on terror. The choice for war in Iraq was therefore to some extent a fluke. It reflected the peculiar way in which the figures that happened to dominate an accidental administration, especially Cheney and Rumsfeld, viewed the world. It flowed from the conviction of a few aging Cold War hawks, solidified long before 9/11, that the only truly dangerous beasts roaming the international jungle were well-organized states. His belief that no nonstate actor could have possibly organized a serious strike against the United States, to choose another example, is apparently what convinced Wolfowitz that Saddam must have been behind the 1993 bombing of the World Trade Center. This conviction is no neoconservative eccentricity, to be sure. Something like it has been deeply ingrained in Western national-security institutions and doctrine since the consolidation of the modern European state system in the mid-seventeenth century. An inherited rule of thumb does not explain what happened after 9/11, however.

The state-centered focus of traditional national-security thinking survived into the George W. Bush Administration not because it still made perfect sense (it did not), but because it appealed to particular individuals with particular life stories. Having come to political maturity during the Cold War, as recounted in Chapter Four, Cheney and Rumsfeld remained to some extent hostages to a Cold War mentality. When they returned to public office from the well-upholstered wilderness of corporate America, they were no longer young, were set in their ways and past the age when mental updating comes naturally. Their personal career trajectories meant that they had had scant experience dealing with newly emergent threats such as those posed by nonstate terrorists operating without state support. What still obsessed them, by contrast, was a need to overcome the crippling legacy of Vietnam. This pent-up need, peculiar to their circle, surely played a role in their post-9/11 rush to demonstrate that the United States can easily obliterate hostile regimes and is not afraid of losing soldiers in the process.

One fruit of these inherited obsessions and agendas was an Administration more alert to the dangers posed by saber-rattling rogue states than to dangers impossible to destroy militarily. This biased and selective perception of the threat environment was evident not only before but also after 9/11. In the first nine months of the Administration, George Tenet and Richard Clarke made repeated efforts to mobilize serious preemptive action against al Qaeda, to no avail. After the Taliban fell, the

Cheney-Rumsfeld group quickly reassigned some of the specialty intelligence forces that had been hunting for Osama bin Laden and Ayman al-Zawahiri to the Iraqi theater. It was as if they could simply not see a free-standing al Qaeda as a serious threat. They recognized al Qaeda as supremely dangerous, but only when harnessed in some way to a rogue state. Nonstate terrorism, in their clouded eyes, appeared to be much less dangerous than "terrorist tyranny." Osama alone did not pose an existential threat, although that bicephalous monster, Osama-Saddam, did.

What blinded the war party, until it was too late, to the potential for disaster in postwar Iraq? State-centered thinking about strategic threats certainly played a role. From the plausible observation that hostile regimes are dangerous, it does not necessarily follow that the destruction of a hostile regime will reduce the level of danger, for the simple reason that regime destruction may engender dangers of its own. That possibility seems to have been beyond the ken of the war planners. During the run-up to the invasion, from all reports, they believed that Iraq would no longer imperil American interests once Saddam's tyranny had been dismantled. They saw in vivid colors the danger posed by a hostile state ostensibly bristling with weapons of mass destruction. The problems that would predictably result from state collapse, however, including a proliferation disaster involving those same fantasized stockpiles of WMD, apparently eluded the war party. Nor did they give much thought to the possibility that anarchy in Iraq could indirectly endanger the United States by providing an inspiration and training ground for anti-American jihadists. The Administration's morally shameful and strategically obtuse failure to prepare for stabilizing Iraq after the fall of the dictatorship may well have stemmed from its tunnel vision. It overestimated the threat posed by a hostile tyranny and underestimated the threats posed by state collapse. It hyped the problem that the Pentagon was designed to handle and minimized a problem that should have been assigned to the State Department, which Rumsfeld wanted to keep out of the loop. These are some of the skewed threat assessments that helped pave the road to disaster.

The cognitive biases inseparable from any powerful government agency also contributed substantially to this general pattern of skewed optics and murky misperceptions. Bureaucratic politics enforced and reinforced an already distorted vision of the threats facing the country after 9/11. According to Francis Fukuyama, remember, "Bureaucratic tribalism rose to poisonous levels in Bush's first term."[33] Rather than testing their ideas in a free-wheeling adversarial process, partisan loyalists around Cheney and Rumsfeld barred the doors, lowered the shades and denigrated their

critics (including distinguished Republicans who had served in the Administration of Bush's father), sometimes smearing them as myopic appeasers
of America's implacable foes. Making an implicit claim to infallibility,
they also downplayed facts that challenged their preconceived ideas. This
retreat of the Administration's principal decision makers into a windowless bunker, with little creative input from critics and dissidents, naturally
entailed a self-stultifying loss of knowledge. In Bush's first term, a cadre of
political appointees was largely responsible for the Administration's disastrously blurred image of the enemy, Osama superimposed on Saddam. To
understand with somewhat greater precision how this blurring occurred,
however, we need to begin at a higher level of generality.

Each agency in government has its own specific set of instruments and
capacities. Capacities and instruments, in turn, affect cognition, including
the assessment of threats. Each agency inside America's sprawling national-
security bureaucracy will naturally see the country's threat environment
somewhat differently, and each will tend to emphasize the threats that it is
best positioned to counteract. It will see precisely "its" threats as the ones
that are objectively the most urgent and pressing. This skewing of priorities is not necessarily the result of calculating deception – it is just as likely
to result from cognitive bias. Active people frequently see vividly the problems they are well equipped to solve, consigning the problems that they do
not know how to handle, or handle effectively, to the backburner. It would
be very surprising if the same were not true of national-security agencies.

This cognitive bias came into play because the Pentagon, by historical
happenstance, was the one agency in the government largely controlled
by Cheney and Rumsfeld. Because the Department of Defense operates
under a formal military command structure, pressure tactics applied from
above could easily silence voices from the uniformed military with the
potential to dissent. Largely because of longstanding personal relations
between the Vice President and the Secretary of Defense, as discussed,
OSD was given an improperly dominant role in shaping America's counterterrorism policy. The disastrous consequences of this irresponsible concentration of unaccountable power ranged from an exaggerated hostility
to international cooperation and an aversion to peacekeeping to a stifling
of healthy debate not only in the country at large but also within the
executive branch itself. Once the center of gravity of its counterterrorism
policy had shifted to OSD, the Administration was bound to put excessive
emphasis on targets that could best be "taken out" by military force. The
suburbs of Hamburg may be incubating another serious terrorist conspiracy against the United States, but the suburbs of Hamburg will never land

high up on OSD's ranking of threats, because military force is utterly use-less for dealing with the problem. What will rank very high are countries such as Iraq with many inviting military targets, easy to strike from the air.

In an ideal world, a strong and independent-minded National Secu-rity Advisor would have first helped the White House define the various distinct missions that, taken together, should make up a comprehensive and coherent counterterrorism strategy and would have then selected, on a case-by-case basis, the agency that was best equipped to perform each task. Of course, this happened to some extent. Too often the relationship was reversed, however. Instead of the ends establishing the means, the means set the ends. Instead of the mission determining the agency, the agency selected the mission. Not surprisingly, OSD – chosen for extrane-ous reasons to take the lead – focused on the threats that the Pentagon alone could effectively parry. In effect, OSD magnified the importance of those threats that made OSD's own capacities seem most valuable. OSD applauded the choice of itself to lead the counterterrorism effort and, in justifying itself, helped take the country to war. The step from conceiving the overall struggle with terrorism as a "war" to commencing a real war in Iraq was dismayingly quick.

Two personal considerations are also worth mentioning in this con-text. First, some members of Bush's war cabinet, during the 1990s, had argued for the overthrow of Saddam Hussein. Some had denigrated Clin-ton's "obsession" with swatting flies such as Osama bin Laden. To admit that al Qaeda alone was behind the 9/11 attacks would have been tanta-mount to admitting their own negligence and incompetence as self-styled guardians of U.S. national security. Even worse, it would have meant admitting that Clinton was right. To avoid confessing or recognizing their own blindness to a looming threat, they were naturally drawn to the idea that Osama could not have acted without Saddam. Blurring the newly revealed threat (nuclear terrorism by nonstate actors) with an old neo-conservative hobby-horse (the threat posed by rogue states and especially by Saddam's Iraq) may have helped them hide and/or repress this humil-iating realization. Fusing the two threats relieved a painful dissonance, allowing them to defend their threatened self-image and to fortify their delusions of infallibility. This psychological hypothesis is just speculative, admittedly, as are the ones offered earlier, but it, too, is fuller and more interesting than conventional accounts that stress the cynical opportunism of the Administration's response to 9/11.

Second, over the course of their careers, these same individuals have often expressed mysteriously intense anger at minor and militarily weak states, such as Cuba, that have dared to challenge or defy the United States. High up on the list of such states was Iraq, a country that was to some extent dangerous but that irritated the principal members of Bush's national-security team as much for its in-your-face defiance as for the actual threat it posed. This provides yet another reason why Cheney, Rumsfeld, Wolfowitz, and the rest might have been psychologically compelled to imagine the hand of Saddam behind the actions of Osama. Their inexplicable excess of fury against Iraq, otherwise embarrassing to admit, would finally make sense if Iraq were capable of facilitating a horrifying atrocity.

Ideological Blinders, Electoral Ambitions

Alongside personal agendas and bureaucratic politics, ideology, too, helped distort the Administration's picture of the threat environment after 9/11. One often-discussed way in which ideology justified the Administration's swerve from al Qaeda to Iraq is revealed in the Administration's curious claim, cited above, that "democracy is the opposite of terrorist tyranny." For Wolfowitz, in particular, absence of democracy was the hidden link between Osama and Saddam. The root cause of anti-American terrorism, according to neoconservatives in and around the Administration, was Arab authoritarianism. By democratizing the Middle East, starting with Iraq, the fount of terrorism would be dried up. The facile optimism of this so-called analysis has been examined above, especially in Chapter Nine. Two themes needs re-emphasizing here. First, Bush's "forward strategy of freedom," the grand plan to democratize the Middle East, permitted and encouraged the Administration's fatal slippage from the threat of al Qaeda to the threat of Iraq. If anti-American terrorism is "caused" by the lack of democracy in the Arab Middle East, then establishing a democracy in Iraq will self-evidently remove terrorism's principal cause. Second, a dogmatic belief that unelected leaders lack legitimacy encouraged the American authorities in Iraq (in sharp contrast to their counterparts in Afghanistan) to waste precious months attempting to build a new Iraqi government from the ground up, by organizing popular elections rather than negotiating from the start with unelected religious and tribal leaders such as Ayatollah Ali al-Sistani.

Ideology entered into the picture in a second way as well. It will become gradually more feasible, as time passes, for terrorist groups with substantial financial resources (perhaps funneled through mosque-based networks) to purchase weapons of terrible destructiveness on the unregulated, underground arms market. Nuclear terrorism that draws on markets and mosques for logistics and supplies, not old-style state-sponsored nuclear terrorism, may be the grimmest nightmare darkening mankind's collective future. To push it out of mind and keep the hope of deterrence alive, the war party may have unconsciously harped upon a single militarily vulnerable source – namely, rogue states – from which terrorist groups could acquire fissile materials. Such wishful thinking, if it was a factor, was powerfully reinforced by a frozen-in-time conservative ideology, in particular an implicit and empirically unjustifiable belief that unregulated markets and private religious charities are basically innocent, that they cannot possibly pose serious strategic threats to American national security. The Administration's entire public philosophy assumes that the world will be better off with more private religious charities and more unregulated markets. To admit that both could be Trojan Horses for "evil" would violently explode its conservative worldview.

The traumatic effect of 9/11 on Administration thinking may be disputed. That personal agendas, bureaucracies, and ideologies all contributed to the decision to invade Iraq is perhaps less controversial. Electoral considerations obviously worked to the same effect. The Commander-in-Chief is an irresistible campaigner on the domestic front. Voters, too, want to hear that "we will win," and the Administration surely embraced the war paradigm for electoral purposes to reassure the electorate as well as itself. Likewise, voters appreciated the chance to see America's military superiority field-tested in the Iraqi arena. A dazzling show of force helped ordinary citizens, too, recuperate from the trauma of 9/11 even if the savage government smashed by the U.S. military had no relation at all to the freelancers who had attacked America.

The Administration's unilateralist tendencies, which undoubtedly greased the skid from al Qaeda to Iraq, were not only reinforced by personal, bureaucratic, and ideological factors. Unilateralism also had an electoral payoff. After 9/11, in particular, Bush was able to increase public support for his policies by making it clear that he would never take the interests of other countries into account when defending American security. Neither the manhunt for terrorists nor the interdiction of the illicit transfer of WMD can be conducted unilaterally, of course. The invasion of Iraq, by contrast, is basically an American show. Whether they were conned by the Administration's attempt to suture together Osama and Saddam, voters seemed eager to invest American blood and treasure in an invasion of Iraq. When they were told that Iraq had possessed no WMD with which to threaten America and had had no role in the 9/11 plot, many voters continued to express their support for the invasion. The resilience of prowar sentiment even when the causes of war began to be discredited one by one is simply breathtaking. One reason why public support for the war lasted as long as it did may be that many Americans are emotionally excited by the U.S. military's violent and ostensibly noble actions abroad that do not require accommodating the interests of foreign allies.

At the outset, in any case, support for the war was fueled by the public's craving for revenge, and that necessarily means for collective punishment. A shadowy group of Arabs flew airplanes into American buildings and killed thousands of innocent Americans. The revenge instinct, in response, fueled an American desire to desecrate the skyline of a representative Arab city and dole out misery to generic Arabs. It did not matter, for the logic of revenge, that the Arabs whom Americans attacked were not the same Arabs who attacked America. What matters, in a blood feud, is that some members of the same group who harmed us are harmed by us. Because many Americans seem to think that all "Arabs" are the same, the Administration's blurred image of the enemy, Osama melting into Saddam, resonated strongly with public perceptions. This is why the logic of revenge could be shamelessly twisted to justify a leap from 9/11 to Iraq. Viewed from a detached perspective, the "logic" of revenge is simply the strong tendency, apparently hard-wired into human nature, for violence to breed violence. What goes around comes around, however. America's gratuitous violence in Iraq is bound to breed anti-American violence in the future. Responsibility for fueling this archaic cycle lies not with the Cheney-Rumsfeld group alone, therefore. It lies partly with the public as well.

Threats Before Enemies

What does the foregoing analysis imply about the way forward? For one thing, to frame the terrorist threat properly we need to abandon the crime-war polarity altogether. The best way to escape it is to replace it. I propose, in its stead, the distinction between *enemy-centered counterterrorism* and *threat-centered counterterrorism*. The Administration hastily, impulsively, reflexively chose the former instead of the latter, and that mistaken choice explains most of what has gone wrong since 9/11. Choosing correctly may just possibly be the beginning of a more effective, or at least less ruinous, policy.

Enemies can be threatening, but not all threats are enemies. Two of the most dangerous elements in our current threat environment, for example, are global warming and contagious disease. These are impersonal processes, governed by laws of nature that entertain no sympathy or antipathy to mankind. Human negligence may exacerbate such processes, of course, but the processes themselves exhibit no detectable aggression, no hostility toward humankind, or wish to do us harm. The absence of *mens rea* in global warming and contagious disease does not make either of them any less dangerous, however. They both have the potential to destroy the human race.

For evolutionary reasons, human beings seem more alert to some dangers than to others. Degree of dangerousness is not the only factor that triggers human acts of precaution and self-defense. One additional and highly important factor is displayed aggression. The human mind seems programmed to pay more attention to a danger that appears accompanied by a snarled threat to do us intentional harm than to a danger accompanied by silent indifference to our pleasure or pain. Such a bias in threat perception can itself be dangerous, however, especially if it makes us worry more, say, about the malicious handoff of a nuclear device than about the sale of a nuclear device carried out with no aggressive purpose, or hostility to us, but only to reap a windfall profit.

The human tendency to overestimate threats made by hostile actors and to underestimate threats posed by impersonal forces, with no malice aforethought, can have seriously negative consequences in the current war on terror. This is because the United States is faced with relatively weak enemies who seem to be devoted to taunting us into a violent overreaction. I have analogized the 9/11 attack to a matador's cape in the hands of a homicidal maniac. The attack was carried out, in part, to provoke America into reacting recklessly. Al Qaeda was successful to the extent that it lured the United States into using military force indiscriminately and exposing its troops to unforgiving guerrilla attacks in relentlessly hostile territory. The most important rule for conducting an effective counterterrorism campaign is not to be provoked, to keep a cool head when the matador's cape is flashed before the eyes. This rule is crucial because at least some terrorist attacks are explicitly designed to induce a "phobic" response, that is, to create fear out of proportion to the terrorist group's actual capacity to do harm. The danger lies not in "overreacting" to a puny or essentially nonexistent threat, as John Mueller has wittily argued.[34] The danger lies in "mis-reacting" to an all-too-real, if not yet imminent, threat of nuclear terrorism by attacking a substitute target without calculating the enormous potential costs.

Embracing threat-centered counterterrorism and rejecting enemy-centered counterterrorism is the best way to keep a cool head. It is a difficult choice to make for both political and psychological reasons, however. Fighting an enemy allows the U.S. government to "strut its stuff," to frighten others, and to reassure itself by displaying how destructive it can be. Enemies surrender or can be publicly showcased, stripped naked and hanged before a jeering crowd. The appeal of such displays of force is the appeal of enemy-centered counterterrorism. Militarizing counterterrorism is attractive because it promises, deceptively, to "end evil." We cannot promise anything of the kind when combating global warming or Avian Flu or SARS.

Threat-centered counterterrorism also lacks the eye-catching electoral benefits of war-centered counterterrorism. Resolving complex problems is a thankless grind. This is equally true with problems that involve national security such as unsecured highly enriched uranium (HEU) in Russia, lack of domestic preparedness, and political instability in Afghanistan. Confronting such looming threats is an onerous process, requiring multilateral cooperation and negotiations. It may possibly never be brought to a definitive conclusion.

This is also true of "someone else's civil war." Violent conflict between rival militias in an Iraqi town presents a serious problem for occupying forces. It would be preposterous for outside forces to classify such strife as an "enemy" to be defeated, however. Iraqi fratricide may be America's fault and curse, but it is not America's enemy. Managing this particular problem means either getting between the warring groups or taking sides. Lacking the capacity to protect civilians from rival paramilitary formations and unwilling, for moral reasons, to become a full-fledged party to ethnocracy and ethnic cleansing, the occupying forces have effectively stepped aside and let the internecine struggle rage. All the more absurd does it sound, therefore, when, back in Washington, the Administration rehearses its mantra that America will "win" by "defeating the enemy." America cannot "defeat" factional warfare in Iraq, any more than America can "defeat" a proxy war between Saudi Arabia and Iran. Fratricidal conflicts may or may not have winners, but there is certainly no chance that America will emerge a winner from this particular civil war.

Al Qaeda's Global Reach

An additional reason for the war party's disastrous shift of attention from al Qaeda to Iraq may have been its understandable desire to avoid self-blame. After 9/11, some left-wing commentators rushed to allege that the United States had somehow "provoked" the attacks. They associated al Qaeda's cause with the cause of anticolonial insurgency, with conflicts in which the West was notoriously at fault. Such "blaming the victim" did not go over well with most Americans. Nor was a Republican Administration interested in being reminded that the United States had helped the Afghan mujihadeen in their battle against the Soviets.[35] It was even less eager to hear this: "Through years of both tacit and overt support, the West helped create the Saddam of today, giving him time to build deadly arsenals and dominate his people."[36] Refusal to accept blame for a murderous attack on the United States is understandable, and so is reluctance to revisit embarrassing episodes of complicity with current enemies. But these natural impulses should not be allowed to distort the nature of the threats we face.

Why do terrorist groups, such as al Qaeda, have "global reach"? The answer is that we gave it to them, not in a covert transaction but as an unintended by-product of our own economic and technological development. The industrialized world, with America in the lead, has created the global systems of communication, transportation, and banking on which transnational terrorism thrives. Cell phones, the information superhighway, cheap air travel – these are the existential conditions of our lives. They are possibilities inextricable from the modern world. They are also the tools of trade of terrorists who, as the *9/11 Commission Report* explains, "simply could buy off the shelf and harvest the products of a $3 trillion a year telecommunications industry."[37] We are effectively selling to enraged anti-American conspirators the rope with which to hang us. The commercialization for mass consumption of astonishing technological innovations helps make the threat posed by relatively unimpressive groups of killers loom disproportionately large. The instruments and opportunities provided by the advanced industrial world transform what would be a nuisance into a strategic threat. The permeability of the industrialized world, inseparable from its prosperity, makes infiltration by determined apocalyptic saboteurs ultimately unstoppable, because an open economy entails an open demography. By drawing immigrants from Muslim countries with the lure of jobs, political asylum, social security, and a better life, the industrialized states of Europe, especially, have exposed themselves to the resentment of jobless and alienated second-generation Muslims and so forth.

We cannot declare war on cell phones, the information superhighway, or cheap air travel. Nor can we drain the cyber-swamp where a virtual jihadist training camp can be found. The flow of tourists and visitors and immigrants might be slowed, but it cannot be stopped. We cannot "defeat" our vulnerabilities, declare mission accomplished, and bask in "victory." We cannot slash and burn our way out of our current security dilemma, as Cheney still seems to hope. Yet if the sources of our vulnerability are so deeply intertwined with our lives, how can we respond rationally to the threats to American national security disclosed on 9/11? A perfectly understandable and even healthy psychological defense mechanism may be what leads some people, even well-meaning ones, to focus on enemies who can be defeated rather than concentrating on vulnerabilities that we have created for ourselves and that we cannot possibly eliminate.

Succumbing to this temptation would be a grave mistake, however. It would be a mistake because some parts of the complex threat environment that we have created by our own efforts are "optional." Two in particular stand out: petrodollars and nuclear weapons. The river of petrodollars that we continue to pour into politically unstable countries is a matter of political choice, not destiny. The same can be said, to some extent, about the proliferation of WMD, unguarded nuclear storage sites, and the weakness of interdiction efforts aimed to halt nuclear smuggling. Petrodollars and nuclear technology are not enemies that we can defeat. Rather, they are "factors of destruction," Western inputs into the strategic threat against the West. They are disasters in the making that only an enemy-fixated superpower would allow to fester unaddressed.

A counterterrorism policy attuned to a wide variety of potential threats is superior to single-minded enemy-centered counterterrorism. The difficulty is that the former is harder to sustain, politically as well as psychologically, than the latter. We obviously need to focus less on enemies who can be definitively defeated by America's own military power and more on threats that must be managed cooperatively over time. This is not a message that is easy to convey to voters – but it is the correct message, nevertheless. The Administration's failed policy toward North Korea exemplifies what is at stake. Because Bush's security hawks could not safely attack that country, they apparently decided to ignore it. The subsequent disaster reveals what happens when enemies who can be defeated fill the radar screen and problems that require patient management are left to languish in neglect.

If we transferred some of the national-security assets currently devoted to "fighting enemies" to the task of reducing impersonal threats (such as securing Russian HEU), we would actually be making ourselves measurably safer. When confronting the threat of nuclear terrorism, the Administration seems to believe that "HEU doesn't kill. Terrorists do." But terrorists would be defanged if we could deprive them of access to the world's most devastating weapons. Instead of mobilizing our military to destroy the enemy, we should be mobilizing the entire range of our national-security assets to "incapacitate" the enemy, and that means to deny all potential enemies the most lethal capacities that they could use against us.

James Fallows, among others, makes exactly this point: "If nuclear weapons constitute the one true existential threat, then countering the proliferation of those weapons themselves is what American policy should address, more than fighting terrorism in general."[38] It also makes good sense to concentrate our counterterrorism resources on unsecured stock-piles of nuclear weapons and materiel, because we know where to find them. This is more than we can say about the terrorists. So, what is stand-ing in the way of this eminently sensible readjustment in national priorities? The principal obstacle seems to be the political and psychological desire to confront enemies who can be dramatically gunned down in bloody confrontations, rather than taking up problems that must be laboriously and collaboratively managed over time. Human beings need enemies, as Huntington would say. Lethal enemies strengthen social solidarity and valorize manliness.

Asking the Administration to forgo its enemy-centered counterterror-ism policy, therefore, is asking a great deal. It would require a political leadership able and willing to explain why a serious effort is worth under-taking, even though it does not involve the thrill of a battle in which the public can participate vicariously via cable news, or the promise of a victory to be celebrated on battleships. It would require the Pentagon to loosen its monopoly on national-security policy, giving a much larger role to diplomacy. It would force our leaders to explain to the public that American security can be enhanced by accommodating the inter-ests of other nations. It would also require a massive and sustained U.S. investment in the skills of its officials, because political solutions presume greater cultural and linguistic knowledge than military solutions. Above all, realism would require a frank acknowledgement by the government that the threat of nuclear terrorism can be reduced or postponed but not definitively removed. Vice President Dick Cheney has repeatedly said that staying the course in Iraq, despite that country's descent into uncontrol-lable sectarian butchery under U.S. supervision, will take "strong nerves." What would really take "strong nerves," however, is the candid admission by our political leadership that the United States must abandon its infantile hopes for "victory" and must concentrate instead on managing and reduc-ing, in collaboration with capable allies, largely self-created vulnerabilities that can never be completely removed because they are simultaneously the sources of liberal civilization's identity, prosperity, and creative resilience in the face of ominously evolving threats.

NOTES

Introduction

1. Bernard Lewis, "The Roots of Muslim Rage," *Atlantic Monthly* (September 1990).
2. Full transcript of bin Ladin's speech, *Aljazeera* (November 1, 2004).
3. David Fromkin, "The Strategy of Terrorism," *Foreign Affairs* (July 1975), reprinted in James F. Hoge, Jr., and Fareed Zakaria (eds.), *The American Encounter: The United States and the Making of the Modern World* (New York: Basic Books, 1997), p. 344.
4. James A. Baker III, Lee H. Hamilton et al., *The Iraq Study Group Report* (New York: Vintage, 2006), p. 95.
5. Patrick D. Healy, "Rove Criticizes Liberals on 9/11," *New York Times* (June 23, 2005).
6. Michael A. Ledeen, *The War Against the Terror Masters: Why It Happened, Where We Are Now, How We'll Win* (New York: St. Martin's Press, 2002), p. 221.
7. Max Boot, "For Better and Worse," *Newsweek International* (April 11/18, 2006).

1. Did Religious Extremism Cause 9/11?

1. Arrested in Pakistan in March 2003, Khalid Sheikh Mohammed was transferred in 2006 from a secret CIA prison to Guantánamo Bay, allegedly for trial before a military tribunal.
2. For the suggestion that Khalid Sheikh Mohammed also played an organizational role in the failed 1993 attack on the Twin Towers, and not only in the successful 2001 attack, see Yosri Fouda and Nick Fielding, *Masterminds of Terror: The Truth behind the Most Devastating Terrorist Attack the World has Ever Seen* (New York: Arcade Publishing, 2003). p. 95. Richard Clarke states flatly that KSM planned the 1993 attack (Richard A. Clarke, *Against All Enemies: Inside America's War on Terror* [New York: Free Press, 2004], p. 153). *The 9/11 Commission Report* disagrees, concluding on the basis of evidence of uncertain reliability that KSM played only a peripheral role in the 1993 attack (*The 9/11 Commission Report:*

Final Report of the National Commission on Terrorist Attacks upon the United States [New York: W.W. Norton, 2004], p. 147).

3. Information to help us answer these questions comes from post-attack police investigations in many countries, leaked portions of detainee interrogations, unearthed documents, investigative journalism, court proceedings in the U.S. and Germany, wiretaps revealed in such proceedings, interviews with people who met the hijackers and the latters' close friends and relatives, filmed and written "wills," a slew of al Qaeda propaganda material (including training films, pamphlets, websites, proclamations, communiqués, *fatwas*, and amateur post-attack videotapes), published speculations by psychologists, dozens of "the mind of a fanatic" newspaper and magazine articles, Internet searches, and a slew of books. It is worth mentioning that the 9/11 Commission was denied direct access to Khalid Sheikh Mohammed and other American detainees involved in the attacks. Explaining the restrictions placed on the Commission's inquiries, the *Report* revealingly adds: "Nor were we allowed to talk to the interrogators so that we could better judge the credibility of the detainees and clarify ambiguities in the reporting. We were told that our requests might disrupt the sensitive interrogation process" (*The 9/11 Commission Report*, p. 146).

4. Michael Scheuer, *Through our Enemies' Eyes: Osama bin Laden, Radical Islam, and the Future of America*, revised edition (Washington, D.C.: Potomac Books, 2006), p. 19.

5. Daniel Benjamin and Steven Simon, *The Age of Sacred Terror* (New York: Random House, 2002), p. 159.

6. Nancy Kobrin, "The Death Pilots of September 11th, 2001: The Ultimate Schizoid Dilemma," in J. Piven, C. Boyd, and H. Lawton (eds.), *Jihad and Genocide: Psychological Undercurrents of History*, vol. 3 (New York: iUniverse/Bloomusalem, 2002).

7. "Dawn Interview with Usama bin Ladin (November 10, 2001)," in Barry Rubin and Judith Colp Rubin (eds.), *Anti-American Terrorism and the Middle East* (New York: Oxford University Press, 2002), p. 261.

8. "Broadcast by Usama bin Ladin (October 7, 2001)," in Rubin and Rubin, *Anti-American Terrorism and the Middle East*, p. 249.

9. Osama bin Laden, interview with Tayseer Alouni (October 2001), cited in Benjamin and Simon, *The Age of Sacred Terror*, p. 157.

10. David Hume, "Of Suicide," *Essays: Moral, Political and Literary* (Indianapolis: Liberty Classics, 1985), p. 577.

11. Rohan Gunaratna, *Inside Al Qaeda: Global Network of Terror* (New York: Berkley Books, 2002), p. 10.

12. "Scoundrels rule fanatics, placing the knife in their hands. Such scoundrels resemble the 'Old Man of the Mountain,' who, it is said, fooled imbeciles into thinking that they had tasted the joys of paradise, promising them an eternity of pleasures if only they would go assassinate all those whom he named." Voltaire, *Dictionnaire philosophique*, "Fanatisme," (Paris: Flammarion, 1964), p. 190.

13. Charles M. Sennott, "Before Oath to Jihad, Drifting and Boredom," *Boston Globe*, March 3, 2002; Marc Sageman, who is generally dismissive of the role of mental illness in suicide terrorism, admits that Wail al-Shehri suffered "some form of psychotic disorder in early adulthood" (Marc Sageman, *Understanding Terror Networks* [Philadelphia: University of Pennsylvania Press, 2004], p. 81).

14. "Suicide," in *The Oxford Encyclopedia of the Modern Islamic World* (Oxford University Press, 1995), p. 134.
15. Aristotle, *Nichomachean Ethics,* 1116a, 12–14.
16. Conversion stories are told about many of the other hijackers. In 1999, for instance, Ahmed Alnami "began a rapid change, becoming obsessively pious after returning home from a Saudi-government sponsored religious summer camp" (Sennott, "Before Oath to Jihad, Drifting and Boredom," *op. cit.*).
17. Jason Burke, *Al-Qaeda: Casting a Shadow of Terror* (London: I.B. Tauris, 2003), pp. 214–215.
18. "Atta's Last Will," reprinted, among other places, in Stefan Aust and Cordt Schnibben, *Inside 9–11: What Really Happened* (New York: St. Martin's Press, 2002), pp. 304–7.
19. The only pilot not a member of the Hamburg cell was Hani Hanjour, a Saudi who had been in the United States, on and off, since 1996, revealing that Germany was not the sole forward operational base for 9/11 and that the attack was coordinated at a higher level.
20. John Cloud, "Atta's Odyssey," *Time* (October 8, 2001); Burke, *Al-Qaeda,* p. 216.
21. Jane Corbin, *Al-Qaeda: In Search of the Terror Network that Threatens the World* (New York: Nation Books, 2002), p. 121.
22. Terry McDermott, *Perfect Soldiers: The 9/11 Hijackers: Who they Were, Why They Did It* (New York: Harpers, 2005), p. 31.
23. Joseph Conrad, *The Secret Agent* (New York: The Modern Library, 2004), p. 68.
24. Miller and Stone, *The Cell,* p. 252.
25. Peter Finn, "A Fanatic's Quiet Path to Terror," *The Washington Post* (September 22, 2001).
26. Aust and Schnibben, *Inside 9–11,* p. 186.
27. Cloud, "Atta's Odyssey."
28. His dissertation was titled "Khareg Bab-en-Nasr: Ein gefährdeter Altstadtteil in Aleppo. Statteilentwicklung in einer islamisch-orientalischen Stadt" (Khareg Bab-en-Nasr: An Endangered Ancient Urban District of Aleppo: Urban District Development in an Islamic Oriental Town").
29. Cited in Gunaratna, *Inside Al Qaeda,* p. 140.
30. About Jarrah, we learn that "'He was different,' said Mzoudi. 'A mixture of Westerner and real Muslim. Sometimes you couldn't tell him apart from the Europeans'" (John Miller and Michael Stone, *The Cell: Inside the 9/11 Plot, and why the FBI and CIA Failed to Stop It* [New York: Hyperion, 2002], p. 264); he is consistently reported to have been "Fun-loving" (Corbin, *Al-Qaeda,* p. 135) and, unlike Atta, gifted in human relations. As 9/11 approached, however, he did begin to pressure his girlfriend to wear the veil. It is curious that his great uncle had served in the Stasi, East Germany's secret police (Fouda and Fielding, *Masterminds of Terror,* p. 85).
31. The other important member of the Hamburg cell was Ramzi bin al-Shibh. Originally from Yemen, he was arrested in Karachi in 2002 and transferred from a secret CIA prison to Guantánamo Bay in 2006.
32. Daniel Benjamin and Steven Simon, *The Next Attack: The Failure of the War on Terror and a Strategy for Getting it Right* (New York: Times Books, 2005), p. 201.

33. Cloud, "Atta's Odyssey."
34. Per capita GDP of Saudi Arabia went from $28,600 in 1981 to $6,800 in 2001 (Robert Baer, "The Fall of the House of Saud," *Atlantic Monthly*, May 2003, p. 55).
35. Russian anarchists were the first suicide bombers of modern times. Anna Geifman, *Thou Shalt Kill: Revolutionary Terrorism in Russia, 1894–1917* (Princeton: Princeton University Press, 1993), pp. 130–138.
36. Michael Mann, *Incoherent Empire* (London: Verso, 2003), p. 109.
37. Ahmad al Haznawi al-Ghamidi's "Pre-Attack Videotape" (Summer 2000), in *Anti-American Terrorism and the Middle East*, p. 276).
38. Eden Naby and Richard N. Frye, "The Martyr Complex," *NYT* (Sept. 14, 2003), section 4, p. 11.
39. Ariel Merari, "The readiness to kill and die: Suicidal terrorism in the Middle East," in Walter Reich (ed.), *Origins of Terrorism: Psychologies, Ideologies, Theologies, States of Mind* (Washington, D.C.: Woodrow Wilson Center Press, 1998), p. 197.
40. Br. Abu Ruqaiyah, "The Islamic Legitimacy of the 'Martyrdom Operations'," *Nida'ul Islam* (December-January, 1996–1997), http://islam.org.au/articles/16/martyrdom.htm.
41. Joyce M. Davis, *Martyrs: Innocence, Vengeance, and Despair in the Middle East* (New York: Palgrave, 2003), p. 94.
42. Albert Camus, *Les justes* (Paris: Gallimard, 1977), act 4, p. 119; cf. "Celui qui tue n'est coupable que s'il consent encore à vivre. . . . Mourir, au contraire annule la culpabilité et le crime lui-même" in Albert Camus, *Réflexions sur le terrorisme* (Paris: Nicolas Philippe, 2002), p. 112.
43. Martha Crenshaw, "'Suicide' Terrorism in Comparative Perspective," *Countering Suicide Terrorism* (Herzilya, Israel: International Policy Institute for Counter Terrorism, 2001), p. 28.
44. Avishai Margalit, "The Suicide Bombers," *New York Review of Books*, vol. 48, no. 13 (August 9, 2003).
45. Rather than being too secular to understand religious motives, as Benjamin and Simon contend in *The Age of Sacred Terror*, many Americans may be too individualistic and hedonistic to understand strong corporate identity and the glorification of self-sacrifice it allows.
46. "Nous perdons encore la vie avec joie, pourvu qu'on en parle." Pascal's *Pensées* (first edition, 1669), J. Chevalier (ed.), *Oeuvres completes* (Paris: Pléiade, 1954), p. 1128.
47. Merari, "The readiness to kill and die: Suicidal terrorism in the Middle East," pp. 207, 206.
48. Georg Simmel, "Secrecy," *The Sociology of Georg Simmel*, translated and edited by Kurt Wolff (New York: Free Press, 1950), p. 330.
49. Merari, "The readiness to kill and die: Suicidal terrorism in the Middle East," p. 198.
50. Ibid., p. 197.
51. Corbin, *Al-Qaeda*, p. 188.
52. S. J. Rachman, *Fear and Courage* (New York: W. H. Freeman and Company, 1990), pp. 49–50.

53. Thomas Hobbes, *Behemoth or the Long Parliament* (Chicago: University of Chicago Press, 1990), p. 26.

54. Ian Buruma, *Murder in Amsterdam: The Death of Theo van Gogh and the Limits of Toleration* (New York: Penguin, 2006), p. 201.

55. Malise Ruthven, *A Fury for God: The Islamist Attack on America* (London: Granta B Books, 2001), p. 21.

56. Benjamin and Simon, *The Age of Sacred Terror*, p. 165.

57. Ibid.

58. Mark Juergensmeyer, "Sacrifice and Cosmic War," in Mark Juergensmeyer (ed.), *Violence and the Sacred in the Modern World* (London: Frank Cass, 1992), p. 111.

59. Olivier Roy, *The Failure of Political Islam* (Cambridge, Mass.: Harvard University Press, 2001), p. 65.

60. Kanan Makiya and Hassan Mneimneh, "Manual for a 'Raid'," in Robert Silvers and Barbara Epstein (eds.), *Striking Terror* (New York: New York Review of Books, 2002), p. 317.

61. Ahmad al Haznawi al-Ghamidi's "Pre-Attack Videotape" (Summer 2000), in *Anti-American Terrorism and the Middle East*, p. 276).

62. Euripides, *The Bacchae*.

63. Makiya and Mneimneh, "Manual for a 'Raid'," pp. 308–309.

64. Miller and Stone, *The Cell*, p. 269.

65. "Interview with Ayman al-Zawahiri (October 7, 2001), in *Anti-American Terrorism and the Middle East*, p. 288.

66. This is the principal theme of Fouda and Fielding, *Masterminds of Terror*, a book based to some extent on KSM's boastful account, delivered before his arrest, of his own heroic exploits. While largely in agreement with Fouda and Fielding, *The 9/11 Commission Report* attributes a larger operational role to Osama bin Laden, depicting him as a micromanager, for instance, personally selecting the commandos and so forth.

67. Robert Pape, "The Strategic Logic of Suicide Terrorism," *American Political Science Review*, vol. 97, p. 344.

68. Gunaratna, *Inside Al Qaeda*, p. 296.

69. According to some reports, "Yousef wasn't a particularly religious man – or perhaps not religious at all – but he was able to speak the language of religious men and make their goals seem akin to his own," in Terry McDermott, *Perfect Soldiers*, p. 132. Whatever Khalid Sheikh Mohammed's involvement in the first attack on the WTC, he was not closely affiliated with Osama bin Laden in 1993. The tight collaboration between them probably began sometime around 1996 (Fouda and Fielding, *Masterminds of Terror*, p. 92).

70. As was the attack on the synagogue in Djerba, Tunisia, in April 2002. The suicide terrorist in that case telephoned Khalid Sheikh Mohammed three hours before completing his mission (Frantz and Butler 2002).

71. Scott Atran, "The Moral Logic and Growth of Suicide Terrorism," *The Washington Quarterly* (Spring, 2006).

72. Diego Gambetta, "Can We Make Sense of Suicide Missions," *Making Sense of Suicide Missions* (Oxford: Oxford University Press, 2005).

73. Bruce Hoffman, "The Logic of Suicide Terrorism," *Atlantic Monthly* (June 2003), p. 42.

74. Ayman al Zawahiri, "Knights under the Prophet's Banner," in Laura Mansfield, *His Own Words: A Translation of the Writings of Dr. Ayman al Zawahiri* (TLG Publications, 2006), pp. 200, 223.

75. David Guttman, "Killers and Consumers: The Terrorist and his Audience," *Social Research*, vol. 46, 1979, pp. 517–26.

76. G. W. Bowersock, *Martyrdom and Rome* (Cambridge University Press, 1995), pp. 42–43.

77. "Videotape of a Private Meeting (December 13, 2001)," in *Anti-American Terrorism and the Middle East*, p. 244.

78. Zawahiri, "Knights under the Prophet's Banner," pp. 200–201.

79. Ahmad al Haznawi al-Ghamidi's "Pre-Attack Videotape" (Summer 2000), in *Anti-American Terrorism and the Middle East*, p. 276.

80. Burke, *Al-Qaeda*, p. 211.

81. Ahmad al Haznawi al-Ghamidi's "Pre-Attack Videotape" (Summer 2000), in *Anti-American Terrorism and the Middle East*, p. 276.

82. Zawahiri, "Knights under the Prophet's Banner," p. 224.

83. Alan Cullison, "Inside Al-Qaeda's Hard Drive," *The Atlantic Monthly* (September 2004).

84. Zawahiri, "Knights under the Prophet's Banner," p. 46.

85. Conrad, *The Secret Agent*, p. 61.

86. David Fromkin, "The Strategy of Terrorism," *Foreign Affairs* (July 1975), reprinted in James F. Hoge, Jr., and Fareed Zakaria (eds.), *The American Encounter: The United States and the Making of the Modern World* (New York: Basic Books, 1997), p. 343.

87. Fromkin, "The Strategy of Terrorism," p. 345.

88. See Andrew Macdonald (pseudonym for William Pierce), *The Turner Diaries* (Fort Lee, N.J.: Barricade Books, 1996) p. 51 (originally published in 1978).

89. "Dawn Interview with Usama bin Ladin (November 10, 2001)," in *Anti-American Terrorism and the Middle East*, p. 261.

90. Reuven Paz, "The Islamic Legitimacy of Suicide Terrorism," *Countering Suicide Terrorism* (Herzilya, Israel: International Policy Institute for Counter Terrorism, 2001), p. 97.

91. Interview with Osama bin Laden, October 20, 2001, in Bruce Lawrence (ed.), *Messages to the World: the Statements of Osama bin Laden* (London: Verso, 2005), p. 124.

92. "Videotape of a Private Meeting (December 13, 2001)," in *Anti-American Terrorism and the Middle East*, p. 244.

93. Ibid.

94. "Conversations with Terror," *Time* (October 8, 2001), cited in *Anti-American Terrorism and the Middle East*, p. 161.

95. "Statement: Jihad against Jews and Crusaders (February 23, 1998)," in *Anti-American Terrorism and the Middle East*, p. 150.

96. "Broadcast by Usama bin Laden (November 3, 2001)," in *Anti-American Terrorism and the Middle East*, p. 257.

97. "Videotape of a Private Meeting (December 13, 2001)," in *Anti-American Terrorism and the Middle East*, p. 244.

98. "Broadcast by Usama bin Laden (November 3, 2001)," in *Anti-American Terrorism and the Middle East*, p. 259; in the November 2002 audiotape

attributed to bin Laden, Bush is referred to as "the modern-day pharaoh" (James Risen and Neil MacFarquhar, "New Recording May be from bin Laden," *NYT*, November 13, 2002, p. A18).

99. "Broadcast by Usama bin Ladin (October 7, 2001)," in *Anti-American Terrorism and the Middle East*, p. 249.
100. Ibid., p. 262.
101. *Qur'an*, Surah 2: 190–1; Surah 22: 39–40.
102. "Broadcast by Usama bin Ladin (October 7, 2001)," in *Anti-American Terrorism and the Middle East*, p. 249; the Ottoman Caliphate was abolished in 1924.
103. Bruce Lawrence (ed.), *Messages to the World: The Statements of Osama bin Laden*, p. 239.
104. "Al-Qa'ida Statement (October 10, 2001)," by Suleiman Abu Ghaith, in *Anti-American Terrorism and the Middle East*, p. 252.
105. Ibid., p. 256. It is curious to observe that both Osama bin Laden and George W. Bush oscillate, in their descriptions of the ongoing conflict, between two mutually incompatible analogies: fighting a war and prosecuting a crime.
106. "Interview with Ayman al-Zawahiri (October 7, 2001)," in *Anti-American Terrorism and the Middle East*, p. 288.
107. "Broadcast by Usama bin Laden (November 3, 2001)," in *Anti-American Terrorism and the Middle East*, p. 260.
108. Christoph Reuter, *Mein Leben is eine Waffe* (Munich: Bertelsmann, 2002), p. 29.
109. Zawahiri, "Knights under the Prophet's Banner," pp. 210–211.
110. NATO suffered a similar identity crisis after the collapse of the U.S.S.R. but, unlike Al Qaeda, the Atlantic alliance has proved unable to regroup and reinvigorate itself by identifying a new common enemy.
111. Zawahiri, "Knights under the Prophet's Banner," p. 220.
112. *The 9/11 Commission Report: Final Report of the National Commission on Terrorist Attacks upon the United States*, p. 58. David J. Kilcullen refers to this consortium as "a globalized insurgency, initiated by a diffuse confederation of Islamist movements" in "Countering Global Insurgency," *The Journal of Strategic Studies*, Vol. 28, No. 4 (August 2005), p. 614.
113. "Broadcast by Usama bin Laden (November 3, 2001)," in *Anti-American Terrorism and the Middle East*, p. 260.
114. Friedrich Nietzsche, *The Genealogy of Morals*, III, 15, in *The Birth of Tragedy and the Genealogy of Morals* (New York: Doubleday, 1956), p. 263.
115. "Broadcast by Usama bin Laden (November 3, 2001)," in *Anti-American Terrorism and the Middle East*, p. 259.
116. Peter Bergen, *Holy War, Inc.: Inside the Secret World of Osama bin Laden* (New York: Free Press, 2001), p. 26.
117. James Gilligan, *Violence: Reflections on a National Epidemic* (New York: Vintage, 1997), p. 55.

2. Why Military Superiority Breeds Illusions

1. Robert Kagan, *Of Paradise and Power: America and Europe in the New World Order* (New York: Knopf, 2003), p. 3.
2. Robert Kagan, "Power and Weakness," *Policy Review* (June 2002).

3. Kagan, *Of Paradise and Power*, p. 96.
4. Ibid., p. 32.
5. Ibid., p. 31.
6. Ibid., p. 10.
7. Ibid., p. 41.
8. Ibid., pp. 73–74.
9. Ibid., p. 101.
10. Kagan's contrast between the garden and the jungle, oddly enough, seems to contain a distorted echo of the distinction between *dar al-Islam*, the house of submission and *dar al-Harb*, the house of war.
11. *Of Paradise and Power*, p. 73.
12. Ibid., pp. 98, 57.
13. Ibid., p. 27.
14. Ibid., p. 98.
15. Ibid., p. 22.
16. Ibid.
17. Daniel Benjamin and Steven Simon, *The Next Attack: The Failure of the War on Terror and a Strategy for Getting it Right* (New York: Times Books, 2005), p. 202.
18. Louise Richardson, *What Terrorists Want: Understanding the Enemy, Containing the Threat* (New York: Random House, 2006), p. 101.
19. *Of Paradise and Power*, p. 39.
20. *The Iraq Study Group Report* (New York: Vintage, 2006), p. 92.
21. Cited in Thomas E. Ricks, *Fiasco: The American Military Adventure in Iraq* (New York: Penguin, 2006), p. 272.
22. *The Iraq Study Group Report*, p. 92.

3. How the War was Lost

1. Bob Woodward, *State of Denial* (New York: Simon & Schuster, 2006), p. 469.
2. Michael Gordon and Bernard Trainor, *Cobra II: The Inside Story of the Invasion and Occupation of Iraq* (New York: Pantheon Books, 2006).
3. Gordon and Trainor, *Cobra II*, p. 259.
4. Ibid., p. 229.
5. Ibid., p. 497.
6. Ibid., p. 82.
7. Ibid., p. 502.
8. Ibid., p. 46.
9. Ibid., p. 501.
10. Ibid., pp. 502–503.
11. L. Paul Bremer, *My Year in Iraq: The Struggle to Build a Future of Hope* (New York: Simon and Schuster, 2006), p. 39.
12. *Cobra II*, p. 65.
13. Ibid., p. 58.
14. Ibid., p. 61.
15. Ibid.
16. Ibid., p. 60.
17. Ibid., p. 8.

18. Ibid., p. 505.
19. Ibid.
20. Ibid., p. 497.
21. Ibid., p. 499.
22. Ibid., p. 142.
23. Ibid., p. 477.
24. *The Iraq Study Group Report* (New York: Vintage, 2006), p. 38.
25. John Gray, "The Mirage of Empire," *The New York Review of Books* (January 12, 2006), p. 6.
26. *Cobra II*, p. 517.

4. Radicals Trapped in the Past

1. James Mann, *Rise of the Vulcans: the History of Bush's War Cabinet* (New York: Viking, 2004).
2. Francis Fukuyama, *America at the Crossroads: Democracy, Power, and the Neoconservative Legacy* (New Haven: Yale University Press, 2006), p. 193.
3. Ibid., p. 61.
4. Ibid., p. 93.
5. Ibid., p. 152.
6. Ron Suskind, *The One Percent Doctrine: Deep Inside America's Pursuit of its Enemies Since 9/11* (New York: Simon and Schuster, 2006), p. 225.
7. Mann, *Rise of the Vulcans*, p. 51.
8. Ibid., p. 67.
9. Ibid., p. 242.
10. Ibid., p. 35.
11. http://www.pbs.org/newshour/bb/terrorism/july-dec01/wolfowitz-9–14.html
12. *Rise of the Vulcans*, p. 107.
13. Richard A. Clarke, *Against All Enemies: Inside America's War on Terror* (New York: Free Press, 2004), pp. 231–232.
14. *Rise of the Vulcans*, p. 218.
15. Ibid., p. 21.
16. Ibid., p. 30.
17. Jeanne Kirkpatrick, "Neoconservatism as a Response to the Counter-Culture," in Irwin Stelzer, *The Neocon Reader* (New York: Grove Press, 2004), p. 235.
18. Jeane J. Kirkpatrick, *Dictatorships and Double Standards: Rationalism and Reason in Politics* (New York: Simon and Schuster, 1983), p. 34.
19. Ibid., pp. 29–30.
20. Condoleezza Rice, "Remarks at the American University in Cairo" (June 20, 2005).
21. Kirkpatrick, *Dictatorships and Double Standards*, p. 44
22. Ibid., p. 30.
23. Ibid., p. 92.
24. Ibid., p. 31.
25. *Rise of the Vulcans*, pp. 335–336 (citing Scowcroft's speech to the Norwegian Nobel Institute on April 8, 2003).
26. Ibid., p. 230.

27. Charles Krauthammer, "Democratic Realism: An American Foreign Policy for a Unipolar World," American Enterprise Institute Annual Dinner, Washington, D.C. (February 10, 2004).

28. L. Paul Bremer III, *My Year in Iraq: The Struggle to Build a Future of Hope* (New York: Simon and Schuster, 2006), p. 397.

29. George Packer, *The Assassins' Gate* (New York: Farrar, Straus and Giroux, 2005), p. 42.

30. Richard N. Perle, "Iraq: Saddam Unbound," Robert Kagan and William Kristol (eds.), *Present Dangers: Crisis and Opportunity in American Foreign and Defense Policy* (San Francisco: Encounter Books, 2000), p. 102.

31. *Rise of the Vulcans*, p. 308.

5. A Self-Inflicted Wound

1. Condoleezza Rice, "Promoting the National Interest," *Foreign Affairs* (January/February, 2000), p. 53.

2. Mann, *Incoherent Empire*, p. vii.

3. Michael Mann, *Incoherent Empire* (London: Verso, 2003), p. vii.

4. Ibid., p. vii.

5. Ibid.

6. See, for example, Charles Krauthammer, "The Bush Doctrine," *Time* (March 5, 2001).

7. *Incoherent Empire*, p. 20.

8. Ibid., p. 24.

9. Ibid., p. 253.

10. Ibid., p. 265.

11. James Risen, *State of War: The Secret History of the CIA and the Bush Administration* (New York: Free Press, 2006), p. 64.

12. *Messages to the World: The Statements of Osama bin Laden*, edited by Bruce Lawrence (London: Verso, 2005), p. 96.

13. *Incoherent Empire*, p. 82.

14. Ibid., p. 177.

15. Ibid., pp. 265, 39.

16. Ibid., p. 12.

17. Ibid., p. 265.

18. Ibid., p. 40.

19. Ibid., p. 235.

20. George Kennan, cited in Jane Mayer, "A Doctrine Passes," *The New Yorker* (Oct. 14, 2002).

21. *Incoherent Empire*, p. 97.

22. Ibid., p. 95.

23. Ibid., p. 190.

24. Ibid., p. 159.

25. Ibid.

26. Ibid., p. 186.

27. Ibid., p. 160.

28. Ibid.

29. Ibid., p. 163.

30. Ibid., p. 177.

31. Ibid., p. 104.
32. Ibid., p. 245.
33. Ibid., p. 261.
34. Ibid., p. vii.
35. Ibid., p. 263.
36. Ibid.
37. Ibid.
38. Ibid., p. 260.
39. Ibid., pp. 15–16.
40. Ibid., p. 252.
41. Ibid., p. 257.
42. Ibid., p. 260.
43. Ibid., p. 149.
44. Ibid., p. 76.
45. Ibid., p. 266.
46. Ibid., p. 93.
47. David J. Kilcullen, "Countering Global Insurgency," *The Journal of Strategic Studies*, Vol. 28, No. 4 (August 2005), p. 604. Kilcullen, it should be said, echoes Mann almost word for word, arguing that the United States should above all strive to de-link transnational terrorists and nationalist guerrillas; but his analysis of the role of globalization in making the fatal linkages possible shows why this strategy is largely chimerical.
48. *Incoherent Empire*, p. 266.
49. Ibid.
50. Ibid.
51. Ibid., pp. 265, 111.
52. Ibid., p. 13.
53. Ibid., p. 2
54. On the Administration's incoherent amalgam of best-case and worst-case reasoning in the run-up to the invasion of Iraq, see Thomas Ricks, *Hubris: The American Military Adventure in Iraq* (New York: Penguin, 2006), pp. 58–59.
55. *Incoherent Empire*, p. 87.
56. Ibid., p. 85.
57. Mark Danner, "Iraq: The War of the Imagination," *New York Review of Books* (December 21, 2006), p. 82.
58. *Incoherent Empire*, p. 84.
59. Ibid., p. 259.

6. Searching for a New Enemy after the Cold War

1. Interview with Osama bin Laden, October 20, 2001, in Bruce Lawrence (ed.), *Messages to the World: the Statements of Osama bin Laden* (London: Verso, 2005), p. 124.
2. Larry Wright, *The Looming Tower: Al-Qaeda and the Road to 9/11* (New York: Knopf, 2006), p. 8.
3. Samuel Huntington, "The Clash of Civilizations?," *Foreign Affairs* (Summer, 1993), vol. 72, no. 3.
4. Samuel Huntington, *The Clash of Civilizations and the Remaking of World Order* (New York: Simon and Schuster, 1996).

5. Huntington, *The Clash of Civilizations*, p. 207
6. Ibid., p. 304
7. Ibid., p. 100.
8. Ibid., p. 82.
9. Ibid.
10. Ibid., p. 125.
11. Ibid., p. 21.
12. Ibid., pp. 67, 130.
13. Ibid., p. 246.
14. Ibid., p. 184.
15. Ibid., p. 126.
16. Ibid., pp. 126, 138.
17. Ibid., p. 308.
18. Ibid., p. 311.
19. Ibid., p. 242.
20. Ibid.
21. Ibid., p. 320.
22. Ibid., pp. 310, 321.
23. Ibid., p. 156.
24. Ibid., p. 311.
25. Ibid., p. 303.
26. Ibid., pp. 308, 302.
27. Ibid., p. 318.
28. Ibid., p. 239.
29. Ibid., p. 312.
30. Ibid., p. 232.
31. Ibid., p. 58.
32. Ibid., p. 258.
33. Ibid., p. 256.
34. Ibid.
35. Ibid., p. 264.
36. Ibid., p. 258.
37. Ibid., p. 242.
38. Ibid., p. 213.
39. Ibid., p. 154.
40. Ibid.
41. Ibid., p. 178.
42. Ibid., pp. 179, 162.
43. Ibid., p. 309.
44. Ibid., p. 153.
45. Ibid., p. 66.
46. Ibid., p. 309.
47. Ibid., p. 162.
48. Ibid., p. 265
49. Ibid., p. 113.
50. Ibid., p. 147, citing Eric Rouleau.
51. Ibid., p. 273.
52. Ibid., p. 174.
53. Ibid., p. 175.

54. Ibid., p. 126.
55. Ibid., p. 172.
56. Ibid., p. 262.
57. "The Clash of Civilizations?," *Foreign Affairs* (summer, 1993), vol. 72, no. 3.
58. *Clash of Civilizations*, p. 20.
59. Ibid., p. 267.
60. Ibid., p. 307.
61. Ibid.
62. Ibid., p. 232.
63. Ibid., p. 225.
64. Ibid., p. 107.
65. Ibid., p. 229.
66. Ibid., pp. 218, 231.
67. Ibid., p. 281.
68. Ibid., p. 185.
69. Ibid., p. 69.
70. Ibid., p. 92.
71. Ibid., p. 306.
72. Ibid., p. 52.
73. Ibid., p. 42.
74. Ibid., p. 260.
75. Ibid., p. 259.
76. Ibid., p. 261.
77. Ibid., p. 36.
78. Ibid., p. 268.
79. Ibid., p. 281.
80. Ibid., pp. 296, 290.
81. Ibid., p. 286.
82. Ibid., p. 287.
83. Ibid., p. 309.
84. Ibid., pp. 252, 291.
85. Ibid., p. 298.
86. Ibid., p. 51.
87. Ibid.
88. Ibid., p. 84.
89. Ibid., p. 264.
90. Ibid., p. 198.
91. Ibid., p. 101.
92. Ibid., p. 82.
93. Ibid., p. 91.
94. Ibid., p. 186.
95. Ibid., p. 86.
96. Huntington has subsequently developed this theme in *Who Are We: The Challenge to America's National Identity* (New York: Simon & Schuster, 2004).
97. *Clash of Civilizations*, p. 304.
98. Ibid., p. 305.
99. Ibid., p. 206.
100. Ibid., p. 304–305.
101. Ibid., p. 204.

102. Ibid., p. 170.
103. Ibid., p. 205.
104. Ibid., p. 306.
105. Ibid., p. 321.
106. Ibid., p. 156.
107. Ibid., p. 321.
108. Ibid.
109. Ibid., p. 320.
110. Ibid., p. 321.
111. Ibid.
112. Ibid., p. 95.
113. Ibid., p. 174.
114. Ibid., p. 35.
115. Ibid., p. 63.
116. Ibid., p. 95.
117. Ibid., p. 276.
118. Ibid., p. 66.
119. Ibid., p. 54.
120. Ibid., p. 111.
121. Ibid., p. 264.
122. Ibid.
123. Ibid., p. 188.
124. Ibid.
125. Ibid., p. 321.
126. George Packer, *The Assassins Gate: America in Iraq* (New York: Farar, Straus and Giroux, 2005), p. 43.
127. Gilles Kepel, *The War for Muslim Minds: Islam and the West* (Cambridge, Mass.: Harvard University Press, 2004), p. 62.
128. Roy, *Globalized Islam*, p. 154.
129. *Globalized Islam*, p. 9.
130. Anatol Lieven and John Hulsman, *Ethical Realism: A Vision for America's Role in the World* (New York: Pantheon Books, 2006), p. 46.
131. Lieven and Hulsman, *Ethical Realism*, p. 39.

7. Humanitarianism with Teeth

1. Lawrence F. Kaplan and William Kristol, *The War Over Iraq: Saddam's Tyranny and America's Mission* (San Francisco: Encounter Books, 2003), pp. 9–10.
2. Kaplan and Kristol, *The War Over Iraq*, p. 17.
3. Ibid., p. 15.
4. Ibid., p. 13.
5. James A. Baker III, Lee H. Hamilton et al., *The Iraq Study Group Report* (New York: Vintage, 2006), p. 95.
6. Samantha Power, *"A Problem from Hell": America and the Age of Genocide* (New York: Basic Books, 2002).
7. Power, *"A Problem from Hell": America and the Age of Genocide*, p. 251.
8. Ibid., p. 503.
9. Ibid., p. xv.

10. Ibid., p. 334.
11. Ibid., p. 236.
12. Ibid., p. 464.
13. Ibid., p. 277.
14. Ibid., pp. 278, 279.
15. Ibid., p. 449.
16. Ibid., p. 8.
17. Ibid., p. 518.
18. Ibid., p. 68.
19. Ibid., p. 519.
20. Ibid., p. 57.
21. Ibid., p. 383.
22. Ibid., p. 468.
23. Ibid., p. 67.
24. Ibid., p. 146.
25. Ibid., pp. 146–147.
26. Ibid., p. 534.
27. David Halberstam, *War in a Time of Peace: Bush, Clinton and the Generals* (London: Bloomsbury, 2001), p. 424.
28. Halberstam. *War in a Time of Peace*, p. 3.
29. Ibid., p. 6.
30. Ibid., p. 32.
31. Ibid., p. 7.
32. Ibid., p. 34.
33. Ibid., p. 497.

8. The War of the Liberals

1. Anatol Lieven and John Hulsman, *Ethical Realism: A Vision for America's Role in the World* (New York: Pantheon Books, 2006), p. 43.
2. Paul Berman, *Power and the Idealists: Or, The Passion of Joschka Fischer, and its Aftermath* (Brooklyn, NY: Softskull Press, 2005), p. 194.
3. Berman, *Power and the Idealists*, p. 283.
4. Ibid., p. 63.
5. Ibid., p. 82.
6. Ibid., p. 84.
7. Ibid., p. 83.
8. Ibid., p. 89.
9. Ibid., pp. 170–1.
10. Ibid., p. 259.
11. Ibid., p. 194.
12. Ibid., p. 124.
13. Ibid., p. 256.
14. Ibid., p. 125.
15. Ibid., pp. 124–5.
16. Ibid., p. 258.
17. Ibid., p. 123.
18. Ibid., p. 66.

19. Ibid., p. 198.
20. Ibid., p. 232.
21. Ibid., p. 68.
22. Ibid., p. 233.
23. Ibid., p. 242.
24. Ibid., p. 64.
25. Ibid., p. 256.
26. Ibid., p. 127.
27. Ibid., p. 257.
28. Ibid., p. 256.
29. Ibid., p. 258.
30. Ibid., p. 97.
31. Ibid., p. 259.
32. Ibid., p. 262.
33. Ibid., p. 260.
34. Ibid.
35. Ibid., p. 261.
36. Ibid., p. 262.
37. Ibid., p. 264.
38. Ibid., p. 262.
39. Ibid., p. 124.
40. Ibid., p. 197.
41. Ibid., p. 283.
42. Ibid., p. 281.
43. Ibid., p. 221.
44. Ibid., p. 164.
45. Ibid., p. 162.
46. David Rieff, *A Bed for the Night: Humanitarianism in Crisis* (New York: Simon & Schuster, 2002), p. 197.
47. David Rieff, *At the Point of a Gun: Democratic Dreams and Armed Intervention* (New York: Simon & Schuster, 200?), p. 253.
48. Rieff, *At the Point of a Gun*, p. 254.
49. Ibid., p. 254.
50. Ibid., p. 57.
51. Ibid., p. 252.
52. Ibid., p. 56.
53. Ibid., p. 57.
54. Ibid.
55. Ibid., p. 162.
56. Ibid., p. 82.
57. Michael Barnett, *Eyewitness to a Genocide: The United Nations and Rwanda* (Ithaca: Cornell University Press, 2002), p. 175.
58. *At the Point of a Gun*, p. 63.
59. Ibid., p. 144.
60. Ibid., p. 19.
61. Ibid., p. 33.
62. Ibid., p. 35.
63. Ibid., p. 251.
64. Ibid.
65. Ibid., p. 164.

66. Ibid., p. 169.
67. Ibid., p. 160.
68. Ibid., p. 166.
69. Ibid., p. 163.
70. Ibid., p. 166.
71. Ibid., p. 167.
72. Ibid.
73. Ibid.
74. Ibid., p. 171.
75. Ibid., p. 170.
76. Ibid., p. 9.
77. Ibid., p. 168.
78. Ibid.
79. Ibid., p. 169.
80. Ibid., p. 171.
81. Ibid., p. 35.
82. David Rieff, "No Exit Strategy," *The Nation* (August 1, 2005).
83. *At the Point of a Gun*, p. 231.
84. Ibid., p. 34.
85. Ibid., p. 4.
86. Ibid., p. 47.
87. Ibid., p. 36.
88. Ibid.
89. Ibid., p. 35.
90. Ibid., p. 3.
91. Ibid., p. 161.
92. Ibid., p. 37.
93. Ibid., p. 39.
94. Kenneth Roth, "War in Iraq: Not a Humanitarian Intervention," *Human Rights Watch, World Report 2004* (http://hrw.org/wr2k4/3.htm).

9. The Neoconservative Intifada

1. Here is the entire passage from the open letter to the President signed by Fukuyama: "It may be that the Iraqi government provided assistance in some form to the recent attack on the United States. But even if evidence does not link Iraq directly to the attack, any strategy aiming at the eradication of terrorism and its sponsors must include a determined effort to remove Saddam Hussein from power in Iraq. Failure to undertake such an effort will constitute an early and perhaps decisive surrender in the war on international terrorism" (http://www.newamericancentury.org/Bushletter.htm). Cosignatories included Richard Perle and Robert Kagan.
2. Francis Fukuyama, *America at The Crossroads: Democracy, Power, and the Neoconservative Legacy* (New Haven: Yale University Press, 2006). p. 3.
3. Fukuyama, *America at the Crossroads*, p. 182.
4. Ibid., p. 189.
5. Ibid., p. 105.
6. Ibid., p. 185.
7. Ibid., p. 62.
8. Ibid.

9. Ibid., p. 51.

10. Ibid., p. 105.

11. Ibid., p. 63.

12. Ibid., p. 47.

13. Ibid., p. 83.

14. Ibid., p. 184.

15. Charles Krauthammer, "Democratic Realism: An American Foreign Policy for a Unipolar World," American Enterprise Institute Annual Dinner, Washington, D.C. (February 10, 2004).

16. Charles Krauthammer, "In Defense of Democratic Realism," *The National Interest* (Fall 2004).

17. *America at the Crossroads*, p. 83.

18. George W. Bush, speech, 88th Annual American Legion National Convention, Salt Lake City, August 31, 2006.

19. Terry McDermott, *Perfect Soldiers: The 9/11 Hijackers: Who they Were, Why They Did It* (New York: Harpers, 2005), p. 18.

20. *America at the Crossroads*, p. 117.

21. Ibid., p. 116.

22. Ibid.

23. Ibid., p. 47.

24. James Kurth, "America's Democratization Projects Abroad," *The American Spectator* (November 14, 2006).

25. *America at the Crossroads*, p. 53.

26. Ibid., p. 25.

27. Ibid., p. 29.

28. Full Transcript of bin Ladin's Speech, *Aljazeera* (November 2, 2004).

29. *America at the Crossroads*, p. 19.

30. Ibid., p. 28.

31. Ibid., p. 19.

32. Ibid.

33. Ibid., p. 47.

34. Ibid., p. 114.

35. Ibid., p. 178.

36. Ibid., p. 116.

37. Ibid.

38. Ibid., p. 184.

39. Ibid., p. 30.

40. Ibid., p. 145.

41. Ibid., p. 124.

42. Ibid., p. 137.

43. Ibid., p. 148.

44. Ibid., p. 124.

45. Ibid., p. 148.

46. Ibid., p. 210.

47. Ibid., p. 183.

10. Liberalism Strangled by War

1. Geoffrey Stone, *Perilous Times: Free Speech in Wartime From the Sedition Act of 1798 to the War on Terrorism* (New York: W.W. Norton, 2004), p. xxiii.

2. Stone, *Perilous Times*, p. 23.
3. Ibid., p. 111.
4. Ibid., p. 121.
5. Ibid., p. 122.
6. Ibid.
7. Ibid., p. 185.
8. Ibid., p. 139.
9. Ibid., p. 138.
10. Ibid., p. 304.
11. Ibid., p. 296.
12. Ibid., p. 302.
13. Ibid., p. 12.
14. Ibid., p. 438.
15. Ibid., p. 237.
16. Ibid., p. 552.

11. The Unilateralist Curse

1. Charles Krauthammer, "Democratic Realism: An American Foreign Policy for a Unipolar World," American Enterprise Institute Annual Dinner, Washington, DC (February 10, 2004).
2. George Friedman, *America's Secret War: Inside the Hidden Worldwide Struggle between America and its Enemies* (New York: Doubleday, 2004), p. 258.
3. G. John Ikenberry, *After Victory: Institutions, Strategic Restraint, and the Rebuilding of Order After Major Wars* (Princeton: Princeton University Press, 2001), p. 258.
4. Ikenberry, *After Victory*, p. 19.
5. Ibid., p. 257.
6. Ibid., p. 163.
7. Ibid., p. 9.
8. Ibid., p. xiii.
9. Ibid., p. xiii.
10. Ibid., p. 19.
11. Ibid., p. 104.
12. Ibid., p. 83.
13. Ibid., p. 63.
14. Ibid., p. 205.
15. Ibid., pp. 52, 19.
16. Ibid., p. 257.
17. Ibid., p. 6.
18. Ibid., p. 9.
19. Ibid., p. 181.
20. Ibid., p. 210.
21. Ibid., p. 203.
22. Ibid., p. 266.
23. Ibid., pp. 270, 214.
24. Ibid., p. 266.
25. Ibid., p. 65.
26. Ibid., p. 5.
27. Ibid., p. 270.

28. Ron Suskind, *The One Percent Doctrine: Deep Inside America's Pursuit of its Enemies since 9/11* (New York: Simon & Schuster, 2006), p. 186.

29. *Ibid.*, pp. 43–48, 53, 75, 187, 221–22, 263, 266, 270.

30. Terry McDermott, *Prefect Soldiers* (New York: Harper, 2005), p. 95.

12. Battling Lawlessness with Lawlessness

1. Danielle S. Allen, *The World of Prometheus: The Politics of Punishing in Democratic Athens* (Princeton University Press, 2000), p. 104.

2. Walter Ullmann, "Reflections on Medieval Torture," *Juridical Review* (vol. 56, 1944), p. 123.

3. *The Digest of Justinian*, trans. Alan Watson (Philadelphia: University of Pennsylvania Press, 1985), vol. IV., pp. 843; this extract is drawn from Aurellius Arcadius Charisius, a jurist from the age of Constantine.

4. Edward Gibbon, *Decline and Fall of the Roman Empire*, vol. I, p. 549.

5. Aristotle, *Rhetoric* 1376b 26–1377a 26 (Cambridge, Mass.: Loeb Library, 1926), trans. by John Henry Freese, p. 163.

6. Ibid.

7. Cicero, *Pro Sulla*, 78, in *In Catilinam I-IV, Pro Murena, Pro Sulla, Pro Flacco*, translated by C. MacDonald (Cambridge, Mass.: Loeb Library, 1977), p. 391.

8. *The Digest of Justinian*, trans. Alan Watson (Philadelphia: University of Pennsylvania Press, 1985), vol. IV., pp. 841.

9. Augustine, *City of God*, XIX, 6 (Cambridge, Mass.: Loeb Library, 1960), trans. William Chase Greene, pp. 145–147.

10. Michel de Montaigne, *The Complete Essays*, translated by M.A. Screech (London: Penguin, 1991), p. 414.

11. La Bruyère, *The Morals and Manners of the Seventeenth Century, being the Characters of La Bruyère* (Chicago: McClurg, 1890), p. 272.

12. William Blackstone, *Commentaries on the Laws of England* (Chicago: University of Chicago Press, 1979), vol. IV, p. 321.

13. Cesare Beccaria, *On Crimes and Punishments* (Indianapolis: Bobbs-Merrill, 1975), p. 31.

14. Ibid.

15. Ibid., p. 32

16. Ibid, p. 35.

17. Ibid., p. 33.

18. "Memorandum for Alberto R. Gonzales Counsel to the President" (signed by Jay Bybee, but written by John Yoo), in Karen J. Greenberg and Joshua L. Dratel (eds.), *The Torture Papers: The Road to Abu Ghraib* (Cambridge: Cambridge University Press, 2005), p. 210.

19. "Memorandum for Alberto R. Gonzales," *The Torture Papers*, p. ???

20. Blackstone, *Commentaries on the Laws of England*, vol. IV, p. 184.

21. "Memorandum for Alberto R. Gonzales," *The Torture Papers*, p. 208.

22. Ibid., p. 208.

23. Ibid., pp. 208–209.

24. Ibid., pp. 211–212.

25. Beccaria, *On Crimes and Punishments*, p. 33.

26. Indictment before the International Military Tribunal (October 6, 1945) in Michael Marrus (ed.), *The Nuremberg War Crimes Trial 1945-46* (Boston: St. Martin's, 1997), p. 65.

27. Beccaria, *On Crimes and Punishments*, p. 32.

28. Leonard Levy, *Origins of the Fifth Amendment: The Right Against Self-Incrimination* (New York: MacMillan, 1986), p. xi.

29. Blackstone, *Commentaries on the Laws of England*, vol. IV, p. 321.

30. Harold Nicolson, "Marginal Comment," *The Spectator* (May 10, 1946), p. 478.

31. Richard Posner, *Not a Suicide Pact: The Constitution in a Time of National Emergency* (New York: Oxford University Press, 2006), p. 85.

32. Interview with Secretary of State Colin Powell by Barry Schweid and George Gedda, September 10, 2004.

33. The United Nations Convention Against Torture and Other Inhuman and Degrading Acts, Article 2.2.

34. Mark Danner, "We are all Torturers Now," *New York Times* (January 7, 2005).

35. George J. Andreopoulos, "The Age of National Liberation Movements," Michael Howard, George J. Andreopoulos, Mark R. Shulman (eds.), *The Laws of War: Constraints on Warfare in the Western World* (New Haven: Yale University Press, 1994), p. 205.

36. Charles Krauthammer, "The Truth about Torture," *The Weekly Standard* (December 5, 2005).

37. James Risen, *State of War: The Secret History of the CIA and the Bush Administration* (New York, Free Press, 2006). p. 33.

38. Cited in Bob Woodward, *State of Denial* (New York: Simon and Schuster, 2006), p. 408.

39. William Pfaff, "The Truth about Torture," *The American Conservative* (Feb. 14, 2005).

40. Elaine Scarry, *The Body in Pain* (Oxford University Press, 1985), p. 28.

41. Ibid., p. 27.

42. Thomas E. Ricks, *Fiasco: The American Military Adventure in Iraq* (New York: Penguin, 2006), p. 278.

43. Judith N. Shklar, *Ordinary Vices* (Cambridge, Mass.: Harvard University Press, 1984), p. 29.

44. David Rennie, "God put Bush in charge, says the general hunting bin Laden," *Telegraph* (November 17, 2003).

45. Cited in Mark Danner, "Torture and Truth," in *Abu Ghraib: The Politics of Torture* (Berkeley: Terra Nova, 2004), p. 32.

46. Cesare Beccaria, *On Crimes and Punishments* (Indianapolis: Bobbs-Merrill, 1975), p. 30.; cf. "An infallible dogma assures us that the stains contracted through our human frailty...must be purged by an incomprehensible fire" (Ibid., p. 35).

47. "New Accounts of Prisoner Abuses," BBC News World Edition (May 21, 2004).

48. George F. Kennan, "Where Do You Stand on Communism?," *New York Times Magazine* (May 27, 1951).

49. Martin van Creveld, *The Transformation of War* (New York: Free Press, 1991), p. 225.

50. His complete warning is this: "Whoever fights monsters should see to it that in the process he does not become a monster. And when you are looking into an

abyss, the abyss also looks into you." Friedrich Nietzsche, *Beyond Good and Evil* (New York: Vintage, 1966), §146, p. 89

51. Lou Dubose and Jake Bernstein, *Vice: Dick Cheney and the Hijacking of the American Presidency* (New York: Random House, 2006), pp. 187–205.

52. Laura Mansfield (trans.), *His Own Words: A Translation of the Writings of Dr. Ayman al Zawahiri* (TLG Publications, 2006). pp. 30, 33.

53. *His Own Words*, p. 204.

54. "Takfîr," John L. Esposito (ed.), *The Oxford Encyclopedia of the Modern Muslim World* (Oxford: Oxford University Press, 1995), vol. 4, p. 179.

55. Pierre Hassner, *La violence et la paix: Tome 2, La Terreur et l'Empire* (Paris: Seuil, 2006), p. 400.

13. The Infallibility Trap

1. Michael Isikoff and David Corn, *Hubris: The Inside Story of Spin, Scandal, and the Selling of the Iraq War* (New York: Crown Publishers, 2006), p. 9.

2. John Yoo, *The Powers of War and Peace: The Constitution and Foreign Affairs After 9/11* (University of Chicago Press, 2005), p. 294.

3. Yoo, *The Powers of War and Peace*, pp. 104–105.

4. Ibid., p. 100.

5. Ibid., p. 66.

6. Ibid., p. 323; citing Max Farrand (ed.), *The Records of the Federal Convention of 1787*, Vol. 1 (New Haven: Yale University Press, 1966), p. 70.

7. *The Powers of War and Peace*, p. 110.

8. Ibid., p. 113.

9. William Blackstone, *Commentaries on the Laws of England* (Chicago: University of Chicago Press, 1979), Vol. 1, p. 234. (Blackstone's *Commentaries* were originally published in 1765).

10. *Ibid.*, p. 238.

11. *The Powers of War and Peace*, p. 45.

12. Clinton Rossiter (ed.), *The Federalist Papers* (Mentor, 1966), Paper No. 47, p. 302.

13. *The Powers of War and Peace*, p. 22.

14. Ibid., p. 99.

15. Ibid., p. 92, citing Farrand (ed.), *The Records of the Federal Convention of 1787*, Vol. 1, pp. 65–66.

16. *The Powers of War and Peace*, p. 327.

17. Ibid., p. 121.

18. Ibid., p. 99.

19. Ibid., p. 22.

20. Ibid., p. 119.

21. Ibid., p. 136.

22. Ibid., p. 127.

23. Ibid., p. 114.

24. Ibid., p. x.

25. Ibid., p. ix.

26. Ibid., p. x.

27. *The Federalist Papers*, No. 81, p. 484.

28. *The Powers of War and Peace*, p. 327.

29. Vice President Dick Cheney, speech before the Veterans of Foreign Wars in Nashville, Tennessee, Aug. 26, 2002.

30. *The Powers of War and Peace*, p. x.

31. Ron Suskind, *The One Percent Doctrine: Deep Inside America's Pursuit of Its Enemies Since 9/11* (New York: Simon and Schuster, 2006), p. 308.

32. James Risen, *State of War: The Secret History of the CIA and the Bush Administration* (New York: Free Press, 2006), p. 65.

33. *Arab Human Development Report 2002* (New York: United Nations Publications, 2002), p. 2.

Conclusion

1. Statement by the President in his Address to the Nation (September 11, 2001).

2. Olivier Roy, *Globalized Islam: The Search for a New Ummah* (New York: Columbia University Press, 2004), p. 328.

3. George Orwell, "Politics and the English Language," *The Collected Essays, Journalism and Letters, Volume IV, In Front of Your Nose* (Harmondsworth: Penguin, 1970), p. 166.

4. James Bamford, *A Pretext for War: 9/11, Iraq, and the Abuse of America's Intelligence Agencies* (New York: Doubleday, 2004), p. 285; the notes of Rumsfeld's uncensored remarks referenced by Bamford are well-known, but bear re-citing: "best info fast; judge whether good enough to hit S.H. [Saddam Hussein] at same time. Not only U.B.L. [Osama bin Laden]." "Go massive." "Sweep it all up. Things related, and not."

5. Richard A. Clarke, *Against All Enemies: Inside America's War on Terror* (New York: Free Press, 2004), p. 30.

6. Max Rodenbeck, "How Terrible is It?," *The New York Review of Books* (November 30, 2006), p. 38.

7. Frank Rich, *The Greatest Story Ever Sold* (New York: Penguin, 2006), p. 223.

8. President George W. Bush, "Address to the Nation" (September 11, 2006).

9. President Bush, discussing terrorism with Colombia President, the Oval Office, September 25, 2002.

10. Clarke, *Against All Enemies*, p. 268.

11. Thomas E. Ricks, *Fiasco: The American Military Adventure in Iraq* (New York: Penguin. 2006), p. 274.

12. *The National Security Strategy of the United States* (March 2006), p. 11.

13. Clarke, *Against All Enemies*, pp. 264–265.

14. Daniel Benjamin and Steven Simon, *The Next Attack: The Failure of the War on Terror and a Strategy for Getting it Right* (New York: Times Books, 2005), p. 154.

15. President George W. Bush, "State of the Union," January 29, 2002.

16. Vice President Dick Cheney, Remarks, Town Hall Meeting, Des Moines, Iowa, Sept. 7, 2004.

17. John R. Bolton, "Beyond the Axis of Evil: Additional Threats from Weapons of Mass Destruction," in Irwin Stelzer, *The Neocon Reader* (New York: Grove Press, 2004), p. 235.

18. *The 9/11 Commission Report: Final Report of the National Commission on Terrorist Attacks upon the United States* (New York: W.W. Norton, 2004),

p. 116; for more on insider fear of a nuclear nightmare scenario, see pp. 380–381.

19. Martha Crenshaw, "The Psychology of Political Terrorism," Margaret Hermann (ed.), *Political Psychology* (San Francisco: Jossey-Bass, 1986), p. 401.

20. Cass Sunstein, "Terrorism and Probability Neglect," *Journal of Risk and Uncertainty* (2003) 26 (2/3) March-May, pp. 121–136.

21. *The National Strategy for Homeland Security* (2002), p. vii.

22. George Friedman, *America's Secret War: Inside the Hidden Worldwide Struggle between America and its Enemies* (New York: Doubleday, 2004), p. 258.

23. Vice President Richard Cheney, Meet the Press interview, 9/14/03.

24. President Bush Addresses American Legion National Convention in Salt Lake City, Utah (August 31, 2006).

25. Roy, *Globalized Islam*, p. 338.

26. René Girard, *Violence and the Sacred* (Baltimore: Johns Hopkins University Press, 1977), p. 2.

27. Daniel Henninger, "George Bush Talks About 'The Next Attack on America'," *The Wall Street Journal* (October, 27, 2006).

28. Ron Suskind, *The One Percent Doctrine: Deep Inside America's Pursuit of its Enemies Since 9/11* (New York: Simon and Schuster, 2006), p. 123.

29. Friedman, *America's Secret War*, p. 305.

30. Benjamin and Simon, *The Next Attack*, pp. 145–148.

31. President Bush Discusses Global War on Terror, Wardman Park Marriott Hotel, Washington, D.C. (September 29, 2006).

32. Suskind calls this "the Cheney doctrine" (*The One Percent Doctrine*, pp. 62, 150–151).

33. Fukuyama, *America at the Crossroads: Democracy, Power, and the Neoconservative Legacy* (New Haven: Yale University Press, 2006), p. 61.

34. John Mueller, *Overblown: How Politicians and the Terrorism Industry Inflate National Security Threats, and Why We Believe Them* (New York: Free Press, 2006).

35. For Arundhati Roy's entertaining but inaccurate claim that "Bin Laden has the distinction of being created by the CIA," see "The algebra of infinite justice," *Guardian* (September 29, 2001).

36. Christopher Dickey and Evan Thomas, "How the U.S. Helped Create Saddam Hussein," *Newsweek* (September 23, 2002).

37. *The 9/11 Commission Report*, p. 88.

38. James Fallows, "Declaring Victory," *The Atlantic Monthly* (September 2006), p. 5.

INDEX